Introducing Psycholinguistics

How humans produce and understand language is clearly introduced in this textbook for students with only a basic knowledge of linguistics. With a logical, flexible structure *Introducing Psycholinguistics* steps through the central topics of production and comprehension of language and the interaction between them.

- Students will gain an understanding of the processes and representations involved in language use, aided by a comprehensive glossary, concepts defined in the margins and online flashcards that allow students to check their understanding of all the key terms and concepts of the subject.

- Examples and exercises throughout each topic reinforce understanding and encourage students to consider what language users might carry around in their heads as part of their linguistic knowledge, and how this stored knowledge relates to the structures and rules proposed by theoretical linguistics.

- Students will gain hands-on experience of experimental methods, with online demonstrations of techniques. This supports the theory within the book, reinforces a student's grasp of the concepts and allows the student to apply their understanding to the analysis of data.

PAUL WARREN is an Associate Professor in the School of Linguistics and Applied Language Studies at Victoria University of Wellington.

Cambridge Introductions to Language and Linguistics

This new textbook series provides students and their teachers with accessible introductions to the major subjects encountered within the study of language and linguistics. Assuming no prior knowledge of the subject, each book is written and designed for ease of use in the classroom or seminar, and is ideal for adoption on a modular course as the core recommended textbook. Each book offers the ideal introductory material for each subject, presenting students with an overview of the main topics encountered in their course, and features a glossary of useful terms, chapter previews and summaries, suggestions for further reading, and helpful exercises. Each book is accompanied by a supporting website.

Books published in the series
Introducing Phonology David Odden
Introducing Speech and Language Processing John Coleman
Introducing Phonetic Science Michael Ashby and John Maidment
Introducing Second Language Acquisition Muriel Saville-Troike
Introducing English Linguistics Charles F. Meyer
Introducing Morphology Rochelle Lieber
Introducing Semantics Nick Riemer

Forthcoming:
Introducing Language Typology Edith Moravcsik

Introducing Psycholinguistics

PAUL WARREN

Victoria University of Wellington

CAMBRIDGE
UNIVERSITY PRESS

CAMBRIDGE
UNIVERSITY PRESS

University Printing House, Cambridge CB2 8BS, United Kingdom

One Liberty Plaza, 20th Floor, New York, NY 10006, USA

477 Williamstown Road, Port Melbourne, VIC 3207, Australia

314-321, 3rd Floor, Plot 3, Splendor Forum, Jasola District Centre, New Delhi - 110025, India

79 Anson Road, #06-04/06, Singapore 079906

Cambridge University Press is part of the University of Cambridge.

It furthers the University's mission by disseminating knowledge in the pursuit of education, learning and research at the highest international levels of excellence.

www.cambridge.org
Information on this title: www.cambridge.org/9780521130561

First published 2013
6th printing 2018

A catalogue record for this publication is available from the British Library

Library of Congress Cataloging in Publication data
Warren, Paul, 1958–
Introducing psycholinguistics / Paul Warren.
   pages   cm. – (Cambridge introductions to language and linguistics)
Includes bibliographical references and index.
ISBN 978-0-521-11363-2
1. Psycholinguistics – Textbooks.   I. Title.
P37.W35   2013
401′.9 – dc23   2012017769

ISBN 978-0-521-11363-2 Hardback
ISBN 978-0-521-13056-1 Paperback

Additional resources for this publication at www.cambridge.org/paulwarren

Contents

Figures

Tables

Preface

This book introduces key issues in the production and comprehension of spoken and written language. Its focus is on how adult native speakers carry out the everyday but complex tasks involved in generating an utterance from an idea or in deriving a meaning from a sentence.

Using data from observation, from experiments, and more recently from brain imaging, the field of psycholinguistics has contributed significantly to our understanding of the uniquely human ability to communicate through language. *Introducing Psycholinguistics* summarises key findings from the field, such as the fascinating study of spontaneous speech errors and misperceptions, and carefully controlled experimental investigations of the details of how we produce and understand language.

Introducing Psycholinguistics is written by a linguist primarily for students of linguistics. The book therefore assumes no prior familiarity with psychology. Although readers would find a basic understanding of linguistic concepts helpful, explanations of key linguistic terminology are provided. As a consequence, this text is also a useful introduction for students of psychology with an interest in language processing.

The book is arranged in two main clusters of chapters. Chapters 2 to 5 cover aspects of language production, starting with the speaker's (or writer's) intention, moving through the stages of sentence planning and word selection to the construction of words. The final chapter in this first cluster considers the monitoring and repair that speakers carry out of their own speech output. Chapters 7 to 12 deal with language perception and comprehension, starting with the perceptual skills relevant for language processing, before looking at word recognition, syntactic and other aspects of sentence analysis, as well as discourse processing. A bridge

between these two clusters of chapters is provided by Chapter 6, which discusses how the study of gesture can inform us about both production and comprehension. Chapter 13 brings together issues from earlier chapters, linking the study of the production and comprehension of spoken and written language in a discussion of how it all fits together.

The structure of the book allows some flexibility in how it can be used in the teaching of psycholinguistics. That is, in addition to the existing sequencing of chapters, the book could be used to support a course that starts by looking at issues in language perception and comprehension (using Chapters 7 to 12), before considering language production (Chapters 2 to 5). The choice of ordering may hinge on other aspects of a course, such as assessment, and on what material needs to be covered before assignment topics can be tackled.

Note that this book does not give extensive coverage to (first or second) language acquisition or to language breakdown. Instead, it focuses on normal adult language processing. What we know about normal language processing is of course informed by our knowledge of how infants become adult users of language and also by what we understand of impaired language use. But these are vast subject areas in their own right.

The chapters have a common structure. Each chapter opens with a preview summarising what the reader should expect to learn. This is followed by a list of key terms that will be introduced in the chapter. These and further key terms are also highlighted in bold blue text when they first occur. The most important key terms are explained in the glossary at the end of this book, and all key terms are explained in the fuller glossary on the accompanying website. The main text for each chapter consists of a short introduction and a number of sections covering the subject matter of the chapter. A short summary then reviews the main points, and is followed by a set of exercises to reinforce the reader's learning, as well as a section indicating where to look for relevant further reading.

The chapters include many illustrative examples and figures, as well as sidebars that convey more detail than is in the main text. Sidebars with blue shading introduce technical terms or matters of notation, while those shaded in grey provide additional background information of interest.

The online glossary on the website for *Introducing Psycholinguistics* (www.cambridge.org/paulwarren) provides definitions and examples for the key terms, and also includes functions that allow users to test their own understanding of the entries. The website also includes audio and video files illustrating ideas introduced in the text, solutions to some of the exercises, and examples of some of the main experimental techniques used in psycholinguistics, as well as links to other useful resources. When the following symbols appear in the margin they indicate that at the time of publication links were available on the website to resources relevant to the material under discussion. Other resources will be added over time.

 General web resource

 Sound file

 Video or image file

 Demonstration

 Solutions to problems

1 Introduction

PREVIEW

This chapter provides an overview both of the field of psycholinguistics and of the book itself. By the end of the chapter you should have a better understanding of, amongst other things, the appeal, significance and subject matter of psycholinguistics.

KEY TERMS

mental lexicon
process
psycholinguistics
representation

1.1 Introduction

Although there is little agreement on how many words an adult native speaker of English might know, let us take a conservative estimate of 20,000 (based on Nation, 2006, but see Section 8.2), and let us also assume that *splundle* is not one of them. Imagine such a native speaker searching through their 20,000-word mental lexicon, as we call the dictionary in our heads. Let's assume that they do so at a seemingly impressive rate of 100 words per second (which incidentally is 20 times faster than a good reading pace of 300 words per minute). At this rate, if they searched exhaustively through their mental lexicon, it would still take over 3 minutes to confirm that *splundle* is not there. Yet if you ask someone if they know the word *splundle*, they will be able to tell you more or less instantly that they do not. Clearly something is wrong with the assumptions we have just made about how rapidly we can look up words in our mental lexicon, or about the way in which we search through it, or both.

Ask someone to tell you what they had for breakfast, and then ask them to explain the workings of their coffee machine, and you are likely to find that their speech is much more hesitant in the second task than in the first, with more errors and restarts as well as pauses and *uhms* and *ahs*. The differences here reveal something about the nature of planning involved in different speaking tasks. The locations of the hesitations might also tell you which kinds of words and/or sentence structures the speaker finds more difficult to find or to put together.

Have a conversation with someone while they are carrying out a difficult task like driving a car, and you will find that both their language production and their language comprehension is less fluent than at other times (Becic *et al.*, 2010).

If you listen out for speech errors, or slips of the tongue, you are much more likely to hear an error where the beginning sounds of two words have been swapped over, as in 'tip of the slongue', than one where the beginning of one word and the end of another have been exchanged, as in 'slit of the pongue'.

When you see a sign like that in Figure 1.1, or one that says 'Please go slowly round the bend', you might well chuckle, but your experience of misreading the sign shows that there are certain preferred patterns of analysing the structure and meaning of sentences in English.

Consider what is wrong with the following interaction between speakers A and B, in which <SILENCE> indicates noticeably long periods of silence, and CAPITALS indicates the part of the word that receives word stress:

A. Could you tell me the time of the next train to Palmerston North and how much a single fare costs?
B. <SILENCE>
A. Hello?
B. <SILENCE> Invisible tables sleeeeep violently

Figure 1.1
Thank goodness our young ones are not breaking the speed limit.

A. When does the next train go to Palmerston North and what is a single ticket?
B. <SILENCE> PalMERston North trains from platform 3 leave. A single ticket licences a one-way journey.

There are of course a number of odd features here – there is meaningless and irrelevant content, there are long silences with odd patterns of pausing, there are infelicities of vocabulary and structure ('A single ticket <u>licences</u> a one-way journey', 'Palmerston North trains from platform 3 leave'), there is strange stress placement ('PalMERston') and another odd pronunciation ('sleeeeep'). Looking at 'odd' speech like this (the example is fabricated but the principle remains valid) sheds some light on what we need to do in order to speak. That is, speakers usually aim to produce utterances that have appropriate meaningful content, that use appropriate lexical items and grammatical structures, and that have appropriate pronunciation, intonation and phrasing. Speakers aim to do this fluently and in real time, and rarely have opportunity to rehearse. They also have to relate what they say to the context, including to previous speech in a conversation.

Speakers are generally very good at doing this. For example, one experiment was explicitly designed to elicit subject-verb agreement errors like (1.1), where the subject is plural (*efforts*) but is followed by a singular verb (*is*). The reason for the error is that the most recent noun before the verb is singular (*language*). In the experiment, fewer than 5% of the stimuli designed to produce agreement errors like this actually did so (Bock & Miller, 1991).

(1.1) Efforts to make English the official language is gaining strength throughout the US.

In spontaneous speech, it has been found that sound errors (e.g. saying 'par cark' for 'car park') occur only about 1.5 times per 10,000 words, and word errors (where the wrong word is chosen or words change positions in a sentence) occur only about 2.5 times per 10,000 words (Deese, 1984). Clearly we are generally pretty good at what we do when we produce and understand language.

1.2 What is psycholinguistics?

The rather disparate observations in the preceding section illustrate just a few of the areas of interest in psycholinguistics. Psycholinguistics can be defined as the study of the mental representations and processes involved in language use, including the production, comprehension and storage of spoken and written language. A number of issues arise from this definition. Some are to do with *representations*, such as:

- How are words stored in the mental lexicon, i.e. the dictionary in our heads? Is the mental lexicon like a dictionary, or more like a thesaurus? For instance, is *cat* listed near the similar sounding word *catch* or near the meaning-related word *dog*? Or neither? Or both?
- Do we have phoneme-sized chunks of language in our heads? That is, as part of recognising the word *cat* do we also recognise the component sounds /k/, /æ/ and /t/?
- Do literate people have letter-sized chunks filling equivalent roles for the processing of written language?
- How is the meaning of a sentence represented in our memory?
- Is *government* a single word or *govern* + *ment*?
- Is the plural form *cats* represented in the lexicon, or just the singular *cat*?

Other questions concern the *processes* that might operate on those representations:

- How do we recognise words so effortlessly?
- Do we analyse the speech signal phoneme-by-phoneme or do we identify complete syllables or even larger units?
- Do we recognise *government* as a complete form or do we have to construct it from *govern* + *ment*?
- If *cats* is not represented in the lexicon, does that mean that we use a rule to get the plural form of *cat*, and how does this work for irregular plurals like *children*?
- When we speak, how do we convert an idea into an utterance?
- As listeners, how do we get from hearing an utterance to developing our own representation of the idea(s) being expressed by that utterance?
- What stages do we have to go through during the construction of utterances? For example, do we first generate a sentence structure and only then populate it with words from our mental lexicon, or do we first choose words and then build a structure around those words?
- Do the processes involved in language production and comprehension influence one another, and if so in what ways?

The outline sketch of language use in Figure 1.2 gives an overview of areas of interest in psycholinguistics as well as providing the basic structure of this book, which has chapters on language production (roughly following the progression shown in the second column) and on comprehension

Processes	Production		Comprehension	Areas of linguistics
				discourse analysis
central	intention	message ('idea')	interpretation	syntax/semantics
	planning	sentence structure	parsing	morphology/syntax
	lexicalisation	words	word recognition	phonetics/phonology
peripheral	articulation	sounds/letters	perception	

Figure 1.2
An outline sketch of language use.

(fourth column). Psycholinguistics clearly has links to other areas of linguistic study, and some of these are shown in the final column.

From the language producer's (speaker's, writer's) perspective, the production of a message takes us from an underlying intention, through stages of planning sentence structures and selecting words, to the articulation of that intention as a sequence of sounds or letters, as shown by the arrow.

From the comprehender's (listener's, reader's) viewpoint, the goal is to perceive or recognise elements such as letters and sounds in the input, to recognise words and to work out the connections between these words in sentence structures, in order to arrive at a message-level interpretation. The arrow in the 'comprehension' column shows such a 'bottom-up' flow of information from the input to an interpretation. This is a simplification, though, as there is evidence for 'top-down' information flow too, e.g. when a listener starts to gain an understanding of the sentence they are hearing this can influence the efficiency with which they recognise subsequent words in the sentence. Most psycholinguists today support the idea of interactive processing in both production and comprehension, with information flowing in both directions (bottom-up and top-down) as well as between elements at the same level (so recognising one word has an effect on the likelihood of recognising similar words).

It is reasonable to claim that the main focal areas of psycholinguistics have tended to be *sentences* and *words*. So production studies have focused on the generation of sentence structure and on syntactic planning, as well as on word finding and word building. Similarly, much of the study of comprehension has dealt with word recognition and sentence parsing (working out the syntactic structure of sentences). The study of these processes has in turn involved consideration of the representation of words and of grammar.

In effect there are many more 'fields' than this, dealing with many subprocesses, such as the perception of letters and of speech sounds, the processing of different kinds of word endings, and so on. In addition, these fields are not always clearly distinct, neither in terms of research nor in terms of the ways in which the processor operates. For instance does our choice of words influence our choice of sentence structure, does sentence-level interpretation influence phonetic perception, does the spoken form of a word affect our silent reading of it, and so on?

Bottom-up: processing based on information flow from lower levels of processing to higher levels, e.g. from the sensory input (the speech signal) to the lexicon (words).

Top-down: processing guided by information flow from higher levels (e.g. sentence interpretation) to lower levels (e.g. words).

Interactive: processing that involves a combination of bottom-up and top-down flow of information, as well as links between elements at the same level.

Although the discussion above has tried to be inclusive of both spoken and written language, the content of this book shows a bias towards the production and comprehension of spoken language. To an extent this is a personal bias, since the author's own research interests are in this area, but it also reflects the primacy of the spoken language in the development both of the individual and of the species, as well as a general bias in the research literature.

1.3 Who does psycholinguistics?

The term *psycholinguistics* appears to have first been used to refer to the psychology of language in the 1920s. However, the birth of psycholinguistics as a discipline is often linked to a seminar at Cornell University in 1951. The interdisciplinary nature of the field is reflected in the fact that this seminar was reported in both a psychological journal (Osgood & Sebeok, 1954a) and a linguistics one (Osgood & Sebeok, 1954b). Psycholinguistics continues to be taught in both of these disciplinary areas, and is influenced by research and teaching practices and methodologies in both. Courses and research in psycholinguistics are also found in multidisciplinary cognitive science units throughout the world, and the issues studied in this area are also of interest to computer scientists (particularly those interested in Artificial Intelligence and Human–Computer Interaction), philosophers (especially in areas concerning the development and representation of meaning) and others.

Of course, our reasons for studying the psychology of language may differ, according to our starting point, and this will be reflected in the nature of courses and of research agendas. Thus a characterisation of the psychological perspective might be that studying language use can contribute to our knowledge of the workings of the mind. Neuropsychologists might especially be interested in locating the language faculties within the physical structures of the brain. A more linguistic perspective may be that studying language use can inform our theories of language structure, it can provide the performance data to support theories of competence, it can provide psychological validity for linguistic constructs, and so on.

1.4 How do psycholinguists do psycholinguistics?

Although some of our knowledge in this field comes from introspection and the observation of daily behaviour, most of the major insights have come through the generation and testing of hypotheses through experiment. More recently, there has been a marked increase in high-tech observation, measuring brain activity while participants are engaged in language-related tasks. Because of this combination of types of evidence, psycholinguistics tends to blend the theoretical and descriptive insights of linguistics with the experimental methodology and rigour of psychology.

Observation

Sophisticated experimental procedures and equipment have only become available relatively recently, and so it is no surprise that early discoveries in psycholinguistics were based on more observational approaches. Early approaches also focused in particular on speech production, since the spoken output is most easily observed. For instance, we can note and analyse the occurrence of pauses and hesitations in speech, and assess these as indicators of the planning and sequencing of the spoken output. We can observe where speakers make errors, and relate these errors to hypotheses about the speech planning and production processes. We can also look at the correction of errors as an indication that speakers are monitoring their own output. Rather less often, we can note when speakers are in a 'tip-of-the-tongue' state and find out from them what they can remember of an elusive word, and see what this might tell us about the processes involved in finding words.

Some of these observational techniques can be combined with experimental intervention. We will see in later chapters, for example, that researchers have run experiments designed to elicit speech errors or to induce the tip-of-the-tongue state. A range of additional tasks has been used to study both production and comprehension.

Experiment

Experimental methods have become highly sophisticated over the past half century, in particular with the ready availability of software that allows a high level of control over the presentation of stimuli and collection of data, with precise timing. Advantages of experimental over observational approaches include the reduction of observer bias and the increased control over what participants are required to do. This last point means that researchers are more easily able to isolate aspects of the production or comprehension processes that they are interested in. The disadvantage of experimental approaches, however, is the relative lack of ecological validity – it is usually only in experimental settings that participants are asked to make an explicit judgement about whether or not a stimulus they have heard is a word of their language, or makes sense in their language.

Typically, experimental techniques involve some kind of response time measure, where the time taken by participants to carry out some language-related task is recorded, often together with their accuracy in that task. Examples of some of these tasks can be found on the website for this book. Some response time tasks involve the notion of competing attention. That is, it is assumed that the time taken by the participant to complete the task depends on how much spare capacity they have, which will in turn depend on the nature of the linguistic processing going on at the same time. So for instance in the click location task participants listen to an utterance that has had a non-linguistic click or beep sound added to it. Their task is to listen to and understand the utterance and at the same time to mark on a transcript of the utterance where they think the click occurred. Results from such tasks show 'migration' of the click to

Table 1.1 Approximate timing of components involved in picture naming (based on Indefrey & Levelt, 2004).	
Conceptual preparation	175 msec
Word retrieval	75 msec
Phonological code retrieval	80 msec
Syllabification	25 msec per phoneme
Phonetic encoding	145 msec

locations other than where it actually occurred. This migration is at least in part a consequence of the fact that participants' attention was devoted to linguistic processing. Similar effects are found in dichotic switch monitoring. In this task participants have to indicate when the speech they are listening to moves from one headphone channel to the other. They do not always do this accurately because of the linguistic processing load at the point of the switch. (See Chapters 10 and 11 for examples of such tasks and how they contribute to our understanding of sentence comprehension.)

Other response time tasks use reaction times as a measure of the processing speed for the item being attended to. In its simplest form, perhaps, the response time task requires participants to press a button as quickly as possible when they see or hear a word. There may be a choice of buttons, one for a positive response when the word is an actual word of the language and the other for a negative response, when the word is not an actual word. Chapters 8 and 9 discuss how the speed and accuracy of participants' responses depend on factors such as familiarity – well-known words result in faster and more accurate responses than less well-known words.

In another button-pressing task, a participant reads a sentence on-screen, with presentation of each successive word controlled by the participant's pressing of the button. Chapters 10 and 11 give illustrations of how difficulty in interpreting the sentence at any point is reflected in the time taken to press the button to see the next word.

Carrying out a response task involves many components, some of which are assumed to be relatively invariant across different stimuli (e.g. the time it takes to send a motor command from the brain to the hand to execute a button press). One study (Indefrey & Levelt, 2004) broke down the supposedly simple task of saying a word that names a pictured object into the components listed in Table 1.1, starting with a mapping from the picture onto a mental concept and finishing with the initiation of the spoken word. Details will be given in the following chapters, but note for now that the most obvious influence on the time taken to initiate the response is the length of the word, since the stage labelled syllabification in the table has a duration that depends on the number of phonemes, or speech sounds, in the word. But in addition, it is important to remember that the other stages will have variable durations, depending for example on the accessibility of the word, which will vary with factors such as how often or how recently that word has been used. These are the factors that

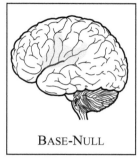 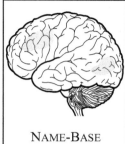 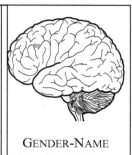

| Base-Null | Name-Base | Gender-Name |

Figure 1.3
Schematic representation of differences in brain activity during different tasks (based on fMRI data published by Heim *et al.*, 2002; see text for explanation).

are often explored in experiments, and which require other aspects of the experiment to be held constant.

Language and the brain

It is becoming more and more usual to find studies which include monitoring of the patterns of blood flow and/or electrical activity associated with neural stimulation in the brain while a participant is carrying out some language production or comprehension task. These measures have a clear advantage over behavioural methods such as response button pressing, since they provide a more direct measure of psycholinguistic processing. Imaging techniques that measure blood flow give an indication of the areas of the brain involved in the tasks being carried out (and of brain areas that have been damaged after strokes or accidents). However, they typically have relatively poor temporal resolution, and so are not ideally suited to tracking the time course of the very fast processes involved in language processing. On the other hand, techniques that measure electrical activity provide better temporal resolution but poor spatial resolution. They are therefore better suited to the measurement of the time course of processing than to the precise determination of which brain areas are responsible for various tasks.

As an example of what we can learn from neurophysiological techniques, Figure 1.3 gives a very approximate depiction of differences in brain activity levels measured in a range of tasks carried out by German participants (Heim, Opitz & Friederici, 2002). Brain activity was measured using functional Magnetic Resonance Imaging (fMRI), which tracks changes in blood flow (see sidebar). An important aspect of German that is being examined here is the fact that nouns have grammatical gender which is marked through the forms of articles (e.g. the word for *the*). For instance the word for *cat* has feminine gender, so *the cat* is 'die Katze', while the word for *dog* has masculine gender and *the dog* is 'der Hund'.

The shaded shapes in each panel show differences in brain activity when two tasks are compared. The first panel shows areas with an increase in activity in a simple baseline speaking task (Base), compared to when the participants are at rest (Null). The baseline task is simply to say 'ja ja' ('yes yes') when they see a simple visual stimulus. The second panel shows areas that are active in a picture naming task (Name), compared with the

fMRI – functional Magnetic Resonance Imaging
   Neurons that are active consume more oxygen from their blood supply than those that are inactive. Oxygenated and deoxygenated blood have different magnetic properties, and though these differences are small they are sufficient to show up in a scanner that generates high magnetic fields. The participant lies in a scanner and changes in neural activity in different brain areas are measured while they perform some language task.

baseline task. In a naming task the participants are not just speaking but are also retrieving a word from memory. For instance, if they see a picture of a cat, then they have to retrieve and produce the word that names that picture, i.e. 'Katze' (*cat*). Clearly additional areas of the brain are involved in this task when compared with the baseline task. Finally, the third panel shows a small additional area (when compared with the naming task) that is active when the participant produces the appropriate definite article. As this is marked for the grammatical gender of the noun in German, the correct form has to be selected, and this seems to involve this small area of the brain (hence the label GENDER in the figure).

fMRI, as used to obtain the data above, is one of the imaging techniques that measures blood flow in the brain. Other types include PET scans (positron emission tomography), which measure emissions from radioactive substances injected into the bloodstream, and CAT scans (computed axial tomography), which are based on a series of X-rays taken from different angles.

Imaging techniques measuring electrical activity in the brain include MEG (magnetoencephalography) and EEG (electroencephalography). The former measures the magnetic fields created by naturally occurring electrical activity in the brain, while the latter measures electrical activity on the scalp. An advantage of the MEG technique is that the magnetic fields it measures are not distorted by surrounding tissues, which can affect the electrical activity measured by EEG. These techniques measure event-related potentials (ERP), the electrical currents passing through the fluid that surrounds neurons as they respond to an event, or event-related magnetic fields (ERF) which measure currents over larger neuronal structures.

Despite the technological advances that now allow us to look in great detail at neurophysiological aspects of language production and comprehension, there are areas of psycholinguistics in which informal observation and relatively simple experimental techniques still provide appropriate means for learning more about the production, comprehension and representation of language. A clear advantage of such techniques for many researchers, especially those housed in linguistics departments in humanities faculties, is their low cost compared with the hugely expensive imaging techniques mentioned above. Where possible, such approaches have been used in the exercise material included in each chapter of this book.

Summary

This chapter has given a short overview of some of the subject matter of psycholinguistics. It has given some examples of the types of phenomena that psycholinguistics explores, as well as examples of how psycholinguists carry out that exploration.

Some of the areas of psycholinguistics that have been highlighted as of relevance to this book are:

- planning a language utterance
- the development of a syntactic structure for the expression of an idea
- the selection of words to express that idea and their insertion into sentences
- the construction of words from smaller parts such as stems and endings, and from sounds and letters
- language-specific aspects of perception
- the recognition of words, whether in speech or writing
- the construction of a sentence structure during comprehension, and the part played in that by meaning and other aspects of sentences

Some of the techniques used by psycholinguists include:

- observation of speakers and listeners, including self-observation
- conducting experiments in production and comprehension, including response time experiments
- measuring brain activity during language tasks

The remaining chapters of this book look in more detail at many aspects of the exploration of language processing set out in this chapter.

Exercises

The exercises below are intended to encourage you to use everyday contexts to explore some of the phenomena investigated in psycholinguistics. Exercises suggested in other chapters will involve more detailed examinations of these and other phenomena.

Exercise 1.1

Newspaper headlines are often incomplete sentences or leave out shorter or less important words. This can result in unintended amusing or ambiguous results, as in 'Man gets nine years in violin case', or 'Sisters reunited after twenty years in checkout queue'. Look out for such instances when you read newspapers, and try to work out why the headlines have the effect they do. Alternatively, Google 'Amusing headlines' to find a number of collections. Think about what it is that we do when we read texts that result in such amusing interpretations.

Exercise 1.2

Listen out for speech errors in the conversations you have during the day. If you can do this without disrupting the conversations, keep a record of these errors in a notebook. These can be errors that other people make, or errors you notice yourself making. See if you can identify any patterns in the errors. In very general terms (we will look at the details later), what do the errors tell you about speech production? Is it always easy to say what the error involves or why the error has come about? How representative and reliable do you think your examples are? Can you think of problems with this way of collecting speech error data?

> **Exercise 1.3**
> If you find yourself (or a conversational partner) in a tip-of-the-tongue state, i.e. you know there is a word for what you want to say but you just can't find it, then write down what you (or the speaker if it is not you) can remember about the word. I.e. how long the word is, what kinds of sounds it has, what the stress pattern of the word is, what other words are similar in sound or meaning. If you subsequently are able to recall the word, how much overlap does it have with the characteristics you were able to remember?

Further reading

There are many introductions to psycholinguistics, with different intended audiences. The following is just a sample. One text that I have used extensively in my teaching and to which I often turn for reference is Harley (2008). A more generally accessible text from the same author is *Talking the Talk* (Harley, 2010). Aitchison has written a number of very readable texts, including an introduction to psycholinguistics (Aitchison, 2008) and an introduction to the mental lexicon (Aitchison, 2003). A text designed for linguistics students, but with different scope to the current book, is Cairns (1999). A strong and detailed textbook from psychology is Carroll (2008). Both of these last two texts differ from the current text in that they include material on language acquisition and on the biological foundations of language. Whitney (1998) is also a text for psychology students, covering language, cognition and neuroscience, and including many exercises.

In addition to these textbooks, there are a number of handbooks that give excellent coverage of key areas with contributions from leading experts. The first of these has appeared in two editions (Gernsbacher, 1994; Traxler & Gernsbacher, 2006), giving a total of 64 original chapters from dozens of leading researchers in the field. The two editions offer interesting snapshots of the field, and a comparison of the two is particularly illuminating for a sense of the rapidity with which the field is developing. The *Oxford Handbook of Psycholinguistics* (Gaskell, 2007) contains 49 chapters from the field's leaders. Altmann (2002) has gathered together seminal publications spanning the twentieth century, originally appearing as journal articles, book chapters and technical reports, into a set of six volumes giving an overview of the scope and history of psycholinguistics.

For more on the teaching of psycholinguistics in a linguistics context, see Warren (2011).

2 Planning utterances

PREVIEW

This chapter looks at how speakers begin the process of producing an utterance. You will learn:

- that constructing an utterance involves different levels of planning;
- that planning is reflected in patterns of pausing and hesitation;
- that speech errors are an important source of information about utterance planning;
- that the way speakers pronounce a sentence indicates more about the grammatical structure of the sentence than is shown by punctuation.

2.1 Introduction

We are so used to speaking that we probably do not think of it as a particularly special accomplishment. But behind what seems to be a fairly automatic process there is a good deal of planning and organisation. In everyday contexts we are only likely to become aware of this planning under certain circumstances, such as when we are unable to find the word or phrase that we would like to use to express some idea, or when we make some kind of an error or 'slip of the tongue'. Along with data from experimental tasks targeting specific aspects of language production, and data from neuroimaging studies, these experiences provide insights into the processes involved in planning and producing utterances. Consider the following text.

Key
· short pause   --- very long pause
- medium pause   <u>underline</u> = filled pause, e.g. *uhm, ah*
-- long pause

1   Yes I went from sleepy old Wellington to - the great bustle of Rome via I think
    the longest route - ever · that anyone has taken from New Zealand to Australia
    cos · I got a -- cheap <u>---</u> a cheap air fare - which · involved me going via
    Amsterdam to get to Rome -- also via Singapore and - most of the - known
5   world - so <u>-</u> I · arrived - in · Rome -- I don't know if you can get jet lag· going
    that way but I was certainly very very tired · having spent forty odd hours on a
    plane or waiting in airports <u>--</u> and - from somewhere where · it's very very
    quiet to somewhere where the bustle and hustle of Rome and people speaking · a
    different language which I had learned · but of course you learn it from books
10 and - written · thing and you don't actually have to speak it to survive -- so I <u>--</u> I
    arrived in Rome -- and <u>---</u> Rome airport is - not actually in Rome - I think it's
    actually in a different country · to Rome because you have to spend about three
    or four hours on · buses and · trains planes in order to be · whereas to actually to
    get into · something that - most people would recognise as being Rome -- So I
15 f-f-finally managed to get myself on a on a - a bus -- and then I actually
    worked · had to work out work out how to pay which was not entirely obvious -
    as anyone that's travelled on foreign buses they all have different system - and -
    - I didn't actually work out until <u>-</u> a couple of months later when I was actually
    living in Florence how you actually pay for buses in Italy which is you buy a
20 ticket before you get on the bus - and then you click it once you're on the bus so
    I could have - you know if someone had checked I probably would have got -
    slammed in jail · having just arrived in the country -- (h)after an hour or so

This text is taken from a short monologue from a young New Zealander describing a journey to Europe. The monologue can be heard on the website for this textbook. There is nothing particularly unusual about this piece of spoken language, and it is perfectly easy to follow when you listen to it. But when it is written down like this, what immediately strikes us is that there are relatively few examples of what we might call well-formed sentences. Some sentences are incomplete (line 17: *as anyone that's travelled on foreign buses…*), some stop and start again as the speaker changes his mind or repairs something that he realises he has got wrong or revises something that is incomplete (lines 13–14: *in order to be · whereas to actually to get into…*), others appear to be full of repetition (lines 15–16: *and then I actually worked · had to work out work out how to pay*). And of course there are errors (*to Australia* in line 2) that hardly seem to matter in the context of the whole passage.

The transcribed text has not been given any conventional written punctuation, but the speaker appears to provide a spoken form of punctuation, by placing pauses at various points in the passage (marked by the dots and dashes – see the key). But if we take a closer look at this pausing, we see that in this respect too the speaker is failing to produce well-formed sentences. The first pause in the transcript is not where we would expect to find a comma: *Yes I went from sleepy old Wellington to - the great bustle of Rome.* Consider also the 'punctuation' in line 5: *so ═ I · arrived - in · Rome.* Clearly pausing is not just about punctuation.

These pauses are a type of hesitation. Notice that some of them contain hesitation noises (these are filled pauses, shown by underlining in the transcript). We can also see other forms of hesitation, like the drawing out of a sound (lines 14–15: *So I f-f-finally …*), and the rather 'empty' use of filler phrases or verbal fillers like *you know* (line 21).

Rather than helping a listener, in the way that punctuation can help a reader work out the structure of a text, many of these pauses and hesitations might actually make it more difficult for us to follow what is going on. For the psycholinguist, though, these hesitation phenomena are far from being a nuisance, since they provide information about how a speaker constructs an utterance and about the choices that speakers have to make as they talk (for a review of some of the early research based on pauses and hesitations see Petrie, 1987). These choices include deciding which words best express the ideas that the speaker wants to convey (Chapter 3 gives additional detail on word selection) and which types of sentence structure are the best vehicles for these ideas. They also include decisions about the very ideas that should be expressed. In this chapter we will look at these types of utterance planning, and the evidence that looking at phenomena such as pausing can provide.

2.2 A sketch of the production process

The task of producing language involves a number of processes and sources of knowledge. A sketch of some of these is given in Figure 2.1, which shows on the left the processes and their outcomes, and on the right some of the knowledge and skills required.

As speakers, we start with some notion or abstract idea of what we want to say, without at first generating the words or sentences to express this.

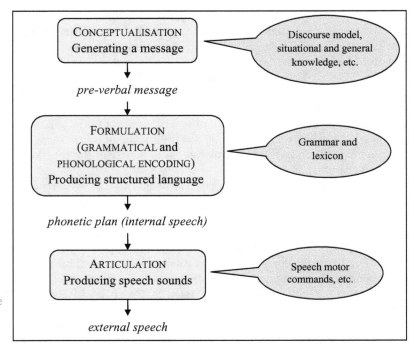

Figure 2.1
Processes and knowledge types involved in language production (Garrett, 1980a; Levelt, 1999).

This is a process of conceptualisation, during which we use what we know about the world, about the current situation etc., in order to sort out our ideas. We then need to put together the elements of language that will express this idea, drawing on our knowledge of our language, including grammar and the lexicon (vocabulary). This involves a process of formulation. Finally, in order to speak this utterance we go through a process of articulation, involving our speech apparatus.

Evidence that the various processes involved in language production are distinct comes from a review of brain imaging studies (Indefrey, 2007). In one study, brain activity was compared in tasks that required syntactic organisation (describing a scenario in full sentences) and in those that did not (listing unrelated words), in order to separate syntactic from lexical processes. In another, the brain areas activated during narrative production were determined, and compared with those used in prompted sentence production. Together, these studies indicate that aspects of language production are distinguishable in terms of brain activity (for example, see Figure 2.2), which supports their separation as stages in the production process.

The material in the remainder of this chapter focuses on the conceptualisation and formulation processes, leaving aside issues to do with choosing and inserting words into sentences, which will be developed in Chapters 3 and 4 respectively. In this book we will have little to say about the articulation processes, for which the reader should refer to texts on phonetics, especially those that include descriptions of articulatory phonetics (e.g. Ashby & Maidment, 2005; Laver, 1994).

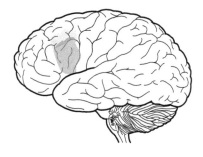

Figure 2.2
Left hemisphere brain areas involved in syntactic encoding (dark blue) and conceptual planning (light blue) (simplified from Indefrey, 2007).

Figure 2.3
The cat hunted the mouse.

2.3 Conceptualisation and planning

Conceptualisation is pre-linguistic. That is, it does not involve forms of language, but is all done 'in the head' in abstract terms. The speaker needs to make some very general decisions about what to say, taking into account facts about the situation that they are in, and relying on their general knowledge as well as on their understanding of how communication (including conversation) works. They will also need to think about whether specific aspects of their message need to be highlighted. The result of the process of conceptualisation is a pre-verbal message, i.e. it is still not language. It consists of a set of ideas in what has sometimes been called mentalese, or the language of thought. These ideas form part of the mental model (Johnson-Laird, 1983) of what the speaker wants to say. They are not yet organised into an ordered string of phrases and words, which will be the task of the formulation component.

Let's imagine the speaker wants to communicate the idea that a cat hunted a mouse (Figure 2.3). For this example sentence, the pre-verbal message will reflect their intention to communicate at least three concepts: the concept of hunting (of one animal by another), the concept of a cat as the entity carrying out this action (the AGENT), and the concept of a mouse as the entity on which the action is carried out (the THEME, sometimes referred to as the PATIENT). It will also include information about whether the speaker wants to highlight any of these concepts, e.g. by focusing on the AGENT or on the THEME.

> AGENT and THEME are types of **thematic role** and relate to the part played by an entity in the action of a verb. This is part of the conceptual structure of a sentence as it relates more to meaning than to syntactic structure

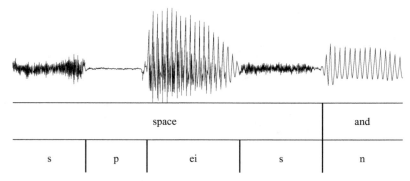

Figure 2.4
Speech waveform and text annotation of '…space and …'. Note the period of silence in the waveform during the /p/ sound. In this case the silence lasts approximately 65 msec.

A key source of information about the processes of conceptualisation and planning in producing spoken output is the pattern of pausing that speakers produce. The argument is that planning involves mental activity that competes for our attention resources with the actual process of speaking. The more planning we need to do, the less easy it is for us to continue speaking and the more likely it is that we will hesitate.

When is a pause a pause?

Before we explore more closely this idea that pauses can tell us about conceptualisation and planning, it is important first to consider what counts as a pause. A key issue concerns how long a silence has to be before we can safely say it is a pause. This is because in the normal articulation of speech we will find silences that we would not want to include in our catalogue of pauses. Take for instance the pronunciation of /p/ in the word *space*. This /p/ requires the speaker to close the lips tightly, preventing any air or sound from coming out, and then to release that closure rather suddenly. During the closure part of this sound, there will be a measurable though very brief silence, as shown in Figure 2.4. This is an articulatory pause. Because of such silences – and also in early research because of the degree of accuracy of the equipment used – researchers tend to use a minimum duration for what counts as a pause, such as 200 milliseconds. At the same time, however, listeners often hear pauses where there are none. This is because speakers sometimes slow down their rate of speaking without actually producing a silence, and this change in rhythm can be enough to lead to the perception of a pause. Not surprisingly, some studies also look at such changes in the durations of syllables or other parts of words as part of the study of pausing.

Note that pauses also have functions other than planning. Delimitative pauses can occur at places where a written text might have punctuation, breaking utterances into constituent parts, possibly to help the listener. Intonation and other aspects of prosody can also contribute to this function. Physiological pauses are those that help speakers to regulate their breathing while speaking. In practice, speakers mostly breathe at points where they might have to pause for some other reason. Accordingly, the use of pausing for breathing is largely disregarded in psycholinguistic studies.

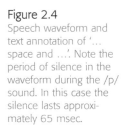

Milliseconds (msec), i.e. thousandths of a second, are a fairly standard unit of time measurement in the psycholinguistic world.

Prosody: the melody and rhythm of speech
Intonation: the melody or tonal modulation of speech

Some researchers have looked in more detail at filled pauses, and in particular at whether different types of filled pause might have different functions. So for example, while Clark and Fox Tree (2002) found a variety of reasons why speakers might use filled pauses – to gain time to search for a word, to indicate that they have not yet finished their turn, etc. – they found that speakers were more likely to use 'uh' to signal a short delay and 'um' to signal a longer delay in speaking. Chapter 5 looks at how such behaviour indicates that speakers are continually monitoring their output and effecting repairs when things go wrong.

Pausing and the amount of planning

Everyone has probably planned an utterance in some detail – a speech, an answer prepared for an interview, a marriage proposal, an apology for that broken vase that has been preying on your mind, and so on. Most speech events are less well prepared but still differ from one another in the amount and types of planning involved. These differences are reflected in the number and distribution of pauses in speech. When the task is reading aloud, most of the planning has already been done in preparing the text in the first place. As a consequence, when fluent readers speak aloud from a prepared manuscript, they do not need to pause for planning purposes but instead pause almost exclusively at points marked by punctuation, with longer pauses at paragraph breaks than at full stops.

This close coordination of pausing and sentence structure during reading can be contrasted with pause patterns in spontaneous speech. Here, it is much more likely that sentence constituents will be interrupted by pausing and other hesitation types (see the transcribed monologue given earlier). Pauses are more frequent and often much longer in spontaneous speech than in reading, but there are also many short pauses. In one of my own unpublished studies of speakers' performance in different tasks, one speaker had average pause durations of 870 msec in spontaneous speech and 479 msec in reading. She spent a total of 31% of her time pausing in spontaneous speech but only 10% during reading aloud.

These rather obvious differences between read speech and unprepared speech reflect the equally obvious differences in the planning involved in the two tasks. When we read aloud a prepared text, we need to plan when to pause in order to mark the structure of the text for our listeners (and to grab an opportunity to breathe). We also need to organise how we are going to articulate the speech sounds that correspond to the words. This is not a trivial task, since it involves recognising the written form of the word, finding a pronunciation for that word, coordinating the movements of various muscles to produce the sounds, and so on. In spontaneous speech, we have to carry out some of the tasks just listed and a whole lot more besides. This is because we also need to decide what we want to say and what sentences and words we want to use in order to say it. Compared with reading aloud, spontaneous speaking involves considerably more planning, and planning of quite different kinds. It is not surprising then that it includes many more pauses, and longer pauses. There are also many more disfluencies and other types of hesitation in

> Prosody, especially pausing, is often regarded as the punctuation of speech. It is important to remember though that not all written punctuation marks will have corresponding prosodic marking, and that not all prosodic marking would be shown through punctuation in text.

spontaneous speech. Since we continuously monitor what we are saying and frequently decide that there is a better or more appropriate way of getting our message across, spontaneous speech also contains more self-interruptions, false starts, and so on.

Between these extremes of reading and spontaneous speech we find other speech tasks that vary in the amount and nature of the planning involved. They also vary in the amount and distribution of pausing. For instance, in a pioneering psycholinguistic study of pausing, Goldman-Eisler (1961) asked speakers to carry out two different tasks using a cartoon story made up of a series of pictures, usually a story with some kind of moral behind it. One task was simply to describe the action in the pictures, and the other was to interpret the story. In the description, speakers do not need to generate the basic ideas (which are given by the pictures), but they do need to find the right words and sentence structures to convey those ideas. In the interpretation, speakers need to explain the moral behind the story. This involves a greater amount of original and abstract thought, and the conversion of this to speech involves more planning than the description task. This difference is reflected in more pause time in interpretations than in descriptions. Goldman-Eisler found that interpretations of cartoon stories had an average ratio of pause time to speech time of 3.31 : 1, while the corresponding figure for cartoon descriptions was just 1.24 : 1.

2.4 Cycles of planning

What, then, is involved in planning unscripted speech? Let us take as a basic unit of planning something that we might call an 'idea'. Researchers have tried to operationalise what is meant by 'idea' by asking naïve participants to look at a tidied-up transcript of spontaneous speech, from which the disfluencies have been deleted, and to mark where new ideas start. There is remarkable consistency in where participants mark these transition points between ideas (Butterworth, 1975).

What is interesting from the point of view of how pause patterns might reflect the processes of conceptualisation is that if we look at the patterns of speaking and pausing that correspond to 'ideas', then we frequently find that the early part of each idea is marked by a lot of pausing, but later parts have more speaking and less pausing (Henderson, Goldman-Eisler & Skarbek, 1965, 1966). This is illustrated in Figure 2.5, from an analysis of the monologue text we saw earlier. Each horizontal segment indicates a period of speaking, and each vertical segment is a period of pausing. These alternate, since each pause comes between two stretches of speech. Two points from the text are marked on this plot. The first, at *so I arrived* in lines 10–11 of the transcript, is at the beginning of a period of the monologue where there is a lot of pausing compared with speaking (see the superimposed line marked A). The second, at *Rome airport* in line 11 of the transcript, is where this relationship of speaking and pausing reverses, as shown by the slope of the line marked B. In unrehearsed speech, these periods of hesitant and fluent speech alternate in this way.

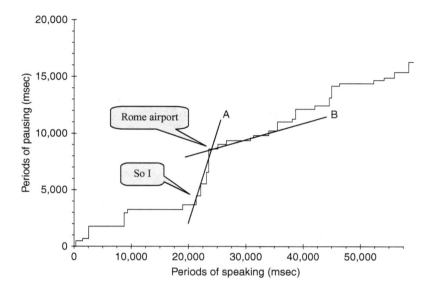

Figure 2.5
Example of hesitant (A) and fluent (B) phases of speech. See text for details.

There was some early criticism of the basic claim that there were cycles of hesitant and fluent periods in speech, since it was shown that naïve judges would detect similar cyclical patterns in graphs based on sequences of randomly generated numbers (Power, 1983; Schwartz & Jaffe, 1968). However, further analysis showed that the speech cycles coincide with 'ideas' (Butterworth, 1980; Merlo & Barbosa, 2010; Roberts & Kirsner, 2000). The greater hesitancy at the beginning of a new idea reflects the fact that the expression of the idea has not been planned in detail in advance, but has to be sorted out once it is started.

Macro- and microplanning

Getting the various ideas organised in a way that is going to best suit their communication is part of macroplanning, i.e. deciding how to achieve an intended communicative goal using relevant speech acts. A speech act is the performance of some action through saying something, such as asking for information, making a promise, and so on (Clark, 1996). Part of our knowledge about how language works is that we know what speech acts work well in achieving particular goals in a given context and for given addressees.

Not all goals have single corresponding speech acts. Some goals require multiple speech acts, such as giving route directions. Some speech acts achieve multiple goals, such as saying *I saw the bastard last night*, which tells the listener that the speaker saw the person in question at a particular time, and also conveys the speaker's opinion of that person. When a communicative goal requires a series of speech acts, such as route directions, then the speaker needs to both select and sequence those speech acts. This involves linearisation, i.e. choosing the order in which information should be expressed. There may be different consequences to saying

Walk towards the sea and stop at the edge of the cliff and *Stop at the edge of the cliff and walk towards the sea.*

Some ordering is largely natural – e.g. relating a sequence of events, or the route from A to B (Filipi & Wales, 2004; Klein, 1981). Other ordering appears to follow certain conventions that keep the structure of what is said as simple and as transparent as possible, perhaps to minimise the processing and memory load for the listener. Illustrations of these conventions come from studies that have used network description tasks where speakers are asked to describe a set of interconnected colour nodes so that the listener can draw the node pattern from their description (Levelt, 1982). Chapter 5 gives more detailed description of how these node structures have been used in collecting production data, and in particular looks at their use in generating data relating to how speakers monitor and repair their speech.

When speakers get to points where a node network splits into two parts, they usually describe a shorter arm first, because this means that the description can return to the choice point sooner than if they had first described the longer arm. Also, they tend to follow a principle of connectivity in describing these node patterns (as in other tasks such as route descriptions, or descriptions of the layout of furniture in a room). That is, rather than making jumps, speakers tend to describe things that are near to one another or somehow connected. As well as physical connections, this connection might involve the functions of the things being talked about, which may be important in the description of the contents of a room.

Another aspect of macroplanning is the selection of which information will go into the *main* structure of the utterance and which will go into *side* structures, e.g. additional comments, asides and embellishments not central to the main communicative intention.

The speaker also needs to decide how much and what sort of information to include. This depends on the important notion of instrumentality – speakers select information that helps them to achieve their communicative goals. Equally, they leave out information if they can assume the listener can make the appropriate inferences. For instance, if we can infer that the listener will know that the Beehive is a landmark building in Wellington (it is a beehive-shaped government building), then it is suitably efficient to give a route direction that does not include detail about what the Beehive is, like *Turn left at the Beehive*. But giving an equivalently informative set of directions to an overseas visitor to New Zealand will require the planning of additional information structures to explain what the Beehive is.

It is clear then that considerable planning is involved in speech production. Some of this planning can be carried out prior to beginning speaking (as in anticipating what you might say before you go to an interview), but most will be carried out once speech performance has started. If the information you have to express is readily available (e.g. visible to you at the time of utterance), then you do not have to do a lot of macroplanning to decide what to express. But a more complex task, such as planning a route, giving a narrative account, making a speech, etc., involves more

> Memory limitations are important factors in speech production and comprehension. It is widely accepted that there are different types of memory, involved in different ways in language processing. An important type is short term memory (STM), also known as working memory. In comprehension, items (e.g. words) are held in STM before being processed at a higher level (e.g. into idea units).

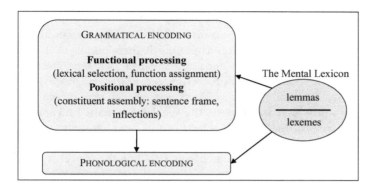

extensive searches for information and more ordering of utterances. These types of discourse tend to reveal the cyclical patterns of hesitant and fluent phases of speech.

As well as sorting out the type and order of speech acts in macroplanning, speakers carry out detailed planning of each individual speech act, known as microplanning. This involves determining the perspective and information structure that is most appropriate for a given speech act, and deciding what should be highlighted as new or topical information. Macro- and microplanning should be thought of as two levels of planning, rather than temporally distinct stages. That is, once a speaker has made initial decisions about the sequence of speech acts required to achieve some communicative goal, individual acts can be planned in more detail, even before the overall plan has been finalised.

The outcome of macro- and micro-planning is still not 'language'. It is a pre-verbal message representing the speaker's ideas or propositions, and which still needs to be converted to linguistic form. In terms of the sketch of a language production model in Figure 2.1, we have reached the output of the conceptualisation process.

2.5 Formulation

The formulation processes are the linguistic powerhouse of language production. Formulation involves grammatical encoding i.e. where the speaker uses their (implicit) knowledge of grammar to create sentence structures that will convey a message. Chapter 4 examines how formulation also involves phonological encoding, which allows us to construct the appropriate sequences of sound to express the message. Other encoding processes will be involved in producing handwritten or typed text outputs. Grammatical and phonological encoding are linked to different aspects of lexical entries, as shown in Figure 2.6. Words are accessed from the mental lexicon on the basis of their meanings. These content-based or semantic aspects of words are known as lemmas. The lemmas are linked to the forms of words, known as lexemes, which can be the spoken shape of words, or their written forms.

Grammatical encoding

Grammatical encoding is an important aspect of taking the message generated by the conceptualiser and turning it into language. It has been claimed that grammatical encoding involves two separate but related components – functional processing and positional processing (Garrett, 1980a). The aim of functional processing is to give the appropriate jobs to words that will express the speaker's intended meaning. This involves two processes: lexical selection and function assignment, i.e. choosing the words and giving them their jobs in the sentence. Initially, abstract forms of words are chosen, based on the concepts that the speaker wants to express. These lemmas are fleshed out into actual word forms, or lexemes, at a later stage. For our example in Figure 2.3, the speaker might select the lemmas {hunt}, {cat} and {mouse}. As we have seen, in terms of thematic structure the cat is the AGENT and the mouse is the THEME of the action conveyed by {hunt}. Depending on exactly how the speaker wants to convey the message, different possible grammatical roles could be given to these lemmas in the sentence. So for one possible sentence, i.e. *the cat hunted the mouse*, the AGENT {cat} is assigned the job of grammatical subject, and the THEME {mouse} is set up to be the grammatical object. In an alternative sentence expressing the same concept, but with a different focus, i.e. the passive sentence *the mouse was hunted by the cat*, {cat} is the grammatical object, even though it is still the AGENT or do-er of the action, and the THEME {mouse} is the subject.

> Braces { } conventionally indicate that we are referring to a concept rather than to an actual word.
> Angle brackets < > are used to indicate spelled forms of words.
> Slashes / / are used to indicate aspects of the spoken forms of words.
> In this text, linguistic examples are also distinguished from normal text by italics or by being indented and numbered.

In either of these versions of our example sentence, both the SUBJECT and OBJECT concepts are marked as singular and definite (which will ultimately lead to the selection of *the* rather than *a* as the determiner, so *the cat*, not *a cat*). The time of the event being described will be 'past'. If we had access to the output of the functional component, then we might find there an unordered set of lemmas, together with the functions that they have in the sentence, as in (2.1).

(2.1)   VERB = {hunt}; SUBJECT = {cat}: singular, definite;
         OBJECT = {mouse}: singular, definite; TIME = past

In the next component of grammatical encoding, positional processing, the selected set of lemmas is organised into an ordered string. As part of this process, constituent assembly creates a sentence frame for the message. The details of this sentence frame depend on a number of things, including grammatical considerations (such as making sure that tenses are marked using verb inflections, but also specific constraints associated with particular words), as well as the speaker's decisions about which items to place in focus. A possible sentence frame for our example is given in (2.2), where N stands for noun and V for verb, and 'determiner' is a word like 'a' or 'the'.

(2.2)   (determiner) N_1 $V_{[past]}$ (determiner) N_2

Next, the lemmas for the content words are accessed from the mental lexicon and slotted into this frame, as in (2.3).

(2.3)   (DETERMINER) {cat}[singular; definite] {hunt}[past]
         (DETERMINER) {mouse}[singular; definite]

Function words and grammatical endings are then specified, before the process of phonological encoding accesses the word-forms and generates a phonetic plan, which will drive the articulators (the speech organs).

Evidence from speech errors

Much of the evidence for the distinction between functional and positional processing as components of grammatical encoding comes from speech errors. (Chapters 3 and 4 give more detailed discussions of speech errors and show that errors can provide rich information about language production.) Studies of speech errors show that word exchanges like example (2.4) are highly likely to involve two words that have the same grammatical category but which appear in different syntactic phrases. In this case these are the noun phrases that form the subject and object in the sentence. (See sidebar for a description of how error data are presented in this book.)

(2.4)   this <u>seat</u> has a <u>spring</u> in it → this <u>spring</u> has a <u>seat</u> in it
         (Garrett, 1980a)

We have just seen that word lemmas (content-based aspects of words) are selected at the functional level of the grammatical encoding system, and are assigned functional roles within the sentence. These roles include grammatical functions that are frequently linked to grammatical characteristics of specific word classes. It is therefore not surprising if exchanges involve two words from the same grammatical category and which could assume the same roles. Let us assume that the abstract pre-verbal message structure of the intended sentence in (2.4) involves concepts in the roles of subject and object of the verb, and let us assume also that at the functional level the two noun lemmas {seat} and {spring} have been selected to express the meanings required of these roles. The error in (2.4) arises when these noun lemmas are assigned to the wrong functional roles, so that when the sentence is subsequently put together at the positional level, they appear in the wrong positions.

Other errors, such as those in (2.5) and (2.6), support the idea that the error in (2.4) results from the wrong function assignment rather than just a superficial misordering of words.

(2.5)   <u>they</u> must be too tight for <u>you</u> → <u>you</u> must be too tight for <u>them</u>
         (Stemberger, 1982)

(2.6)   a <u>floor</u> full of <u>holes</u> → a <u>hole</u> full of <u>floors</u> (Fromkin, 1973a)

In (2.5) we see that the misplaced items (in this case both pronouns) have the grammatical marking that is appropriate to the functions they now have, not the functions they should have had. A simple misordering would

---

Content words are nouns, verbs, adjectives and adverbs. These are also known as the **open class** of words, since the set can easily be added to (e.g. by new product names.).

Function words are determiners, prepositions, conjunctions, particles, etc. Also known as the **closed class** of words, since the sets they come from are small and not easily extended with new vocabulary.

For speech error examples in this book, the words to the left of the arrow show the speaker's intended utterance and the words to the right of the arrow show the actual utterance.

Sources for error examples are given after each example. Errors labelled FSED are taken from the speech error database set up by Vicki Fromkin and maintained by the Max Planck Institute for Psycholinguistics (see references). If no source is given, then the error is from the author's own observations.

have produced the error *you must be too tight for <u>they</u>*. Example (2.6) shows stranding – the plural marker *–s* at the end of the phrase has not moved with the rest of the word (Chapter 4 discusses stranding in more detail and shows how this demonstrates that the base forms of words are inserted into a grammatical framework). Let us assume for this case that the pre-verbal message for the phrase is something like an abstract version of 'X(singular) full of Y(plural)'. If the functional process has to assign roles to the two nouns *floor* and *hole* and incorrectly assigns these roles (i.e. swaps X and Y but not their number marking), then we can understand how we get the error with stranding as in (2.6), rather than *a holes full of floor* or *holes full of a floor*.

(2.7)   on a <u>h</u>ot <u>s</u>oldering iron → on a <u>s</u>ot <u>h</u>oldering iron (Garrett, 1980a)

> **Double-object constructions** are sentences with two objects, one of which is the direct object, i.e. the thing or person directly affected by the action of the verb. The other is the indirect object, often the recipient of the direct object. In English the indirect object can also be expressed as a prepositional phrase

In contrast, sound exchanges like example (2.7) do not respect the grammatical class of the words they come from, and are most likely to affect words within the same syntactic phrase. Such errors occur at a more local level, during the phrase-by-phrase assembly of the utterance. We will return to a more detailed consideration of sound errors and the construction of the spoken forms of sentences in Chapter 4.

Further evidence that sentence frameworks are developed at least in part independently of the words that are placed into them comes from studies of syntactic priming. One form of this task requires participants to read aloud a sentence (the prime) before then describing a picture (Bock, 1986). Typically, the kind of sentence frame that participants choose for describing the picture is biased towards the structure of the prime sentence. So if participants read the prime sentence in (2.8) and then have to describe a picture of a man reading a story to a boy, then they are more likely to use a sentence like (2.10) than one like (2.11). Sentences (2.8) and (2.10) both use a prepositional phrase to show the recipient, i.e. the phrase starting with *to*. But if the prime is the sentence in (2.9), known as a double-object construction, then participants are more likely to describe the same picture with a sentence like that in (2.11), also a double-object construction.

(2.8)   The rock star sold some cocaine to an undercover agent.

(2.9)   The rock star sold the undercover agent some cocaine.

(2.10)   The man is reading a story to the boy.

(2.11)   The man is reading the boy a story.

Importantly, this syntactic priming appears to involve the syntactic structures, rather than the actual words in the sentence. So for instance the prime sentence in (2.12), which uses a different preposition (*for*), is just as effective as that in (2.13) in priming the use of the sentence in (2.10) rather than that in (2.11) to describe the picture.

(2.12)   The secretary baked a cake for her boss.

(2.13)   The secretary took a cake to her boss.

2.6 Sentence complexity

The previous section has looked at how the abstract word entities (lemmas) that are selected at the functional level are inserted into positional-level sentence frames. It was mentioned earlier that one of the determinants of the sentence frame might be the perspective being taken by the speaker, such as which elements in the message are being placed in focus. So the speaker might choose the passive form *The mouse was hunted by the cat* to place the mouse in focus. However, there may be a cost associated with using the passive form, because it has been argued that the passive form is syntactically more complex than the active.

Indeed, for some time work in psycholinguistics responded to a suggestion from linguistic theory that passives are derived from actives. This syntactic account makes a distinction between underlying or deep structure representations of sentences and the surface structure representations that we actually see and hear (Chomsky, 1965). It was argued that a surface passive form is obtained from an underlying active-like representation by means of a transformation, expressed in a rule such as that in (2.14), where NP stands for Noun Phrase (e.g. the determiner + noun sequence *the cat*), BE stands for the appropriate form of the verb *to be*, and the arrow shows the operation of the rule, changing the string on the left to that on the right.

(2.14) NP_1 V $NP_2 \rightarrow NP_2$ BE Ved by NP_1

The implication is that it is more complicated to produce a passive sentence than an active one, because the passive is further removed from the basic underlying concept. This is encapsulated in the Derivational Theory of Complexity (e.g. Miller & Chomsky, 1963).

However, while results of some early studies suggested indeed that passives took longer to produce than actives, subsequent research showed that the speaker's choice of a passive rather than an active form is based on what is being placed in focus (Tannenbaum & Williams, 1968). Imagine for example that participants are asked to use a passive sentence to describe the cat-chasing-mouse event shown earlier in Figure 2.3. If the picture is preceded by a paragraph that has the mouse as its topic, then it takes no more time to produce a passive than an active sentence to describe the picture. In terms of the model of language production sketched earlier, the pre-verbal message in such a situation includes the intention to present the event from the perspective of the mouse, which combines easily with the instruction to use a passive sentence, such as *The mouse was hunted by the cat*. In fact, both the inherent salience of an entity (which relates to concreteness, animacy, etc.) and its salience in the discourse context (whether it has recently been talked about, has been the focus of discussion, etc.) influence the likelihood that the words expressing this entity will be in syntactically prominent positions, i.e. early in the sentence and/or in subject position. This in turn can affect the likelihood of the speaker producing an active or a passive sentence (Prat-Sala & Branigan, 2000).

> Throughout this book standard abbreviations for word classes and phrase types are used, such as S for sentence (or clause), N for noun, V for verb, P for preposition, Adj for adjective, Adv for adverb, as well as NP, VP, etc. for phrases in which a noun, verb, etc. is the head, or the main element

It has been argued that more specific aspects of theories of sentence structure can be tested by looking at patterns of pausing and other durational patterns in speech production. For instance, the sentences in (2.15) and (2.16) appear to have the same structure, differing only in the verb. Indeed one grammatical analysis (Postal, 1974) argued that *Kate* is the object of the first verb, i.e. of the verb in the main clause, in both sentences. However, Chomsky (1973) argued that in (2.15) *Kate* is the subject of the second verb, i.e. of the verb in the subordinate clause. Intuitively it seems reasonable that the sentences in (2.15) and (2.16) are somehow different, even though they are superficially similar. For example, although it is true that if you persuade someone to do something then you are also persuading that person, it is not the case that if you expect someone to do something then you are also expecting that person. What you are expecting is the complete situation, as reflected in the fact that the sentence in (2.17) is an acceptable alternative to that in (2.15) while the corresponding sentence for *persuade* in (2.18) is simply ungrammatical.

> As the label suggests, a main clause is the clause or sentence that conveys the main idea. A subordinate clause is either dependent on the main clause, or expresses some additional and possibly optional idea

(2.15)   The host expected Kate to be at breakfast.

(2.16)   The host persuaded Kate to be at breakfast.

(2.17)   The host expected Kate would be at breakfast.

(2.18)   *The host persuaded Kate would be at breakfast.

> Sentence (2.18) uses the linguists' convention of an asterisk to mark a sentence as ungrammatical

Chomsky's account for this difference was that the sentences in (2.15) and (2.16) have a different underlying or 'deep' structure, something like (2.19) and (2.20). Crucially, the structure in (2.19) has a boundary (marked by '[') between two underlying clauses after *expected* (i.e. before the subordinate clause), but in (2.20) there is no corresponding boundary after *persuaded*.

(2.19)   [The host expected [Kate be at breakfast]$_S$]$_S$

(2.20)   [The host persuaded Kate [Kate be at breakfast]$_S$]$_S$

> In sentences (2.19) and (2.20), square brackets are used to show some of the sentence constituents. In addition, the subscripted symbol s after a right-hand bracket shows that the constituent finishing at that point is a clause.

Constituent boundaries in sentences are often marked by lengthening of words before those boundaries as well as by pausing, and these effects are more likely at major syntactic boundaries, such as before clauses, including subordinate clauses. With this in mind, Cooper (1976) examined recordings of critical sentences for evidence of such lengthening. Specifically, the duration of *expected* was measured for sentences like (2.15) and (2.17), and compared with its duration in (2.21), where there is no clause boundary immediately after *expected*. Similarly, the duration of *persuaded* in (2.16) was compared with that in (2.22).

(2.21)   The host expected Kate at the big breakfast.

(2.22)   The host persuaded Kate at the big breakfast.

Cooper found that *expected* was longer in both (2.15) and (2.17) than in (2.21), while *persuaded* was not any longer in (2.16) than in (2.22). This supports the idea that *expected* precedes a clause boundary in (2.15), just as it does in (2.17), but the same is not true of *persuaded* in (2.16). This result is claimed as support for the distinction in the grammatical analysis of the sentences that is shown in (2.19) and (2.20). It is interesting as an illustration of how psycholinguistics has often been used as a test-bed for theoretical notions in linguistics.

Another notion of complexity takes into account how many additional clauses are used to express notions related to the main idea in the sentence. Multi-clause sentences consist of a main clause and a number of subordinate clauses. For example, sentence (2.23) has a main clause *The cat hunted the mouse*, and one subordinate clause *which ran away*. The sentence in (2.24) has two subordinate clauses for the same main clause.

(2.23) The cat hunted the mouse, which ran away.

(2.24) Because she was hungry, the cat hunted the mouse, which ran away.

To determine the level of complexity, we can calculate a subordination index (first suggested by Goldman-Eisler, Skarbek & Henderson, 1965), based on the ratio of subordinate clauses to total clauses (so the sentence in (2.24) has a higher level of complexity, at 2/3 or 0.67, than that in (2.23), at 1/2 or 0.5). If greater complexity requires more planning, then this might be one factor determining the amount of pausing in different tasks. Earlier in this chapter we saw that describing a cartoon story resulted in less pausing than interpreting the cartoon. It turns out that the subordination index calculated over the cartoon descriptions is lower (at 0.19) than that calculated over the cartoon interpretations (0.50) (Goldman-Eisler *et al.*, 1965). This is understandable, given that an interpretation of a cartoon story is likely to involve structures that explain cause and effect, i.e. is likely to require multi-clausal structures (such as *The man was shouting because the boy broke the window when he kicked the ball*).

However, it turns out that structural complexity as shown by a subordination index is not the only factor that determines the amount of pausing. Consider a comparison of subordination indices and pause data from cartoon descriptions and interpretations with those from interviews. Interviews had nearly the same degree of structural complexity as cartoon interpretations (0.49), but a lower pause rate than both cartoon tasks (Goldman-Eisler *et al.*, 1965). The crucial difference is that the interviews included a second speaker, the interviewer, who was likely to interrupt the participant. A pause in a dialogue can indicate a transition point between one speaker and the other. When interviewees want to keep the floor, then they need to reduce the opportunities for the interviewer to take a turn, and they can do this by lowering the pause rate.

2.7 Syntax and speech

One intriguing aspect of the formulation processes is how grammatical encoding relates to phonological encoding. That is, are aspects of the grammatical structure of sentences reflected in the way in which those sentences are spoken? What is the relationship between syntax and speech? Do speakers employ some mapping between syntactic structures and speech structures which results in the marking of the constituent structure of the sentence, potentially of benefit to listeners?

The sentences with *expect* and *persuade* discussed in the preceding section involve superficially similar sentences that are actually quite different. The same can be said of other sentences containing structural ambiguity, i.e. which have differences in their sentence structures that correspond to different meanings of the sentences. The example in (2.25) is a global or standing ambiguity, since there is nothing in the sentence itself that resolves the ambiguity, while (2.26) and (2.27) contain a local or temporary ambiguity, hingeing on whether or not *the book* is the grammatical object of *read*, which is confirmed by the final words of the sentences.

(2.25) The spy watched the man with the binoculars.

(2.26) While John was reading the book fell off his lap.

(2.27) While John was reading the book it fell off his lap.

The differences between the two interpretations of each ambiguity correspond to differences in their assumed syntactic structure. In terms of the syntactic trees often used to describe sentence structures in linguistics, and with the omission of irrelevant detail, the two different structures for the prepositional phrase (PP) ambiguity in (2.25) can be represented as in (2.28) and (2.29). (Note that these are not the only tree structures proposed by linguists for these sentence types – see sidebar for implications.) The sentence tree in (2.28) shows that the PP *with the binoculars* attaches to the verb phrase as a modifier of the verb – this is the adverbial use of the PP, describing how the spy watched the man. The tree in (2.29) shows that the PP is part of the noun phrase (NP) headed by *man*, because in this reading the PP is a property of the NP (the man has the binoculars). These tree structures show that the difference between the two meanings of the sentence in (2.25) is related to a difference in the height of attachment of the PP into the syntactic tree. The boundary before the PP is a more major one (i.e. is within a higher-level sentence constituent) in the adverbial treatment in (2.28) than when the PP modifies the N in (2.29).

> It is important to note that any claims about the relationship between syntax and features of speech such as pausing and lengthening will depend on details of the theory of syntax being used, since different theories propose different tree structures for the same sentences. So the examples in this section and elsewhere in the book are not the only possible representations.

> Syntactic trees are one form of representing sentence structure. Another is the labelled bracketing introduced earlier. So instead of using the tree in (2.28), the same structure can be shown with the same level of detail, but arguably with less clarity, as:
> [[The spy]ₙₚ [[watched]ᵥ [the man]ₙₚ [with the binoculars]ₚₚ]ᵥₚ]ₛ

(2.28)

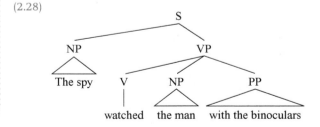

(2.29)

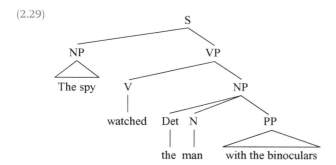

In experiments where participants have to produce sentences like (2.25) with one or other of the meanings, this structural difference is reflected in a greater likelihood of pausing prior to the PP with the adverbial meaning, along with pre-pausal lengthening of the immediately preceding word, compared to the same word in the noun modification reading (Cooper & Paccia-Cooper, 1980). Many studies have also included an acoustic measure of voice pitch, known as fundamental frequency (e.g. Cooper & Sorensen, 1981). Voice pitch falls towards the end of a constituent and re-sets to a higher level at the beginning of the next constituent, often with a 'continuation rise' after the falling tune in the first constituent. Auditory impressions of intonation patterns like this are also used as a measure of prosodic disambiguation (Speer, Warren & Schafer, 2011).

Studies of local ambiguities like that in (2.26) and (2.27) show that these too differ in rhythmic breaks, and also in their intonation patterns, even though the sentences become disambiguated before they end. Chapter 10 discusses the comprehension of such ambiguities and shows that these speech cues are important for listeners working out the intended meaning as efficiently as possible.

Other speech cues that reflect the syntactic differences between these kinds of utterances include the incidence of connected speech processes. These are changes to the speech sounds of words that occur late in the production process, as a consequence of the phonetic environment that the sounds find themselves in. For instance, many varieties of English exhibit flapping, i.e. the pronunciation of /t/ and /d/ as sounds with the briefest of contacts between the tongue and the teeth ridge. This occurs between vowels, and might be found in words like *rider* or *writer*. It even occurs between vowels that are in different words, such as *met Anne*, as long as the boundary between the two words is not a strong syntactic one. So for speakers whose English typically features flapping, this might be found in *Last time we met Anne, she told us a great story*, but not in *Last time we met, Anne told us a great story* (Cooper & Paccia-Cooper, 1980).

Such processes even respect the derivational history of a sentence. Take the ambiguity in (2.30). On the one hand this sentence could mean that

> Pre-pausal lengthening is, as its name suggests, lengthening found before a pause. The term is often also used to refer to lengthening found even in the absence of a pause. What is important is that syntactic boundaries are marked by rhythmic 'breaks', which may or may not include a physical silence

Max wants to leave someone, while on the other it could mean that Max wants someone else to do the leaving.

(2.30)   Who does Max want to leave?

It is argued that these two meanings correspond to different underlying sentences. In the first case, the question in (2.30) is derived from a sentence that might have the structure in (2.31). The question word *who* is asking about the object of the underlying sentence, and if someone answered this sentence with 'Bob', this would be taken to mean *Max wants to leave Bob*. This relationship of the question word to the rest of the sentence is shown in (2.31) by the use of a trace (indicated by *t* in italics) which follows *leave* i.e. in the object position. The trace is co-indexed with the word *who* as indicated by the subscript *i* on both *who* and *t*. The second meaning corresponds to the representation in (2.32), where the question word is now co-indexed with a trace in the subject position before *leave*. The answer 'Bob' to this question would be understood to mean *Max wants Bob to leave*. It is argued that the trace is somehow present in the surface structure of the sentence, and that the version of (2.30) that corresponds to (2.32) therefore has a trace between *want* and *to leave* that blocks the operation of a connected speech process known as wanna-contraction. *Wanna*-contraction results in the realisation of *want to* as *wanna*. In those dialects that regularly have *wanna*-contraction, it is more likely when the sentence has the meaning in (2.31) than when it has the meaning in (2.32) (Nagel, Shapiro & Nawy, 1994; Straub, Wilson, McCollum & Badecker, 2001).

(2.31)   [Who$_i$ does Max want [Max to leave t_i]$_S$]$_S$?

(2.32)   [Who$_i$ does Max want [t_i to leave]$_S$]$_S$?

The examples we have looked at show that the timing structures of speech and the incidence of connected speech processes reflect syntactic sentence structure. They also show that syntactic structure is indicated at more boundaries than those marked by punctuation in corresponding written sentences. But other examples are more complicated. For example, take a sentence from part way through the nursery rhyme *The House that Jack built*. (Those who know this rhyme will know that it can have much longer sentences than this.) Typically this would be recited with breaks as shown in (2.33), but in a traditional syntactic analysis the tree structure for the first part of the sentence would look like that shown in (2.34).

(2.33)   This is the cat / that killed the rat / that ate the malt / that lay in the house / that Jack built.

Notice that the main break in the syntactic tree, i.e. the highest point at which the tree starts to divide, is between *This* and *is*, the next highest break in the tree is between *is* and *the cat*, and so on. In addition, if pauses are primarily used to mark the ends of clauses, it is clear from the tree that there would be no pause until the end of the sentence, since the right-branching structure of this sentence means that no clauses finish until then. In short, the pattern of the syntactic breaks does not match the pattern of the breaks in the spoken sentence. In some treatments, this discrepancy is dealt with through adjustment rules that give the more even structure in (2.33) (Chomsky, 1965; Cooper, 1980). Note that it could also be dealt with by having a different theory of sentence structure than the one represented in (2.34), i.e. one that gives different and flatter syntactic trees. Whatever the solution for this particular sentence, it is clear that the relationship between syntax and speech may not always be straightforward (see also Gee & Grosjean, 1983).

(2.34)

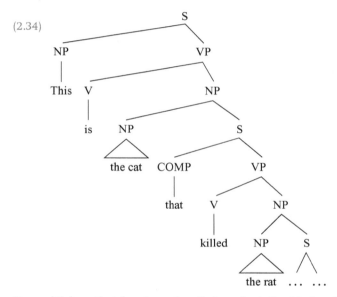

One criticism that has been levelled against the kinds of studies that have been summarised in this section is that they are based on what speakers do when they read sentences aloud (Allbritton, McKoon & Ratcliff, 1996; Haywood, Pickering & Branigan, 2005). This is quite a different task from spontaneous speech, as we have seen above. Not only are there differences in the planning involved in these different tasks, but also the goals of a reader are quite different from those of someone speaking spontaneously, and could include the goal of wanting to produce a clear difference between, say, the two meanings of (2.25), because this is what the reader perceives the experimenter to want. Recent studies have attempted to address this criticism by using speech tasks in which the participant's goals are much more closely aligned to ordinary interactions. These include collaborative game tasks, in which the outcome of the game is dependent on spoken interaction between two participants (Speer *et al.*, 2011). Such studies – on the whole – confirm that speakers produce distinctions such as those discussed in this section, distinctions that are linked to syntactic sentence structure.

Summary

Speaking is something that we largely take for granted, but which requires various types of planning:

- ideas have to be marshalled together and sequenced;
- these ideas have to be converted into language;
- the linguistic expression of the ideas requires appropriate words and these words have to be placed in appropriate sentence structures;
- sentences and words have to be given spoken form.

Looking at the patterns of pausing and other timing structures in spoken language provides us with some insights into the planning of speech, which we can supplement with observations based on speech errors, as well as through experimental studies. The timing structures of speech also reflect syntactic sentence structures, in a manner similar to, but richer than, punctuation in written language.

Exercises

Exercise 2.1

What is the subordination index of the following sentences (see p. 29)?

1. Because he was convinced she liked it, the man bought his wife a CD of a symphony they had heard on the radio.
2. They listened to it the next day.
3. She took it back because it was not the symphony they had heard.
4. The shop replaced it with the one the man should have bought.

Exercise 2.2

Underline and draw a box around the object in each of the following sentences:

1. The man bought the CD.
2. The very suspicious but rather inexperienced spy used the binoculars.
3. The dog chased the cat that had recently brought a mouse into its owner's house.

Exercise 2.3

Check your answers to Exercise 2.2 against the solutions on the website. Using the sentence tree in (2.28) as a model for a sentence with a subject and an object, where is the main division in the tree? Read aloud each of the sentences in Exercise 2.2, breaking the sentence into two parts in the place that seems most natural to you. Did you put the break in the same place as the main division in the tree? If not, why not?

Exercise 2.4

Record some spontaneous speech and some read speech (or use the samples on the website). Transcribe the spontaneous speech using ordinary orthography (or if you are using the website material, copy the text from the site). As far as you are able, and without listening to the speech when you do this, use punctuation to mark sentence breaks etc. on the transcript of the spontaneous speech. Reflect on how easy or difficult it is to do this. Now listen to each recording and mark pauses and hesitation phenomena on the transcripts (devise a key such as the one used for the passage on p. 14 above). Comment on the relationship between pause locations and punctuation for the two recordings.

Exercise 2.5

Using the samples from the previous exercise, measure in seconds how long each sample is (using a speech editor such as Praat, downloadable from www.praat.org). For each sample, count the number of words, and work out the speech rate (in words per second) and a pause rate (either in pauses per second or pauses per word). Comment on your findings.

Exercise 2.6

Ask a friend to give you a verbal list of their relatives. Record your friend while they do this. To what extent does the ordering of the relatives follow the type of organisation suggested in this chapter in the discussion of the linearisation of node-network descriptions?

Exercise 2.7

Ask some speakers to record some ambiguous sentences of your devising but similar to (2.25) or (2.26) and (2.27). How do speakers mark the syntactic differences between sentences?

Exercise 2.8

Run a simple syntactic priming task to investigate the use of active and passive sentences. That is, prepare pairs of priming sentences using active or passive constructions to describe the same event. Show one sentence from each pair to your participants, followed by a simple picture of a different event (such as Figure 2.3 above). Ask your participants to describe the pictured event using a single sentence. Note whether they use an active or a passive sentence. Is their use of active or passive primed by the sentence that came before the picture? (Note: some sample sentences and pictures are included on the website.)

Further reading

A comprehensive study of the processes involved in planning and producing utterances is given by Levelt (1989). The pioneering studies of the relationship between pausing and planning include Goldman-Eisler (1961, 1968), and a summary of these and other early studies can be found in Petrie (1987). Overviews of the processes of grammatical encoding are given by Bock and Levelt (1994) and more recently by Ferreira and Slevc (2007). Cooper and Paccia-Cooper (1980) present a series of experiments investigating the links between syntactic sentence structures and speech structures such as pausing and pre-pausal lengthening. The collaborative game tasks presented towards the end of the chapter are discussed by Speer *et al.* (2011).

3 Finding words

PREVIEW

This chapter provides an introduction to how we retrieve words from the mental lexicon (the dictionary in our heads) for production. You will learn that:

- patterns of pausing and patterns of speech errors both provide evidence for word selection processes during production;
- word finding is affected by the likelihood of a word in a particular context;
- some errors indicate competition between alternatives for a word slot in the sentence;
- some errors show that words associated with the intended word can interfere with the word finding process.

3.1 Introduction

In Chapter 2 we saw that pauses and speech errors are both useful sources of evidence about aspects of the sentence production process. The number and distribution of pauses varies with task complexity and with sentence structure, and can tell us about the amount, type and location of the planning involved in speech production. We also saw that speech errors known as word exchanges, such as (3.1), tend to involve words of the same grammatical category. This indicates that speakers build a sentence frame into which words are positioned according to word-type (e.g. nouns, verbs, etc.).

(3.1)   Older men tend to choose younger wives → Older men choose to tend younger wives (Garrett, 1975)

In this and the following chapter we look in more detail at what pauses, speech errors and other data can tell us about how we put our thoughts into words, the process of lexicalisation. It is argued that there are two stages or levels to this process. The first is the retrieval of the abstract form of a word – its lemma – from the mental lexicon, based on the concepts that the speaker wants to convey. The second stage is the specification of the form of the word (i.e. what it sounds like – or in written language production, its spelling), the lexeme. In Figure 3.1 these stages have been labelled 'finding words' and 'building words'. They are sometimes referred to as lexical selection and phonological encoding, respectively, although this latter term does not cover all aspects of building words. In the current chapter we will focus largely on the process of finding words. Chapter 4 will present a detailed description of building words, including phonological encoding. The important processes involved in recognising words during listening or reading are the subject matter of Chapters 8 and 9.

The separation of the various processes involved in producing words is supported by evidence from brain imaging studies (Indefrey, 2007). By asking participants to carry out various tasks while their brain activity

> One of the founding figures of modern linguistics, Ferdinand de Saussure (1983 [1916]), argued that the word is a sign with two connected aspects, like the two sides of a coin. He called these the *signifié* (signified) and the *signifiant* (signifier). These are similar to the lemma and the lexeme.

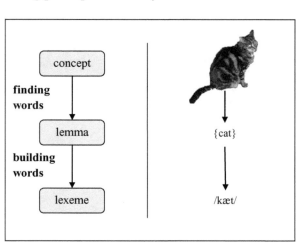

Figure 3.1
A two-stage model of lexicalisation.

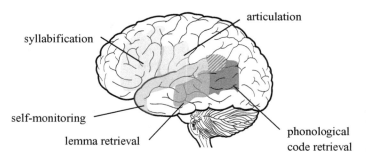

Figure 3.2
Left hemisphere brain areas involved in aspects of word production (simplified from Indefrey, 2007).

is measured, researchers can work out which brain areas have shared activity for tasks which have production components in common (e.g. the three tasks of spontaneously generating a word, naming a picture and reading out a word all involve accessing a stored phonological code for a word, while nonword reading does not, since there is no stored code for non-existent words). Combining the results of such comparisons gives a picture somewhat like Figure 3.2, where different areas are indicated for lemma retrieval, phonological code (lexeme) retrieval, and other functions.

It should be noted that the separation of lexical access into lemma and lexeme retrieval stages is not universally accepted. For instance, Caramazza (1997) argues that a separate lemma retrieval stage is unnecessary. Instead, he suggests a set of interconnected networks for different aspects of word knowledge, including semantic, syntactic, phonological and orthographic knowledge. Activation flows between these networks, and during speaking, the phonological representations for words are activated to the extent that they are connected to the semantic and syntactic information that represents what the speaker plans to say. For the purposes of exposition in this book, however, we will assume the separation of lemma and lexeme illustrated in Figure 3.1.

This chapter starts with a discussion of how patterns of pausing in spontaneous speech show that it is easier to get some words from the mental lexicon than others. We then move to a discussion of lexical selection errors such as substitutions (3.2) and blends (3.3). These are relevant to the consideration of the level at which different types of error take place, and in particular of whether the error results from interference between competing concepts or between competing words.

(3.2)   At low speeds it's too heavy → At low speeds it's too light
        (Garrett, 1975)

(3.3)   I collected my hand baggage/luggage → I collected my hand
        buggage

The study of such phenomena contributes to our understanding of how speakers choose words and insert them into an utterance.

3.2 Pausing and predictability

A central claim in the pausing research outlined in Chapter 2 is that pause patterns vary across speech tasks because these tasks require different amounts and types of planning. A specific instance of this general claim concerns the process of retrieving words from the mental lexicon. Speakers start off with a general abstract idea of what they want to say and they need to find linguistic expression for this, including finding the appropriate words. But not all words are equal – there are some words that are used more frequently than others; and there are some words that fit a particular topic or context better than others. As a result of such frequency and predictability effects, we would expect to find that some words are easier to retrieve from the mental lexicon than others. If lexical retrieval is hard, it may take longer, and may be more likely to result in a pause before the difficult word. Conversely, it has long been known that ease of access to words is associated with greater fluency in speech (Beattie & Butterworth, 1979; Lounsbury, 1954).

Studies of large corpora of pause data have shown that – in general – pauses are more likely and longer before content words than before function words. Recall that the 'closed' set of function words is much more limited than the 'open' set of content words. The finding of more pausing before content words might therefore reflect some additional time needed to select the appropriate word from a larger set of possibilities. There are alternative explanations for this overall effect. One is that function words sit in a separate part of the mental lexicon with faster access. Another is that function words become available at a different stage of the production process, when the grammatical sentence frame is constructed.

To get an experimental measure of the likelihood of different content words in an utterance, researchers have used various sentence completion techniques. In what is known as Shannon's 'Guessing Game' (Shannon, 1951), an incomplete transcript of an utterance is presented to respondents. Initially, they see the beginning portion of the utterance, and have to guess the next word. They carry on making suggestions for each word until they get it right, up to a specified time limit (e.g. one minute). They then go on to guess the next word, and so on. The lower the ratio of correct guesses to incorrect guesses for any particular word, the lower the likelihood of that word in the given context. A variant on this procedure starts at the end of the utterance and works backwards. Another, also known as the Cloze task (Taylor, 1953), deletes a word or words from a transcript and asks participants to fill in the blank(s). One measure taken from such tasks is known as transitional probability. For example, consider the sentence fragments in (3.4). Native speakers familiar with English idioms will find *mouth* highly predictable in the first sentence. There will be a relatively limited set of words that would be likely in response to the second fragment, rather more for the third, and still more for the fourth fragment. Therefore the transitional probability for *mouth* in sentence a. will be higher than that for, say, *shortbread* in sentence c.

Frequency of use and predictability are not the same. A trivial example shows this quite clearly – the word *soup* is more frequent than the word *broth*, but the latter is more predictable in the phrase 'Too many cooks spoil the

_____.'

Psycholinguistic research relies quite heavily on the techniques and results of **corpus linguistics**, i.e. the study of large collections of language data. These corpora provide information on word frequency, as well as on the patterns of phenomena such as pauses.

(3.4)   a. Don't look a gift horse in the _____

         b. The cop drew out his _____

         c. Try some of this delicious _____

         d. She was looking at the _____

Sentences have been taken from transcripts of actual spontaneous speech and used in the types of completion task outlined above. The patterns of transitional probabilities for the content words in these sentences have then been compared with the likelihood and duration of pauses before each of these words. A long-attested effect is that pauses are both more likely and longer when the word is unpredictable (Lounsbury, 1954). But early research also noted a strong relationship of pausing with a likelihood measure derived from the right-to-left, backward variant of the guessing game, and an even stronger relationship with likelihood derived from a combination of forwards and backwards guessing (Goldman-Eisler, 1961). These findings show that predictability (and lexical selection) is based not just on what is the most likely next word in a linear string of words. Rather, it depends also on a more hierarchical structure, with aspects of what we want to go on to say influencing our current word choices.

Note though that words which are unlikely in a given context (such as *opera ticket* after *his* in sentence b. in (3.4)) are also words which have high information value, i.e. they contribute a lot to the meaning. If pauses are also used to highlight less predictable words and make them easier for listeners to make out, then pausing at points of low transitional probability may be a strategy by speakers to help their listeners. (For a general discussion of predictability and speech prosody, see Turk, 2010.)

3.3 Speech errors and lexical selection

Our second source of data relating to lexical selection is provided by speech errors. Several large corpora of speech errors now exist, some of which are available online. What makes speech errors particularly interesting and useful for psycholinguistics is that they are not random. Instead they display patterns. By looking at what errors occur (and possibly those that do not), we can figure out the mechanisms that would have allowed the errors. We could think, for instance, about what linguistic units must be available for the following errors to occur.

(3.5)   This seat has a spring in it → This spring has a seat in it (Garrett, 1980a)

(3.6)   Put it in the car park → Put it in the par cark

In the case of (3.5), the speaker has reached a stage in the sentence production process at which the words *seat* and *spring* have been selected from the mental lexicon, together with relevant information about their grammatical category. These words are in a queue, waiting to be inserted into an utterance frame. Under this kind of slots-and-fillers or scan-copier approach (Shattuck-Hufnagel, 1979), the choice of the wrong fillers (words) for the waiting slots (positions in the sentence frame) can result in an exchange of words, as in (3.5). At another level, we can see the same kind of process applying in (3.6), the difference being that in this case the slots and the fillers are individual speech sounds, rather than complete words. We will return to sound errors like this in Chapter 4.

Before we go any further, it is important to note that the speech errors we are interested in here are the slips that normal competent language users produce as part of everyday speech. That is, we are not looking at clinically impaired language output, although that is also revealing about the so-called 'normal' processes of language production. Nor are we studying the errors that first or second language learners make during the learning process, although again such errors are interesting, but on the whole for different purposes.

Similarly, it is important to distinguish between the causes and mechanisms of speech errors. The causes of speech errors are manifold. Tiredness, distraction, drunkenness, the fear of public speaking – all of these can result in an increase in the count of errors in our speech. What is interesting for psycholinguists when they investigate the process of language production is not the probable cause of such errors, but what the nature of the errors might tell us about the production system. 'Freudian slips' are of course of interest to both psycholinguists and psychoanalysts (and undoubtedly to comedians). Primarily, though, the psycholinguist is interested in the fact that there are slots for words in sentences and slots for sounds (or letters) in words, and that the wrong words, sounds or letters can end up in the available slots. This might make the psycholinguistic analysis of speech errors seem rather bland, but our interest is in the mechanics of errors, which appear to be universal (reflecting aspects of the language production system), while the causes vary with the speaker and with the situation.

Some comments are also required on the reliability of error data. Most speech error corpora have been collected over many years by researchers observing errors in lectures, conferences, café conversations etc. But we need to be certain that these are errors in production rather than in perception (Chapter 7 includes discussion of 'slips of the ear' and of what they can tell us about speech perception processes). Recordings can help here, but are not always available. We also need to be confident in the accuracy of the descriptions not only of the error but also of the intended utterance. Often, the intention is clear from the context or from some sort of self-correction on the part of the speaker once they realise they have slipped. Sometimes, the error is made by the researchers themselves, and they will have a good idea of what their intention had been. But often the intended utterance will be unclear, in which case we need to be careful to avoid any over-interpretation. Chapter 4 illustrates how researchers have also worked with experimentally induced errors, which allows greater control and reliability in reporting, but may result in atypical errors.

> Freudian slips are errors that are claimed to reveal repressed thoughts or feelings, such as writing *I wish you were her* (instead of *here*) on a postcard. Or the 1970s flyer advertising a credit card in the UK that read: *The Access facility can be used at all stores displaying the red and greed symbol.*

Table 3.1 Types of word errors.			
mis-selection	substitution (one word replaces another)	(3.7)	Close it so it doesn't go stale → Close it so it doesn't go fresh (FSED)
	blend (two words are merged)	(3.8)	spaddle (spank/paddle) (Fromkin, 1973a)
mis-ordering	anticipation (a word appears earlier than intended)	(3.9)	I'm not a candidate for a cabinet position → I'm not a cabinet … (FSED)
	perseveration (a word appears again later in the sentence)	(3.10)	How many pints in a pi- … liter (FSED)
	exchange (two words swap places)	(3.11)	Just piece a put of cardboard in it
other	omission (a word is left out)	(3.12)	It's an extremely interesting way to look things up → It's an extremely way to look things up (FSED)
	addition (an extra word appears)	(3.13)	He behaved as like a fool (FSED)

The examples in Table 3.1 illustrate a range of spontaneously occurring word errors, organised into a number of different types. The different types reflect different suggested stages of the production process. Examples (3.7) and (3.8) involve errors during the selection of words from the mental lexicon, while examples (3.9)–(3.11) involve a later stage in the process, when the words that have been selected are positioned in the utterance.

Substitutions and blends

On the whole, substitutions and blends, i.e. errors of mis-selection, involve words that are semantically related, that is words which have a clear meaning relationship to one another. This is not surprising – we select words to express a concept that we want to talk about (see Figure 3.1), and concepts are likely to be linked to a number of related words. What is interesting is the difference in the nature of the relationship in these two types. Substitutions, like (3.2) and (3.7) above and (3.14) below, are quite likely to involve antonyms, words that are some kind of opposite of one another.

(3.14)   Must you leave? It's still so early → It's still so late!

On the other hand, blends more frequently involve words that are synonyms or near-synonyms, i.e. words that have very similar meanings. Example (3.8) above illustrates this, as do the examples in (3.15).

(3.15)   a. slick/slippery → slicker

b. stomach/tummy → stummy

c. stiffer/tougher → stougher (all from Fromkin, 1973a)

Antonyms or words that are opposite in meaning include gradable opposites that allow some in-between value, such as *hot* and *cold*, exclusive or complementary terms such as *dead* and *alive*, and reciprocal terms such as *husband* and *wife*.

Synonyms involve sameness of meaning. Since there would seem to be little advantage in having two words with precisely the same meaning in one language, most synonyms are really near-synonyms, with slight and often subtle differences in meaning.

It has been suggested that the differing nature of the meaning relationships involved in substitutions and blends reflects different stages of the production process at which the errors occur. To understand this, we must distinguish between relationships at the conceptual level and relationships at the lemma level.

Concept-level relationships involve pre-linguistic abstract ideas. Let us assume that during speech production there is sometimes ambivalence as to which of two closely related ideas best represents the speaker's intention. This has been referred to as a situation of 'alternative plans'. In such a situation, the related concepts activate their lemmas at the same time (e.g. {baggage} and {luggage} in (3.3)). If the speaker is unable to resolve the competition between the alternative plans, then these activated lemmas may both be inserted into the same slot, and the lexemes linked to these lemmas become blended at the level of phonological processing (to produce *buggage*).

By contrast, lemma-level relationships tend to be associative. That is, they arise through the associations that words have with one another. Researchers have collected data on native speakers' word associations, as we will see below. Some associations involve collocations (i.e. between words that tend to co-occur in the same phrase or sentence, such as *bread* and *butter*), but many involve some kind of antonymy or oppositeness.

> **Collocations** include words that typically occur together, such as *fish and chips*, and also idioms like *A stitch in time saves nine*.

Unlike the (near-)synonyms involved in blends, words in an associative relationship differ crucially in some core aspect of their meaning. Interestingly, associated words are hardly ever involved in blends, but they do feature quite regularly in substitutions. In substitutions, then, the intended concept activates its lemma, and activation flows through the associative links between lemmas, so that an associate of the initially accessed lemma is also activated, and the wrong lexeme is inserted into the utterance (see Figure 3.3).

We now need to explain why the associate becomes available before the target lemma and replaces it in the utterance. One possible factor is the relative frequency of the lemmas involved. If an associated lemma is more frequent than the target lemma, then it might become available before the target. (Frequency effects are abundant in psycholinguistics, and are discussed in more detail from the perspective of word recognition in Chapters 8 and 9.) The results in this respect seem to be rather mixed, with frequency being a factor in some studies, but not reliably so. Indeed, one study found a stronger effect of imageability, a semantic effect that has independently been shown to influence ease of access to words in production. Substituting words were generally more imageable than substituted words (Harley & Macandre, 2001).

It is also possible that the replacement of a target by an associate comes about because the target lexeme is for some reason unavailable, even if only momentarily. The result is similar to the longer-lasting effects found in the speech of some patients with brain injury (e.g. after strokes), who will often produce words associated with an intended word, often without realising that they have produced the wrong word.

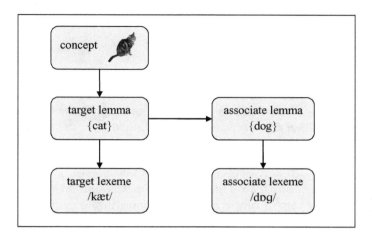

Figure 3.3
Activation flow to an associate lemma in substitution errors.

The discussion above has suggested that blends and substitutions differ in the type of semantic relationship that exists between the words involved: synonyms are blended, while substitutions involve antonyms or other types of associative relationship. This oversimplifies the situation. For instance, there are errors where substitutions involve near-synonyms, including the rather more complicated example in (3.16), where it would appear that a 'footwear' concept has led to lemmas for both *shoes* and *boots* being available, and *shoes* has substituted for *trousers* early in the sentence.

(3.16)   tuck your trousers into your boots → tuck your shoes into your boots

In addition, we have no easy way of determining that substitutions do not also involve synonyms, simply because substitution of one word by another word with a similar meaning is unlikely to be noticed. However, the fact that blends rarely involve anything other than synonyms, while substitutions clearly involve a range of associative relationships, suggests that these two classes of error involve different levels or types of processing.

Malapropisms

A further common observation about blends is that they often involve words that have similar sounds, as was illustrated by the examples in (3.8) and (3.15). These are not the only word-selection errors that involve formal (sound-based) relationships between words. Consider for instance the errors known as malapropisms (Fay & Cutler, 1977). These are errors where the word produced is similar to the intended word in its sound shape, but not necessarily in its meaning, as illustrated in (3.17).

(3.17)   If these two vectors are equivalent, then ... → If these two vectors are equivocal, then ... (Fay & Cutler, 1977)

Malapropisms are named after the character Mrs Malaprop in Sheridan's play *The Rivals* (1775). This character made somewhat ridiculous substitutions

The name Malaprop which led to the term malapropisms was coined on the basis of the word *malapropos* (from the French *mal à propos*) meaning 'unsuitable' or 'inappropriate'.

of words that were similar in form, such as the example from the play in (3.18).

(3.18)   He is the very pinnacle of politeness → He is the very pineapple of politeness

The examples from Sheridan's play are obviously constructed, as are countless others that have been placed by scriptwriters into the mouths of actors over the centuries. However, naturally occurring malapropisms also exist, although they are relatively rare compared with other error types. Some errors infamously produced by former United States President George W. Bush have been described as malapropisms (as well as being called Bushisms). Two of these are listed in (3.19) and (3.20). Many of Bush's examples may of course have their origins in misreading, rather than being spontaneous speech errors.

(3.19)   The law I sign today directs new funds… to the task of collecting vital intelligence… on weapons of mass production [*target*: destruction]

(3.20)   We cannot let terrorists and rogue nations hold this nation hostile [*target*: hostage]

If lexical selection is meaning-based (i.e. based on the conceptual representation of the message), how do form-based word-selection errors occur? One explanation suggests that there are links from the sounds in the target word to other words that contain the same sounds. As the form of the target is retrieved, this activates its component sounds. If activation flows back from these sounds to the other words containing the same sounds, as shown by the dashed arrows in Figure 3.4, then a similar sounding word may become activated. If the activation is strong enough, then this competing word may replace the target in the actual utterance produced. The activation of the substituting word may be higher because it is a more frequent word, as has been demonstrated in an analysis of malapropisms (Vitevitch, 1997). It may even be increased by activation from a conceptual aspect of the context. In this particular case it could be argued that the concept of the word *hostile* is an active one in the context of the sentence in (3.20), and that this has also activated the {hostile} lemma and the /hɒstaɪl/ lexeme. The same process operates in the case of many blends, where the words involved frequently also overlap both in their sounds and in their meaning.

Serial and interactive models of lexicalisation

Notice that Figure 3.4 differs from the simpler model of lexicalisation in Figure 3.1, in that it allows information between the levels to flow in more than one direction. These two figures are rather simplified forms of two theories of speech production. In one type, reflected in Figure 3.1, it is argued that the speaker has access to one word at a time following a rather discrete and unidirectional flow of information between levels.

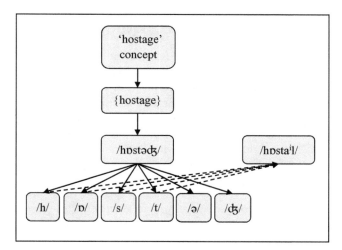

Figure 3.4
Activation flow to a
phonetically similar form
in malapropisms.

Models of this type are variously referred to as symbolic or serial search models. In another type, more like Figure 3.4, information spreads by way of activation from units at one level down to multiple units at the next level, but then also back up to the higher-level units. These are connectionist models, including interactive activation (IA) models. (Chapters 8 and 9 also consider such model types, from the point-of-view of lexical access during word recognition, and explore these models in more detail than is given here.)

As well as the positive or facilitative activation illustrated in Figure 3.4, IA models typically also include the notion of inhibition through competitive links, usually between units at the same level. Such links help to explain the speed with which successful word candidates become available – the more active a candidate word is, the more strongly it inhibits its competitors. For example, a high-frequency word will quickly dominate other candidate words both because it starts off being more active and also because, all else being equal, it will inhibit its competitors and become even more dominant.

In addition to evidence from speech errors, there is also experimental evidence which shows that both meaning- and form-based relationships are important in lexical selection, and which also supports the notion of inhibitory links between words, at least at some levels. For example, Levelt *et al.* (1999) review results from picture/word interference tasks. These are tasks where participants have to name objects in a series of pictures, but at around the time they are about to start producing the name, they either hear or see (superimposed on the picture) a word related to the object name. If this distractor word is related in meaning to the object name (e.g. GOAT if the picture is of a sheep), then it slows the naming response. If the distractor is phonologically related (e.g. SHEET for sheep), then it speeds up the naming response.

> The consequences of the inhibitory connections in IA models are sometimes referred to as 'the rich get richer' effect, or the Matthew effect, after the Bible verse from Matthew, 25:29–30 'For whoever has will be given more, and they will have an abundance. Whoever does not have, even what they have will be taken from them' (New International Version).

> Words are **semantically** related if they share some aspect of their meanings. They are **phonologically** related if they share some aspect of their pronunciation.

3.4 Getting the order wrong

A further group of errors illustrated in Table 3.1 involve mis-ordering. These are errors where the correct words have been selected for production but placed in the wrong position in the utterance. Mis-ordering errors tend not to involve words with strong meaning relationships except insofar as words that are used in the same utterance might very well be associatively related. Errors involving mis-ordering include anticipations (e.g. (3.9) in Table 3.1, along with (3.21) and (3.22) below), perseverations (e.g. (3.10), (3.23) and (3.24)) and exchanges (e.g. (3.11), (3.25)–(3.27)).

(3.21)   Notice there are a number of strings we can associate with these... uh, structures we can associate with these strings (FSED)

(3.22)   combien d'années pardon, combien de groupes y a-t-il en deux-ième année? (FSED) [*how many years sorry, how many groups are there in the second year*]

(3.23)   [weather reporter talking about rainfall] ... twenty-two inches! ... and that not even in 24 hours. most of that fell in twelve inches (FSED)

(3.24)   un jour t'auras des cheveux blancs, t'auras une grand-mère... tu seras une grand-mère (FSED) [*one day you will have grey hair, you will have a grandmother ... you will be a grandmother*]

(3.25)   Seymour sliced the knife with a salami (Fromkin, 1973a)

(3.26)   I got into this guy with a discussion (Garrett, 1980a)

(3.27)   I didn't get a copy with my cover (Fromkin, 1973a)

A common interpretation given for errors of this type is that as a speaker develops an utterance, they access the required lexical items from their mental dictionary, but something goes wrong in assigning an item to the correct position. Often, as in some of the examples cited here, the error is noticed by the speaker and subsequently corrected, which actually makes it easier for the researcher to determine what the intended utterance was. In anticipations, a word is inserted too early into the sentence frame that has been developed. This might be because the word is a particularly frequent one or has somehow become highly activated by the context, and consequently has a higher level of activation than the intended word. In perseverations, a word that has already been used remains 'active' and available for re-insertion. The persistent activation of this word may result from a failure to cross it off the list of words cued for use, again perhaps because it is a frequent word with a high level of activation.

What is interesting about these errors is that they largely involve words from the same grammatical category. For example, in the anticipation errors in (3.21) and (3.22) the noun slots after *of* and *de* respectively are filled by nouns, and in the perseveration error in (3.24) a verb slot after the *t'* form of the pronoun *tu* is filled with a verb used earlier in the utterance.

Anticipations might be incomplete exchanges, where the speaker notices that an exchange of X and Y is happening and blocks the full exchange, so that Y occurs not only early, but also in its intended place.

The exchanges in (3.25)–(3.27) all involve two nouns. It is not always the case that the two words or word-slots involved in an error are of the same category – see for instance example (3.11), where a noun and a verb are exchanged. Nevertheless, in one analysis a clear majority (85%) of a set of 200 word exchanges involved two words from the same grammatical category (Stemberger, 1985). As was pointed out in Chapter 2, the strong likelihood of two words involved in an ordering error being from the same grammatical category indicates that when words are selected for production, their grammatical category information is available, and words of the appropriate category are inserted into the available slots in the sentence frame.

3.5 Association norms

Association norms are lists of the words that are evoked in the minds of native speakers when a target word is presented to them. These lists are a research tool that has proved useful for considering, amongst other things, the nature of the relationships between the words involved in speech errors, and they provide interesting information about the possible connections between words in the mental lexicon. Such norms are established by asking a large number of participants (typically a hundred or more) to write down or say the first word that comes to them when they are presented with the target word. Over the group of participants, a pattern emerges, with some words more frequently given as responses than others. A set of examples from one such study is given in Table 3.2.

What we see from this small selection of targets and their most frequent responses is a range of associative relationships. Some are various types of opposite, such as *high* and *low*, *long* and *short*, *white* and *black*, *boy* and *girl*, *husband* and *wife* (a reciprocal opposite, looking at the same relationship from opposite perspectives), and possibly *king* and *queen*. Others are names of objects that you might expect to occur together in the same sentence, i.e. involve collocational links between words, such as between *hammer* and *nail*, *butter* and *bread* (and some of the other pairings would also fall under this heading). The percentage figures in Table 3.2 reveal a range of strengths of the associative relationship. The responses here are all for the most popular ones to the given words, but range from 25% to 85%. In Table 3.3 the complete lists of responses for two target words, *butter* and *bread*, are given, and these lists show a broader set of

Table 3.2 Most popular association responses to a selection of target words (targets in upper case, responses in lower case; data from the Edinburgh Associative Thesaurus: www.eat.rl.ac.uk; values are percentages of all responses to that target).

HIGH	low	60	KING	queen	45
WHITE	black	55	BOY	girl	78
LONG	short	53	HAMMER	nail	28
HUSBAND	wife	85	BUTTER	bread	25

Table 3.3 Association responses given to two target words (BUTTER and BREAD). Data are from the same source as Table 3.2. Values are percentages of all responses to that target.

BUTTER				BREAD			
bread	25	churn	1	butter	54	floor	1
yellow	9	cutter	1	water	6	flour	1
margarine	8	dish	1	loaf	5	german	1
cheese	6	dripping	1	food	3	heaven	1
milk	6	ham	1	money	3	hungry	1
cup	4	lard	1	bin	2	line	1
eggs	4	mouth	1	board	2	slice	1
jam	4	oil	1	cheese	2	toast	1
knife	3	pat	1	jam	2	waters	1
marg.	3	protein	1	knife	2	wheat	1
cream	2	roll	1	sauce	2		
fingers	2	rolls	1	wine	2		
fly	2	scotch	1	bacon	1		
melt	2	sickness	1	calcium	1		
soft	2	Stork	1	crumbs	1		
spread	2			dough	1		

relationships between targets and responses. They also suggest that collocational links are stronger in a left-to-right direction, since *bread* produces a greater proportion of *butter* responses than vice versa, presumably because of the phrase *bread and butter*.

Summary

Data from pause studies and from speech errors are used to provide evidence for the processes of selecting words and inserting them into sentence frames. The main observations are:

- finding words from the mental lexicon involves a process of selecting a lemma (an abstract representation of the word) to match a concept;
- pauses are more likely before less predictable words, reflecting difficulty of lexical access;
- blend errors reveal competition between alternative concepts;
- substitution errors reveal competition between alternative lemmas – often antonyms – that have been activated based on the conceptual representation;

- lexical properties such as imageability and frequency play a role in the likelihood of meaning- and form-based substitution errors respectively;
- the activation of a word-form (lexeme) corresponding to the lemma can also interfere with the process of lemma selection.

Together, these findings show the complexity of the word retrieval process and indicate that the separation of word finding and word building (see Chapter 4) is to an extent a false one – the various aspects of constructing an utterance interact with one another and do not represent entirely distinct stages of the language production process.

Exercises

Exercise 3.1
What sort of word-level error has taken place in the following examples?

1. to determine what/which → to determine watch (Fromkin, 1973a)
2. a branch falling on the roof → a branch falling on the tree (Fromkin, 1973a)
3. a language learner needs → a language needer learns (Fromkin, 1973a)
4. chamber music → chamber maid (Fromkin, 1973a)
5. wine is being served at dinner → dinner is being served at wine (Fromkin, 1973a)
6. many players think … many people think he's the most underrated player in the nation (FSED)
7. t'as gym tous les jours, sauf le mardi où tu vas à la gym … à la piscine (FSED) [*you have gym every day except Tuesday when you go to the gym … to the pool*]

Exercise 3.2
What are the semantic relationships (antonyms, synonyms, etc.) between the words involved in the errors in Exercise 3.1?

Exercise 3.3
As a simple exercise in measuring predictability, devise some sentences similar to those in example (3.4) and ask a group of your friends to give the first word they think of. You should find that you get fewer and more consistent responses for the more predictable continuation.

Exercise 3.4
Try a version of Shannon's 'Guessing Game' (p. 40), presenting the beginning part of a sentence, and asking participants to guess the next word. Note how many guesses it takes before they get the right word (up to a limit of a certain number of guesses, at which point you should tell them the next word). Then continue for the next word, and so on. This will give you a measure of how predictability changes across a sentence.

Exercise 3.5
Using the same sentences as in the previous exercise, do the backwards version of this task, i.e. starting at the end of the sentence and working forwards.

Do the predictability scores for each word differ from those in the forwards version of the task, or are they more similar than you might have expected?

Exercise 3.6

Select some words that you might predict to have a lot of associates and some others that you would predict to have few associates. Go to the website given in the caption to Table 3.2, and check your predictions. If the results differ from your predictions, why do you think this might be? (NB you could deliberately choose a subset of words that you think might be linked to your own culture, and see whether the results from the Edinburgh association norms differ from your predictions for these words in particular.)

Further reading

One of the leading figures in the study of speech errors was Victoria Fromkin. Her edited volumes (1973c, 1980) set the foundation for later studies. A corpus of her speech error data can be accessed at www.mpi.nl/cgi-bin/sedb/sperco_form4.pl. Fay and Cutler (1977) provided an early model of how we select words and what word substitution data can tell us about this process. Cutler (1982) contains another rich collection of analyses of error data, and includes discussion of the difficulties associated with collecting and interpreting errors. Levelt (1993) provides a collection of useful articles on lexical access in speech production, and Levelt (1999) develops a model of the lexical access process. For a review of the key properties of the word production process see Griffin and Ferreira (2006). Indefrey (2007) reviews neurophysiological aspects of language production, including lemma access.

4 Building words

PREVIEW

This chapter continues our exploration of how we string words together when speaking. We will be looking in particular at how words are constructed from their component parts. You will learn:

- that the stored representation of a word contains structural information about its morphology and phonology, including its stress pattern and its syllable and sound structure;

- that there are stored representations of sub-lexical (smaller-than-word) units, which are phonetic plans used by the 'articulator';

- that building words involves the generation of a string of sub-lexical units, based on information associated with each word. The string is then converted into an articulatory plan;

- that aspects of this process can become confused, leading to a range of speech errors.

4.1 Introduction

The sketch of the lexicalisation process given in Chapter 3 (see Figure 3.1) broke lexicalisation down into two stages – finding words and building words. The process of finding words (lexical selection) was the subject matter of Chapter 3. In this chapter we will look at the process of building words. Again, our evidence will come mainly but not exclusively from speech error data.

The components of the word that need to be fleshed out include its morphology and its phonology. The morphology of the word is its structure defined in terms of the meaningful parts that constitute it – these include the stem or base form of the word and its various possible affixes, such as English -*s* meaning 'plural' in *cats* or *in*- to show 'negative' in *inadequate*. Words are made up of one or more morphemes. The morpheme is the smallest unit of meaning, and can be free-standing such as *cat* or bound to other morphemes as is the case with the plural -*s*. A morpheme, which is often represented using a definition of its meaning and by being conventionally placed inside { }, can have more than one form or allomorph. So the English {plural} morpheme has /s/, /z/ and /əz/ allomorphs occurring in different phonetic contexts (contrast the pronunciation of -*s* in *cats*, *dogs* and *horses*).

The spoken forms of words (and morphemes) are also made up of speech segments, or phonemes. A phoneme can have more than one allophone, or phonetic realisation. So in English the realisation of the /p/ phoneme in *pin* is different from that in *spin* – in *pin* it is typically spoken with a stronger burst of air. (You can feel this yourself if you hold your hand in front of your mouth as you say the words.)

A word's phonology is the individual sounds or phonemes that make up the word, e.g. /k/, /æ/ and /t/ for *cat*, plus other aspects of its sound structure, e.g. the rhyme of *cat* is /æt/, the second syllable of *inadequate* carries the main stress in that word, and so on.

Although morphology and phonology deal with different aspects of word-internal structure, they are treated together in this chapter since they are both relevant to the process of building words. Morphological and phonological production processes occur at the same local level. One study of speech errors (Garrett, 1980a) showed that 70% of morphological stranding errors (where the movement of a word leaves behind an affix, as in (4.1) – see Chapter 2 and the next section) occur within syntactic constituents smaller than the clause, such as verb or noun phrases, rather than across phrases within a clause. Similarly, most (87%) cases of sound exchange (e.g. *par cark* for *car park*) are also within local phrases. Word exchanges, on the other hand, are more likely between (81%) than within phrases.

(4.1)   a floor full of hole<u>s</u> → a hole full of floor<u>s</u> (Fromkin, 1973a)

This patterning has been associated with the different levels in a hierarchical production system, i.e. the *functional* and *positional* levels introduced in Chapter 2. Recall that at the *functional* level the abstract content-based aspects of words, i.e. lemmas, are selected on the basis of their semantic and/or grammatical roles (subject, verb, object, etc). Errors at this level involve whole-words (substitutions, word blends, exchanges, etc.). The *positional* level involves firstly the choice of the local syntactic framework, including grammatical affixes and function words, and secondly the insertion of word-forms into this frame. It is at this level that morphological errors such as stranding take place, as well as errors involving the sound structure of words.

4.2 Tip-of-the-tongue

It might seem odd that words need to be constructed, rather than simply read out of the mental dictionary as complete forms. But there is some fairlycompelling evidence that accessing a word from the dictionary is not an all-or-nothing experience. One source of such evidence is the tip-of-the-tongue (TOT) phenomenon, which was described over a century ago as experiencing 'a gap that is intensely active. A sort of wraith of the name is in it, beckoning us in a given direction, making us at moments tingle with the sense of our closeness and then letting us sink back without the longed-for term' (James, 1893: 243). What is intriguing is that when a speaker has a TOT experience, their 'sense of closeness' means that they can often correctly identify some elements of the word they are looking for (such as its beginning sounds, or its stress pattern), and they can often identify other similar-sounding words. They just seem unable to put together the complete form of the word.

Researchers have conducted experimental studies of word-form access by inducing TOT states. For instance, Brown and McNeill (1966) gave participants definitions of uncommon English words, and asked them to give the word corresponding to each definition. If they could not give the word, they were asked to recall as much as they could about it. Participants were good at recalling the beginnings (around 70% correct) and ends of words, but not as accurate with the middle portions. They could also recall the number of syllables (again around 70% correct) and the position of stressed syllables in polysyllabic words. Better memory for the beginnings of words ties in well with the finding that word beginnings are important for finding words in the mental lexicon during comprehension. The finding that word endings are also recalled better than the middles of words could reflect the important role of suffixes in English as markers of grammatical information and word class.

Vigliocco and colleagues (1997) ran a similar study with native speakers of Italian, which has grammatical gender (i.e. nouns are either masculine or feminine). They chose target words where the gender was arbitrary, i.e. they avoided examples like *man* and *woman* where there would be a semantic reason why a word should be masculine or feminine, and they avoided words where a particular ending indicates the gender of the word, such as *amico* (male friend) vs *amica* (female friend). They found that participants in a TOT state could successfully report the gender of the target word 84% of

> The finding that speakers in the TOT state are better at remembering the beginnings and ends of words than their middles has been dubbed the 'bathtub' effect (Aitchison, 2003), because someone lying in a bath has their head and feet above the water, but their middle submerged.

the time, and their ability to report the gender was independent of whether they could report anything about the sound shape of the word. This last finding supports the idea of the two-stage process of lexicalisation – grammatical information linked to the lemma is available separately from phonological information linked to the lexeme.

Many brain-damaged patients have an experience similar to TOT, called anomia, but for them this happens much more frequently. It has been argued that the TOT experience is really just a special instance of the normal word-building processes, and that word building always involves filling out the details of a word-sketch that has become available during the word-finding stage. Filling out the word-sketch becomes a more obvious process in TOT experiences, because some aspects of the word are for some reason not available to the speaker. The idea that there is a word-sketch that needs to be filled out with the appropriate components is a parallel to the observation in Chapter 2 that there is a sketch of a sentence that needs to be filled out with the appropriate words.

4.3 Speech errors and morphological structure

A key issue in the discussion of the production of morphological structure is whether morphologically complex words are constructed as and when they are needed, rather than being fully listed in the mental lexicon. If we find that at least some complex words are created on the fly, then a subsidiary question is whether this is true only when certain types of morphology are involved. Most frequently, this involves the distinction between inflectional and derivational morphology, and so we shall look at each of these in turn.

Inflectional morphology

(4.1) and (4.2)–(4.7) illustrate stranding errors. The stranded element is underlined in each case. These errors show that word stems and word endings are treated separately during at least some stages of the process of speaking. In Chapter 2 our description of (4.1) (as example (2.6)) was that an abstract version of the phrase, something like 'X(singular) full of Y(plural)', needs to have word stems assigned to the roles indexed by X and Y, and endings produced to indicate {singular} and {plural}. The stranding error suggests that the grammatical marking of {singular} and {plural} is part of the sentence frame, with the error involving the misplacement of the stems into this frame during lexical insertion. That is, *hole* in (4.1) is inserted for X instead of for Y, and is marked for singular, i.e. has no overt affix, while *floor* is inserted for Y instead of X and is given a plural affix, producing *floors*.

(4.2)　He works for a company that makes kitchen<u>s</u> → He works for a kitchen that makes companie<u>s</u>

(4.3)　It just start<u>ed</u> to sound → It just sound<u>ed</u> to start (Garrett, 1975)

(4.4)　I thought the truck was park<u>ed</u> → I thought the park was truck<u>ed</u> (Garrett, 1980a)

(4.5)   She's already pack<u>ed</u> two trunk<u>s</u> → She's already trunk<u>ed</u> two pack<u>s</u> (Garrett, 1975)

(4.6)   Cork bowls, Astle duck<u>s</u> under a bouncer → Cork bowls, Astle bounce<u>s</u> under a duck

(4.7)   … wear<u>ing</u> a name tag → … nam<u>ing</u> a wear tag (Garrett, 1975)

This interpretation of stranding errors suggests that the affixed form is constructed during speech production. If this were not the case, i.e. if in fact the complete affixed form is retrieved from the mental lexicon, then we would predict that the affix remains with the relevant stem, giving *a holes full of floor*. But such errors are extremely rare.

Stranding errors typically involve grammatical endings, i.e. endings traditionally known as inflections. In (4.1) and (4.2) the inflection is a plural marker. This is one of the most frequent elements involved in stranding errors in English, along with tense markers, as in (4.3) and (4.4). Both plural and tense markers are stranded in (4.5). The example in (4.6) involves the third person singular -*s* ending. It is an error noticed by the author in New Zealand. Given that the -*ers* and -*es* endings (as in *villagers* and *villages*) are homophonous for many speakers of New Zealand English, it is possible that the entire base *bouncer* was moved, and that the error word *bouncers* was reinterpreted by the author as *bounces*. In (4.7) the stranded affix is the progressive marker -*ing*.

Not all English plural and past tense forms involve the simple affixation of endings onto stems. English has plenty of irregular plurals, like *feet* or *children* and irregular past tense forms like *swam* or *went*. Such forms cannot be predicted by a rule such as 'add -s for plural', and so it would be reasonable to expect these words to be stored as complete forms in the lexicon and accessed as such rather than being constructed as and when needed. Nevertheless, irregular past tense forms are also involved in English speech errors. Consider the stranding error in (4.8). The exchange is clearly of the underlying morphemes for the stems *know* and *hear*, and not of the full forms, which would have resulted in the error *I'd heard one if I know it*. The location that *know* has been moved to in the error is a location that has been specified at the functional processing stage as 'past', and the subsequent process of specifying word forms results in the insertion of the correct irregular form, rather than a regularised *knowed*.

> There are some instances of regularised versions of irregular past tenses or plurals in English speech errors, such as *swimmed* for *swam*. Such regularisations also occur at the stage in child language development where children have internalised a rule for forming past tense, etc. and are over-applying it.

(4.8)   I'd know one if I heard it → I'd hear one if I knew it (Garrett, 1980b)

Examples like this also show how morphological markers such as {past} are not the same as the phonological realisation of these markers. That is, what is merged with *know* in the error in (4.8) is the abstract entity {past}, rather than a specific form such as /d/.

Words and rules

Because they use the regular, predictable and most widespread way of forming past tenses in English, it seems sensible to suppose that past

The idea that all examples of a particular morphologically complex form of words, such as past tense forms of verbs, are listed in the mental dictionary is known as the **full-listing hypothesis**.

tense forms like *started* and *sounded* (example (4.3)) or plurals like *kitchens* and *companies* (example (4.2)) are constructed when needed. Irregular forms like *knew* or *children*, however, have to be looked up. But does it make sense to have two routes for finding past-tense forms or for plurals – a rule-based route and a lexical look-up route – rather than just assuming that every past tense is looked up in the dictionary? This issue has been a hot topic in psycholinguistics, with many arguments presented for each view (see e.g. Pinker, 1999). Let us consider some of the arguments against the idea that all inflected forms are looked up in the mental lexicon.

First, it is clear that the regular forms are used, in a rule-like way, to form past tenses or plurals of new words. We can quite safely predict that if we asked participants to give a plural form for a nonword that we said was a noun, such as *bafflack*, then they would respond with *bafflacks*.

A second and related argument is that children learn at quite an early stage that forming plurals – an inflectional process – is highly regular and therefore predictable, as is making past tenses. The so-called 'wug test' was used in a study with young children who were shown a cartoon picture of a creature (see Figure 4.1), were told it was a *wug* and were then asked what they would call two of them (Berko, 1958). As predicted, the children said they were *wugs*.

A presumably unintended by-product of the wug test is the popularity of the wug image, the original of which is shown in Figure 4.1. Wugs can now be found adorning t-shirts, mugs, place mats, even pet-food bowls.

A third argument involves morpheme shift errors, such as (4.9)–(4.11). Consider the verb in example (4.10). There is no reason to expect that looking up a stored past tense form of *point out* in the mental dictionary would produce anything other than *pointed out*. So where does *point outed* come from?

(4.9)   It probably gets out a little → It probably get outs a little
        (Garrett, 1980a)

(4.10) pointed out → point outed (Garrett, 1980a)

(4.11) He goes back to → He go backs to (Garrett, 1975)

The error comes about because the regular past-tense rule ('add -ed to the end of the verb') is applied to the entire multiword unit *point out*.

Morphology or phonology?

Since both morphology and phonology involve small bits of words, there will be some errors apparently involving morphemes where an argument in terms of the sound structure of the word might be a plausible alternative to a morphological account. So in (4.10) what might have happened is

Multiword units are lexical items (i.e. individual dictionary entries) that are made up of more than one word, such as the verb+particle form *point out*. They can often be replaced by a lexical item that is a single word, for instance *indicate* in this case.

THIS IS A WUG

Figure 4.1
A wug, as used in the wug test.

not a morpheme shift, but a misplacement of the /əd/ sequence of phonemes corresponding to the <ed> spelling. However, this description is
less convincing than one in terms of a coherent unit of word structure,
the morpheme. In addition, there are parallel cases, like (4.11), where
what <u>looks</u> like the shift of a sound is in fact not. This is because although
in the written version of this speech error an <s> has been moved, in the
intended utterance what would have been a /z/ pronunciation in *goes*,
becomes a /s/ pronunciation in *backs*. This is known as accommodation,
i.e. the allomorph of the morpheme {third person singular present} that
occurs in the error is appropriate to the word on which it occurs, and not
to the word on which it should have occurred. What this suggests is that
such errors do indeed involve the misplacement of a morpheme, rather
than of a speech sound, and that subsequent processes specify the appropriate allomorph for the new context.

Derivational morphology

Much of the inflectional morphology involved in the errors above is predictable by rule, and so it is not surprising to find evidence for productive
word building for these forms. A different situation arises with English
derivational morphology, which is much less predictable. Derivational
morphology involves the construction of new words from base forms. (By
contrast, a plural form *cats* is not a new word, in the sense of having a
separate lexical entry in a dictionary, but a different grammatical form of
the word *cat*.) For example, *derivational* is from *derivation* which is in turn
from *derive*. In English, derivational morphology can involve suffixes,
such as the *-tion* and *-al* endings in the *derive/derivation/derivational* pattern,
the *-hood* in *nationhood* or the *-ness* in *goodness*. It can also involve prefixes,
such as the *un-* in *unkind* or the *in-* in *inadequate*. Both of these prefixes,
un- and *in-* indicate a negative meaning, but note that there is no rule that
tells speakers that they should use *un-* in one case and *in-* in the other. The
use of one or the other is something we have to learn. We can test that this
is the case by asking people to make a negative version of a nonword. So
we might get them to give a negative form of the invented word *armotic*. It
is likely that some of our informants will say *unarmotic*, while others
might say *inarmotic*, or even *non-armotic*. This outcome contrasts with the
unanimous response we would expect to receive for a plural of the nonword *bafflack*.

Errors involving derivational prefixes have also been taken to indicate
that morphological structure is represented in the production lexicon.
Examples (4.12) to (4.14) all involve self-correction, and so we know what
the speaker intended. From the evidence, it seems that the wrong prefix
has been added to a base. However, it is unlikely that naïve native speakers
would for instance know that the target word *assert* in (4.12) is made up of
as+sert, though this may be historically accurate (the form is from Latin
as-serere, in turn from *ad* 'to' + *serere* 'to join, put'). An alternative
explanation is that these errors are a particular type of malapropism (see
Chapter 3), i.e. that the morphological similarity is coincidental, and that
the overall sound similarity is what is important. In (4.13) there could also

be phonological interference from the beginning sounds of the preceding and following words, *director* and *development*.

(4.12)　admitting entails inserting ... entails asserting (FSED)

(4.13)　director of destruc ... instructional development (FSED)

(4.14)　If they had to describe ... subscribe individually they couldn't do it (FSED)

Despite these misgivings, the pattern in such putative prefix errors does seem to be that one prefixed form is replaced by another. That is, prefixes are not replaced by non-prefixes (so we do not find *review* → *maview*). Also, we do not find substitutions involving two non-prefixed words which overlap after the first syllable (so we do not find *kitten* → *gluten*). So the errors do not simply involve words with sound overlap after the first syllable. This suggests that prefixes may be marked as such in the lexicon, even if they may not be involved in productive rules during word building.

A set of prefix errors that has drawn particular attention involves a shift of a negative prefix, as in (4.15) and (4.16). These errors provide further support for the argument that negative prefixes are stored in an abstract form {NEG} in the mental lexicon, so that *imprecise, disregard, unclear, nothing* are stored as {NEG}+stem. At the functional level, the abstract form of the target sentence in (4.15) would include a {NEG} element linked to the object clause (i.e. the clause that forms the object of the verb *regard*). In fleshing out the utterance during positional processing, the {NEG} gets misplaced, and as a result modifies the verb in the main clause. So instead of modifying *precise* (giving *imprecise*), it ends up modifying *regard* (giving *disregard*). In the error it is clearly the abstract {NEG} form that is misplaced, rather than the exact phonological form that would have been attached to the target stem, which would have produced the nonword *imregard*.

(4.15)　I regard this as imprecise → I disregard this as precise (Fromkin, 1973a)

(4.16)　If there was anything that was unclear → If there was nothing that was clear (Fromkin, 1973a)

Notice that there is a model for this shift of negative elements between main clauses and object clauses in English, since there is an equivalence between the two sentences in (4.17) and (4.18).

(4.17)　I think cigarettes are not good for your health

(4.18)　I don't think cigarettes are good for your health

Moving on to suffixes, it has been noted that errors involving the final parts of words – either as the moved elements or as stranded elements – rarely involve derivational affixes. So examples like (4.19)–(4.24) are far less common than errors such as (4.25), which involves sound sequences which are not morphemes, i.e. *-(u)nction* and *-(u)cture*. But note that some of the errors that appear to involve suffixes have plausible alternative or additional explanations. In (4.19) the error could be an anticipation of *-ment* as a syllable rather than as an affix, and similarly the exchanges in (4.20) and (4.21) might be phonological (a syllable) rather than morphological. Indeed, (4.21) is best explained this way, since the *-le* in *single* does not correspond to a morpheme.

(4.19) his dependence on the government → his dependment ...
        (MacKay, 1979)

(4.20) passive usage → passage usive (Garrett, 1980a)

(4.21) the single biggest problem → the singest biggle problem (Garrett, 1980a)

(4.22) I hate hitching on a rainy day → I hate raining on a hitchy day
        (Shattuck-Hufnagel, 1979)

(4.23) The snow makes walking very noisy → The snow makes noising very walky

(4.24) you have to face it squarely → you have to square it facely
        (Garrett, 1980a)

(4.25) structure and function → strunction and fucture (cited by Pillon, 1998)

Productivity

Some affix errors involve both inflectional and derivational endings, as in (4.26) and (4.27). The stranded elements in example (4.26) are the plural inflection *-s* (which accommodates to /ɪz/ when attached to the stem *freeze*) and the instrumental derivational affix *-er*. In (4.27) the stems *nose* and *model* are exchanged, stranding both the inflectional suffix *-ed* and the derivational prefix *re-*.

(4.26) Take the steaks out of the freezer → Take the freezes out of the steaker (Fromkin, 1973a)

(4.27) Fancy getting your nose remodelled → Fancy getting your model renosed (Garrett, 1980a)

Errors like these suggest that the distinction between inflectional and derivational endings in English is not as clear as it has often been made out to be in linguistics. In fact, many linguists see the distinction as a false one, and that morphological processes sit on a continuum that might include purely predictable inflectional endings at one extreme and totally unpredictable derivational endings at the other.

A notion that is important in this context is productivity (Bauer, 2001). Productive affixes are the affixes that are most likely to be used on novel words, such as in the wug test described above, or when a new word is coined in the language and inflected or derived forms are based on this. The more productive an affix is, the more predictable it tends to be. The contention here is that it is also more easily separated from its stem, and that such separability does not discriminate between inflection and derivation. For instance, the instrumental -er ending in (4.26) would count amongst the more productive of the derivational suffixes in English – if we were to invent a new verb, *to spling*, and asked someone to name an object that you might use to perform the action conveyed by that verb, there is a high probability that they will say it is a *splinger*. It is therefore small wonder that this affix – which can be so easily added – is also easily separated from its stem in speech errors.

Morphology and lexical stress errors

Lexical stress errors are errors where the correct word has been produced, but with the wrong stress pattern. Since English has many cases of morphologically related words that have differences in their stress pattern, it is interesting to note whether the incorrect stress pattern is in fact the correct stress pattern for a related word. If this is the case, then it could imply that there are connections between morphologically related words in the mental lexicon, and that during the process of selecting the target word there has been some interference from a linked word. Examples (4.28) to (4.32) illustrate stress errors. The morphologically related word with stress in the error position is shown in parentheses after each example, except for (4.32), which was self-corrected by the speaker, a professor of linguistics.

(4.28)   from my 'prosodic – pro'sodic colleagues ('prosody) (Cutler, 1983)

(4.29)   psycho'linguistic (psycho'linguist)

(4.30)   You think it's sar'casm, but it's not (sar'castic) (Cutler, 1980)

(4.31)   If you have a hie'rarchy of frames, so that … (hie'rarchical) (Cutler, Hawkins & Gilligan, 1985)

(4.32)   de'partment … 'mental meeting

In these errors, the syntactic category specification for the intended word leads to the appropriate ending, but in each case the stress is placed on a syllable which is stressed in a morphologically related word, suggesting confusion between close lexical entries.

4.4 Speech errors and phonological encoding

After the morphological components of a word have been selected, they need to be given form. In speech, this will be the sounds that make up the word. This process of giving sound to the abstract form of the word is widely known as phonological encoding. The lexemes or word-forms are made available via links with the lemmas that have been accessed during the grammatical encoding. So {cat} is linked in the mental dictionary both to the written form <cat> and to the spoken form /kæt/.

In Chapter 2, we started to show the development of the sentence *the cat hunted the mouse*, and had followed this as far as the lemma-based structure

> In examples (4.28)–(4.32) stress is indicated by a raised' mark before the stressed syllable, in line with the standards of the International Phonetic Association. Some dictionaries place the stress mark at the end of the stressed syllable. When using a dictionary to find the stress patterns of words, it pays to check what convention the dictionary-makers have chosen.

Table 4.1 Types of sound errors.		
mis-selection	substitution	(4.36) in his inimitable style → in his inimicable style (FSED)
mis-ordering	anticipation	(4.37) fat and placid → flat and placid (Cutler, 1988)
	perseveration	(4.38) God rest re [for *ye*] merry gentlemen (Harley, 2008)
	exchange	(4.39) like a lilting willy (Cutler, 1988)
other	omission	(4.40) most models of acquired dyslexies – dyslexias (Cutler, 1988)
	addition	(4.41) optimal number → moptimal number (Fromkin, 1973a)

in (4.33). The process of phonological encoding now inserts the appropriate word-forms into the structure, as in (4.34).

(4.33)   (DETERMINER) {cat}[singular; definite] {hunt}[past]
         (DETERMINER) {mouse}[singular; definite]

(4.34)   (DETERMINER) /kæt/[singular; definite] /hʌnt/[past]
         (DETERMINER) /maʊs/[singular; definite]

(4.35)   /ðə kæt hʌntəd ðə maʊs/

Subsequently, the function words are filled in, along with grammatical endings such as the marker of past tense, resulting in (4.35). A phonetic plan is then generated for this string, which will drive the articulators (the speech organs). The detail of the phonetic plan will depend not only on the chosen word-forms but also on the utterance context, because this will affect aspects of pronunciation such as which words will be stressed for emphasis or contrast.

As with morphological aspects of word building, much of the evidence for phonological encoding comes from studying speech errors. Examples of different types of sound errors are given in Table 4.1. As with the word errors discussed in Chapter 3, there are errors that indicate that the wrong element or sequence of elements has been selected, there are errors that show the wrong ordering of selected elements, and there are errors in which elements have been omitted or added. Mis-orderings are the most frequent type of sound error. In error corpora about half of all sound errors are either anticipations (e.g. (4.37) and (4.42)) or perseverations (as in (4.38) and (4.43)), with the next largest group being exchanges ((4.39) and (4.44)).

As we have seen, the majority of sound errors occur within local phrases rather than across larger sentence structures. Unsurprisingly, since there tend not to be many words of the same word class within a phrase, most sound errors also involve two words of different word classes.

(4.42)   role of simplicity → soul of simplicity (Fromkin, 1973a)

(4.43) Fillmore's case grammar → Fillmore's face grammar
(Fromkin, 1973a)

(4.44) copy of my paper → poppy of my caper (Fromkin, 1973a)

Two-thirds of sound errors involve single segments, including initial consonants as in the examples (4.42) to (4.44), as well as final consonants (4.45), and vowels (4.46)–(4.48). Other errors involve consonant clusters (4.49), but whole syllable errors (4.50) are extremely rare (and note that in this case only the *pu* element is an entire syllable, i.e. the other element in the exchange – *ca* – is part of and not the whole syllable, which would be *cat*).

(4.45) cup cake → cuck cape (Shattuck-Hufnagel, 1983)

(4.46) sudden death → sedden duth (Shattuck-Hufnagel, 1986)

(4.47) avoid the tree pruning → avoid the true preening (FSED)

(4.48) Sacco and Vanzetti → Saki and Vanzetto (FSED)

(4.49) start smoking → smart stoking (Fromkin, 1973a)

(4.50) pussy cat → cassy put (Fromkin, 1973b)

> A **nonword** (or nonsense word) is a form that does not exist as a word in the language in question (though it might exist in other languages).

Investigations of sound errors across corpora of error data have pointed out a number of patterns. The non-randomness of these errors leads to some important conclusions concerning language production at this level of phonological encoding. One observation is that there are important constraints – some positional – on sound errors. For example, the elements involved in mis-orderings are more likely than not to come from equivalent positions in two words. Another is that sound errors are more likely to result in real words, rather than in nonwords, although the examples already given show that this is clearly not always the case.

Metrical structure constraints

The sounds involved in sound errors tend to come from syllables that are either both stressed or both unstressed. So in (4.46), (4.47) and (4.49) the exchanged sounds are in the stressed syllables of each word, and in (4.48) they are in unstressed syllables. The interpretation is that the stored specifications of words include information about their stress patterns, in a sort of metrical frame. The good recall of stress position when people are in the tip-of-the-tongue state is a further piece of evidence for the metrical frame. As we will see later, evidence from tongue-twisters also supports this.

> **Metrical structure** includes the stress patterns of words and utterances. **Syllable structure** is concerned with how the segments making up a word or utterance are hierarchically organised into syllables.

Syllable structure constraints

The most widely accepted account of English syllable structure is a hierarchical one. This is illustrated in (4.51), together with some sample English words. The syllable must minimally have a peak, which is usually a vowel – the example word with this minimum is *eye* /aɪ/. The peak is the only obligatory part of the rhyme. The rhyme can also have a final consonant or sequence of consonants, forming the coda. In (4.51) the word *ice* /aᶦs/ has a peak and a coda. A coda-less peak can also combine with an onset consonant (as in *lie*). Finally, both onset and coda positions can be occupied: *lice* /laᶦs/. Syllables in English can be more complex than this, since onsets and codas can contain multiple consonants, as in the word *strengths* /stɹeŋkθs/, which has three onset consonants and four coda consonants.

(4.51)

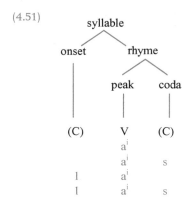

Looking at sound errors in terms of syllable structure, we find that peaks exchange with other peaks (4.46), coda consonants swap with other coda consonants (4.45), and onset consonants exchange with other onset consonants (as in (4.39) and (4.49)). This last class, where onsets swap with other onsets, is the type of speech error known as a spoonerism. Spoonerisms are named after the Reverend William Spooner (1844–1930), who was Warden of New College, Oxford. He is reputed to have frequently committed this kind of error, though it is unclear how many of the examples attributed to him were actually his errors – it has been claimed that some were put on by Spooner for effect, and that some were not uttered by him at all, but constructed by his students. Two classic spoonerism utterances attributed to Spooner are reproduced here as (4.52) and (4.53). The target utterances should be obvious.

(4.52) The Lord is a shoving leopard.

(4.53) You have hissed all my mystery lectures, and were caught fighting a liar in the quad. Having tasted two worms, you will leave by the next town drain.

Spoonerisms seem in fact to be quite noticeable errors, which may reflect a higher frequency of occurrence. But their distinctiveness could equally derive from the fact that the onsets of words are very important for accessing words from the mental dictionary, so that any disruption to onsets will have noticeable effects for the listener. Chapter 8 considers the importance of word onsets in speech comprehension, in particular from the viewpoint of models of spoken word recognition.

Phonetic similarity

> **Phonetic similarity** means that two sounds share some properties, such as both being voiceless sounds (/t/ and /p/), or both being fricatives (/s/ and /z/), or both being labial sounds (/b/ and /m/), and so on.

The third type of constraint on sound errors is that there is a strong tendency for the sounds involved to be phonetically similar and to come from phonetically similar contexts. Clearly, if there is a preference for onsets to swap with onsets, peaks with peaks, etc., then the elements involved will be similar (since for instance the syllable peaks will in most cases both be vowels). But the similarities go beyond this. Although the examples above include some exceptions to this pattern, it has been observed that the onset consonants in spoonerisms are likely to be phonetically similar. The frequently reported error of *par cark* for *car park* is a case in point, since the consonants /k/ and /p/ are both voiceless stops. This example also illustrates the finding that the phonetic contexts in which the sounds are found are frequently highly similar – in this case, both the /k/ and the /p/ are followed by the /a/ vowel.

Slots and fillers

The patterns sketched here, that sound errors tend to involve similar-sounding elements from similar metrical, syllable-structure and phonetic contexts, have been interpreted in terms of a slots-and-fillers approach to phonological encoding (Shattuck-Hufnagel, 1986). This is similar to descriptions given in Chapter 3 and earlier in the current chapter of how sentence structure and morphological structure might be put together. In essence, the approach as applied to phonological encoding suggests that when a lexeme is converted into a sound pattern, phonetic segments are mapped onto a template for the lexeme, in which metrical and syllabic structures are specified. Since the speaker has a number of words lined up for production (as we know from word exchanges), there is potential for the sounds of these words to be misallocated. The fact that the patterns mentioned above are characteristic of sound errors implies that the misallocation is not random. Rather, errors reflect the need to match the properties of the sounds to those of their places in the template. If there are competing similarly-defined positions in the template (e.g. initial voiceless stop consonants in a stressed syllable, as in *car park*), then these are likely to attract the sounds, resulting in error.

Real word bias

> It is sometimes argued that the real word bias (or lexicality effect) is just an example of a frequency effect, since real words are used with some frequency, while nonwords have zero frequency.

We have seen that an important additional aspect to the non-random nature of sound errors is the strong tendency for such errors to result in real words rather than in nonwords. Why should this be the case? One possible answer is that the pattern is illusory. That is, it is possible that many errors do in fact result in nonwords, but because we expect speakers to use existing real words rather than nonwords, we misperceive or reinterpret the nonsense resulting from sound errors as real words. This may be one source of under-reporting of sound errors. In Chapter 5 we will review evidence from experimentally induced errors that relates to this question, amongst others.

Ambiguous errors

The discussion above has assumed that there is no controversy over the interpretation of the errors as being of a certain type, i.e. as either sound errors or word errors. In some cases, though, this is not clear. The self-corrected error in (4.54) could result from the anticipation of the vowel in *way*, or it could be a word substitution of *say* for *speak*. In the example in (4.55) there could be a perseveration of the /v/ in *you've* or a word substitution of *prevented* for *presented*.

(4.54) not much to say – to speak of in the way of wind
        (Cutler, 1988)

(4.55) and you've prevented – presented us with a problem

4.5 Tongue twisters

The morphological and sound errors that have been surveyed above have come from spontaneous speech. As we will see in Chapter 5, the SLIP (Spoonerisms of Laboratory-Induced Predisposition) technique has also been used to induce sound errors in experimental settings (Baars, Motley & MacKay, 1975). A further experimental approach that has been used to investigate word building exploits tongue twisters. In one version, tongue twister effects are achieved by asking participants to spend a short time silently reading a sequence of words such as one of those in (4.56)–(4.58), and then to say them out loud (without reading) repeatedly and as quickly as possible (Shattuck-Hufnagel, 1993).

(4.56) parrot fad foot peril

(4.57) repeat fad foot repaid

(4.58) parade fad foot parole

By careful choice of the words that are included in these sequences, experimenters have been able to explore whether certain properties are more likely to result in confusion and therefore in error. Consider errors involving the phonetically similar sounds /p/ and /f/ in (4.56)–(4.58). Such errors are more likely when both sounds are in word-initial position (4.56) compared to when one is the initial sound in one word and the other is a medial sound in another word (4.57). Errors are also more likely between two sounds that both begin stressed syllables (4.56) than between a sound that begins a stressed syllable and another that begins an unstressed syllable (4.58). This pattern of results provides experimental support for the conclusions based on spontaneous error data on phonological encoding presented earlier.

Summary

Word building includes both morphological structure and phonological structure. As well as combining bases and affixes, the speaker has to provide the phonological form of stored words. Our understanding of the processes of building words is based on regularities in sound error data, on evidence from the tip-of-the-tongue phenomenon, from tongue twisters and from experimentally induced errors. We have seen that:

- words are accessed and assembled phrase by phrase;
- words in these phrases consist of frames, which have a number of slots (for morphemes, phonemes, etc.) that need filling;
- morphological processes are completed at an abstract (i.e. pre-phonetic) level;
- some morphological relationships are best captured by rules, others by assuming full forms of complex words are listed in the lexicon;
- productivity is probably a more useful notion than the distinction between inflection and derivation;
- word frames include stress information and syllable structure;
- word frames include information about phonological and phonetic structure.

Exercises

Exercise 4.1

What sort of word-building error has taken place in the following examples?

1. I've just missed my lift → I've just missed my list
2. I beat the shit out of him → I bit the sheet out of him (Fromkin, 1973a)
3. It's a real mystery → It's a meal mystery (Fromkin, 1973a)
4. the wicked step sisters → the wicked step stisters
5. the zipper is narrow → the nipper is zarrow (Fromkin, 1973b)

Exercise 4.2

Imagine that the following nonwords are nouns in English: *juld, sprenk, spluce, plize, merket, crox, smarg*. What would the plurals of these nonwords be, in their spoken form? See if other native speakers agree with you. What does this tell you about the process of making plurals in English?

Exercise 4.3

Imagine that the following nonwords are verbs in English: *stad, thrim, gleeve, blun, grust, poik, blay*. What would the past tense forms of these nonwords be, in their spoken form? See if other native speakers agree with you. What does this tell you about the process of making past tenses in English?

Exercise 4.4

Were any of the answers to Exercise 4.3 irregular past tense forms? If so, why do you think this was? If not, which do you think might be given irregular past tense forms by some speakers, and why?

Exercise 4.5

Imagine that the following nonwords are adjectives in English: *stummy, blide, hurmy, glong*. Derive from each adjective a noun that you would use to refer to the property shown by the adjective. For example, a *stummy* object is an object that has X (where X is a word derived from *stummy*). Do you use the same type of derivation for all of the nonwords? If not, why not? See if other native speakers agree with you. What does this tell you about the process of making nouns from adjectives in English?

Exercise 4.6

Devise some tongue-twisters similar to those described in this chapter, choosing words where the sounds in the key positions in the words (i.e. where the /p/ and /f/ are in (4.56)–(4.58)) have different amounts of phonetic similarity, or manipulating the stress position or position in the word of these sounds. Ask some friends to carry out the tongue-twister task described earlier, and note the errors. What do the results tell you about phonological encoding?

Exercise 4.7

Find some rare words in a dictionary, and write out the definitions. Present just the definitions to some friends, and ask them to tell you the word that each definition relates to. If any of them experience a tip-of-the-tongue experience, ask them to tell you anything they can about the word, especially anything about how it sounds. What does this tell you about phonological encoding?

....

Further reading

The wug test was first used over fifty years ago by Jean Berko Gleason (Berko, 1958). Levelt's (1993) collection of articles includes Shattuck-Hufnagel's pioneering use of tongue-twister experiments to discover more about the processes and constraints involved in word-building. One of the earliest attempts to elicit tip-of-the-tongue experiences was carried out by Brown and McNeill (1966). The term 'bathtub effect', to describe how people in the tip-of-the-tongue state can best remember the beginnings and ends of words, derives from Aitchison (2003), which is a readable introduction to many aspects of the psycholinguistics of the mental lexicon.

5 Monitoring and repair

PREVIEW

In this chapter you will learn:
- that speakers monitor their own speech for a number of types of well-formedness;
- that the repairs that speakers make to their errors are structured, and that this structure helps listeners;
- that repairs of speech following errors differ from revisions of speech following inappropriateness.

KEY TERMS

covert repair

editing

editing expression

inappropriateness

interruption

main interruption rule

monitoring

prosodic marking

repair

restart

revision

well-formedness rule

5.1 Introduction

A Wellington retailer of electronics goods uses the slogan 'It's the putting right that counts.' This of course promotes the after-sales service of the company as a particular selling point. Cynics might wonder whether it would be better to sell goods that are not likely to break down in the first place.

If we apply this situation to the production of language, what we are looking at is the undeniable fact that language does break down, and that speakers often do something to 'put it right'. Successful communication, as well as successful retail business, depends on this. The preceding chapters have discussed hesitation phenomena and speech errors as two aspects of how spoken language is not always fluent, and have shown how their study can give us insight into the mechanisms of language production. In this chapter, we will focus on what speakers do to correct errors in their own speech. This implies that speakers monitor their own speech output in order to detect that an error has taken place, and in the next section we will look briefly at why speakers might carry out such self-monitoring. We will then look at examples showing how speakers repair or revise their output. We will see that these repairs and revisions have structure, and that in many cases they reflect the speaker's sensitivity to the needs of the listener. Since much of the evidence from the structure of self-repair comes from studies of goal-oriented speech production tasks, this chapter will also introduce a selection of such tasks.

5.2 Self-monitoring

One prompt that might result in speakers wanting to repair errors in their own output is feedback that listeners give when they have not understood something. However, there is plenty of evidence that not all repairs are in response to external feedback. Speakers will repair even when the listener does not give any spoken or visual indication that they have not understood, and they will repair when producing a monologue, or in restricted dialogue situations such as on the telephone. This indicates that speakers carry out monitoring of their own speech as they produce it.

There are a number of aspects of speech that speakers monitor, relating to the levels of the production process that have been discussed in the preceding chapters. At a high level, speakers may check whether the message that they are expressing is the one that they want to utter at this stage. Their monitoring may tell them, for instance, that there is a better or more logical way of organising the message, or that they need to explain some key concept before continuing. In the monologue example in Chapter 1, for instance, the speaker utters the sequence (5.1). He interrupts what he was saying to add the information about where Rome airport is, relative to the city itself.

(5.1)   …so I arrived in Rome – and – Rome airport is not actually in Rome…

At another level, speakers check that the words they have chosen are the best ones for what they want to say. Another extract from the monologue shows this:

(5.2) in order to be – whereas to actually to get into …

Similarly, checks may be made that the correct grammatical structures are being used, that is, the correct syntax and morphology. However, evidence for this is somewhat sparser – speakers and listeners are perhaps more concerned with content than with detail of the form.

Speakers also monitor for errors in pronunciation, including errors in the prosodic patterns of speech, such as stress placement in words. Again, the extent to which such errors are detected and corrected seems to depend on their (mis)communication value.

As data reported in the next section show, there is also monitoring for contextual appropriateness. Speakers check for example whether the words they are using (or are about to use) are the best way of saying something in the present context or conversational setting.

5.3 Induced errors

Using the SLIP (Spoonerisms of Laboratory-Induced Predisposition) technique, a series of studies has induced sound errors, specifically spoonerisms (Baars & Motley, 1974; Motley, 1985; Motley & Baars, 1976; Nooteboom, 2005a). The methodology involves the rapid and brief presentation on a computer screen of pairs of words that have the same repeating pattern of initial consonant sounds. Typically, the consonant sounds used in this task are phonetically quite similar, as errors are more likely if this is the case, just as they are in spontaneous speech. The three pairs in (5.3) all have the /ʃ__/ /h__/ pattern. The word pairs are presented one at a time for silent reading, except that occasionally an additional prompt asks participants to say aloud the pair they last saw. The key condition is when such a pair has a different order of the initial consonants from the sequence that participants have got used to. An example of such a target pair following the sequence in (5.3) is given in (5.4). The prediction is that if a spoonerism is induced by the sequence in (5.3), then the participant will say 'shot hurt' for (5.4).

> /ʃ/ is the phonetic symbol, using the International Phonetic Alphabet, for the sound that is often (but not always) spelled with <sh> in English. For a listing of phonetic symbols and the sounds they represent, consult any good introductory text in phonetics, Table 8.1 on p. 122, or the website for this textbook.

(5.3) ship hull

short haul

sheet hem

(5.4) hot shirt

The issues being addressed in this task are varied, but include the extent and nature of the monitoring that speakers make of their own output. To measure this, the experimenters used different target pairs in the key condition, including examples like those in (5.4) above and (5.5) below, again following a sequence such as that in (5.3).

(5.5)   hide shame

What the experimenters found was that participants, under otherwise identical conditions, would produce a spoonerism 20% of the time when the key condition was like that in (5.4), but only 6% of the time when it was as in (5.5) (Baars *et al.*, 1975). The crucial difference between these conditions is that a spoonerism in the first case would produce a sequence of real words (*shot hurt*), but in the second it would not (*shide hame*). This indicates that speakers monitor their output and filter out nonsense words, even in this rather unnatural task. If this extends to spontaneous language production then it explains the tendency for speech errors to produce real words rather than nonsense, as we saw in Chapter 4. That is, the real word bias may be due at least in part to the speaker filtering out the nonsense.

When confronted by a stimulus like that in (5.6), however, participants were less likely to produce a spoonerism than in either of the other conditions, producing them on only 4% of occasions (Motley, Camden & Baars, 1982).

> Other word pairs with 'taboo' results in the SLIP technique include bunt call, bird tins, smart fell, boar head, duck fate, fits tall, rit club.

(5.6)   hit shed

Although the spoonerism would produce real words, this would be the sequence *shit head*. It seems that the monitoring system excludes inappropriate language, as well as nonsense words.

In a more complex version of this task, properties of the experiment setting were exploited (Motley, 1980). The basic set up again involved sequences of stimulus pairs with the same pattern of initial consonants leading to a possible spoonerism on a target stimulus pair. Within the experiment there were two types of potential spoonerism – one related to the notion of electric shocks (e.g. *bad shock* as a spoonerism of *shad bock*, following a sequence of b__ sh__ pairs), and the other to the notion of glamorous or attractive women (*good legs* as a spoonerism of *lood gegs*, following a sequence of g__ l__ pairs). All participants received the same sets of stimuli, but they were placed in one of two conditions. In one condition, participants were connected to fake electrodes and told that they might receive mild electric shocks during the experiment. The other participants did not receive this instruction, but were instead met by an attractive and provocatively dressed female experimenter. The first group turned out to be more likely to produce errors that related to the electric shock situation. The second group was more likely to produce errors related to the notion of glamorous women. This indicates that the setting in which the participants found themselves had an effect on their ability to filter out the errors – if the error was in some sense 'primed' by the setting, then it was less easy to block.

We will return below to further discussion of the nature of the monitoring for and filtering of errors, but first we will take a closer look at the kinds of repairs that speakers carry out when they detect an error in their output.

5.4 Repair

Repairs typically involve the interruption of an erroneous utterance. With repairs in spontaneous speech it can often be difficult to know what the speaker would have gone on to say if they had not interrupted their utterance. For this reason, a lot of repair data come from carefully controlled speech tasks, where the speaker's original intention is more obvious. One particularly productive source is a series of studies that has used descriptions of networks of coloured nodes, such as that shown in Figure 5.1 (Levelt, 1983).

The speaker has to describe the network so that a listener who cannot see the same network can draw it accurately based on the description. Errors arise when the speaker selects the wrong direction term (*right* instead of *left*, for example) or colour label (*green* for *red*, or *light blue* for *dark blue*). Since the experimenters know what the target node configuration is like, they have an informed idea of what the error is, even when the error is detected and corrected very rapidly, as many are.

Other similar tasks include asking speakers to describe routes around a map (which might be a fictional map invented for the task), or to give route directions from one landmark to another in a locality known to the experimenter and to the participants.

One research project collected nearly a thousand self-repairs using the node network technique, providing enough data for some general patterns to emerge (Levelt, 1983). First, three main phases were identified – interruption, editing and repair. These are illustrated in Figure 5.2 for the repair of an error that relates to the description of the network in Figure 5.1. The moment of interruption is when the speaker breaks off from their original utterance, in this case part way through a word. Taking into account the sounds produced before the interruption together with the likely words in the context of the configuration in Figure 5.1, it is probable that this word was going to be *yellow*. One feature of the editing phase is that the speaker may use an editing expression – in this case it is the vocalisation *uh*. The repair is when the speaker actually makes good the damage of the error from the point of restart onwards.

As well as repairs, which involve the correction of an error in what has been said, speakers also make revisions. A revision is where what has been

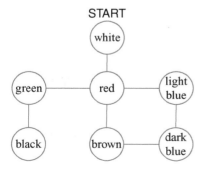

Figure 5.1
An example of a node network as used in experiments collecting repair data. (Labels indicate the colour of the nodes in the experiment.)

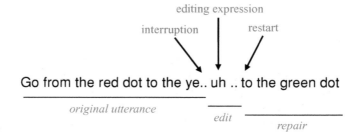

Figure 5.2
The anatomy of a repair.

said is not exactly incorrect, but is in some way incomplete or not fully appropriate to the occasion (hence these are often referred to as revisions of inappropriateness). If we assume that the speaker has been describing the right-hand loop of the node pattern in Figure 5.1, and has got as far as the dark blue node, then the example in (5.7) would be a revision rather than a repair. Although the interrupted utterance fails to distinguish between the two blue nodes in the figure, this is not crucial for the listener since they have added a dark blue node to their version of the figure on the basis of the earlier part of the utterance in (5.7) and are now ready to move on from that node.

(5.7)   From the light blue dot go down to another dot, which is dark blue. Now go left from the blue … the dark blue dot to a brown dot.

Close study of repair data has shown that speakers are very efficient in carrying out repairs. It would seem that we monitor our own speech very closely and interrupt ourselves as soon as we can if we detect an error. This has been encapsulated in the main interruption rule (Nooteboom, 1980), which simply states that speakers interrupt themselves immediately that they detect an error. In fact, self-interruption can be so swift that it occurs before the speaker actually utters the incorrect part of their utterance. These are known as covert repairs, and in Levelt's (1983) study they account for 25% of interruptions. (5.8) illustrates this. We cannot tell from this example what the erroneous utterance would have been, because the speaker does not actually produce an error (contrast the interruptions in Figure 5.2 and example (5.7)). The evidence that suggests that a covert repair has taken place is the presence of a hesitation and the repetition of the word *a*.

(5.8)   To the left of the red dot there is a … a green dot.

This is not the only interpretation of the data, as the hesitation could for instance indicate an uncertainty over word selection (see Chapter 3). Because of difficulties interpreting examples like (5.8), more detailed analysis of repair data tends to focus on overt repairs and revisions, i.e. where the error and repair/revision are available for scrutiny. The immediacy with which errors are detected by the speaker is shown by Levelt's finding that just over half (51%) of interruptions in overt repairs directly

Table 5.1 Examples of different kinds of editing expressions and their suggested functions.

Expression	Function	Example
uh, er	speaker is retrieving something temporarily forgotten	*I saw .. uh .. twelve people at the party*
that is	speaker wants to specify a referent, especially one previously signalled only by a pronoun	*He hit Mary .. that is .. Bill did*
(or) rather	speaker wants to get closer to the intended meaning	*I am trying to lease, or rather, sublease my apartment*
I mean	speaker wants to correct an all-out mistake	*I beg to present to you my half-warmed fish, I mean, my half-formed wish*

followed the error word (Levelt, 1983). A further 18% involved interruptions within the error word itself (as in the example in Figure 5.2). Closer scrutiny of the less immediate interruptions suggests that the additional delay probably arises because the error was not detected right away, rather than because the speaker wanted to complete a phrase or sentence, since even these later interruptions tend to disrupt grammatical constituents. Additional comparison of different repair types shows that interruption during a word is much more likely if the word is one that needs repair (what was said was wrong) than if it is one that needs revision (what was said was incomplete).

The repair sequence frequently includes an editing expression, such as the *uh* vocalisation in the example in Figure 5.2. In the majority of cases, and across a wide range of languages, editing expressions are indistinguishable from the sounds found in filled pauses. Levelt noted that in his database 62% of repairs were accompanied by an editing expression, but only 28% of revisions (Levelt, 1983). It has therefore been suggested that they are a signal to the listener that some dramatic change in the utterance is about to be carried out.

A number of researchers have looked more closely at different types of editing expression, and have suggested that there may be different functions associated with the different types (e.g. James, 1973). A summary is given in Table 5.1.

Following the editing expression, if there is one, the speaker initiates a restart. Because errors need to be undone and repaired, when a speaker makes a repair they tend to backtrack and restart from a point before the error word. It has been argued that the first word of the repair indicates how far back the listener needs to go in backtracking. If there is an identical word before the self-interruption, then they will go back to the last instance of that word, as in the example in (5.9), where the relevant words have been underlined. If the first word of the repair differs from anything in the original, then the repair is taken to be a continuation from the last example of a word from the same syntactic category, as in (5.10), where again the relevant words are underlined.

(5.9)   Now go from the brown dot <u>to</u> the bl ... <u>to</u> the red dot.

(5.10)   Go <u>up</u> from the red dot ... <u>down</u> from the red dot to the brown dot.

It is claimed that the structure of a repair, and how it relates to the error, is subject to a well-formedness rule (Levelt, 1989) which in essence says that the error, or the complete sentence constituent of which it would have been part, must be able to form a grammatically complete coordinated structure (e.g. with *and*) when joined with the repair. So in the case of (5.9) *to the blue dot and to the red dot* would be a complete coordinated structure. What counts here is the grammatical completeness rather than whether the coordinated structure makes sense. It is argued that an example like (5.11) is not likely to occur as a repair structure because *Should I go right and I go left* is not well-formed.

(5.11)   Should I go right, I go left?

In contrast to the repair of an error, revisions, involving something that is incomplete or inappropriate, often need further specification. Consequently they may involve a complete fresh start, sometimes with a completely new sentence construction. This is supported again by statistical data from Levelt's large-scale survey of repair data: 8% of repairs but 44% of revisions involved fresh starts (Levelt, 1983).

Speakers often show important aspects of a repair through prosodic marking (Levelt & Cutler, 1983). This usually involves the spoken emphasis of the repair word. While repairs of sound errors tend not to be prosodically marked, many (38%) repairs of word errors are (Cutler, 1983). One interpretation of prosodic marking is that it helps the words in the repair overwrite the error in the listener's developing interpretation of the utterance. This is supported by the finding that prosodic marking is more likely for repairs than for revisions (Levelt & Cutler, 1983), presumably because in the former case the new text has to replace the error, rather than adding to it. Prosodic marking is also more likely when there is a high degree of contrast between error and repair terms – and presumably a higher cost involved in letting the error go uncorrected – e.g. between *up* and *down* in example (5.10).

Another interesting finding that involves prosody is that an error in a word's stress pattern is more likely to be repaired if the misplacement of stress also results in a difference in the vowels in the word – compare the vowels in the first syllable of 'extract and ex'tract. The repair data show that 63% of lexical stress errors are corrected if they cause a change in vowel quality, but only 23% are corrected if they do not (Cutler & Clifton, 1984). This is almost certainly because misidentification of the speech sounds in a word leads to a greater risk that the word will be misidentified. On a related note, in unpublished data I have found that stress pairs where there is a difference in the vowel qualities are more likely to be

> 'extract and ex'tract form what is known as a **stress pair**, two words with the same spelling and largely the same pronunciation, but a contrasting stress pattern. There are many English pairs such as this one where first-syllable stress indicates a noun and second-syllable stress indicates a verb.

recognised as different in a discrimination task than stress pairs like *'insult* and *in'sult* where the difference is marked – for most speakers – only by stress.

5.5 Editor theories

The finding that speakers monitor their own speech and correct it as they go shows that an editing process takes place during speech production. The precise nature of the editor has been an issue of some debate. Is it, for instance, a mechanism that is specifically geared to self-monitoring and to the editing of the speaker's own output? This would suggest that self-monitoring is a special part of the speech production process, perhaps involving the speaker in a comparison of what they said with what they intended. On the other hand, is self-monitoring simply a particular implementation of a more general monitoring device that is also used when we are listening to other speakers? In this case, self-monitoring may operate without continual reference to what the speaker intended, but might use more general criteria, such as 'does the output I have just heard make sense?'

Neuroimaging studies (Indefrey, 2007) indicate that we actually use similar brain areas in two types of self-monitoring, internal and external, as well as in listening to others. The speed with which errors are detected and corrected also supports the existence of internal as well as external monitoring. The presence of covert repairs reinforces this suggestion, since in covert repairs the errorful word is not even pronounced. Further evidence comes from experimental studies of speech errors using the SLIP technique (see p. 73). As well as spoonerism outcomes, the SLIP technique often results in partial spoonerisms, such as *shide shame* for *hide shame*, as well as interrupted and corrected spoonerisms such as *sh- hide shame* for the same target. Most of the repaired spoonerisms in these tasks are very rapid, with an interruption very early in the error, arguably much earlier than would be compatible with monitoring of and responding to the actual spoken output.

Is this interruption and repair in response to lexical or phonetic monitoring of the speaker's own production? That is, is the repair a response to the realisation that the output is not the word the speaker intended (or indeed not a word at all), or does it follow from a check of the actual sounds produced against the target sounds? One piece of evidence that supports a lexical argument is that there is a greater likelihood that an experimentally induced error will be interrupted if it would have resulted in a nonword. This has been taken as evidence that there is a 'quick and dirty' general check that the output consists of real words rather than nonsense. This is compatible too with the general tendency noted in Chapter 4 for spontaneous sound errors to result in real words more often than they result in nonsense words, and with the finding noted earlier in the current chapter that induced spoonerisms are more likely to be completed if they result in real words (*shot hurt*) than if they result in a nonsense sequence (*sheel helf*). The nonsense word sequences are simply edited out early and efficiently by a general monitor for real word status, but the real word sequences pass this general check and are allowed to proceed.

On the other hand, in cases where an error correction is made, then it is equally fast regardless of whether the error would have produced real words or nonwords. This suggests that from an early stage the monitoring system also makes a phonetic comparison of the speaker's articulation plan with the intended output. So internal monitoring has access to details of the phonetic plan, which it assesses without reference to the lexical status of the output.

Higher-level monitoring, for factors such as the appropriateness of the output, does not seem to come into effect as quickly as the general check for lexical status. In one use of the experimental task, a contrast was made between target pairs in which the first word of a spoonerism was a taboo word (*fits tall* → *tits fall*) and those where the second word was a taboo word (*tool kits* → *cool tits*). Partial rather than full spoonerisms were far more likely in the latter case (leading to *cool kits*), indicating that speakers manage to filter out the taboo word if there is a short delay (the duration of *cool*) before the taboo word would have been produced. As a counter to the claim that the taboo word did not feature at all here, i.e. that this is a sound anticipation error involving the initial consonant of *kits* and not a corrected spoonerism, consider evidence from a measure of emotional arousal. This is the speakers' galvanic skin response. The experimenters found evidence from this emotional response measure that a taboo word had been accessed during the sequence of events that led to the production of *cool kits*, implying that *tits* had indeed formed part of the output plan but had subsequently been edited out (Motley *et al.*, 1982).

> **Galvanic skin response** is a measure of the skin's ability to conduct electricity. For some people, changes in this response measure are highly sensitive to emotional changes.

5.6 Speakers helping listeners

Speakers are generally also listeners. It is not surprising then to find that there are many aspects to the checking and repairing processes that are geared towards making interpretation easier for listeners. So we have seen that speakers use editing terms to signal that a repair is taking place, and that the choice of editing term may convey information about the nature of the repair. We have seen too that speakers repair their errors in a structured way, either by repeating a word that came before the error, or by using a word from the same grammatical category. Both strategies allow the listener to connect the replacement information efficiently into the preceding material. In addition to producing structured repairs, there are other ways in which speakers help listeners. These provide, as it were, some perceptual constraints on production.

Sensitivity to listeners' needs appears to be reflected in the distribution of between-word phonological effects, or connected speech processes (CSPs). CSPs include effects such as palatalisation in English, by which a sequence of /d/ and /j/, as in *would you*, becomes a palatal affricate [dʒ], *wouldja*. Speakers tend not to allow such between-word phonological

> **Connected speech processes** in English include palatalisation (*wouldja*), flapping (*sort of* as *sorda*), assimilations (e.g. *ten people* as *tem people*) and elisions (*intresting* for *interesting*). CSPs are a natural consequence of economy of effort during speaking, though language purists sometimes attribute them to laziness.

effects to occur if they would distort the beginning of a word that listeners particularly need to hear more clearly. This has been shown in a study that manipulated the frequencies (as measured from frequency norms) of the first word in such sequences, i.e. the word ending in /d/, or of the next word, beginning with /j/. It was found that palatalisation did not vary according to the frequency of the first word, but that it was much less likely when the word after the boundary was a low-frequency word. Because the beginnings of words are particularly important for their access from the mental lexicon, allowing the initial consonant to be modified by CSPs is likely to contribute to poorer recognition (Cooper & Paccia-Cooper, 1980). This is especially important for low-frequency words, which are already at a disadvantage. See Chapter 8 for further discussion of these points.

As shown in Chapter 12, speakers tend to pronounce with greater clarity words that are new to the discourse, and to speak less clearly words that convey people, objects or ideas that have already been introduced into the conversation. This difference in clarity also helps the listener – it is important to hear quite clearly any novel information. What is more, while it might seem at first blush that clarity of diction will help comprehension, it turns out that if old or given information is spoken clearly it can actually impair the listener's understanding, since they expect old information to be spoken less clearly.

Finally, in one early experiment, speakers were asked to read sentences from cards and were told that they might be asked to repeat the sentences by the experimenter, who was in an adjoining room and listening to the sentences over headphones with – they were told – varying levels of noise. Some of the sentences on the cards had less explicit grammatical structures (e.g. (5.12)) than others (e.g. (5.13)). The experimenters found that speakers will choose a 'clearer' syntactic structure when asked 'What?' by a listener, so saying something like (5.13) if they had previously read out the sentence in (5.12) (Valian & Wales, 1976).

(5.12)   The treasure she found was valuable

(5.13)   The treasure that she found was valuable

Summary

In previous chapters we have discussed the use of speech errors in providing evidence about the speech production process. In this chapter we have seen:

- that speakers monitor their inner speech as well as their spoken output;
- that there are many different reasons for output monitoring, including the detection of speech errors;
- that speech production tasks such as network descriptions and

experimentally induced errors provide rich data on monitoring and repair;

- that speakers detect and repair errors in their speech efficiently and rapidly;
- that the structured manner in which repairs are carried out is one way in which speakers help listeners.

Rather than it simply being the putting right that counts, it is the principled way in which the putting right happens that really counts.

Exercises

Exercise 5.1

Mark the structure of the following repairs, indicating the point of interruption, the editing expression, and the point of restart, as well as the phases of original expression, edit and repair. Are all the repairs well-formed (see p. 78)? Could any of these examples be considered revisions, rather than repairs?

1. first I need to find out um I need to get an engine
2. Well, I think it's you know, I think this has gone beyond, as it were, Al Qaeda as a specific network
3. in order to be whereas to actually get into something that most people would recognise as being Rome
4. a lot more good for you than European continental European youth hostels

Exercise 5.2

Record some unrehearsed speech data from a friend, who you have asked to describe a network of coloured nodes such as that given above, or whose task is to describe from memory the walking route from one well-known place in your town or city to another well-known place. Listen to the recording and note any occurrences of repairs and revisions. Try to apply to these the framework for analysis of repairs outlined in this chapter. Comment on how easy or difficult you found it to apply this framework. Alternatively, analyse a recording from television or radio in the same way. Use unrehearsed speech for this task.

Exercise 5.3

Devise some sentences with /d/-/j/ sequences across word boundaries (like *did you*), where the information value (e.g. the importance in the context, or the overall lexical frequency) of the words beginning with /j/ varies between sentences. Ask participants to say these sentences as fluently as possible, and note whether they palatalise the /d/-/j/ sequence as in the study mentioned on p. 80. What appear to be good predictors of palatalisation in your data? As an alternative, if your dialect of English allows it, you could look at the incidence of flapping, by which a /t/ between two vowels becomes an alveolar flap.

Further reading

Levelt (1989: Chapter 12) provides detailed descriptions and explanations of self-monitoring, repairs and revisions, including a summary of his extensive research using the corpus of repair data from node network descriptions. Further analyses of repair data and what it can tell us about the processes of language production can be found in the work of Nooteboom (e.g. 1980; 2005a; 2005b).

6 The use of gesture

PREVIEW

This chapter considers how speakers accompany their speech with gestures, and the functions that these gestures have. By the end of the chapter you should understand:

- that gestures have at least two different types of function – to contribute content to what the speaker is saying, and to help manage the conversation;
- that there are different types of gesture – some have symbolic meaning, some direct the listener's attention, and some depict some aspect of what is being talked about;
- that gestures help the speaker as well as the listener;
- that gestures vary cross-linguistically not only because of cultural differences but also because gestures are linked to language output and the vocabulary and structure of languages differ from one another.

KEY TERMS

beat/batonic gesture

icon/iconic gesture

index/indexical gesture

symbol/symbolic gesture

6.1 Introduction

This chapter gives a brief overview of the relationship between our spoken output and the gestures that accompany our speech. It considers the different roles that gestures can have. It also looks at how gestures can both contribute to the content of the message and play an organisational role in helping speakers and listeners to manage conversation. Finally, it considers the relationship between gestures, language production and cognition.

Research into the use of gestures falls into two broad camps (Beattie, 1980). First, there is research that takes a psychoanalytic approach, looking for gestures that reveal something about the speaker's emotional state. Second, there are linguistic and psycholinguistic approaches to gesturing, including a discourse analysis view. This latter view assumes that gestures provide an additional channel of information, complementing the spoken channel. These two approaches parallel those found in the study of speech errors, as outlined in Chapters 3 and 4. There we similarly saw that there are psychoanalytic (Freudian) and psycholinguistic approaches. As in our treatment of speech errors, we will focus here on the evidence that gestures can provide for the mechanisms of language processing, particularly language production, rather than on the possibly hidden truths that they might reveal about our mental or emotional situation.

It needs to be stressed that while gestures and sign languages may share some properties, the material covered in this chapter does not involve the psycholinguistics of sign languages. As complex linguistic systems, sign languages can provide legitimate material for psycholinguistic research, and much of what is written in this book about the processing of spoken and written languages can also be applied to sign languages (Emmorey, 2007). Here, however, our focus is on the gestures that accompany spoken language. These should be seen as an integral part of the interactional event, which cannot be fully studied simply by looking at a written transcription: 'A written discourse is to a face-to-face conversation as a stuffed grizzly bear is to a live one' (Clark, 1994: 987).

6.2 Gestures as content

In a more detailed analysis of the linguistic use of gestures, we can distinguish between two main functions, which have been associated with two parallel 'tracks' (Clark, 1996). One of these tracks carries the subject matter or content of the discourse, while the other is used for discourse management. Of course, it is not just gestures that can be analysed onto these two tracks. The error repairs described in Chapter 5 can also be looked at in these terms. For instance, the example in (6.1) could be analysed onto two tracks as shown in (6.2).

(6.1)   I beg to present to you my half-warmed fish, I mean, my half-formed wish ...

(6.2)   *Management*:   I mean

> *Content*: I beg to present to you my half-warmed fish   my
> half-formed wish ...

Gestures can have a number of functions, relating to either or both of these tracks. In this section we look at the use of gestures to convey content. Experimental work suggests that content-related gestures make a significant contribution to fluency in production, since preventing speakers from using gestures can result in reduced fluency and reduced vocabulary size (Krauss, 1998). Speakers who are prevented from gesturing also rely more on spoken expressions denoting spatial relationships, presumably because their hands are not free to play this role.

Content-related gestures can include symbols, indices and icons, i.e. gestures that stand for something, indicate something, or depict something, respectively (McNeill, 1992).

Symbols

Gestures as symbols (sometimes referred to as emblems) 'stand for' something. Indeed, such gestures can often correspond to and be used instead of a complete utterance, though they can also be used alongside information that is contained in the speech. They are used for interpersonal control (e.g. 'hello', 'be quiet'), to express personal states ('I approve', 'I don't know') and for evaluations of others ('he's crazy'). Less frequently they stand for objects or actions.

A small sample of such gestures and their possible meanings is given in Table 6.1. As the examples show, gestures can involve the use of various body parts including parts of the face and head, fingers and thumbs, the entire hand, shoulders, and so on.

It is clear that for these gestures to be successful there must be some implicit agreement between speaker and listener as to their meaning. This is part of the common ground between the participants in an interaction, just like the common understanding of what words mean. It is often naïvely assumed by speakers that gestures are universal, and that they can use the same gestures when speaking a foreign language as they would use with their native language. However, there are cultural differences in the meanings that gestures have, not only between languages but also between varieties of a language used by different cultural groups. These

> A joke that exploits caricatures of cultural differences in the amount (rather than the meaning) of gestures relates to the perception that Mediterranean people gesture a lot. It is about how a group of shipwrecked Italians kept their boat afloat until they were rescued: by talking to one another.

Table 6.1 Examples of symbolic gestures (Clark, 1996: 163).			
Gesture	Meaning	Gesture	Meaning
head nod	'yes'	head shake	'no'
thumb up	'I approve'	thumb down	'I reject'
greeting wave	'hello'	farewell wave	'goodbye'
shoulder shrug	'I don't know'	wink	'I'm kidding'
thumb and index finger in circle	'excellent'	index finger to protruding lips	'be quiet'

differences can result in differences in interpretation. For instance, crossing the middle finger over the index finger can mean 'may I be protected' in England, Scandinavia, parts of Sicily and in (former) Yugoslavia, but 'I am breaking a friendship' in Turkey and Corfu (Morris, Collett, Marsh & O'Shaughnessy, 1979). The 'thumbs up' gesture that carries a positive meaning ('okay', 'well done', 'awesome') in many European cultures is a very insulting gesture in some Middle Eastern countries as well as in parts of West Africa and South America (Morris *et al.*, 1979).

Note also that sounds can carry similar functions to gestures. That is, there are also auditory emblems, such as clap ('I approve'), hiss ('I disapprove'), tongue-click ('shame on you'), and so on.

Some gesture use usually requires more than one person to be actively participating. These have been called 'junctions' (Clark, 1996) and are typically joint physical actions, such as shaking hands, hugging, kissing. These junctions are often ignored in discussions of communication, because they involve joint action, but it has been noted that other types of communication are no less dependent on joint action. For instance, a successful spoken conversation depends on the listener paying attention as well as on the speaker articulating.

Indices

Indexical or indicative gestures direct the perceiver's attention to particular objects. These gestures usually involve an instrument, frequently a body part, as well as a locative action. For example, a common instrument for indicating is the forefinger (the 'index' finger), and a frequent locative action is to point at something (Schegloff, 1984). Again, though, the gesture is culturally determined. Some cultures point with the middle finger and many can also use the thumb, sometimes when pointing to something behind the speaker. To add to the confusion, in Western cultures where the index finger is used to indicate, it is frequently considered rude to use it to point directly at a person. Instead, indicating a person would be done by using the open hand. In addition to finger, thumb or hand, there are many other ways to point, for example with a nod of the head, or by directing your gaze towards someone. Some cultures point with the nose or lips. A sweeping gesture with the whole arm can be used to point towards a group of people. Simply turning your body towards someone or something in coordination with what you say can also have an indexical function.

Indexical gestures typically accompany speech, and may be timed to coincide with a spoken reference to the thing or person being indicated, as in (6.3). (Examples (6.3)–(6.6) are from the author's own observations.)

(6.3)   Can you just put the saw down there [pointing to a workbench when saying the word *there*].

However, it is not essential that there is also spoken reference to the thing being indicated. In the example in (6.4), it is clear that the speaker has painted two of the walls in the room, though these are not mentioned. (In the actual utterance context it was also obvious that the remaining two walls had not been painted, which is perhaps implied but certainly not explicit from the utterance.) In this example, the gesture complements the utterance, and could be seen as standing for some spoken referential act (e.g. saying the word 'walls' in the appropriate place in the utterance).

(6.4)   I've painted both those now [pointing to two of the walls in a room].

Iconic gestures

Iconic gestures are gestures that depict what is being talked about. Most are executed by speakers, though listeners sometimes use them as part of their responses, such as when they smile or give a look of surprise. Iconic gestures are clearly a descriptive part of the basic message. In example (6.5) the gesture forms part of the description of the road.

(6.5)   An' an' we went down this dusty an' [pause] rough road [with an iconic 'wavy' gesture during the pause before *rough*].

Iconic gestures tend to be closely linked in time to relevant sections of what the speaker is saying. Interestingly, they often anticipate the words they belong to. This can lead to ambiguity in how analysts interpret the gestures. For instance, the gesture in (6.5) might be truly iconic, i.e. depicting perhaps the undulating and not just rough nature of the road, in which case it appears in the right place for an adjective in English, just before the noun. Or – unlikely perhaps in this case – it could be serving a speech production purpose (see below), i.e. helping the speaker to access the word *rough* from their mental dictionary.

An iconic gesture can run alongside spoken information, with speech and gesture concurrent. Alternatively, the gesture can be embedded in the utterance, forming a component of what the speaker is saying in much the same way as words do. This second type is illustrated in (6.6).

(6.6)   Then the big guy went ... [gesture of someone pushing someone out of the way], and I just got outta there.

Iconic gestures mainly function as signals by which speakers mean things. For this reason, most iconic gestures are informative; they generally express something not found in the accompanying words. A useful exercise for becoming aware of this is to consider a description of something that is technically quite complex but which might be more easily described visually through gestures. So for instance you could think about the gestures that might accompany an explanation of how a lock works, and about how difficult it would be to complete such an explanation without gestures.

Another example of how a gesture conveys additional information comes from the utterance in (6.7), part of a description of a Sylvester and Tweety Bird cartoon (McNeill, 1992; McNeill & Duncan, 2000).

(6.7)   and Tweety Bird runs and gets a bowling b[all and ... drops it down the drainpipe]

In the example, the square brackets show the entire period over which the hands were involved in gesturing, the bold face indicates when the main gestural movement took place, and the double-underline shows pre- and post-movement 'holds'. In these holds the hands were in a position which indicated holding a large round object. The gestural movement was a sharp downwards one. The interesting observation made about this example is that the speaker selected a verb *drop* to characterise Tweety Bird's actions, but chose to align the gesture with the words *it down*. This alignment, it is argued, is deliberate, because what is important in the narrative is the consequent action of the ball, which is that it is swallowed by Sylvester the cat and subsequently flushes him out of the drainpipe. The combination of lexical and gestural information therefore conveys more about the event than either alone.

Despite the iconicity of many gestures, it is often the case that the interpretation of gestures depends on the utterance context, just as individual words can often only be fully understood in the context of the utterance of which they are part. This can be experienced by viewing a speaker gesturing on a video with the sound turned off – some of the gestures will be obvious, but many can only be properly interpreted with the spoken utterance.

Interestingly, there is some automaticity to gesturing. Although speakers gesture less when the addressee cannot see them (e.g. when they are talking on the telephone), they do not cut out their gestures altogether (De Ruiter, 1995). Research shows that Japanese native speakers sometimes bow at the end of telephone conversations, and that in America people nod on the telephone. Congenitally blind speakers also gesture, though not as much as sighted people. Such findings show how gestures are an integral part of a composite signal.

6.3 Gesturing for discourse management

Many gestures are used for managing the conversation that the speaker is involved in. As with content gestures, discourse management gestures come in different flavours. There can be gestures which are *symbols* in discourse management, such as shaking or nodding of the head. Gestures can be *indices* such as eye gaze, pointing, nodding. And they can be *icons*: smiling, frowning or putting on a thinking face. These gestures perform a number of discourse management functions. One analysis distinguishes delivery, citing, seeking and turn-taking (Bavelas, 1994).

A delivery gesture indicates that the subject matter is being communicated to the listener, often by a specific 'handing-over' gesture directed towards a particular recipient. Similarly, there are gestures which are associated with a change in topic or which are used when new information is being delivered. These gestures often involve changes in body position or leg position (Beattie, 1980).

Gestures that are used in citing refer back to an earlier contribution to the conversation, e.g. by pointing at an addressee who made the earlier contribution, indicating something like 'as you said earlier'.

A seeking gesture usually requests a response. That is, the speaker is trying to get a particular response from an addressee; e.g. by looking at the addressee as if to say something like 'can you give me the word for …?'

Turn-taking gestures contribute more obviously to the management of conversation. An example would be a gesture that indicates that another speaker may now have a turn, a 'ceding the floor' gesture. For instance, a speaker might 'hand over' the floor to the addressee with one of the indicative gestures discussed earlier under the heading 'indices'. This can include eye gaze or body orientation. These gestures can either be expressing content (by referring to the addressee) or managing discourse (by inviting the addressee to take the floor), or both.

It is not only the speaker who manages conversation – listeners can contribute through their use of what are referred to as collateral gestures, e.g. head-nods as acknowledgment or some kind of mimicry related to the content. This kind of feedback manages conversation in that it confirms for the speaker that their turn is being understood and followed. It may also be used to express sympathy, such as when an observer grimaces when either witnessing or being told about an accident. The grimace does not mean that the listener is in the emotional state expressed by the facial gesture, as shown by experimental observations from a role-play situation. This involved a staged accident where it looks to the observer that an experimenter has dropped some equipment on his finger (Bavelas, Black, Lemery & Mullett, 1986). Observers typically and quickly form a grimace. If the experimenter looks up and makes eye-contact, the grimace continues, presumably to display sympathy. If the experimenter remains hunched-up the grimace is dropped.

6.4 Gestures for emphasis

When we talk we place greater emphasis or stress on some words than on others, usually because they carry more important information, or because we wish to reinforce some idea. Batonic (or beat) gestures tend to coincide in time with the stressed syllables of speech and probably therefore reinforce the stresses, helping to bring home a point. Consider the example in (6.8) (from the author's own observation).

(6.8)   I've told you before, but it looks like I need to tell you again [pause] you must not use other people's work in your essays without giving references [pause] you must not go over the word limit [pause] and you must not hand your work in after the due date without getting clearance from me first.

This utterance was accompanied by a downward chopping gesture on each instance of *not*, and on the final word, *first*. These gestures serve to accentuate the importance of meeting the requirements being described, but also perhaps indicate the exasperation felt by the speaker.

One study looked at the incidence of beat gestures in different phases of the hesitant and fluent speech cycles discussed in Chapter 2, and suggested that beat gestures are more likely when the speaker has their output under greater control, since they occurred more frequently in fluent than in hesitant phases. This is compatible with the idea that batonic gestures are a deliberate emphatic device.

6.5 Gestures, conceptualisation and lexicalisation

Languages clearly differ from one another in many respects, and researchers have made use of these differences in their exploration of the relationship between gestures and language production. Languages differ from one another in their vocabulary. If gestures are at least in part linked to what can be expressed through words, do vocabulary differences relate also to differences in how gestures are used? That is, as the speaker moves from pre-linguistic conceptualisation to language formulation, the lexicalisation processes may vary between languages, and so too may the gestures (Kita, 2009).

Linguistic differences

In a comparative study of English and Japanese native speakers, Kita (2000) looked at the gestures associated with a description of a sequence in a cartoon story where a cat is swinging on a rope across a street from one building to another, where he has seen a bird in a window. A linguistic difference between English and Japanese is that while English has an intransitive verb that depicts the down-then-up trajectory of the cat across the street (*the cat swings across the street*), Japanese does not. Therefore, when Japanese participants talked about this part of the cartoon, they did not use expressions that encoded the arc of the swinging action. Instead, they used phrases which might be translated as 'jump across to' or 'go in the direction of the bird', etc.

Interestingly, the analysis of their gestures showed that the Japanese participants were likely to use straight-line gestures to show the movement of the cat from one building to the other, while the English-speaking participants almost exclusively used arc-like gestures. While some of the Japanese speakers did use a separate arc-like gesture in addition to the straight-line gesture, only the latter coincided with the words indicating the movement.

Recall that the model of language production sketched in Chapter 2 distinguished pre-linguistic conceptualisation and linguistic encoding as different components of the production process. It has been argued that gestures can reflect both the conceptual mental model of what is being depicted and the linguistic encoding of that model. In the case of English, these coincide, since the verb *swing* has the arc-like movement encoded in it. In Japanese, however, the linguistic expressions have a straight-line movement, hence the straight-line gesture, while the pre-linguistic mental model of the message has the arc-like movement, and hence the additional arc-like gestures made by some of the participants in this study. So gestures can relate either to the pre-linguistic conceptualisation of what

Although Japanese does not have an intransitive verb like *swing* (as in *the monkey swings from tree to tree*), it does have transitive verbs for swing (approximating *I swing the cat*) and intransitive verbs for types of swinging where someone or something else has caused the swinging motion (*the pendulum swings*).

is being talked about, or to the linguistic formulation of this model (which may be more restrictive, as in the Japanese example here), or to both (as for the English speakers).

In addition to lexical differences, syntactic differences between languages can be reflected in gestural practices. Again, the focus has been on expressions showing movement. In particular, researchers have looked at how languages convey the manner or type of the movement and the direction or pathway of the movement. As shown in (6.9), the tendency in English is for the manner to be contained in the meaning of the verb (*roll*), while the direction or pathway is expressed using an adverbial construction within the same clause, such as a prepositional phrase (*down the slope*). In other languages, such as Japanese and Turkish, the path is typically expressed in the verb and the manner by an additional clause. So to express the same idea in those languages speakers would use a sentence that would look like (6.10) in English (Kita & Özyürek, 2003).

(6.9) The ball rolled down the slope.

(6.10) The ball descended as it rolled.

These two pieces of information – the manner of movement and the pathway – are clearly part of the speaker's intention during the conceptualisation stage of planning an utterance, in either type of language. However, the grammatical encoding processes differ depending on how the language expresses these two components, with different sequencing in the sentence structures for the two languages. This encoding difference is also reflected in the gestures used in different languages – English speakers use a single hand-gesture combining a circling movement for the roll with a sideways movement of the hand for the direction. Kita & Özyürek (2003), however, showed that Japanese and Turkish speakers are more likely to show the path and the manner in two separate gestures, coordinated with the two clauses of the speech.

Cultural differences

The comparative studies of gesturing in languages such as English and Japanese are examples of a number of studies that have looked at the relationship between gesture, language and cognition. A further set of findings points to cultural differences in how spatial relationships are referred to. These have been attributed to cognitive differences in the conceptualisation of such relationships.

On the one hand, there are largely western cultures where spatial orientation relative to the perceiver is important. This is reflected in both linguistic and non-linguistic tasks. So if a speaker from one of these cultures is describing a series of objects, then they will say that one object is to the left or right of another, and so on. If that speaker is shown a group of objects and is then asked to turn around and draw that group of objects then the drawing will keep the relative orientation (so the object that is on the left will still be on the left in the picture).

On the other hand, there are cultures where what is important is the absolute spatial orientation. An example of absolute orientation is compass directions. So for example one object is to the west (or north, etc.) of another object. This is encoded in some languages, so that a description of three objects in a line will say that one is to the west of another and the third is to the east of the middle one. Interestingly, when speakers of such languages are asked to turn around 180 degrees and draw the objects, they will preserve the absolute orientation, so the first object is still to the west of the second one. From the western left-to-right way of thinking the drawing will appear to be the reverse of the reality (Levinson, 2003; Levinson, Kita, Haun & Rasch, 2002).

What happens when speakers from these different language communities use gestures to accompany their speech? Not surprisingly, westerners will use left-to-right gestures for a left-to-right description, in relative space and regardless of which way they are looking. Speakers of languages that use absolute spatial relationships will change the direction of their gestures, depending on which direction they are facing. They keep the absolute direction. The cultural difference between relative and absolute spatial orientation is reflected both in the patterns of language and in the nature of the accompanying gestures.

6.6 Who do we gesture for?

Do gestures communicate information to listeners, or do they help speakers formulate and manage their utterances (De Ruiter, 2003)? Most of the discussion so far in this chapter has considered how gestures are used by speakers to communicate something to listeners, either in terms of content or conversation management. It has also been claimed that gestures help speakers to find words and formulate utterances (Beattie, 1980; Hadar & Butterworth, 1997). One study has explicitly tested who gestures are for, and the findings indicate that they have a strong listener focus (Jacobs & Garnham, 2007).

In this study, participants were asked to describe cartoons. They were placed in one of four conditions. The conditions differed as to whether the cartoon was already known to both the speaker and the listener, was known only to the speaker, was known only to the listener, or was known by neither. Speakers tended to gesture much less in the first and third conditions than in the other two. In other words, when the listeners already knew what was being described (either by having heard it described before or by dint of being able to see the cartoons themselves), then the speaker used fewer gestures. This suggests that gestures – at least in this task – are primarily listener-oriented.

Neurophysiological studies of participants listening to and watching speakers who are gesturing reinforce the close link between speech and gesture for the listener. Stimuli in one study included verbs which either matched (*wrote*) or mismatched (*hit*) a preceding object noun phrase (*shopping list*) (the stimuli were in Dutch, using constructions in which the object precedes the verb). The gesture in the video recording that accompanied the speech also matched or mismatched that object (i.e. was a writing or hitting gesture). The crucial finding from the comparisons of matching and mismatching conditions was that key language processing areas (in Broca's area, see Chapter 13) were involved in the integration of both gesture and speech with the preceding object noun phrase (Willems, Özyürek & Hagoort, 2007).

However, there is also strong evidence that gestures can have facilitative functions for the speaker, helping them to carry out the speech production task. At a most basic level, this notion is supported by findings from experiments where gesturing was impeded. Under such circumstances, speakers showed reduced fluency. This seemed particularly marked if what they were talking about had a lot of spatial content, such as describing the layout of a room. This reduction in fluency may be a result of inhibiting the word retrieval processes. A range of other research supports this idea that gestures facilitate word retrieval. One study found that the less familiar a word was, the greater the time lag between the onset of the gesture and the onset of the spoken word (Morrel-Samuels & Krauss, 1992). This is compatible with the idea that the gesture occurs at the initiation of the lexical retrieval process, with the less familiar words taking longer to find, measured from that point. In another study, speakers taking part in a tip-of-the-tongue elicitation experiment (see Chapter 4) were more likely to enter the tip-of-the-tongue state if they were prevented from using gestures.

It has been proposed that gestures help speakers maintain an image of the concepts that they are trying to express, thus helping the language formulation processes to make the connection between concepts (lemmas) and linguistic expressions (lexemes). One interpretation is that gestures may reinforce certain semantic properties in a way that affects their salience in the pre-verbal message. Another is that a gesture helps the speaker access a word from their mental dictionary by a mechanism of visual priming, just as seeing a picture of an object helps speakers access the spoken form of a word used in naming that picture. It is interesting to note in this context that iconic gestures are found most often before nouns, but also fairly frequently before verbs and adjectives. Fewer than one in five are found before other types of word. In other words, gestures are predominantly found before content words, the words which we have earlier seen are most likely to involve more difficult word retrieval.

In addition, although iconic gestures typically precede the spoken material to which they are linked by about one second, the asynchrony can be longer and is quite variable (in one study from less than half a second to almost four seconds). Gesture duration is also variable and is usually long enough to mean that a gesture is still continuing when the speaker produces the related speech material. This suggests that the gesture is initiated as the speaker enters the lexicalisation process and might be terminated once the lexical search has been completed. The variability in the duration of the gesture arises because the speaker cannot predict how long a specific lexical search will take.

Iconic gestures are also highly frequent during pauses in the fluent phases of speech cycles (see Chapter 2 for a discussion of speech cycles), i.e. at the points where lexical selection is argued to be taking place, rather than higher-level planning. This, together with the iconic nature of the gesture, is compatible with the idea that the speaker knows in advance the semantic specification but not the form of the word they are going to utter. This is explicitly the case in the tip-of-the-tongue experiments mentioned above. The conclusion from all these findings is that the gesture is helping the speaker access the word-form or lexeme, rather than the lemma.

Summary

In this chapter we have seen that speakers not only speak, but they also use gestures as part of their communication. Gestures can:

- communicate some of the content the speaker wants to convey to the listener;
- help speaker and listener manage the conversation;
- represent iconically some part of the content being communicated;
- direct the addressees' attention;
- convey physical aspects of what is being communicated (size, shape, etc.);
- emphasise parts of the message;
- help the speaker retrieve words from their mental lexicon.

In addition we saw that gestures are linked to linguistic and cultural differences and can provide interesting insights into the processes of conceptualisation and formulation that we have outlined in earlier chapters.

Exercises

Exercise 6.1

Think of two places you might want to get to from your home. Ask someone who lives with you to describe the route to each of these places. For the first description, don't give your informant any further instruction. For the second one, tell them to do this while sitting on their hands or holding their hands behind their backs. Do you notice any difference in their fluency? Do they report finding one task any easier to complete than the other?

Exercise 6.2

Sentences 1 and 2 below are English and Spanish versions of the same sentence.

1. The bottle floated into the cave.
2. La botella entró a la cueva flotando.
   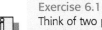
   the bottle entered the cave floating

What sort of gestural patterns would you expect native speakers of each language to use when saying the sentence in their language?

Exercise 6.3
The Jacobs and Garnham experiment referred to on p. 94 had a companion experiment in which the listeners were told to be either attentive or inattentive. What effect would you predict this manipulation to have on the speakers' gestural behaviour?

Further reading

An early review of gesture research is provided by Beattie (1980). The separation of gestures into the content and discourse management tracks derives from the work of Clark (1996). For some of the most significant work in the field of language and gesture see McNeill (1992), Bavelas (1994), Kendon (2004) and McNeill's edited collection (2000), which includes a report of the Tweety Pie study by McNeill and Duncan (2000), and the comparative study of English and Japanese by Kita (2000). A review of cross-cultural gestural research and of the relationship between gesture and cognition is provided by Kita (2009).

7 Perception for language

PREVIEW

This chapter introduces some key issues in both visual and auditory perception that relate to language processing. By the end of the chapter you will know that:

- there are similarities as well as crucial differences in the perceptual processes involved in spoken and visual language comprehension;
- there are perceptual skills that are particularly important for efficient language processing;
- the language system influences the interpretation of perceptual cues.

KEY TERMS

categorical perception

fixation

Ganong effect

hemispherical specialisation

McGurk effect

phoneme restoration

right ear advantage

saccade

segmentation

variability

7.1 Introduction

In this chapter, we consider some significant findings in both visual and auditory perception studies. In particular we consider those skills that are specifically language-oriented and which act as a pre-requisite for successful language processing. The chapter will also consider some of the findings from language acquisition that indicate the early stage at which these perceptual skills develop.

There are some issues that are common to both visual and spoken language processing, but – as we will see – there are also some issues that are unique to either modality. The common questions concern the nature of the information extracted in the early stages of the recognition process and how this information is extracted, the mapping from the input to the lexicon and the nature of any intervening units of analysis, and the time-course of the flow of information throughout the system.

7.2 Basic issues in perception for language

Some basic tasks for successful language comprehension are that language users must recognise the signals that reach the brain (from eye or from ear, or even from the fingers in the context of Braille) as being language rather than non-language, they must recognise them as being in a language that they understand, and they must interpret them as meaningful. In the comprehension of written and spoken language, these tasks involve knowledge about how letters and sounds are used, but also knowledge about writers and speakers, about the processes of writing and speaking, and about the structures and units of language. In this section we will focus on some of the general issues that exist for perception for language.

Hemispherical specialisation

It is clear that as a species, humans have become specially adapted for language. Our upright posture, the position of our larynx (voice box) in the throat and the shape and dimensions of our vocal tract all contribute to our ability to produce a rich and well-controlled range of speech sounds. Our hearing for language is helped by the fact that these speech sounds have sound frequencies and amplitudes to which our auditory system is especially sensitive. There is also neurophysiological evidence that humans have perceptual specialisation for language. This includes hemispherical specialisation, where the two halves of the brain have different specialisations. It is typically (though not always) the case that language faculties are predominantly in the left hemisphere of the brain. Interestingly, and following the general pattern that the left hemisphere is responsive to and responsible for the right-hand side of the body, this is linked to a right ear advantage (REA) for speech for most people. This was demonstrated in the 1960s and 1970s in dichotic listening experiments (e.g. Kimura, 1961; Studdert-Kennedy, Shankweiler & Pisoni, 1972;

> **Hemispherical specialisation** Various tasks are under the control of certain brain areas, and there is considerable evidence that one hemisphere (half) of the brain is responsible for some tasks, and the other for other tasks. It is quite well known for instance that there is a cross-over whereby motor commands to the left body side – e.g. mental instructions to move the left arm – are controlled by the right brain hemisphere, and vice versa.

Studdert-Kennedy & Shankweiler, 1970). In these experiments, participants hear competing sequences of words presented over headphones to each ear. More accurate identification occurs for words presented to the right ear, as long as participants have no basic hearing imbalance between the ears.

An interesting question is whether the REA arises because we hear better with the right ear, or because we hear speech sounds better with the right ear, or because we process language better when we receive it through the right ear. That is, at what processing level does the left hemisphere get its advantage? To test this, dichotic listening experiments have been carried out with a number of different kinds of stimuli. Musical stimuli fail to show the REA, and indeed have been found to give a left ear advantage (Bryden, 1988). This shows that the REA is not a reflection of auditory processing per se, as this would predict an REA for any kind of auditory input. In addition, neurophysiological studies using speech and equivalently complex non-speech sounds found differences in left brain hemisphere activation for the speech and non-speech, but equal activation levels for the two types in the right hemisphere (Parviainen, Helenius & Salmelin, 2005).

The REA is also clearly not phonetic, i.e. not an advantage specifically for speech sounds, because Morse code signals (sequences of short and long tones acting as a code for letters of the alphabet) also show the REA (Papcun, Krashen, Terbeek, Remington & Harshman, 1974). It is most likely therefore that the REA reflects the linguistic processing that takes place in the left brain hemisphere, and which will apply to both speech and Morse code input. It also turns out that speech-like but unintelligible stimuli also show an REA (i.e. more can be remembered about these stimuli when presented to the right ear). Even though these stimuli are unintelligible, our linguistic processing system attempts to make sense of them, and so we can recall more about them as a consequence.

If participants are instructed to pay greater attention to one ear than the other, then this can enhance or decrease the REA, suggesting again that the advantage is not an automatic peripheral effect (Hugdahl & Andersson, 1986). In addition, the REA for simple syllables in dichotic listening tasks is affected by the nature of a preceding prime stimulus presented to both ears simultaneously (Sætrevik & Hugdahl, 2007). If the prime differs from both of two test items, one presented to each ear, then the REA persists, i.e. the item presented to the right ear is recalled more accurately. If the prime is identical to the left-channel test item, then the REA increases, and if the prime is identical to the right-channel test item, the REA decreases, i.e. there is inhibition of the previously presented prime item. Inhibition has been shown independently for primes that have to be ignored (i.e. where no response is expected for the prime item, as in this task). Sætrevik & Hugdahl argue that after the prime item is presented, cognitive control inhibits it because it is a potential interfering factor, and this leads to a recognition advantage for the novel item. Interestingly, this effect is found in this dichotic listening task even when the primes are visually displayed on a computer screen (e.g. <ga> before

In **priming** tasks researchers are interested in how quickly and/or accurately participants respond to a stimulus (the probe) that has been preceded by another stimulus (the prime) that might be related to it in some way. Priming can include for example identity priming (the same stimulus is presented twice) or semantic priming (the prime word is related in meaning to the probe, e.g. DOCTOR then NURSE).

dichotic auditory stimuli consisting of /ga/ to one ear and /ba/ to the other).

Mapping from the input to the linguistic system

An important part of perceptual processing for language is how the listener or reader gets from the input signal to the linguistic system. In Chapters 8 and 9 we discuss this process more closely in the context of spoken and visual word recognition respectively, building on assumptions that words provide a significant linguistic building block and that recognising words in the input stream is therefore an important objective of the perceptual system.

An issue that is common to both visual and auditory processing, though different in its specific workings, is the nature of pre-lexical processing, i.e. what kinds of units need to be identified before words can be accessed. We are so used to a particular way of thinking about how written words are made up that it might seem obvious that word recognition would involve the recognition of a word's component letters. However, there is evidence that practised readers recognise individual letters only in the case of relatively uncommon words, and that a lot of word recognition is based on overall word shape. While this suggests recognition units larger than the letter, other approaches to visual word recognition argue that there are smaller recognition units than letters, and that letter features (such as horizontal, vertical or diagonal lines at various heights on a text line) form an important part of the recognition process.

Similarly, models of spoken word recognition argue for different types of intervening representation between the input and the word. The most obvious is the phoneme, or distinct speech sound, as the nearest equivalent in speech to the letter in visually presented words. But smaller units, e.g. phonetic features have also been claimed to have perceptual validity. In addition, pre-lexical units larger than the phoneme have also been proposed, such as the syllable or the diphone.

In both the visual and auditory domains there are also peripheral perceptual processes that must take place before linguistically relevant information can be extracted from the input. These more automatic processes do not generally form part of the subject matter of psycholinguistics, except insofar as they may be relevant to the extraction of linguistically relevant features.

Variability

A significant issue in perception for language is variability. That is, the input that we receive can be highly variable in its detail. This variability adds to the difficulty of identifying the units of writing or of speech.

Writing styles and legibility vary from one person to the next. The care taken over writing depends on the nature of the writing task and the intended reader of the material (notes written by a student during a lecture will differ from a scholarship application letter from the same student). The choice of font in a typed document will affect letter shape, as Figure 7.1 illustrates.

Phonetic features usually involve the presence or absence of a feature, such as [±voice], i.e. whether or not the sound is voiced, as in the contrast between /z/ (voiced) and /s/ (voiceless).

A **diphone** is a sequence of two sounds, capturing the important transitions from one sound to the next. Diphones are often used to create more natural sounding speech synthesis.

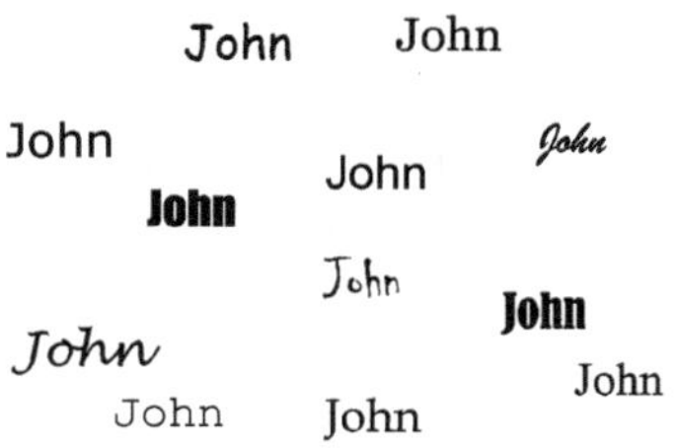

John   John

John

John   John   *John*

John   *John*

John   **John**

John   John

John   John   John

Figure 7.1
Variability in the input.

Variability is very obviously present in speech too. Speakers have different vocal tract shapes and sizes and different chest cavity sizes. These and other physical factors will contribute to variation in the sounds produced by different speakers. Even the same speaker will produce qualitatively different versions of the same sound on separate occasions, depending on a range of factors such as health, emotional state, the situation of speaking, the phonetic and linguistic context in which a sound is found, and so on.

Variability is a potential problem for perception, as too much variability will result in difficulty identifying the intended letter or sound or word or message. Researchers in speech perception and automatic speech recognition have often struggled to identify invariant cues to the identity of individual speech sounds. Of course, some variability is predictable and therefore potentially useful. Predictable variation in speech can indicate differences between speakers in terms of their age, sex, size, social class, place of origin, and many other demographic, social and personal factors. Some variation, both in writing and in speech, results from the effects of the context in which a letter or sound is found, and can therefore provide information about that context which can actually help perception. For instance, nasalisation on an English vowel may make that vowel different from other instances of that vowel, and therefore increase the vowel's variability, but at the same time this nasalisation may be informative, because it may tell you that the following consonant is nasal.

Exemplars

Rather than assume that the input is matched against a single template for a phoneme, word or other recognition unit, recent approaches to language perception and comprehension have argued that our memory systems allow us to store multiple representations for a given unit. These are known as exemplars, and are assumed to be rich in information that relates to the actual utterances on which they are based. For example, it has been argued that we have exemplar representations for words which include information about the speaker who uttered the word, such as their age, sex, social grouping, dialect, etc., as well as possibly about the time and place of the utterance, and so on (Hay, Warren & Drager, 2006; Johnson, 1997; Pierrehumbert, 2001; Strand, 1999). Exemplars provide a possible mechanism for coping with variation, because the latter becomes part of the richness of the set of representations rather than a problem to

Nasalisation occurs when the velum, or soft palate, is lowered during speaking, allowing air to flow through the nose. English has no nasal vowels, though it does have nasal consonants (e.g. the final consonants in *sum, sun* and *sung*). When a vowel in English precedes a nasal consonant, then the vowel often has a nasal quality as a result of assimilation to (i.e. becoming more like) that consonant. In this case we say the vowel is nasal*ised*, but not that it is a nasal vowel.

be overcome. Since social information is also associated with the exemplars, speech perception has a built-in mechanism for recognising social variation and for normalising for it. As new exemplars are encountered, they are added to our exemplar sets, and older exemplars that are not reactivated fade over time.

Segmentation

If language comprehension involves the recognition of basic units of writing or of speech, then these units need to be separable from adjacent units. But segmentation of the input is not always straightforward.

(7.1)   *Some joined up writing*

Take for instance the example in (7.1). Although this is a highly regularised version of connected letters, using a computer font rather than actual handwriting, there are areas of ambiguity and uncertainty concerning where one letter finishes and the next begins. For instance, the beginning of the final word could be a <u>, the second letter in the first word might be <a>.

Likewise, speech sounds run into one another as the articulators move from the position for one sound to that for the next. Figure 7.2 gives a visual representation – a spectrogram (see sidebar) – of speech, for the utterance *Pete is keen to lead the team*. An approximate segmentation into words is shown below the spectrogram. Note that there are seldom any clear 'boundaries' between the words in the spectrogram, i.e. segmentation of the speech into words is difficult, let alone into individual sounds within these words. In this respect, speech is different from most instances of writing, in that writing – even joined up writing as in (7.1) – usually places spaces between words. Note also that Figure 7.2 includes a good example of variability resulting from the context in which a sound is uttered – there are four instances of the /i/ sound in this utterance, and the portions of the spectrogram corresponding to those instances are not identical, as shown in Figure 7.3. They differ both in their duration and in the shape of the darker bands showing how the sound energy is distributed, though there are also some common features.

This section has highlighted some of the common issues for the perception of written and spoken language. These issues relate to the fact that the perceiver has to extract linguistic information from the input signal, and that this can be made difficult by two major problems. One is the lack of invariance in how the 'same' letter or sound is produced on different occasions or by different people. The other is how to segment a piece of text or an utterance into its constituent parts. We have noted above that the segmentation of speech into words is more problematic than the segmentation of written or printed text. In addition, the transitory nature of speech means the initial re-coding of the input into linguistic units is likely to be more critical with speech than with writing, where the reader can go back and look again at the input. In the next section we will look at further issues for speech perception.

Spectrograms are based on the analysis of the sound energy present in speech at different frequencies. Time is represented on the horizontal axis, frequency on the vertical axis, and the darkness of the shading shows how much energy is present at any frequency at a given point in time during the utterance.

The darker bands during the vowels shown in the spectrogram show the resonant frequencies, known as formants, of the vocal tract. These differ for different vowels because of the position of the tongue, the shape of the lips, the height of the lower jaw, etc. They also differ for what seems to be the same vowel, depending on what sounds precede and follow that vowel.

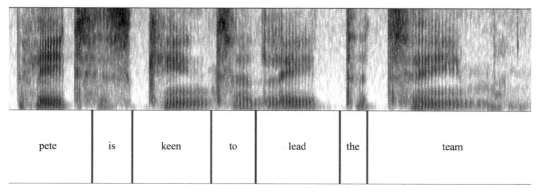

| pete | is | keen | to | lead | the | team |

Figure 7.2
Spectrogram for the utterance *Pete is keen to lead the team*.

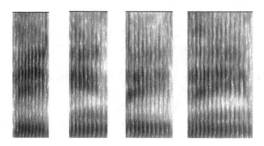

Figure 7.3
Four /i/ sounds from the utterance in Figure 7.2.

7.3 Basic issues in speech perception

As already mentioned, human auditory perception is especially well tuned to speech sounds. Our hearing is most sensitive to sounds in the frequency range in which most speech sounds are found, i.e. between 600 Hz and 4000 Hz.

It is also the case that the human perceptual system streams language and non-language signals, i.e. treats them as separate inputs, thereby reducing the distracting effect of non-speech signals on speech perception. This has been shown through phoneme restoration effects (Samuel, 1990). When listeners hear words in which a speech sound (phoneme) has been replaced by a non-speech sound such as a cough, they are highly likely to report the word as intact, i.e. the cough is treated as part of a separate stream. There is a clear linguistic influence here, as the restoration effect is stronger with real words than with nonsense words. It has also been shown that when the word-level information is ambiguous, then the word that is restored is one which matches the sentence context. For example, the sequence /#il/, where # indicates a non-speech sound replacing or overlaid on a consonant, could represent many possible words (*deal*, *feel*, *heal*, etc.). In the different conditions shown in (7.2), a

> Hz = Hertz, or cycles per second. It is the rate at which a sound-wave repeats itself, and is the standard measure of frequency for sounds.

word will be reported that is appropriate to the context shown by the final word in the utterance (originally demonstrated by Warren & Warren, 1970). So if that word is *orange*, then *peel* is reported, if it is *table*, then *meal*, and so on. Linguistic effects on perception are powerful, and will be discussed in more detail later in this chapter.

(7.2)   It was found that the /#il/ was on the { shoe | orange | table }

> Click consonants are found in a range of languages in southern and eastern Africa. Speakers of English use click sounds, such as the 'tut-tut' noise of disapproval, or the 'gee-up' clicking sound made to encourage a horse. In click languages, such sounds are used as parts of words.

The language-specific nature of streaming effects is indicated by anecdotal evidence from students who are asked to listen to recordings from a language with a very different sound inventory from their own, and who experience some of the sounds as non-speech sounds external to the speech stream. A good example of this is when English-speaking students first listen to recordings of a click language, with many students reporting the click consonants as a tapping or knocking sound happening separately from the speech.

Despite the evidence that listeners segregate speech and non-speech signals, it is also clear that the perceptual system will integrate these if at all plausible. That is, if a non-speech sound could be part of the simultaneous speech signal, we will generally perceive it as such. For example, if the final portion of the /s/ sound in the word *slit* is replaced by silence, then this silence is interpreted as a /p/ sound, resulting in the word *split* being heard (see the exercises at the end of this chapter). A stretch of silence is one of several cues to a voiceless plosive such as /p/ (the silence results from the closure of the lips with no simultaneous voicing noise), and is sufficient in this context to result in the percept of a speech sound.

Frequently there are multiple cues to a speech sound, or to the distinction between that speech sound and a very similar one. The voiceless bilabial plosive /p/ sound is cued not just by the silence during the lip-closure portion of that consonant, but also by changes that take place in the formant structure of any preceding vowel as the lips come together to make the closure, by the duration of a preceding vowel (voiceless stops in English tend to be preceded by shorter variants of a vowel than voiced stops such as /b/), by several properties of the burst noise as the lips are opened, and so on. While some of these cues may be more important or more reliable than others, it is clear that the perception of an individual sound depends on cue integration, involving a range of cues that distinguish this sound from others in the sound inventory of the language.

A fascinating instance of cue integration comes from studies of speech perception that involve visual cues. We are often able to see the people we are listening to, and their faces tell us much about what they are saying. A particular set of cues comes from the shape and movements of the mouth. For a bilabial plosive (/b/ or /p/) there will be a visible lip closure gesture; for an alveolar plosive (/d/ or /t/) it might be possible to see the tongue making a closure at the front of the mouth, just behind the top teeth; for a velar plosive (/g/ or /k/) the closure towards the back of the mouth will be visually less evident. Normally, these visual cues will be compatible with the auditory cues from the speech signal, and therefore will supplement them. If however, the visual cues and the auditory cues have been experimentally manipulated so that they are no longer compatible, then they can merge on a percept that is different from that signalled by either set of cues on their own. This is known as the McGurk effect, after one of the early researchers to identify the phenomenon (McGurk & MacDonald, 1976). For instance, if the auditory information indicates a /ba/ syllable, but the visual information is from a /ga/ syllable, showing no lip closure, then the interpretation is that the speaker has said /da/. Examples of this effect are available on the website for this book (and see also the exercises at the end of this chapter).

Another and at first glance somewhat bizarre cue integration effect has been reported in what have been referred to as the "puff of air" experiments. In these experiments participants listen to stimulus syllables that are ambiguous between, say, /ba/ and /pa/. For speakers of English and many other languages, one of several characteristics that distinguish the /b/ and /p/ sounds in these syllables is that there is a stronger puff of air that accompanies the /p/ than is found with the /b/. In phonetics terminology, the /p/ is aspirated and the /b/ is unaspirated. In the experiments, it was found that participants were more likely to report the ambiguous stimulus as /pa/ if they also felt a puff of air that was presented simultaneously with the speech signal. The effect was found whether the puff of air was directed at the hand or at the neck (Gick & Derrick, 2009), or even at the ankle (Derrick & Gick, 2010).

It has also been shown that cue trading is involved in speech perception. For instance, if the release burst of a /p/ is unclear, perhaps because of some non-speech sound that happened at the same time, then the listener may assign greater perceptual significance to other cues such as the relative duration of the preceding vowel and movements in the formants at the end of that vowel.

These cues in the formant movements are a result of coarticulation – the articulation of one sound is influenced by the articulation of a neighbouring sound. It appears that our perceptual system is so used to the phenomenon of coarticulation that it will compensate for it in the perception of sounds. For instance, Elman and McClelland (1988) asked participants to identify a word as *capes* or *tapes*. Their experiment hinged on the fact that a /k/ is pronounced further forward in the mouth, so closer to a /t/, when it follows /s/ (as in *Christmas capes*) than when it follows /ʃ/ (as in *foolish capes*). This is because /s/ is itself further forward in the mouth than /ʃ/ and there is coarticulation of the following /k/ towards the place of articulation of the /s/. Elman and McClelland manipulated the first speech sound in *capes* or *tapes* to make it sound more /k/-like or more /t/-like. One of the cues to the difference between the /k/ and /t/ sounds is the height in the frequency scale of the burst of noise that is emitted when the plosive is released – it is higher for front sounds like /t/ than it is for back sounds like /k/. In the experiment, the noise burst of the initial consonant in *tapes* or *capes* was manipulated to produce a range of values that were intermediate between the target values for /t/ and /k/. Participants heard tokens from this range of *tapes*/*capes* stimuli after either *Christmas* or *foolish*, and had to report whether they heard the word as *tapes* or *capes*. The

Aspiration is the puff of air that accompanies the release of certain stop or plosive consonants such as /p/ in English. You can demonstrate aspiration to yourself by dangling a piece of paper loosely in front of your mouth and saying /pa/ and /ba/. The paper should move more with /pa/. It should also move more with /pa/ than with /spa/, since another characteristic of /p/ in English is that it is aspirated at the beginning of a syllable, but not when it follows /s/.

Burst noise as a cue to place of articulation – The spectrogram in Figure 7.2 contains /k/ in *keen* and /t/ in *team*. Notice that the dark band of acoustic energy for /k/ covers lower parts of the frequency range than the corresponding band of energy for /t/.

Figure 7.4
Compensation for
coarticulation (based on
Elman and McClelland,
1988).

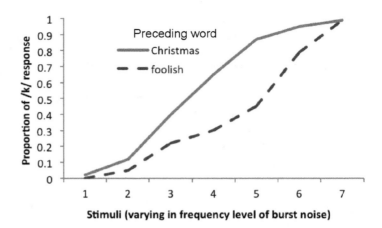

Figure 7.4
Compensation for coarticulation (based on Elman and McClelland, 1988).

results were very clear – after the word *Christmas*, tokens on the /t/–/k/ continuum were more likely to be heard as /k/ than when the same tokens followed *foolish* (see Figure 7.4). That is, the participants expected the coarticulation effect to lead to a 'fronted' /k/ after /s/, and compensated for this in their interpretation of the frequency level of the burst noise.

Our perception and comprehension of speech is also affected by signal continuity. That is, listeners are better able to follow a stream of speech if it sounds like it comes in a continuous fashion from one source. This lies behind the cocktail party effect, where we are able to follow one speaker in a crowded room full of conversation despite other talk around us (Arons, 1992). This effect can be demonstrated in various ways. In one task, participants hear two voices over stereo headphones, and are asked to focus on what is being said on just one of the headphone channels, the left channel for example. If the voice on the left channel switches to the right part way through the recording, then participants find that their attention follows the voice to the right channel. They then report at least some of what is then said on the right channel, despite the instructions to focus on the left channel (Treisman, 1960). The strength of this effect is reduced if the utterance prosody is disrupted at the switch. The importance of signal continuity is also demonstrated in the relative unnaturalness of some computer-generated or concatenated speech, such as is found for instance in the automated speech of some phone-in banking systems.

Active and passive speech perception

There have been numerous attempts to frame aspects of speech perception in models or theories (some of these are reviewed by Klatt, 1989). One distinction that has been made between different models concerns the degree of involvement of the listener as speaker, characterised as a difference between active and passive perception processes.

Passive models of speech perception assume that we have a stored system of patterns or recognition units, against which we match the speech that we hear. Depending on the specific claims of the model, these stored patterns might be phonetic features or perhaps templates for phonemes or diphone sequences, and so on. A phoneme-based perception model might for example include a template for the /i/ phoneme that shares some of the common characteristics of the spectrogram slices shown in Figure 7.3. A feature-based model might include a voicing detector that examines the input for the presence of the regular repetition of speech waves that corresponds to vocal cord vibration, and would have similar detectors for other features that define a speech sound.

Incoming speech data is matched against the templates, and a score given for how well the data matches the templates. These scores are evaluated and a best match determined. Many automatic speech recognition systems operate like this – they have templates for each recognition unit and match slices of the input speech data against these templates. Such systems perform best when they have had some training, usually requiring the user to repeat some standard phrases so that the speech processing system can develop appropriate templates.

Active models of speech perception argue that our perception is influenced by or depends on our capabilities as producers of speech. One model of this type involves analysis-by-synthesis. Here, the listener matches the incoming speech data not against a stored template for input units of speech, but against the patterns that would result from the listener's own speech production, i.e. synthesises an output (or a series of alternative outputs) and matches that against the analysis of the input.

7.4 Basic issues in visual perception for language

We have seen that speech perception involves some pre-linguistic analysis of the auditory input, the precise details of which vary according to the model of perception. In visual perception for language, some sort of preliminary analysis of the input is also assumed to take place. The whole word-shape is probably important, as shown by the fact that we can recognise words containing misspellings or ordering errors, jsut as long as the overoll shape of the word is relatively unaffected. This can even result in errors remaining undetected. For instance, if you have been reading this paragraph quickly, for meaning rather than to identify the detail of every word, you might not have noticed the misspellings of *just* and *overall* two sentences ago.

It seems that the visual input is not recognised on a straightforward letter-by-letter basis. This is shown by the word superiority effect. This is the finding that individual letters (e.g. D) are recognised more rapidly and reliably when they occur in words (e.g. in WORD) than when they are either in nonwords (legitimate sequences of letters that happen not to make a word, as in WROD) or in jumbled letter strings (WLOD). Nevertheless, individual letters and letter shapes are important in visual perception for language, and form an important part of approaches to visual

Several years ago a passage was published in the press and on the internet that began "Aoccdring to rscheearch at Cmabrigde Uinervtisy it deosn't mttaer in waht oredr the ltteers in a wrod are". Crucially, though, the disruptions in that text involve local reorderings within the word, keep the overall word shape reasonably intact, and have no effect on shorter words. Information from the context (the overall meaning) further reduces the disruptive effect.

word recognition (see Chapter 9). It has also been argued that letter features are significant. Letter features might include horizontal and vertical lines (as in <H>), sloping lines (in <M>), various loops (<P, p, B>) and so on. Evidence for the importance of letter features comes from studies that show that it is more difficult to find a letter if it is embedded in a set of letters with similar features.

The specific nature and level of detail that is claimed to be important in the initial visual analysis varies according to the particular theory of perception. It may also depend on the automaticity of visual word recognition, which varies with reading experience.

Stages during visual perception

It is generally assumed that there are stages in the visual perception of language. The initial visual analysis transfers the input into some sort of buffer. This is followed by further analysis in working memory, and then by integration of the analysed input with the linguistic and cognitive interpretation of the text.

Evidence for these stages comes from a number of sources. As we will see below, reading normally proceeds by means of a series of eye fixations, where different portions of text are in the visual field. Although these fixations are relatively brief, at around 250 msec, they are actually longer than is needed to recognise a word. We know this because studies that use very brief presentations of words show that we only need to see a word for about 50 msec in order to be able to recall it quite well. It seems that we fixate on a stretch of text for longer than this because it takes longer to transfer information from a visual buffer into working memory. This was demonstrated in some early experiments where participants were asked to report which letter in a series of letters had been marked by having a vertical line placed next to it (Sperling, 1960). The letters were presented very briefly, and could be recognised from such a brief presentation. The vertical mark was not presented simultaneously with the letters, but after a very short delay. The experience for the participants, though, was that the mark appeared at the same time as the letters, and so they were able to report accurately which letter was marked. But this only happened if the interval between the letters and the vertical mark was not too long. The interpretation of these results is that it takes a short while to transfer information from the visual buffer to working memory, where further processing can take place. If further visual input is received too soon, then the first lot of visual information is added to or overwritten, resulting in the marking of a letter. It follows therefore that if the eyes skip ahead too soon during reading, then the visual information relating to one set of words will be merged with or replaced by the information relating to the next fixation, before it can be shuffled into working memory.

The letter recall experiments worked like this:

First presentation:

G D J P S K W A

\<short delay\>

Second presentation:

|

Percept:
G D J|P S K W A

If the delay was too long (over half a second), then the two presentations were not integrated in this way.

Eye movements during reading

It is clear that the initial visual analysis of text is different from other kinds of visual perception. There are some obvious differences between text and much other visual input, such as the fact that text is generally

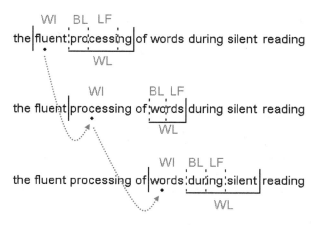

Key:
• = fixation point; WI = word identification; BL = beginning letters;
LF = letter features; WL = word length

Figure 7.5
Eye movements during silent reading (adapted from Rayner & Balota, 1989: 268).

stationary and can easily be looked at again, text is usually sharply defined but two-dimensional, and so on. There are some important differences in how text is read, compared with other visual processing. An obvious external indication of this can be gained by comparing people's eye movements when reading text and when watching someone walking across a room. The following summary of eye movements during reading is based on Rayner and Balota (1989). (See also Balota, Yap, & Cortese, 2006.)

During reading, eye movements are characteristically not smooth, but demonstrate sequences of fixations and saccades (jumps). Most of the time readers' eyes are not in fact moving, since the fixations last about 250 msec while the saccades are very quick, taking between 10 and 20 msec. Each jump moves the eyes forward by approximately 8–9 characters, as shown by the example in Figure 7.5, although the size of the jump can depend on the complexity of the text. The example in the figure is based on data from reading studies using precision cameras that measure the movements of the eyes. It shows three consecutive fixations on a piece of text, and illustrates the information that is available during each fixation.

As indicated by the key in the figure, WI shows that word identification can take place for the word(s) in question, i.e. those at or near the fixation point. BL indicates that the beginning letters of following words can be identified, and LF shows that some of the letter features of the next few letters are discernible. WL means that the reader can judge the relative lengths of words to the right of the fixation point. The solid vertical lines show the total perceptual span of the fixation, which is clearly greater than the size of the jump between fixations, and includes more words than the one(s) that can be readily identified. The span also takes in more information to the right of the fixation point than to the left. These aspects of the perceptual span during reading have been measured in

The perceptual span asymmetry, where more information is taken in from one side of a fixation than the other, depends on the direction of reading. Readers who deal with scripts that are read from right-to-left, such as Hebrew, show the opposite asymmetry to those shown by English readers. In other words, the fixation is 'looking ahead' in terms of what is to be read.

tasks controlling the amount and nature of information available on-screen as a reader progresses through a text, and assessing the impact on the speed and success of reading that results from changing the available information.

The look-ahead evident in Figure 7.5 plays an important part in reading. Being able to tell the difference between shorter and longer words (using the word length information marked by WL in the figure) helps the reader to distinguish function and content words (the former tend to be quite short) and to determine which words should be the landing point for the next fixation. Identification of the beginning letters of words (BL) and some of the letter features in the rest of the word (LF) allows the lexical search to be started before the word itself is looked at more closely during a subsequent fixation.

This preview effect is one of many factors that influence fixation times and jump distances during reading. Others include the difficulty of the text, the predictability of the fixated words from the prior context, how frequent the words are and how recently they have been encountered, whether the words are ambiguous, and whether there is any priming of the words by previous mention of related words or other material (see Chapters 8 and 9 for further discussion of some of these parameters in the context of word recognition).

The nature of the input

It is important to note at this point that languages do not all use the same writing system as English, and that many of the differences between writing systems will have consequences for the visual perception of words or for their recognition. The following are some of the differences. First, there is a range of orthographic writing systems, i.e. of writing systems that represent some aspect of the sounds of words. As we will see in Chapter 9, pronunciation plays a role during reading, and so the relationship between letters and sounds is important. English uses an alphabetic system, but one in which there are many irregularities in the correspondences between letters and sounds. For instance <c> has a /s/ pronunciation in *cease*, but a /k/ pronunciation in *cat*. Languages with a high degree of irregularity are said to have a deep orthography. They contrast with languages in which there is a reasonably direct letter-sound correspondence, and therefore a shallow orthography, such as Italian, Serbo-Croatian or Māori, as well as with languages in which the pronunciation of a particular letter string is reasonably predictable but where there may be many letter strings with the same pronunciation (e.g. French, in which the spellings <o>, <au>, <aux>, <eau>, <eaux> can represent the same sound).

Other orthographic writing systems include consonantal systems, such as Hebrew and Arabic, in which the letters often represent the consonants only, and syllabic systems, such as Kannada and the Japanese *kana* writing system, in which each orthographic symbol represents a syllable. Looking beyond orthographic systems, we find ideographic systems, such as in Chinese, where a symbol corresponds to a word (or a portion of a word in a morphologically complex form); with the exception of diacritic markers, the symbol does not bear a direct representation of the sounds of the word.

The range of different writing systems and of the relationships of these writing systems to pronunciation adds to the complexity of the study of visual perception and visual word recognition.

7.5 Influence of the linguistic system on perception

There are many ways in which our perception is influenced by the linguistic system, i.e. by the fact that the sounds or visual shapes we are processing might be considered part of language. We saw evidence of this earlier (p. 105) where phoneme restoration effects depended on the sentence context in which the replaced phoneme occurred. We see it also in the perceptual advantages that language-relevant stimuli have. For example, studies in which sounds are embedded in noise have shown that speech sounds are more reliably identified or recalled than non-speech sounds. On top of this, if the speech sounds make up real words rather than nonsense, then they have an even greater processing advantage. Neurophysiological studies, using EEG and MEG to measure electrical activity in the brain, show that this processing advantage for real words over nonsense words becomes distinct as early as 150 msec after the point at which a word can be recognised (Pulvermüller *et al.*, 2001). The fact that this is a linguistic effect rather than a consequence of differences in the sounds involved is shown by the fact this is found for native speakers of the language being tested (Finnish in this case) but not for foreigners who do not know the language.

A very significant area in which a linguistic influence on speech perception has been demonstrated is categorical perception. Work in this area dates back to the 1950s (Liberman, Harris, Hoffman & Griffith, 1957), but our understanding of what is involved in categorical perception has been refined over the intervening decades. As the name suggests, categorical perception relates to the finding that we hear speech sounds as belonging to categories. That is, if we are presented with a series of speech stimuli that vary along some linguistically relevant phonetic dimension, then we will classify some of them as belonging to category X and some as belonging to category Y, rather than hearing a particular stimulus as being X-ish, another as being a little more Y-like, and so on.

Although categorical perception has been demonstrated for a range of contrasts, the one most widely cited is the distinction between voiced and voiceless plosive consonants, e.g. between /b/ and /p/. This distinction is actually signalled by a range of different parameters, but the one that has usually been explored is voice onset time (VOT). Voice onset time is the lag between the release of the closure for the plosive consonant (in this case the opening of the lips) and the beginning of voicing for a following vowel. This is shorter for a voiced plosive like /b/ than for a voiceless one like /p/ – in English typically less than and more than 30 msec respectively.

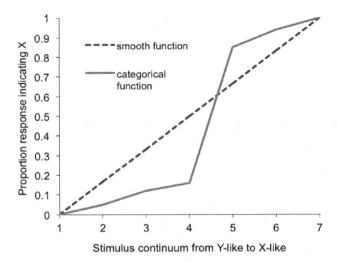

Figure 7.6
Smooth and categorical
response functions.

In experiments, participants are given synthesised /ba/-like or /pa/-like syllables to respond to. The response can either be an identification one (is this /ba/ or /pa/?) or a discrimination one (are two stimuli the same or different?). The identification responses show that rather than there being a gradual change of responses from /ba/ to /pa/ as VOT increases, there is a dramatic switch of response preference part-way along the continuum. In terms of the hypothetical responses shown in Figure 7.6, responses to VOT continua follow a categorical function – also referred to as an S-curve because of the shape of the line in such a figure – rather than a smooth or straight-line function.

Responses in the discrimination tasks show that participants treat as 'same' two stimuli that fall on the same side of the dramatic shift in the identification response, e.g. in terms of Figure 7.6, stimuli 2 and 3, or 3 and 4, or 5 and 6, but will label as 'different' two stimuli that fall on either side of the shift, i.e. stimuli 4 and 5 in the figure. They do this even if in terms of VOT the difference between 4 and 5 is of the same magnitude as the difference between 3 and 4 or between 5 and 6. This is evidence that sounds are placed into perceptual categories, with rather sharp boundaries between the categories. These findings have been supported by neurophysiological studies that have demonstrated different brain responses (measured through changes in event-related magnetic fields, or ERFs) to tokens either side of a category boundary, but similar responses to stimuli within a VOT category (e.g. Simos *et al.*, 1998).

Categorical perception makes sense from the point of view of language perception and comprehension. This is because we expect spoken sound to indicate linguistic entities as part of the comprehension process.

Studies with infants have shown that they are able to discriminate categories, e.g. between /b/ and /p/, at a very young age (around 3 months old), before they can speak (Eimas, Siqueland, Jusczyk & Vigorito, 1971). While an initial reaction to this finding was to conjecture that phonetic distinctions are a specially evolved and innate human characteristic that serves as a precursor to speech, a number of factors indicate that this is not the case. First, it turns out that there is nothing special about speech – other stimuli, including non-speech sounds, can also be distinguished categorically, with appropriate training (as demonstrated in early work by Lane, 1965). Second, it was found that humans are not alone in making categorical perceptual distinctions between speech sounds – chinchillas for instance can also do this, even though they have not evolved to speak (Kuhl, 1987). Third, there are cross-linguistic differences in where the VOT category boundary between, say, /b/ and/p/ is found. This implies that the categories themselves, and the boundaries between the categories, have to be learned (Abramson & Lisker, 1973), although some studies have demonstrated that infants may initially be more sensitive to certain category boundaries than to others (Aslin, Pisoni, Hennessey & Perey, 1981).

In further categorical perception studies with adults, it has been shown that category boundaries are not fixed, even within a language, but can be affected by the linguistic context. We saw this earlier in this chapter in the discussion of listeners' compensation for coarticulation (see Figure 7.4), where the /k/ identification function for *tapes* vs *capes* was shifted depending on the nature of the consonant at the end of the preceding word.

The Ganong effect (named after the author of the first famous study of this phonemenon) is a good demonstration of how the boundaries between phonetic categories can be affected by linguistic information (Ganong, 1980). In this case, it is the lexical status of the word containing the manipulated segment that is important. For a /d/–/t/ continuum, for instance, the category boundary falls nearer the /d/ end of the continuum if the stimulus is /?ask/ (where ? indicates the manipulated segment). This is because *task* is a word and *dask* is not, so more of the stimuli towards the /d/ end of the continuum are accepted as falling within the /t/ category. Conversely, the boundary falls nearer to the /t/ end if the stimulus is /?esk/, i.e. more *desk* responses are given overall, because *desk* is a word and *tesk* is not.

> The perceptual abilities of infants are measured using methods such as High Amplitude Sucking. An infant sucks on a dummy connected to equipment that measures how hard she is sucking and controls the presentation of stimuli. When the infant gets bored with the same stimulus, her sucking intensity reduces, at which point a new stimulus is presented. If she hears this as different, then she becomes excited and her sucking increases.

Summary

We have seen that there are some clear commonalities in language perception in the auditory and visual modalities:

- the input has to be segmented and analysed into linguistically useful units;
- variability in the input has to be overcome.

But there are also some differences in how speech and writing are processed, which result from the obvious differences between the modalities:

- speech is transitory;
- speech lacks many clear boundaries between the linguistic units it contains;
- writing has greater permanence and can be re-inspected with relative ease;
- writing contains clearer boundaries between words and within words between letters.

We have also seen some key issues relevant to perception for language:

- the human brain is specialised for language processing;
- the perceptual system streams language and non-language stimuli;
- but will integrate stimuli if this makes linguistic sense;
- cue integration includes visual and tactile cues as well as auditory ones;
- the linguistic system can have an influence on perception, leading to effects such as real word advantages and/or biases in perception;
- infants begin to tune-in to the relevant cues for the language they are learning at a very early age.

Exercises

Exercise 7.1

If you replaced some of the end of the /s/ in the words *soil*, *suit* and *seep* with silence, would you expect to hear a /p/ in each case? Why? If not, why not? (If you want to hear this for yourself, the website has examples of these words in the original and manipulated forms. Alternatively, use a speech editing package such as Praat (www.praat.org) to record and manipulate words like this yourself.)

Exercise 7.2

The sound file represented in Figure 7.2 shows two nasal sounds (at the end of *keen* and of *team*). Can you identify a characteristic of nasal sounds from the spectrogram?

Notice that the vowel portions of the words *to* and *the* look very similar to one another in the spectrogram. Why do you think this is the case? Figure 7.3 showed four examples of the /i/ vowel from this sound file. Can you explain any of the differences between these examples? What do they have in common that might tell you that the same vowel is involved?

Exercise 7.3

Work with two fellow students, friends or relatives for this exercise, forming a group of three – A, B and C. A watches B's eyes as B either reads a text or watches C walking across the room. A should note any differences in the patterns of B's eye movements. What differences are there? Swap roles and do this again.

Exercise 7.4
The perceptual integration of visual and auditory inputs known as the McGurk effect is a powerful effect. Would you expect it to happen if the face you see is clearly not the origin of the voice you hear (e.g. if the face is female and the voice is male)? Look at the example of this on the website.

Further reading

Samuel (1990) provides a review of phoneme restoration effects. The McGurk effect has been reported in many places, and a short and accessible overview is given by McGurk & MacDonald (1976). An excellent review of eye movements during reading, with particular reference to word recognition, is provided by Rayner and Balota (1989). A recent review of work in speech perception, including discussion of the recent interest in episodic exemplar representations, can be found in Pisoni and Levi (2007).

8 Spoken word recognition

PREVIEW

This chapter introduces some key issues involved in the process of recognising spoken words. You will learn that spoken word recognition:

- involves a series of stages, including contact between the input speech and the representations for words stored in the mental lexicon, the activation of these stored representations, and the recognition of a single word as the outcome of this process;
- involves both the analysis of the input and the interpretation of the context in which words are encountered;
- is affected by how often and how recently words have been encountered, and by their similarity to other words.

KEY TERMS

activation
cohort
competitor
contact
frequency
inhibition
lexical access
lexical frequency
mental lexicon
neighbour(hood)
pre-lexical analysis
selection
variability
word recognition

8.1 Introduction

Words are often regarded as the basic building-blocks of language. Although in theory they are not the minimal unit of meaning, in practice we think of different words as conveying different meanings, and therefore of the word as a unit of meaning. In addition, the 'first word' is a landmark in most parents' appraisals of their children's language development. Words are what we look up in dictionaries and what we learn for spelling tests. When we learn a second or foreign language, words are what we study on vocabulary lists. A good author is sometimes known as a wordsmith.

The purpose of this chapter is to present some of what we know about how people recognise words. The focus will be on the recognition of *spoken* words, though some of the claims that we will encounter can be extended to the discussion of visual word recognition in Chapter 9. To provide a framework for the discussion we will assume that the overall process of spoken word recognition can be broken down into neat and manageable stages (following Tyler & Frauenfelder, 1987): pre-lexical analysis – the operations that are carried out on the speech input in order to organise it into useful units; contact – establishing links between the input and the stored forms of words; activation – getting contacted words excited about the fact that they have been contacted; access – getting hold of the information about a word that is stored in the mental lexicon (e.g. its meaning, grammatical category, etc.); recognition – knowing which word it is that we have heard. These stages are not necessarily temporally distinct, and we will see that the processes involved here also interact with other processes that contribute to the comprehension of larger stretches of language (e.g. sentences). Wider reading will show that there are in fact many models of word recognition and that the differences between them reflect differences in the detail of the analysis that is argued to take place at each of these stages, and also in the way in which these stages relate to one another.

8.2 What are words?

We can be impressed by the number of words someone knows. But how many words do native speakers know, on average? This is one of the questions that many linguists hate to have to answer, but love to be able to ask. There are at least two notions that need defining before the question can even be addressed – what is a 'word', and what does it mean to 'know' a word? The first of these seems trivial but is not. One important issue is that the notion of 'word' is different when applied to different languages (see the example in the sidebar). But even if we gloss over language differences and reach a tacit agreement that words are what are separated by spaces in printed text (so that in these parentheses there are nine words), then we still have to face the question of whether *cat* and *cats* are two entirely separate words or two 'versions' of the same word. Or whether *foot*

The minimal unit of meaning is the **morpheme**, which can include for instance endings that cannot be used on their own, but which can convey meanings, such as 'plural' -*s* or 'past' -*ed*.

As an example of how the notion of 'word' varies between languages, consider Aymara, a language of the Chilean Andes. In this language, *uta* means *house*, but endings can be added to form words that in English would require a complete sentence, so that for instance *utawa* means *it's a house*, *utamanwa* means *I see it's in your house*, and the single word *utamanpachawa* is best translated as something like *I see evidence to suggest that it's in your house*.

and *feet* are two words. Or whether *houseboat* is a different word from both *house* and *boat*. Or whether *phone-tree* is two words or one. Or whether *old* is the same word in *old news* and *old friend*.

The second issue we need to consider is what 'knowing' a word entails. A distinction can be drawn between passive and active vocabularies – most speakers can understand more words than they are likely to use in their own speech. But also there are words that we see and understand in print, but have never encountered in speech (and occasionally vice versa).

Given these uncertainties about what words are and what it means to know them, it is not surprising that estimates of the average vocabulary size vary considerably. You will easily find estimates in the range of 20,000 to 75,000 words. In the Introduction (p. 2) we took an estimate at the conservative end, of 20,000 words (Nation, 2006). We saw how with a vocabulary of that size and a search speed of 100 words per second, it would take someone 3 minutes to search exhaustively through their mental lexicon to discover that they did not know the word *splundle*. Trivial though it may seem, this example is useful as an illustration of how efficiently we recognise words (or in this case recognise that a word-like beast is not a word we know), and it immediately suggests some key aspects of how we look for words in our mental lexicons. At the very least it shows that we do not do this by matching some input (e.g. the spoken form of *splundle*) against each and every word that we know.

8.3 Pre-lexical analysis

Pre-lexical analysis involves automatic peripheral perceptual processes which analyse the spoken input into linguistically relevant units. These units are then used in the course of word recognition and in further language comprehension processes. As we have seen in Chapter 7, the perceptual cues and processes that we use for these language-related tasks are special, and infants become selectively attuned to these cues very early on in their lives.

It is widely accepted that the speech input is analysed into phonemes. The phoneme is the smallest unit that when changed can result in a change in meaning by signalling a different word, as shown by minimal pairs (see sidebar). Since a difference in one phoneme can signal a difference in the word in question, it makes sense if the pre-lexical analysis of the speech input has the job of identifying these word-differentiating units.

But why not let the word be the unit of pre-linguistic analysis, since this is after all the unit that is to be recognised? There are a number of very good and practical reasons why this would be ill-advised. To start with, in spoken language it is very often extremely difficult to know where one word finishes and the next begins – the segmentation problem we saw in Chapter 7. This is reflected in 'slips of the ear' or misperceptions of speech, which often involve the misplacement of word boundaries, e.g. when *a coke and a Danish* is misheard as *a coconut Danish* (Bond, 1999). So if we are often unable to determine the boundaries between words in

---

The minimal pair test helps establish the **phoneme** inventory of a language. A minimal pair is a pair of words which are accepted as different because they mean different things and which differ only in one sound. For instance, the two English words *cat* and *cap* mean different things and differ in their final phoneme – /t/ vs /p/. Or the difference between *cat* and *cot* in the author's English is marked by the difference in the vowel phonemes /æ/ vs /ɔ/. From these two comparisons we know that English has at least the four phonemes /t/, /p/, /æ/, /ɔ/. It in fact has many more than four (see Table 8.1).

Table 8.1 Consonant and vowel phonemes of New Zealand English, with example words containing these phonemes (as underlined).

consonants				vowels			
p	p̱in	ʃ	s̱hore	ɪ	hi̱d	eɪ	ha̱y
b	ḇin	ʒ	leis̱ure	ʊ	ho̱od	əʊ	ho̱e
t	ṯin	h	ẖam	ɛ	he̱d	ɔɪ	bo̱y
d	ḏin	tʃ	c̱hore	ɔ	ho̱d	aɪ	hi̱gh
k	ḵin	dʒ	ju̱dge	ʌ	bu̱d	aʊ	ho̱w
g	g̱one	m	m̱ow	æ	ha̱d	ɪə	he̱re
f	f̱an	n	ṉow	ə	a̱gain	ɛə	ha̱ir
v	v̱an	ŋ	si̱ng	i	he̱ed	ʊə	to̱ur
θ	ṯhin	l	ḻow	u	bro̱od		
ð	ṯhan	r	ṟow	ɜ	he̱rd		
s	s̱ue	w	w̱oo	o	ho̱ard		
z	ẕoo	j	y̱ou	a	ha̱rd		

Note that even though there are many irregularities in the correspondences between letters and sounds in English, it is still to a large extent true that letters 'stand for' sounds, and that spoken forms of English words are very often predictable from their written form. This is shown by the fact that speakers will generally agree on the pronunciation of nonsense words such as *splundle*.

speech, then the task of identifying whole word-sized units in the spoken input before we try to find them in the dictionary will be problematic.

In addition, word-by-word analysis of the input also implies that a word will not be recognised until its entire speech pattern has been identified. As we will see later in this chapter, there is plenty of convincing evidence that we frequently recognise a word before the speech signal corresponding to that word is complete.

The advantages of analysing speech pre-lexically into something like phonemes are not only that we will be able to start the process of recognition on the basis of a shorter portion of speech than if the analysis unit were an entire word, but also that there will be fewer units that we need to recognise. This leads to more efficient and more rapid processing. If we take New Zealand English as an example, we find that there are 44 phoneme units (24 consonants and 20 vowels, see Table 8.1). This is a considerably smaller number of units for an initial analysis system to deal with than the tens of thousands of words that we might know.

A number of researchers have questioned the assumption that phonemes are significant units of pre-lexical analysis (Marslen-Wilson & Warren, 1994). Some argue that phonemes are linguistic constructs, and that if they exist at all as psychologically valid entities, then this is a consequence of learning to read and making connections between the sounds of spoken words and the shapes of written words. Interestingly, this implies that illiterate speakers and speakers whose writing system does not represent phoneme-sized chunks of sound will not use phonemes in their processing of speech. So languages like Chinese have ideographic writing systems, where a character stands for a word, and there is little representation of individual sounds in the writing system. Indeed, if speakers of such languages are asked to perform tasks that involve phoneme-sized chunks of speech (e.g. a phoneme monitoring task in which subjects might be instructed to press a button as soon as they hear a particular speech sound, such as /p/), they perform far worse than literate speakers of alphabetic languages like English (Morais, Cary, Alegria & Bertelson, 1979). This suggests that awareness of phonemes and the ability to perform phoneme-related tasks is in part a result of literacy in an alphabetic language. Since speakers who are not literate in an alphabetic language are nevertheless capable of recognising and understanding spoken words, this demonstrates that phonemes are not a <u>necessary</u> part of spoken word recognition.

Smaller units of pre-lexical analysis

Alternatives to the phoneme as a pre-lexical unit of analysis include both smaller and larger units than the phoneme. Amongst the smaller units is the phonetic feature, such as the voicing feature that distinguishes /p/ and /b/ in English. There are many cues to this contrast in voicing, and it would be possible to break down phonetic features into smaller units of difference, such as the voice onset time (VOT) considered in Chapter 7 as one perceptual cue to voicing. For illustrative purposes, however, let us remain at the level of phonetic features, and consider whether it makes sense to propose a unit of this type as an appropriate unit of pre-lexical analysis.

The feature that is shared by /m, n, ŋ/ and makes them a class distinct from other sounds in English is nasality. That is, during the production of these sounds, the soft palate or velum at the back of the mouth is lowered, so that the passageway between the mouth and nose is open, and air can flow out through the nose. Unlike many other languages, English does not have contrasting oral and nasal vowels (so, for instance, it would not be possible to create a new word in English that differed from *cat* only by having a nasal vowel, i.e. a vowel during which air can pass through the nose). But vowels in English can be nas<u>alised</u>, meaning that their essentially oral (non-nasal) property can be modified by allowing air to pass through the nose during part or even the entire duration of the vowel. This has a noticeable effect on the sound of the vowel. One context in which this is likely to happen in the speech of many native English speakers is when the vowel is followed by a nasal consonant. So in the word *soon*, the lowering of the velum might start during the vowel. Listeners are able to utilise this information to anticipate what the final consonant is. We know this from the results of gating experiments, which show that a word like *soon* becomes identifiable as this word and not as, say, *soup*, *suit* or *sued*, during the vowel portion of the word, i.e. before the final /n/ consonant itself has been heard (Warren & Marslen-Wilson, 1987, 1988). On the other hand, in languages that contrast oral and nasal vowels, such as

> **Phonetic features** are the distinctive properties of speech sounds. Phonemes can be distinguished from one another, and also grouped into classes, on the basis of phonetic features, which are often expressed in binary terms (i.e. ± values). For example, the difference between the /p/ in *pin* and the /b/ in *bin* is that the former is voiceless [−voice] and the latter is voiced [+voice]. The sounds /p, t, k, f, s, ʃ, θ/ (and others) all have in common that they are voiceless.

> In **gating** experiments, truncated portions of a recorded word are played to participants for identification. Typically, longer and longer fragments are presented, with an identification response at each 'gate'.

Bengali and Hindi, the nasal quality of a vowel informs the listener about the identity of the vowel and not necessarily about the following consonant. This is confirmed in gating experiments in those languages (Lahiri & Marslen-Wilson, 1991; Ohala & Ohala, 1995).

The early use of phonetic featural information in word recognition suggests that pre-lexical analysis might be in terms of phonetic features and not phonemes, and there are in fact models of spoken word recognition that argue for lexical access from such featural cues or similar sub-phonemic units of analysis (Klatt, 1989). It is difficult, however, to entirely disprove the possibility that what listeners are doing pre-lexically is using such features in order to generate predictions about phonemes in the speech stream, and then using these phoneme hypotheses to access word-forms from the mental lexicon. Phonetic features, after all, cannot exist on their own, whereas phonemes do have pronounceable realisations in the form of individual speech sounds.

Larger units of pre-lexical analysis

Pre-lexical units of analysis that are larger than the phoneme have also been suggested, either instead of or as a supplement to phonemes. Such units include diphones and syllables, especially stressed syllables. Because diphones include the transition from one phoneme-sized segment to the next, they encapsulate the variation in pronunciation of speech segments that results from the influence of neighbouring sounds. As we have seen, the /u/ sound in *soon* is likely to show nasalisation because of the following nasal. Similarly, the end of this /u/ sound in *soon*, and also in *suit*, will have a different quality from the quality it has in *soup*, because in the latter case the next consonant involves a lip closure, while in *soon* and *suit* it involves a closure between the tongue and the alveolar ridge (the bony structure just behind the top teeth).

The structure of syllables varies from language to language. As illustrated in Chapter 4, an English syllable can be a single vowel (*eye*), a vowel with a single preceding or following consonant (*my*, *up*), or a vowel with multiple preceding and/or following consonants (*strengths*). Māori, on the other hand, has a more limited choice of syllable types. The Māori syllable has to have a vowel, which can be preceded, but not followed, by one and no more than one consonant. This means that if the unit of pre-lexical analysis is the syllable, then speakers of different languages will be monitoring the input for differently sized and structured units.

There are also cross-linguistic differences in the positioning of stress on the syllables of words. Some languages have fixed stress, with the position of the stressed syllable of a content word entirely predictable. So in Czech the first syllable is stressed; in Polish it is the last but one syllable in the word. Other languages have no word stress at all. English has word stress, but while it is predictable for each word and can therefore be indicated in a dictionary (with a comparatively small amount of variation between varieties of English), it is not in the same position for all words. For example, English contrasts the noun 'import with first-syllable stress and the verb im'port with second-syllable stress. Nevertheless, corpus analyses of

---

The metrical structure of English contrasts strong and weak syllables, where 'strong' includes either primary or secondary stress. For instance, the word ,immi'gration has secondary word stress on the first syllable (marked by ,) and primary stress on the third syllable. Both these syllables are strong, and typically have full or non-reduced vowels. Weak syllables have reduced vowels, usually the central schwa vowel. The word *immigration* has a strong-weak-strong-weak pattern. This alternation of stronger and weaker units is a notable characteristic of English rhythm.

English have shown that a clear majority of content words – some 90% – have a strong, i.e. stressed, first syllable (Cutler & Carter, 1987). One approach in spoken word recognition recognises this pattern, and suggests that in English word searches are started each time a strong or stressed syllable is encountered. This approach is known as the Metrical Segmentation Strategy or MSS (Cutler & Norris, 1988).

It has been argued that the MSS applies to all languages, but that the type of unit used for segmentation depends on the metrical or rhythmic structure of the language in question. Researchers have looked for evidence for the application of the MSS in a range of languages of differing rhythmic types. These include Dutch, which has a similar rhythmic structure to English with an alternation between stressed and unstressed syllables but without the same distinction between full and reduced vowels (Quené & Koster, 1998; van Zon & de Gelder, 1993); French, which has relatively simple syllable structures and a rhythmic pattern that is based more on each syllable, i.e. it has syllable-based rather than stress-based timing (Cutler, Mehler, Norris & Segui, 1986; Mehler, Dommergues, Frauenfelder & Segui, 1981); Japanese, where the rhythmic unit is the mora, which is a unit of syllable weight such that a long syllable (e.g. a syllable with a long vowel) has two moras, so that *Tōkyō* has the four moras *to-o-kyo-o* (Otake, Hatano, Cutler & Mehler, 1993); and Finnish, where both stress and vowel harmony have been argued to play a role in word segmentation (Suomi, McQueen & Cutler, 1997; Vroomen, Tuomainen & de Gelder, 1998). Studies have also considered the acquisition of the MSS by infants exposed to different languages (for a review see van Kampen, Parmaksiz, van de Vijver & Höhle, 2008).

It has also been suggested that the MSS applies only in conjunction with another principle, the Possible Word Constraint (PWC), which is also claimed to be found across different languages (Norris, McQueen, Cutler, Butterfield & Kearns, 2001). This constraint ensures that the speech input is exhaustively segmented into words without leaving any residual sounds. For instance, it is more difficult for English listeners to detect the real word 'see' when they hear the nonsense word /siʃ/ than when they hear the nonsense word /siʃʌb/ because the residue 'sh' in the first case is not a possible word of English, but the residue 'shub' in the second case is a possible word, though it happens not to exist as a current word of English (Norris, McQueen, Cutler & Butterfield, 1997).

In the application of the MSS to English, pre-lexical analysis needs to determine which syllables are strong and therefore likely to trigger a new word search. Evidence for the MSS has been claimed in experimental studies. In one experiment (Cutler & Norris, 1988), participants were asked to listen to a series of nonword stimuli and to press a button as quickly as possible whenever they heard a real word within a nonword stimulus. Participants were slower in making such a response for the stimulus *mintave* (/ˈmɪnˌteɪv/) than for the stimulus *mintesh* (/ˈmɪntəʃ/). The difference between these stimuli is that the first has two strong syllables, with the second such syllable starting at the /t/, while the second stimulus has one strong syllable and one weak syllable. It is claimed that participants start

> **Vowel harmony** exists in some languages and can be thought of as a type of agreement between vowels in the relevant syllables. In some cases it can affect all the syllables in a word, with all vowels being, for instance, front vowels (/i/, /e/, /y/).

a second lexical search when they encounter the second strong syllable in the first stimulus, i.e. at the /t/ in *mintave*, so that the stimulus is segmented as *min-tave*, making it more difficult to recognise the word *mint* contained in that stimulus than in *mintesh*, where this new lexical search is not initiated. Different results are found for this type of experiment in different languages, and the proponents of this model argue that this is because there are different language-specific instantiations of a MSS, depending on the rhythmic structure of the language.

As we have seen, the size of the units of pre-lexical analysis ranges across models of spoken word recognition from sub-phonemic units like phonetic features, through phonemes, to entire syllables. It is worth remembering, though, that even if the lexical search is based on a larger unit such as the syllable, this does not rule out the importance of a smaller unit in pre-lexical analysis, since it is possible to hypothesise the identity of a larger unit on the basis of information deriving from smaller units. Nevertheless, since the output of pre-lexical analysis provides the entities that will be used in retrieving words from the mental lexicon, the size of the unit has implications for the granularity of the lexical search process. On the one hand, larger units imply greater delays before a lexical search can be initiated (e.g. if the recognition system has to wait until a syllable has been identified, rather than a phoneme). On the other hand, larger pre-lexical units will result in a smaller set of items produced by the search (on average, fewer words will be known that start with a particular syllable than start with a particular phoneme).

8.4 Contact and activation

After the pre-lexical analysis of the speech input, the next stage of the word recognition process is the contact stage, involving a mapping from the output of pre-lexical analysis onto forms stored in the mental lexicon. Such mapping from the input to the lexicon is an example of bottom-up processing. Many models of word recognition argue that this initial contact is based solely on automatic bottom-up processing, while others also claim a role here for top-down processing, e.g. the use of context to pre-select words from a particular area of meaning.

Simultaneous contact with more than one stored word is a characteristic of parallel models of lexical processing. The alternative is a class of models that can be characterised as serial search models, where one word is considered at a time, such as Forster's Search Model (Forster, 1976), discussed in Chapter 9. Support for the notion of parallel processing of all lexical entries that match the input comes from studies using a cross-modal priming technique. One study (Zwitserlood, 1989) presented visual targets after either a test prime such as *captain* or a control prime such as *justice*. The test primes all had partner words which started with the same sequence of phonemes (e.g. in this case *capital*), but which were never heard in the experiment. The test and control prime were each combined with three types of target. One (*ship*) was related to the test prime (*captain*), the second (*money*) was related to the partner word (*capital*), and the third (*lamp*) was related to neither the test prime nor its partner. (The study was actually done in Dutch, but the examples are similar.)

The experimental measure of interest is whether the targets show facilitation, i.e. faster and more accurate responses, after test primes compared with after control primes, and whether this varies depending on how much of a prime has been heard. In an Early condition, the targets were presented part way through the prime, i.e. before the whole prime word had been heard. For a test prime, this was a point that included all the material which the word shares with its partner word – for *captain / capital* this would be at the end of the /p/. In the Late condition the targets were shown at the end of the prime. Facilitation was found in the Early condition for targets related either to the test prime or to the partner word. So in our example both *money* and *ship* would be responded to more rapidly and with fewer errors after the initial portion of *captain* than after the initial portion of the control word *justice*. The control target (*lamp*) showed no such facilitation. In the Late condition, when all of the prime word has been heard, only *ship*, related to *captain*, shows facilitation. The earlier facilitation shown for *money* has now disappeared.

The Cohort Model

The above result shows that during the early stages of the processing of the spoken word *captain*, both this word and the phonetically similar word *capital* have been contacted, and words related to both of these are primed. In other words, the initial contact is with multiple words matching the input, i.e. there is parallel lexical processing. Note that further experiments with rhyming word pairs shows that it is the overlap of the <u>initial</u> portion of the word that is important, and not just any portion of the word. That is, while *bee* is primed by *honey*, it is not primed by *money*, which has most of the same sounds as *honey*, but does not start with the same sound. It makes good sense for the beginning sounds of words to carry primary responsibility for making contact with words in the mental lexicon, since we hear these parts of the word first. The set of words contacted in this way has been referred to as a word-initial cohort.

The word-initial cohort is a key feature of the parallel and primarily bottom-up approach to spoken word recognition known as the Cohort model (Marslen-Wilson, 1987; Marslen-Wilson & Welsh, 1978). In this model, once the initial sounds of a word have been heard, all words in the listener's mental lexicon that have the same initial sequence of sounds will be contacted. Once initial contact has been made with the cohort members, the lexical entries for these words become activated, making available further information about these words that is stored in the lexicon (as discussed in more detail below).

Zwitserlood's experiment described above also shows that as the input continues, further bottom-up information concerning the next sounds becomes available, so that some of the initially contacted words no longer match this input, and fall out of contention. This is sometimes referred to using a directional metaphor from reading (at least as applies

> The **Cohort** model of word recognition has been developed over many years by Marslen-Wilson and his colleagues. One of its attractions is that it makes testable predictions about key aspects of the word recognition process. As these predictions have been tested experimentally, so the model has been further developed to include many of the features discussed in this and subsequent sections.

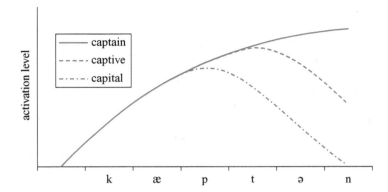

Figure 8.1
Illustration of changing
activation levels of word
entries as more of a
word (*captain*) is heard.

to the reading of languages such as English), i.e. that there is left-to-right processing of spoken language. By the end of the spoken word, it is clear that the word is *captain* and not *capital*, and so only *ship* is primed.

In early versions of the Cohort model, it was assumed that a word was either available or not available, depending on whether the sounds matched the input (and on whether the lexical information about that word matched the developing utterance context, as we will see later). However, it soon became widely acknowledged that lexical entries in the mental lexicon are not just 'on' or 'off', but that they assume levels of activation (Marslen-Wilson, 1987). The more input there is that supports a particular lexical item, the higher the level of activation for that entry. So the activation levels of both *captain* and *capital* increase as the first few sounds (/kæp/) are heard, but once the sound pattern of the input diverges from that expected for the word *capital*, then the activation of this word falls, while that for *captain* continues to rise. This is illustrated in Figure 8.1, which shows what might happen to the activation levels of *captain*, *captive* and *capital*, as examples of the word-initial cohort of *captain*, as more of the word *captain* is heard.

One of the advantages of an activation-based model rather than an all-or-nothing model of recognition is that it can more easily allow for partial matches and for recovery from mispronunciation or perhaps from unexpected pronunciations. So for example if a speaker says 'shtudent' for 'student' (an increasingly common pronunciation in New Zealand English), the initial 'sh' sound partially activates the similar /s/ and the subsequent input (/tju.../) continues to increase the activation of words such as 'student', which we might suppose is represented in the lexicon as /stjudənt/.

8.5 Selection

If multiple word candidates have been contacted on the basis of the initial sounds of an input word, then some kind of selection process must choose between them so that a word can be recognised. The illustration in Figure 8.1 suggests that as further bottom-up information becomes available, i.e.

as more of the word is heard, then the appropriate word will eventually emerge as the only one that still matches the input. For each word we can identify a uniqueness point, i.e. a point in the word where it no longer overlaps with other words in the initial cohort. Depending on the speaker's pronunciation, for *captain* (/kæptən/) this point could be the second vowel sound (/ə/), where this word becomes distinct from *captive* (/kæptɪv/). Theoretical uniqueness points can be determined by searching through pronunciation-based dictionaries or lexical databases. These can be confirmed through gating experiments (see above), which indicate that the actual recognition points of words correlate highly with these uniqueness points. There has been some debate about the mechanism that results in the decision that a particular word has been heard. In our illustration this might require that a word's activation passes some threshold level. Alternatively, there may need to be some difference between the relative probabilities of the words in the cohort (expressed as some measure of the differences between the curves in Figure 8.1).

But what about nonwords – how are these 'recognised'? That is, how do we know when we hear *splundle* that it is not a word of our language? Clearly there is no stored representation in our mental lexicon for a word that does not exist. It is claimed, though, that the recognition of nonsense words follows the same process as the recognition of real words. This is a process that is optimally efficient, in that decisions are made as rapidly as possible. It makes sense that the same process should apply to real and nonsense words, because we do not know before we hear a word whether it will be one that we know or not, so we are not able to deploy different strategies in advance of hearing it. In the case of a nonword input, a set of words matching the initial input is activated, and the activation levels of the members of this set change as more of the input is heard and processed, until there is no remaining strong candidate word. This will be at the point in the nonsense word where it diverges from known words. This is known as the deviation point.

The significance of the deviation point was first demonstrated in an experiment in which participants were required to press a response button whenever they heard a nonsense word in a list of stimulus words. It was found that response times were reasonably constant (at around 450 msec) when measured from the deviation point (Marslen-Wilson, 1980). Other studies, however, have cast a shadow of doubt over that result, since they have found some variation in the response times from the deviation point, variation which depends both on the nature of the task that participants are doing and also on the word-likeness of the material after the deviation point (Goodman & Huttenlocher, 1988; Taft & Hambly, 1986). It seems that listeners continue to monitor the input after the deviation point, so that a more word-like ending, such as a regular affix like *-ise* or *-ic* will slow down the 'no' responses in the lexical decision task. Such continued monitoring of the input is of practical value in ordinary speech comprehension situations, since we are able to recognise words even under noisy conditions (e.g. at parties or with machinery operating in the background). We can also recognise words when sounds within them are mispronounced. As we will see below, this is facilitated by the use of information from the utterance context in which the word is heard.

8.6 Lexical access

The selection process discussed above simply refers to the decision that what we have heard is word-form X rather than word-form Y. But word-forms or lexemes are linked to lemma-based content information, e.g. the meaning of the word, its grammatical type (noun, verb, etc.), and so on. Lexical access is used here to refer to the point at which this lexically stored information becomes available. Note though that there is some ambiguity in the use of the term 'access', since it is sometimes used to mean the point at which lexical entries are first contacted. To an extent this ambiguity is understandable, because in many models of recognition contact and access amount to the same thing. That is, such models argue that as soon as a word-form has been contacted, all of the information associated with that word becomes available.

Lexical access clearly occurs before the selection of a unique candidate word. This is demonstrated in the priming experiment referred to above (Zwitserlood, 1989). Participants were able to respond more rapidly to both the test targets *ship* and *money* when they had heard the onset fragment /kæp/ of the test prime *captain* than when they had heard an equivalent amount of a control prime. The explanation for this is that the onset fragment allows the listener to make contact with lexical representations for both *captain* and *capital*, with consequent access to the semantic content of these representations. Without such access, priming of the related words *ship* and *money* would be difficult to explain.

8.7 Recognition and context effects

In many models of word recognition, including the Cohort model, lexical access is only possible after a word has been activated on the basis of the input speech signal, i.e. on the basis of bottom-up information. This seems to run counter to the intuitive notion that there is pre-selection of words based on information from the contexts in which they are uttered. That is, we often find ourselves able to complete or continue someone else's sentence for them. This suggests that we can predict a word on the basis of top-down or contextual information.

(8.1)   The men stood around for a while and watched their captain...

However, there is little evidence that contextual information leads to the pre-selection of candidate words during the normal rapid word recognition process. For instance, when sentence contexts such as (8.1) are used in cross-modal priming experiments and a related visual target word (*ship*) is presented immediately before participants hear the actual prime word (*captain*), then there is no facilitation of *ship*, relative to a control condition. But if the target word is presented later in the prime word (e.g. after /kæp/), then there is facilitation. (For discussion of the efficacy of using the cross-modal priming technique with sentence primes, see Nicol,

Swinney, Love & Hald, 2006.) It seems, then, that bottom-up information (the phonetic input) has priority over contextual information in the initial stages of making contact with stored lexical forms.

It is argued that the experience of being able to finish someone's sentence for them reflects processes that are slower than the normal processes of word recognition. That is, just as words can be primed by other words related in meaning, so the interpretation of a sentence context can activate a field of meaning and can cause a set of words to become available, just as they are during language production. However, this process is not as fast as bottom-up activation.

A further argument against pre-selection is the sheer quantity of words that would be activated in many contexts (see examples discussed under Predictability in Chapter 3).

Although context might not pre-select words, it is involved in efficient word recognition, as follows. Words are activated on the basis of bottom-up information; lexical access makes available lexical (i.e. grammatical and semantic) information associated with these words; this lexical information is assessed against the developing interpretation of the sentence, resulting in changes in the activation levels of the activated words. The rapid integration of contextual and lexical information means that words can be recognised earlier in sentence contexts than in isolation. That is, the recognition point of a word can be earlier than its uniqueness point, if contextual information rules out other candidate words before this point. An oft-cited example is the word *trespass*. In isolation this word's recognition point is the same as its uniqueness point, at the /p/. It is at this point that other members of the word-initial cohort, such as *tress* and *trestle*, can be eliminated. If this word is heard in a context such as that in (8.2), then its recognition point is earlier, at the /s/, since *tress* and *trestle* do not fit the context and so the activation levels of their lexical representations will have dropped away.

> Note that it is assumed in this section that words from a single word family are activated together. That is, words morphologically related to *trespass*, such as *trespasser*, *trespassing*, etc. are activated together with *trespass* and do not count as separate cohort members. Other work in word recognition has explored more fully how morphologically related forms are accessed, as discussed later in this chapter.

(8.2)   The poacher was found guilty of tres-.

Not all contexts are the same, and some may have a greater constraining influence of this type than others. This is revealed in word monitoring experiments using the same target words in different spoken sentence contexts (Marslen-Wilson, Brown & Tyler, 1988). In one example, participants were told to listen out for the target word *guitar* and to press the response button as soon as they heard this word. Depending on which participant group they were assigned to, they would have heard the word in one of the four contexts in (8.3)–(8.6):

(8.3)   The crowd was waiting eagerly. The young man grabbed the guitar ...

(8.4)   The crowd was waiting eagerly. The young man buried the guitar ...

(8.5)   The crowd was waiting eagerly. The young man drank the guitar ...

(8.6)   The crowd was waiting eagerly. The young man slept the guitar ...

Participants' response times (RTs) were measured from the onset of the word *guitar*. The results showed that across sentences (8.3) to (8.6) response times got increasingly longer. This reflects the changing contextual constraints across these sentences, as determined by the changes in the verb. In (8.3), a *guitar* is something that very plausibly can be *grabbed* (mean RT was 241 msec, measured from the onset of the word being monitored for, and averaged across a set of examples with the properties of (8.3)). In (8.4), while a *guitar* can be *buried*, this is a somewhat unusual thing to do (mean RT was 268 msec). In (8.5), although the verb *drink* can have an object noun phrase (the thing that is consumed by drinking), this noun phrase usually denotes a liquid, and *guitars* are not liquid (mean RT was 291 msec). Finally, in (8.6), *sleep* is a verb that does not take an object (mean RT was 320 msec). An additional finding was that word monitoring times tended to decrease the later a word is in a sentence, as long as that sentence is grammatically well-formed. This shows that as we hear more words in a sentence, we are able to develop a more complete interpretation of the context sentence, which becomes more constraining on the possible words that can occur.

A neuroimaging study (Kuperberg *et al.*, 2000) also used sentences such as those in (8.3)–(8.6). Participants had to listen to the entire sentence and say whether it made sense. The study found that all of the violation conditions ((8.4)–(8.6)) showed increased activation in a brain area which has also been associated in brain-damaged patients with comprehension difficulties. In addition, separate areas of increased activity were found for the different types of violation. It is conjectured that the area showing activation increases for all three violation types is the area that is responsible for integration of information, which is of course important in the context effects on recognition that we have discussed in this section.

8.8 Frequency, competition and neighbourhoods

 The earlier illustration of the activation of word candidates needs an important supplement, since a regular and very robust research finding is that there are frequency effects in word recognition (Forster & Chambers, 1973; Monsell, 1991; Murray & Forster, 2004). That is, words that we encounter more often have an advantage over words that we do not see or hear so often. This is reflected in faster response times and greater accuracy for common words in tasks such as lexical decision. In Figure 8.2, this frequency effect is shown by a slower increase in activation for *captive* and *capital* relative to *captain*, so that even when the phonetic information still matches both *captain* and *captive* (e.g. at /kæpt/), the former already shows an activation advantage. This advantage is also reflected in the detailed results of the cross-modal priming experiments referred to earlier – more frequent word candidates showed greater priming effects than less frequent candidates.

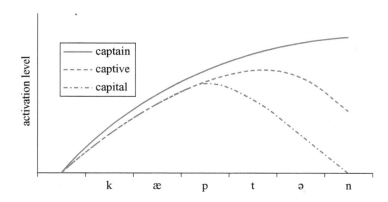

k　æ　p　t　ə　n

Figure 8.2
Modification of the illustration in Figure 8.1 to account for the greater frequency of *captain* relative to *captive* and *capital*.

The illustration in Figure 8.2 suggests that frequency effects might be accounted for in terms of the rate of increase of activation for the different word candidates. Alternative mechanisms have been suggested, including different 'resting levels' of activation for different words, so that frequent words have an initial advantage by having a higher resting level than rare words. Under such a mechanism, if the same input (e.g. the /kæpt/ onset in our illustration) results in the same rate-of-change in activation of word candidates, the resting-level advantage will persist for more frequent words, so that these cross some activation threshold and achieve recognition before the less frequent words. An effect that is related to the frequency effect, and which can probably be accounted for in a similar manner, is that of recency (Oliphant, 1983). That is, words which we have encountered quite recently seem to gain – at least temporarily – an advantage over similar words that have not been heard for a while. If using a word causes an increase in its activation, and if it takes a while for this activation to return to its resting level, then hearing or seeing the word a second time may take place at a point where the activation is still above its normal resting level, resulting in faster recognition.

In neurophysiological studies, it has been demonstrated that frequency effects (and those of other factors discussed in this chapter and the next) are reflected in the size of the electrical response to words (in ERP studies), but also in the speed of certain components of this response (see Kutas & Federmeier, 2007). Both of these findings indicate greater neural stimulation in response to higher frequency words.

Competition

The recognition of a word depends quite clearly not only on the properties of that word itself (its sound form, its frequency, and so on) but also on the properties of other words that compete with it. We saw earlier that the use of nasalisation information on a vowel in an English word like *soon* helps listeners to distinguish this word from similar-sounding words such as *suit* or *soup*. This means that given the input /sũ.../ (~ above the vowel indicates nasalisation), listeners may already be forming a strong hypothesis that the word is *soon* and not *suit* or *soup*. This is reflected in the results of gating experiments with words like this. However, the same nasalisation information has a different information value if it occurs on the vowel in *fruit*, since there is no word that has a nasal consonant after the /u/ vowel here. If it tells us anything, nasalisation here would probably indicate that the speaker is one who typically has a nasal setting to their speech, i.e. it might help us identify the speaker, but not the word. What this boils down to is that the informativeness of properties of the signal depends on the alternative possibilities that exist and whether these alternatives can be ruled in or out by these properties. This is the notion of contingency of choice – knowing you have heard the word *cat* depends not just on the sounds of *cat*, but also on knowing that you have <u>not</u> heard the words *cap*, *can*, *cash*, etc. (Warren & Marslen-Wilson, 1987, 1988).

Such considerations make it obvious that we need to take into account not just individual words, but also the relationships of these words to their competitors. The notion of competition is an important one in models of word recognition, and has been studied in considerable depth. Like frequency effects, competitor effects have been modelled in different ways by different researchers. One of the most popular notions is that a result of competition between two words is that the words inhibit one another. That is, competition has a negative impact on the activation levels of competitor words. The size of this inhibition effect might depend on the relative activation levels of the words that are in competition with one another. Given an ambiguous input like /kæpt/, for instance, the more frequent word *captain* will have a higher activation level than the less frequent *captive*, and this greater activation level will allow *captain* to exert a stronger inhibitory influence on *captive* than vice versa. This will in effect boost the activation difference between the two words, making it more certain that *captain* will be recognised, in the absence of any further differentiating information.

Neighbourhoods

Another important aspect of competition is the size of the competitor set. A word belongs to a neighbourhood of words that share similar properties (Luce & Pisoni, 1998; Pisoni, Nusbaum, Luce & Slowiaczek, 1985; Vitevitch, Stamer & Sereno, 2008). A word-initial cohort is of course a type of neighbourhood, but more extensive neighbourhoods than these have been examined, for instance neighbourhoods that consist of all words that are just one phoneme different from the target word under consideration, regardless of where in the word the differentiating phoneme is (see example in sidebar). The recognition of a word (in tasks such as lexical decision and naming, i.e. reading aloud) is affected by how many neighbours it has, by the phonetic similarity of these words to the target word (i.e. the extent of the overlap of the forms of the words), and by the frequencies of the words in the neighbourhood. For instance, a word with a lot of high-frequency neighbours is identified more slowly and less accurately than a word with only a few neighbours or with only low-frequency neighbours. These factors contribute to what has become known as the neighbourhood density of a word, which has been shown to have an

As an example of a **neighbourhood** for a word consider the following list of words that differ from the word *money* by a single phoneme: *month, munch, mucky, muddy, mummy, mushy, muzzy, many, meanie, moony, bunny, funny, gunny, honey, runny, sonny, sunny, tunny.*

influence on both word recognition (Vitevitch & Luce, 1998) and word production (Vitevitch, 2002).

8.9 Recognising morphologically complex forms

Our discussion of word recognition processes has so far largely avoided the issue of how we recognise, process and store words that are made up of more than one meaningful element, i.e. morphologically complex words like *cats*, *children* or *predisposition*. A determining factor in this context is the relative productivity of morphological processes, that is, the predictability of a certain way of constructing a morphologically complex form. As discussed in Chapter 4, productivity is sometimes also linked to the distinction between inflectional morphology (adding affixes to mark grammatical information such as plural [*cat–cats*], past tense [*jump–jumped*], or subject-verb agreement [*he swims* vs *I swim*]) and derivational morphology (adding affixes to make a different kind of word, such as making a noun *disposition* from a verb *dispose*) (Bauer, 2001; Frauenfelder & Schreuder, 1992).

Inflections tend to be more productive than derivations, though there are differences within each of these sets. For instance, examples of making a plural in English by adding -*s*, as in *cats*, are plentiful, but making a plural by adding -*ren* and changing the vowel in the word (as in *child–children*) is very unusual. The more frequent or regular patterns are the ones that children identify for themselves as they learn their native language(s), and which for a while they apply inappropriately in their own speech. So for instance children learning English as their first language will produce forms like *foots* (or even *feets*) instead of *feet*. (See also the discussion in Chapter 4 of the wug test.)

The corresponding rule-governed process in word recognition would be to look for a form like *cats* under the entry for *cat*. Just as it is claimed that the language production system assembles *cats* from the base word *cat* and the highly productive affix -*s*, following a rule like 'to make a plural add -*s* to the stem', so the word recognition system would disassemble the input *cats* through a process of morphological decomposition. This is reasonably straightforward in the kind of 'left-to-right' processing system that we have been considering for spoken language processing, since the base word *cat* would be contacted on the basis of the first three phonemes of *cats* in any case. Indeed, surveys of the morphological characteristics of the world's languages suggest that accessing an inflected form via its stem may be a common strategy, since inflectional affixation is predominantly done through suffixes, i.e. adding elements to the ends of words rather than to their beginnings or to some point within the word.

Processing inflections
There is considerable evidence from both spoken and visual word recognition studies concerning how we process inflected forms. We have seen

above how the frequency with which a word has been encountered can influence recognition speed and accuracy. It has also been shown that the important frequency statistic is not that of a base form (e.g. *cat*) on its own, but the combination of the base form and its inflected forms (so *cat* and *cats* together). This combined frequency can be a better predictor of recognition time. This suggests that each time we encounter an inflected form we also encounter the base word, adding to its frequency count. It has also been shown that inflected forms are hard to access – out of context, /deɪz/ and /pækt/ tend to be reported as *daze* and *pact* rather than *days* and *packed*, even though the latter are of higher frequency. Note though that this may be a consequence of presenting words in isolation – citation forms tend to be uninflected forms.

There is clearly a difference between regular and irregular inflection. As we have seen, children tend to regularise irregular forms, suggesting that these do not have a strong hold on their processing system, even for frequently encountered irregular forms like *went*. In addition, evidence from repetition priming in adults supports this processing distinction as well as providing further evidence for the close links between inflected forms and base words. Equally strong priming is found for identical prime–target pairs (so the word *pour* preceded several items earlier by the same word *pour*, compared to a condition without this earlier instance of *pour*) and for a condition where the form *pour* is preceded not by the same word but by the inflected word *poured*. Compare this with the finding that although there is some priming of *swim* by its irregular past form *swam*, it is not as strong as priming of *swim* by *swim* itself.

Differences in the processing of regular and irregular forms are reflected in ERP studies. These have indicated that different brain areas are activated, with the regular forms showing activation in areas known to be involved in rule processing and the irregular forms leading to activation of areas that are associated with lexical storage (Newman, Ullman, Pancheva, Waligura & Neville, 2007).

Processing derivations

If we turn now to derived words, we find that recognition of a word like *account* appears to be affected by the combined frequency of words that are related to it in terms of some base meaning, like *accountant* and *unaccountable*, but not by less obviously related words like *count*, *counter* and *viscount*. It has also been found that derived words like *ability* can prime their base forms like *able*, but that the priming effect is not as strong as that found between inflected forms and their base forms. More detailed investigation of priming effects amongst derivationally related words paints a more complex picture. It appears that a distinction needs to be made between transparent and opaque derivational relationships. That is, priming effects exist between a base form and a morphologically related word only if the meaning relationship between the two is transparent, or clear. So *mature* and *maturity* prime each other, but *casual* and *casualty* do not (Marslen-Wilson, Tyler, Waksler & Older, 1994). Since we would not imagine that most language users know about the relationship between *casual* and *casualty*, this result is not surprising.

Repetition priming results in a particular word being processed more easily (e.g. recognised more rapidly and/or more accurately) if it has been heard a short time previously.

Transparent relationships exist between words if these relationships are obvious. Otherwise they are described as being **opaque**. Transparency can relate to form (so the spoken forms of *sign* and *signature* are not as transparently related as *mature* and *maturity*), or meaning (so *mature/maturity* are a more transparent pair than *casual/casualty*).

Amongst transparently related words we also find that prefixed words prime and are primed by their base forms, so *disloyal* primes *loyal* and vice versa. Also, prefixed words prime other prefixed words that are morphologically related to them, so that *remount* primes *dismount*. But suffixed words do not prime morphologically related suffixed words – *maturity* does not prime *maturation*. An explanation given for this last result is that any priming that might result from the morphological relatedness of *maturity* and *maturation* is offset by competition that arises between them because they are members of the same word-initial cohort. Since priming is however found for the *mature/maturity* pair, it would seem that the relationship between base forms and words derived from them is rather special.

Words and rules

As with the production of morphologically complex forms (Chapter 4), so the recognition of complex words is often discussed in terms of a distinction between a rule-based recognition system, where the input word is analysed into its meaningful constituent parts, and a full-listing system, where every word, whether simple or complex, is listed in the mental lexicon (Marslen-Wilson, 2007). The processing differences between regular and irregular inflected forms, and those between transparent and opaque derived forms, along with the complex interactions between words in priming studies, suggest that the mental lexicon probably relies on both systems. This is supported by the neurophysiological studies referred to above. Rule-based analysis of productive and regular affixation exists alongside stored representations of complex forms that do not lend themselves to easy morphological analysis.

Summary

Words are an important building block of language, and word recognition needs to be efficient and reliable, since it gives access to the meanings and grammatical information required for comprehension. The word recognition process has a number of stages:

- pre-lexical analysis of the input into recognition elements;
- mapping of these recognition elements onto entries in the mental lexicon;
- consequent activation of candidate words and access to information associated with these words.

Lexical information is assessed against the developing context, speeding both the word recognition process itself and the overall interpretation of the message. Recognition of words thus depends both on bottom-up input-driven processes and top-down interpretative processes. Competition and neighbourhood effects show that recognition also depends on the structure of the mental lexicon itself and the relationships between words in the lexicon. Finally, we have seen how morphologically complex words are almost certainly recognised through a combination of rule-based and storage-based mechanisms.

Exercises

Exercise 8.1

Based on the first two sounds (phonemes) of the words *monkey* and *swing*, what words are in the *word-initial cohort* of each?

Exercise 8.2

What are the *uniqueness* points of the words *monkey* and *swing*? In the sentence context below, is the *recognition* point for each word likely to be the same as its uniqueness point? Justify your answers by saying what kinds of information might be used in recognising the words.

All the children loved watching the long-tailed monkey as it started to swing through the trees.

Exercise 8.3

What are the deviation points of the following nonwords?

blorsilize, breganist, brondation, munart, pytel, shrortile

Exercise 8.4

A lexical decision experiment included two sets of nonwords of different length (i.e. two or three syllables long – see Exercise 8.3) which were otherwise matched for their deviation points. (For example, equal numbers of nonwords in each set became nonwords at the first vowel.) Correct response times (responding 'no, this is not a word') were measured from the deviation point, and turned out to be significantly longer for three-syllable nonwords than for two-syllable nonwords. Is this what the Cohort model would predict? Why (not)? Can you think of an explanation for the result? Note also that adjusting the response times so that they were measured from the end of the nonword gave shorter response times for the three-syllable nonwords than for the two-syllable nonwords.

Further reading

Aitchison (2003) provides a very readable introduction to issues concerning the mental lexicon, including the recognition of words. A summary of some of the basic notions in spoken word recognition can be found in Tyler and Frauenfelder (1987), an overview that is still relevant today. For further summaries of features of the Cohort model see Marslen-Wilson (1989), and for discussion of some of the key questions in spoken word recognition see McQueen (2007). An extensive discussion of the question of whether complex words are stored as complete forms or accessed through analysis of their meaningful parts is given by Pinker (1999), who also draws on evidence from fields such as language acquisition and language impairment. A review of morphological processes in word recognition is found in Marslen-Wilson (2007).

9 Visual word recognition

PREVIEW

In this chapter we consider how readers access words from written or printed input. By the end of the chapter you should understand:
- that reading involves both letter recognition and whole-word recognition;
- that one route for reading involves converting spellings to sounds;
- that the reading process can be affected by a range of types of dyslexia, which in turn provide important information about the skills involved in reading.

KEY TERMS

automatic word recognition

autonomous search model

consistency

dual route model of reading

dyslexia

grapheme-to-phoneme conversion

logogen model

phonological recoding

regularity

9.1 Introduction

Chapter 7 introduced some basic issues in perception, including issues that are relevant to the visual processing of written language. We saw that the visual perception of language involves a series of processing levels, including an input buffer for the visual stimulus, the transfer of information from there to working memory, and the linguistic interpretation of the analysed input. Studies of eye movements show that the input of text during reading involves a high level of control. In Chapter 8 we considered some of the key aspects of spoken word recognition. In this chapter we look at the processing of visual information in order to access words from written or printed input.

The chapter starts with a summary of some important factors that have been found to affect visual word recognition. It then briefly reviews three main attempts to capture some of these effects in word recognition models. This review includes comparison with the Cohort model of spoken word recognition outlined in the preceding chapter. We then consider one particular issue for reading aloud, the conversion of print to sound, which then leads to discussion of the dual-route model of reading. Finally, some principal types of dyslexia, or reading disability, are summarised, with reference to this model of reading.

9.2 Factors affecting visual word recognition

There are a number of factors that influence both spoken and visual word recognition. These include lexical frequency (or the familiarity that participants have with a word) and context effects (the more constraining the context, the faster and more reliable the recognition of a word). Since these are discussed in Chapter 8, little more will be said about them here, except insofar as they interact with other factors to be discussed in this section. As more is discovered about the process of visual word recognition, so more and more factors have been identified that seem to exert some influence on the process. In this section, we review some of these factors, both because they are in themselves of great interest, but also to provide some background information that will be of relevance in the subsequent discussion of word recognition in the context of reading.

Word superiority effect

The word superiority effect was introduced in the discussion of visual perception for language in Chapter 7. The effect was noted a long time ago (Cattell, 1886). Not only is it easier to identify words than nonwords, but the recognition of letters within a string of letters is easier and more accurate if the string constitutes an existing word. This is reflected in response times and error rates in a range of tasks. So recognition of the letter <d> is faster if it is contained within a word such as <word> than if it is in a legal nonword (e.g. <wrod> in English) or an illegal nonword (<wlod>). The word superiority effect indicates that we do not simply process a word letter-by-letter, but

> **Legal nonwords** are sequences of letters (or sounds, in speech) that would be possible words in the language but which happen not to exist (e.g. <wrod> in English). **Illegal nonwords** contain a sequence or sequences of letters (or sounds) that do not occur in equivalent positions in real words (e.g. <wlod> is illegal, as <wl> cannot start a word in English).

rather that recognising a word makes the letters in that word more readily available. That is, there is some top-down processing pathway from words to their constituent letters (McClelland & Johnston, 1977).

Word length effect

A pervasive effect in word recognition is that the size of the word, measured in terms of its length in letters, affects participants' memories for words they have seen (Baddeley, Thomson & Buchanan, 1975) as well as recognition times for individual words. It has been claimed that longer words take longer to recognise, as reflected in both lexical decision and naming tasks (O'Regan & Jacobs, 1992), although at least one study found this effect for naming but not for lexical decision (Frederiksen & Kroll, 1976). A more recent study was based on responses to over 33,000 words collected in a collaborative project involving six American universities, and with an average of 29 responses to each word (New, Ferrand, Pallier & Brysbaert, 2006). The data revealed a U-shaped pattern of responses – increases in word length between 3 and 5 letters resulted in faster responses, there was no effect of changes from 5 to 8 letters, and responses to words from 8 to 13 letters were increasingly slow. The authors suggest that this pattern may go some way to explaining the somewhat mixed results previously reported, with some authors failing to find a length effect in lexical decision tasks.

While the general finding of a relationship between word length and the processing of and/or memory for words is not in itself very surprising, it is nevertheless an effect that needs to be remembered, because research that plans to explore other effects such as those outlined below needs to control for word length in the experimental materials used.

Frequency effect

The frequency effect was discussed in Chapter 3 with respect to lexical access during language production, and in Chapter 8 in connection with spoken word recognition. High-frequency words are recognised more easily and more reliably than low-frequency words. This is reflected in response times and error rates in tasks like lexical decision. It is also the case (for English at least) that high-frequency words tend to be shorter than low-frequency words. This is known as Zipf's law, after one of the early researchers to identify this relationship between word length and frequency (Zipf, 1935). Clearly, this is one area where it is particularly important to control for word length when devising experimental materials. So in a study of frequency effects <dog> should be compared with <ewe>, rather than with <elephant>, since <elephant> is not only less frequent than <dog> but also longer, and if we compared response times to <dog> and <elephant> it would be unclear how much of any effect we observe is due to frequency or length.

Regularity effect

The regularity effect in visual word recognition concerns the relationships between spelling and pronunciation. A regular spelling–sound correspondence means that a word follows the general rules for arriving at a

> The **body** of a word is the final vowel and any following consonant(s), and is the written equivalent to the rhyme.

pronunciation based on the spelling. So the <ea> spelling in English most usually has an /i/ pronunciation, so <meat> is a regular word, while <threat> is not. The <ave> spelling usually has an /æⁱv/ pronunciation, so <save> is regular and <have> is not. The basic regularity effect (Baron & Strawson, 1976) is that visually presented words with a regular spelling–sound correspondence are easier to process than those with an irregular correspondence. However, the regularity effect and the frequency effect interact. High-frequency words are not particularly affected by regularity, while low-frequency ones are strongly affected by regularity. We will see later that this is an important finding for advocates of the dual-route model of reading.

Once researchers started looking in more detail at regularity in English, they found that the regularity effect is more complex than previously thought. In particular, they found that consistency of spelling–pronunciation correspondences is also important (Patterson & Morton, 1985). That is, visual word recognition is influenced not just by whether the spelling–sound correspondences reflect a set of 'rules', but also by the language user's knowledge of similar lexical entries. The examples in Table 9.1 illustrate the types of consistency and inconsistency that can exist in spelling–sound relationships.

What is particularly important is that there are sets of words, described as 'gangs' in Table 9.1, where there is an irregular spelling–sound correspondence for almost all words with that spelling. The example of <look> in the table illustrates this nicely. Most spellings with <oo> have an /u/ pronunciation, such as <soon>, <root>, <scoop>, and so on. The <ook>

Table 9.1 Some word types based on regularity and consistency of the relationship of spelling and pronunciation of the word body (based on Patterson & Morton, 1985: 340).

word type	example	characteristics
consistent	gaze	all words receive the same *regular* pronunciation of the body
consensus	lint	all words with one exception receive the same *regular* pronunciation
heretic	pint	the *irregular* exception to the consensus
gang	look	all words with one exception receive the same *irregular* pronunciation
hero	spook	the *regular* exception to the gang
gang without a hero	cold	all words receive the same *irregular* pronunciation
ambiguous: conformist	cove	*regular* pronunciation with many *irregular* exemplars
ambiguous: independent	love	*irregular* pronunciation with many *regular* exemplars
hermit	yacht	no other word has this body

body is different. With the exception of <spook> and the rather infrequent <snook> and <dook> (known as 'heroes' because of how they defy the gang and obey the rules), all <ook> words have the /ʊ/ vowel. If we were therefore to encounter a new word (e.g. a name coined for a new product), such as <wook>, we would expect the pronunciation to follow the pattern of the gang, rather than that of the hero(es). That is, the pronunciation would be consistent, but in terms of the overall pattern of the language, it would be considered irregular because of the general tendency of the <oo> spelling to have an /u/ pronunciation.

Neighbourhood effects

The notion of the neighbourhood was introduced in Chapter 8 in the discussion of competition effects between the activated words in a cohort. In the context of visual word recognition, neighbours are words with similar spelling patterns to the target word. One definition is that these are words sharing all but one letter with the target word, and where letter position is the same (Coltheart, Davelaar, Jonasson & Besner, 1977). So <work>, <ward> and <ford> would all be orthographic neighbours of <word>. A number of properties of the neighbourhood are important for visual word recognition, the most important of which are the neighbourhood size or density, and the lexical frequency characteristics of the neighbourhood, as well as of the target itself. These properties interact with one another, and their effects seem to be to some extent task-dependent (Andrews, 1997; Perea & Rosa, 2000).

A general finding is that responses to low-frequency words, but not those to high-frequency words, are affected by neighbourhood size. The nature of this effect for low-frequency words is not the same in all tasks. First, responses in naming tasks (i.e. where the word is read aloud) are generally faster for low-frequency words that come from large or dense neighbourhoods (such as *rink*, which has 15 neighbours, including *sink, rank, risk, ring*) than for low-frequency words from small or sparse neighbourhoods (e.g. *tact*, with 6 neighbours) (Andrews, 1989). This shows a facilitatory effect of neighbourhood size. Second, inhibitory effects have emerged in tasks which require the unique identification of a target word. Such a task is progressive demasking, where more and more of a word is exposed on repeated presentations until the participant is able to uniquely identify the target. The more neighbours there are for a word, the longer the exposure to a word needs to be before it can be recognised (Carreiras, Perea & Grainger, 1997). Third, lexical decision tasks have variably shown facilitation or inhibition from neighbourhood size, depending on other aspects of the task, including the degree of word-likeness of the nonwords used in the task (Andrews, 1992), an emphasis of speed over accuracy (Grainger & Jacobs, 1996), and the language being studied. A further effect is that the frequency characteristics of words in the neighbourhood also have an impact on recognition – words with high-frequency neighbours are recognised more slowly than comparable words with low-frequency neighbours (Pollatsek, Perea & Binder, 1999).

Note that the discussion of regularity and consistency here is in terms of a fairly standard Southern British English pronunciation of the example words. The consistency or otherwise of the pronunciation of these words clearly depends on accent.

9.3 Models of visual word recognition

The various findings from research on visual word recognition have led to a number of models of the process of recognising words. A selection of three dominant models will be presented in this section, in order to illustrate the different mechanisms that have been suggested for accounting for some of the basic effects outlined above.

Morton's Logogen model

In the Logogen model (Morton, 1969), words are represented by logogens, recognition units that are activated on the basis of different types of input information. One way of conceptualising this is to see the logogens as containers, into which the input information is poured (see Figure 9.1). Because this information can include phonological input as well as orthographic, the Logogen model is also a model of spoken word recognition. The logogens can also be activated by appropriate contextual input information. Word recognition occurs when the activation level of a recognition unit climbs above some threshold.

The logogen-as-container analogy in Figure 9.1 shows how different words may have different thresholds (the dotted lines), so that the same input information (the shaded content of the units) brings one word over its threshold before the others. Such threshold differences might result from the frequency with which words are encountered, with repeated exposure to a word causing a lowering of the logogen threshold.

Since there is no interaction between the recognition units, the Logogen model has no obvious mechanism for accounting for the effect of neighbourhood size.

In some respects the Logogen model is similar to the Cohort model. It is clearly a parallel model, with more than one word candidate activated at any one time. It also proposes that the initial activation of candidates is a result of bottom-up input (i.e. in this case orthographic or phonological input), with context effects only coming into play once logogens have been activated.

Forster's Search model

The Search model is a serial search model (Forster, 1976; Murray & Forster, 2004). It differs in this respect from both the Cohort model discussed in

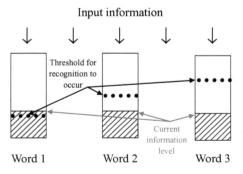

Input information

Figure 9.1
Representation of
logogens as containers.

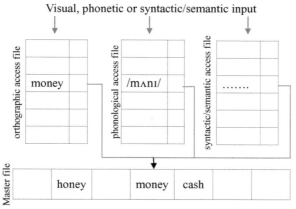

Visual, phonetic or syntactic/semantic input

Figure 9.2
Forster's bin or search model of word recognition.

Chapter 8 and the Logogen model presented above, which are parallel models. In serial search models, the checking of the input against a candidate set of words is done one word at a time. Frequency effects are easily accounted for in a serial model by the ordering of words in the candidate set being checked. High-frequency words are checked first, and so high-frequency words are recognised more quickly than low-frequency ones.

The candidate set that is being checked is determined in the Search model by the type of input, which depends on the task at hand. The model has access files for orthographic, phonological and syntactic/semantic input (see Figure 9.2). There are multiple access files of each type, organised according to relevant factors, so that for instance words with the same sequences of beginning letters will be listed in the same bin. Only one access file of each type is shown in the figure. The access files or 'bins' have links to a master file, i.e. a complete listing of words in the mental lexicon. This arrangement is somewhat similar to the organisation of a library, with the access files being a type of catalogue, giving a code for each word just as the library catalogue gives a code for each book. These codes allow the processor to find the word in the master file, in the way that book codes allow the user to locate the book in the relevant stack or shelf.

Although different in other respects, the Search model is similar to the Logogen model in that it cannot easily account for neighbourhood effects. In this case this is because the serial search process means that words are considered one at a time and are not compared all at once to the set of their potential competitors. In particular, there is difficulty accounting for the finding noted above of facilitatory effects of neighbourhood size on lexical access. As noted by Andrews (1992), an increase in neighbourhood size would be expected to result in slower responses because of the increased number of similar words to be checked. At best, there would be no effect of neighbourhood size, if the neighbours were not sufficiently similar to the target word to influence the search for it.

An Interactive Activation model

The models outlined above assume that the visual recognition of words follows a linear process whereby recognition elements such as letters are

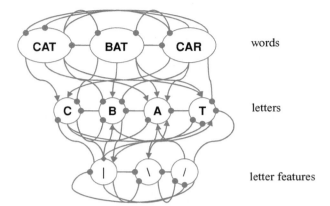

Figure 9.3
Partial sketch of an
Interactive Activation
model of word
recognition.

detected in the input and mapped onto representations for words in the lexical system. In Chapter 7, however, we saw that the perception of both the spoken and the visual input is affected by linguistic information. This included the Ganong effect (Ganong, 1980), which we saw resulted in a shift in perceptual boundaries between two categories (e.g. /d/ and /t/ phonemes), depending on which category resulted in a real word (e.g. *desk* vs **tesk* and **dask* vs *task*). In an attempt to characterise such findings, computer-based implementations of word recognition models have been constructed which allow the flow of activation not only from the recognition elements at the input stage to the lexical system but also from the words in the lexical system back to the recognition elements. These are known as Interactive Activation (IA) models (McClelland & Rumelhart, 1981; Rumelhart & McClelland, 1982; Seidenberg & McClelland, 1989).

The workings of such a model (cf. the TRACE model) are illustrated in Figure 9.3, where the three levels of units are letter features, letters and words. The connecting lines between the units in the model are of two types. Some links, ending in arrows in the figure, are excitatory. That is, if one unit receives activation, then it will pass this activation on to units at the other end of such excitatory links, following the direction of the arrow. The other type of link is inhibitory, and is shown by lines ending in dots. If two units are connected by such a link, then activation of one will cause inhibition, i.e. reduction of activation, in the other.

As input activation is received at the level of letter features, it is passed up through the model to units for letters that contain those features. At the same time, inhibitory connections ensure that letters which do not contain those features, i.e. which are in this respect incompatible with the input, have their activation levels lowered, making them less likely for recognition. Similar activation and inhibition links are found between the letter units and the word units. Note also that in this illustration links between units at the same level are inhibitory in nature, so that if one letter feature, letter or word unit is activated, then it suppresses the activation of competing units. In addition, there are links that allow activation or inhibition effects to flow down through the model from words to

Interactive Activation models have a complex network of connections. The partial network in Figure 9.3 is incomplete. Clearly many more words, letters and letter features would be needed for a complete model, and even in this simplified illustration many of the connecting lines between units have been omitted.

letters and from letters to letter features. This means for example that as a word receives activation on the basis of its initial letters, so this word in turn feeds activation down to each of its component letters. This raises the activation level of letters not yet encountered, with the effect that these letters are more readily recognised. It is easy to see how such a system would predict the Ganong effect – letters or phonemes are more easily recognised if they receive activation from the lexical level.

Although this is not shown in the illustration, IA models can be extended to include units representing the semantic and syntactic properties of words, so that words are more readily recognised if they fit the context in which they are found. Note also that some IA models, such as that proposed by Seidenberg and McClelland (1989) are 'distributed' models, and do not have representations corresponding to linguistic entities such as words. Instead, letters, words, etc. emerge as patterns of activation across elementary processing units in the interactive network. Additional refinements of this class of model include variations in the strengths of the connections between units, to better reflect specific patterns of competition and support. Individual units can also have different resting levels of activation, capturing the frequency effects found in behavioural research. Using such manipulations, researchers have run computer implementations of this type of model to test their hypotheses about a range of possible effects in word recognition and other aspects of comprehension.

9.4 Routes to read by

Except in experimental settings, visual word recognition does not usually take place in isolation, but is rather part of the process of reading. Chapters 10 to 12 present some discussion of how sentences and longer stretches of text and speech are understood. This section, by contrast, focuses on the specific skill of reading aloud from text. This is important because reading aloud is something that many of us do on a fairly regular basis, and therefore is a learned skill that might reveal some of the psycholinguistic processes involved in both word recognition and spoken word production. It is also important because a range of research findings have suggested that the pronounced forms of words are important even in silent reading, under certain conditions.

The grapheme–phoneme route

One of the most extensively studied issues in research on reading aloud is the use, in various tasks, of grapheme–phoneme conversion (GPC), also referred to as graphophonic transposition (GPT) or phonological recoding. Under discussion is first, whether there is a pathway that takes readers through a rule-based system that converts written strings into forms for pronunciation; second, whether this conversion happens prior to lexical access; and third, the extent to which the use of such conversion is under strategic control.

One extreme position concerning the grapheme–phoneme route is that it is obligatory, and involves what is known as an articulatory loop

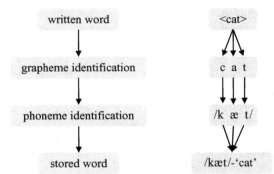

Figure 9.4
The grapheme–phoneme
route in reading.

between the visual buffer used in visual processing and the lexicon. As a consequence, the pronunciation of words we read has to become available, even if only inwardly, before we can recognise them from our lexicon. Inward rehearsal of the spoken forms of words is known as subvocalisation. Less extreme positions do not insist on this subvocalisation, but still maintain that there is conversion between spelling and sound during reading, even when this is silent reading.

A key question is therefore whether lexical access in visual processing is mediated or at least influenced by sound forms. I.e. do we first recognise the graphemes, then the phonemes corresponding to those graphemes, and then from there follow the same route as is used in spoken word recognition, as shown in Figure 9.4?

Orthographic (written) forms are of course historically and developmentally secondary to spoken forms. Children normally learn spoken words first and only subsequently learn written words and thus make the connections between written forms and meanings. It is therefore tempting to think that for visual word recognition to be successful a grapheme–phoneme conversion system just needs to be plugged onto a pre-existing spoken word recognition system. However, a link between the written and spoken forms of a word does not have to involve recoding of subword units such as conversion of letters to phonemes. Instead, the whole written word may give access to a spoken form of the complete word, which then leads to lexical access, as in Figure 9.5.

On top of this, even if the process of learning to read suggests some kind of mediation of sound forms (as in Figure 9.4), the mature skill of reading may not be based on mediation, but may rather proceed from whole word-forms (as in Figure 9.5).

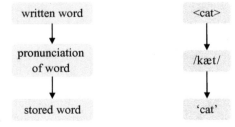

Figure 9.5
Lexical access through
whole-word pronunciation.

Additionally, of course, the irregularity of grapheme–phoneme corre-spondences in many languages (as well as differences in writing systems as outlined in Chapter 7) casts doubt on the reliability of the grapheme–phoneme route for those languages.

Evidence for grapheme–phoneme conversion

We can pronounce nonwords. For instance, you can probably find a pro-nunciation for <florp> even though you may not have encountered this form before, and it is likely that native speakers will agree on the pronun-ciation of this form. This suggests that there may be some element of subword translation that takes us from spelling to pronunciation. Note that this need not involve recoding from individual letters to individual sounds, but might instead involve larger subword elements such as the onsets of words (e.g. the initial consonant cluster <fl>) and the rhymes or word bodies (e.g. <orp>).

The regularity effect noted above also supports some sort of spelling-to-sound recoding. The processing advantage for words with a regular spelling–sound correspondence falls naturally out of a system in which the regularities are represented in terms of rules used during the process-ing task. In early research using a naming task (Baron & Strawson, 1976), it was found that participants can initiate their reading aloud of words with regular grapheme–phoneme correspondences more quickly than that of words with irregular correspondences (compare *cowl-fowl-howl* and *bowl*; *boss-loss-moss* and *gross*).

Note though that the task involves both the recognition of the written form and the production of a spoken form of the word. The regularity effect could therefore originate in the production process rather than in recogni-tion. It turns out that if participants' productions of the word are delayed (i.e. they are not allowed to say the words as soon as they see them) then the advantage for regular words is removed (Gough & Cosky, 1977). This sug-gests that the regularity effect is indeed in the initial recognition of words, not in their production. However, other research removed the speaking component altogether, using a visual lexical decision task with regular and irregular forms. Such tasks showed no consistent effect of regularity on real word decisions, but a clear effect on nonword decisions (Coltheart, 1978).

A particularly robust effect turned out to be the pseudohomophone effect (Rubinstein Lewis & Rubinstein, 1971). Pseudohomophones are non-words that would sound like real words if they were pronounced, such as <blud>. Such nonwords take longer to reject in a lexical decision task than other nonwords, indicating that there is some obligatory spelling–sound recoding that makes the corresponding real word available (in this case *blood*), and this then interferes with the lexical decision response. The effect is clearly influenced by the spelling–sound correspondences that speakers have been exposed to, since the pseudohomophone effect is not found for word bodies that do not exist in actual words, even though their pronunciation might be predictable. For example, the effect is found for <beaf> (as a pseudohomophone for <beef>) but not for <befe> (Vanhoy & Van Orden, 2001).

Such a collection of findings has been taken to suggest that there is both a direct route from the written input to the lexicon, without any spelling–sound conversion, and a mediated route which uses spelling–sound correspondences. This second route is used in nonword recognition and in certain tasks that require reading aloud. The pseudohomophone effect then arises when the mediated route produces a form that *could* be a real word, and which has to be re-checked against the written form, leading to longer processing times.

Dual-route models

Such a dual-route model (Coltheart, Rastle, Perry, Langdon & Ziegler, 2001), with a whole-word route for practised forms, and a grapheme–phoneme route for novel forms, is shown in Figure 9.6. This type of model has received widespread discussion in the context of how children should be taught to read, in particular in the debate between an alphabetic or phonic method, which involves identifying spelling–sound correspondences, and a whole-word or 'look-and-say' method, in which children learn to associate the sound of a word with its overall visual pattern. Our focus will be on the role of such a model in adult reading, and in particular on the part it has played in the discussion of various types of acquired dyslexia (see later in this chapter).

Evidence that both routes are used comes from studies that looked at the interaction of regularity and frequency effects in naming tasks. The regularity effect reported in naming tasks is robust only for infrequent words (Seidenberg, Waters, Barnes & Tanenhaus, 1984). If the words are of high frequency then irregular words (<have>) are read aloud just as rapidly as regular words (<make>). The account given for this is that although both routes shown in Figure 9.6 are used, the direct route from the written word to the stored word is faster, particularly for high frequency words with high activation levels (or low recognition thresholds). There is no reason to suppose that the access speed to stored words via this whole-word route is different for regular and irregular words, and this is confirmed by the absence of a regularity effect for the high-frequency words. For low-frequency words, however, it is argued that the spelling–sound conversion route might produce a candidate for pronunciation at about the same time as the whole-word route, which is slow for these low-frequency words. The two candidate pronunciations are then checked against one another. If they agree, as in the case of low-frequency regular words, then the

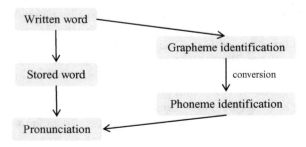

Figure 9.6
A dual-route model of reading.

pronunciation of the word takes place. For irregular words, though, the two outputs disagree. For example, the low-frequency irregular word <deaf> would be predicted to have the pronunciation /dif/ (rhyming with *leaf*) following the spelling–sound rules, but will have the pronunciation /def/ according to the pronunciation information for this word that is contained within its lexical entry. This disagreement needs to be resolved before the word can be pronounced, and this leads to a delay in naming low-frequency irregular words compared to low-frequency regular forms.

Reading for meaning

During normal reading we clearly do not just recognise the form of a word, but we also need to access its meaning. One question is whether access to meaning, i.e. reading for meaning, is phonologically mediated, even in silent reading. One way in which this has been tested is through a category monitoring task (Van Orden, 1987). In this task, participants see individual words and have to indicate whether or not each word belongs to a particular semantic category. For instance, if the category they were classifying for was 'types of food', then participants should answer 'yes' to <meat>. The results show misclassification of words that were **homophones** of within-category words, so that <meet> was for instance often wrongly classified as a type of food. This effect was even found for pseudo-homophones, with <soop> also being classified as a type of food.

Such results indicate that phonological mediation does take place. However, the category monitoring task may be sufficiently different from normal reading that it might allow unusual effects to arise. For instance, the task involves a late (post-lexical) decision about whether the word is a member of the target category. This means that a decision has to be made after the word is accessed from the lexicon, which typically results in a slower response than in many other tasks. During the time taken for this task, phonological forms generated by a spelling–sound conversion process might also become available for lexical search, so that at least some words are accessed based on the routes typically used for spoken word recognition. That is, phonological mediation during visual word recognition may be a rather indirect and marked process. It is nevertheless noteworthy that word activation based on spelling–sound correspondences takes place even when it is counter-productive.

Other evidence for the influence of meaning on word recognition comes from a range of studies showing that words with richer semantic representations are recognised more easily or more rapidly than those with weaker semantic representations. So there are processing advantages, for instance, for words with greater imageability (Balota, Cortese, Sergent-Marshall, Spieler & Yap, 2004), or those with a greater number of related meanings (Rodd, Gaskell & Marslen-Wilson, 2002).

Visual access to words

During normal silent reading, it is almost certainly the case that practised readers access familiar visually presented words via a direct route, without spelling-to-sound coding. If it is in fact the case that most real words

> **Homophones** are distinct words that have the same spoken form but not necessarily the same written form, like <meet> and <meat>.
>
> **Homographs** are distinct words that have the same written form but not necessarily the same spoken form, like <lead> the verb and <lead> the metal. Both are types of **homonym**, which can also include words that both sound and look the same, such as <bear> the verb and <bear> the animal.
>
> **Polysemy** differs from homophony, as polysemes are different related meanings of the same word, such as *point* as the tip of a pencil or a headland.

Figure 9.7
Whole form vs
letter-by-letter word
identification.

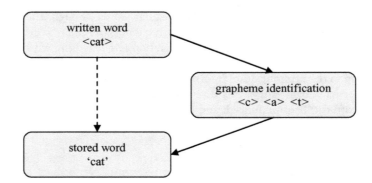

are recognised visually without such coding, then a further question concerns precisely how they are accessed visually, and whether this involves letter units. That is, do readers get from the written word to the stored word using the right-hand grapheme identification route in Figure 9.7, or via a more direct whole-word recognition route? And if words are accessed via grapheme identification, what is the nature of these letter-sized representations, i.e. how abstract are the letter shapes, allowing for variation in font and handwriting (Rapp, Folk & Tainturier, 2001)?

Whole-word recognition relies on visual evidence concerning the word-form as a complete unit, such as its overall word shape. Evidence that word shape is important in word recognition includes the finding that words are recognised more quickly if they are presented in lower case than if they appear in upper case. It is argued that lower case letters, with ascenders (as in the letters <l, t, d>, etc.) and descenders (as in <p, q, y>, etc.) make the word shape more distinctive than UPPER CASE, where all letters are the same height. Similarly, typing mistakes are less likely to be detected if they preserve the overall word shape. So for the intended word *test*, an oversight during proof reading is more likely for <tesf> than for <tesc>. Note though that both these sources of evidence could also be evidence for easier discrimination and faster recognition of individual letters, and hence that words are recognised letter-by-letter.

9.5 Dyslexia

In this section we will summarise some of the main findings from the investigation of adult reading problems, focusing particularly on what these findings might tell us about models of word recognition and reading. This is in line with attempts that have been made to characterise types of dyslexia in terms of parts of a 'normal' model of reading aloud that have been affected by damage (Caplan, 1992: Chapter 5; Marshall & Newcombe, 1981; Morton & Patterson, 1980; Patterson & Morton, 1985).

Dyslexia affects reading processes and is therefore different from, but will often co-exist with, dysgraphia, which affects writing processes. Dyslexia can be acquired or developmental. In developmental dyslexia

(Snowling & Caravolas, 2007), there is no obvious single event such as head trauma that has resulted in the problems faced by the dyslexic, and it is usually the case that the full range of normal reading skills has never been present. Acquired dyslexia on the other hand is usually the result of brain damage, resulting from a blow to the head (e.g. in a motor vehicle accident) or from a stroke (which affects the brain's blood supply). In this form of dyslexia, there is disruption of previously intact reading processes. Most of the research relevant to this section has been on acquired (adult) dyslexia. Some types are referred to as 'peripheral', affecting e.g. attention, visual processing, letter identification, and so on. Our focus here is on 'central' types.

The study of acquired dyslexia, as is common with much study of impaired language processing, often involves the argument of double dissociation. If one patient (A) performs well in one area of processing (Task 1), but not in another (Task 2), while another subject (B) performs well in the second area but not in the first, then there is a dissociation between the skills involved in these two tasks – either can be impaired while the other remains intact. Often evidence is also sought that patients A and B differ in the type or location of physical damage. It can then be argued that certain areas of the brain are the loci of certain types of processing.

Attempts have been made to characterise different types of dyslexia in terms of which parts of a 'normal' model of reading aloud might have been affected by brain injury. The normal model considered in this section is an extension of the dual-route model of reading aloud discussed above (Coltheart, Patterson & Marshall, 1980; Coltheart *et al.*, 2001). It envisages that reading aloud can occur via the three routes shown in Figure 9.8. Routes (a) and (b) are the whole-word and grapheme–phoneme routes common to most dual-route models. Route (a) involves access of lexical forms, including meaning, via orthography; pronunciation is accessed through the output route from the lexicon to articulation. Route (b) proceeds from sub-word orthography (letters) to sub-word phonology (phonemes) via a grapheme–phoneme coding (GPC) route, and bypasses content-based aspects of lexical representations. It is the route that has to be used for nonword pronunciation. Note that the additional route in this model compared to the simpler dual-route model presented earlier is route (c). This takes the reader from whole-word orthographic representations to whole-word phonology, without involving access to the meanings associated with a word.

A number of types of dyslexia have been described in terms of disruptions of the routes marked in this model. It is worth looking at a selection of these as illustrations of how the patterns of disrupted language processing are used to provide support for a particular model of processing, using the notion of double dissociation.

Patients with surface dyslexia typically have good reading aloud of nonsense words, indicating that they are able to make use of the spelling-to-sound conversion route marked as (b) in Figure 9.8. However, they show poor recognition and reading aloud of real words, particularly irregular

Typically, **acquired dyslexia** is part of a bundle of problems faced by a patient, i.e. is one symptom of some larger syndrome in which other skills are disrupted. The fact that these other skills include other language skills can often make diagnosis difficult. For instance, it may not be clear whether a patient's inability to read aloud is due to impaired visual word recognition skills or impaired speech production skills, or a combination of both.

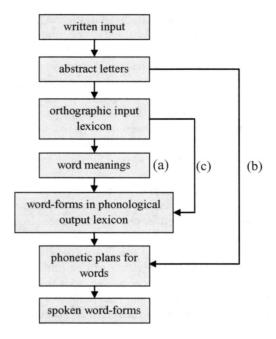

words, i.e. words that do not follow the spelling–sound rules. The errors they make when reading such words aloud tend to involve over-regularisation of the spelling–sound rules. So for instance they might read <love> as though it were *loave*, <head> as *heed*, <steak> as *steek*. In some patients, this difficulty particularly affects low-frequency words.

This pattern of good reading of nonsense words and regularisation of irregular words suggests that such patients have to rely on the spelling–sound route, and that there is therefore some impairment involving the lexical routes (a) and (c). Note also that comprehension is good for the words these patients can accurately read aloud, i.e. regular words. Irregular words on the other hand are often understood on the basis of how they are pronounced, so that if there is a match between the forms that the patients produce and a known word, then the visual form will be misunderstood (e.g. <head> as *heed*), rather than rejected as a nonword (which might be the case with reading <steak> as though it were *steek*). This suggests that semantic lexical representations are still available, so that meanings can still be accessed in these cases, but via the pronunciation, presumably by means of the route used in recognising spoken words.

The opposite pattern to surface dyslexia is shown in phonological dyslexia, where patients demonstrate a good ability in reading real words, whether regular or irregular, but are poor at reading pronounceable non-words. This seems to indicate an impairment of the spelling–sound route (b). Surface and phonological dyslexics taken together provide the double dissociation required to provide a functional distinction between reading routes within the lexicon (i.e. (a) and (c) in Figure 9.8) and the external route (b).

Evidence for the separate route marked as (c) comes from patients who show nonsemantic reading. Such patients have good reading aloud skills, but they do not seem to have any understanding of what they read. Amongst such patients, cases have been identified where both regular and irregular words are pronounced correctly, but no meanings seem to be accessed (as shown in tasks where patients have to match the word they read to the appropriate picture). These cases have the whole-word reading route (c) intact, as shown by success with irregular as well as regular words, but the semantic access route (a) is impaired.

Our final type of dyslexia under consideration here is deep dyslexia. Again, this is characterised by a combination of symptoms (Coltheart *et al.*, 1980). First, patients cannot read aloud nonsense forms, even pseudohomophones such as <seel>. In fact they will often substitute visually similar real words for nonsense forms, such as 'sift' for <sife>. This indicates a breakdown in the spelling–sound rule system (b). This is supported by the finding that such patients are often also unable to identify a spoken nonword as matching a written one, e.g. that /dit/ and <deet> might match. Second, deep dyslexics show moderately good reading comprehension for concrete and imageable words, but are less good with abstract and grammatical words. Third, they exhibit a large number of substitutions, or paralexias (see sidebar), of different types. Interestingly, such misreadings of real words very rarely produce non-existent forms.

The puzzle with deep dyslexia is why these symptoms co-occur. On the one hand, it is possible that the damage to the brain has affected neighbouring areas, each responsible for one or more of the symptoms listed. On the other, there may be a functional relationship between the symptoms. Some research indicates that the pattern hinges on the semantic errors, and it has been suggested that routes (c) and (b) (non semantic whole-word and spelling–sound routes) are damaged, and that words can only be read via the meaning route (a). In addition, there may be some disruption in the output of this meaning route, resulting in the observed substitutions. Interestingly these substitutions are very similar to those found in spontaneous speech errors (see Chapter 3). The higher incidence of such errors in the patient data suggests either a more permanent type of disruption, or that while the normal reading processes involve a check of the output of route (a) against those of routes (b) and (c), this checking is not possible for the patients because of the damage to these routes.

> **Semantic paralexias** result in a word that is semantically related to the target, such as <paddock> being read out as *kennel*. In **derivational paralexias**, one affixed form is substituted for another. For example, <edition> may be misread as *editor*. In **visual paralexias**, there is a visual similarity between the target and the error, such as <typing> being read out as *taping*. There are also instances of a mix of visual and semantic paralexias, for instance where <sympathy> is misread as *orchestra* (presumably via *symphony*).

Summary

In this chapter we have seen that visual word recognition and reading involve a range of skills. These include:

- individual letter recognition;
- whole-word recognition;
- the mapping between letters and pronunciation.

Different skills are used in different tasks, and different aspects of the reading package are affected by different types of dyslexia. Studying patterns of difficulty in dyslexia has been a productive avenue of research for modelling normal visual word recognition and reading processes.

Exercises

Exercise 9.1

Explain, in terms of the patterns of spelling–sound correspondence shown in Table 9.1, why some speakers of New Zealand English pronounce *worry* with the vowel in *jog* rather than the vowel in *jug*, even though most speakers of the same dialect pronounce it with the *jug*-vowel.

Exercise 9.2

Work out how many orthographic neighbours (words differing by one letter) the following words have, and place them in two groups of three words each according to neighbourhood size: *bash, deem, lust, maul, mope, romp*.
Given that all these words have quite low frequencies of use, what outcome would you predict for the relative speed of naming them (reading them out loud)? What about for their speed of recognition in a task like progressive demasking?

Exercise 9.3

What sort of paralexias are involved when a patient says (a) *dad* when reading the word <father>, (b) *tantrum* for <tandem>, (c) *scent* for <perfect>, (d) *helpless* for <helpful>?

Exercise 9.4

Explain with reference to models of reading presented in this chapter how it is that parents can sometimes find themselves reading a bedtime story to their children without taking in the meaning of what they are reading, and yet also without making any pronunciation mistakes.

Further reading

Rastle (2007) and Balota *et al.* (1999) provide useful overviews of visual word recognition. Caplan (1992) is a good source for additional information on dyslexia and on the dual-route model of reading. Developmental dyslexia, not discussed in this chapter, is reviewed by Snowling and Caravalos (2007), and the processes involved in learning to read by Treiman and Kessler (2007). Frequency and neighbourhood effects have been explored by Andrews (1992).

10 Syntactic sentence processing

PREVIEW

This chapter considers how readers and listeners assign syntactic structure to strings of words. By the end of the chapter you should understand that:

- determining syntactic structure is an important aspect of sentence comprehension;
- markers of syntactic structure can help readers and listeners in this process;
- there are claims that comprehenders have certain preferred strategies that they can use in assigning syntactic structure to sentences.

10.1 Introduction

Chapters 8 and 9 assume that the word is a basic building block of language comprehension, and describe some of the psycholinguistic evidence for the recognition of spoken and written words respectively. The focus of this chapter is on how, during comprehension, we build a sentence structure using the sequence of words we have recognised. Although much of what is covered in this chapter can be applied equally to spoken and visual input, the evidence comes chiefly from studies of visual sentence processing, using techniques such as reading time measures and the tracking of eye movements during reading. Specific properties of spoken sentences, such as their prosodic structure, will be part of the material covered in Chapter 11.

The current chapter begins with discussion of how syntactic complexity affects processing and of how syntactic structure can be explicitly marked to facilitate processing. It then explores the notion of parsing strategies, i.e. that comprehenders have grammatical preferences for how sentence structures are built up from words during reading. We will see that this can lead to a 'garden path' experience, where readers find that they have made the wrong analysis and need to carry out some revision of this analysis. The discussion of parsing strategies and garden path experiences takes place largely in isolation from issues concerning meaning and appropriateness, issues which will be taken up in Chapter 11.

10.2 Complexity and sentence processing

Certain sentence structures are claimed to be more difficult to process than others. During the time of the transformational approach to grammar that was current in the 1960s and 1970s, it was argued that the more difficult structures were those that had undergone some change(s) in the history of their derivation. This is part of the Derivational Theory of Complexity, which is discussed in the context of language production in Chapter 2. One derivational process in this grammatical framework produced passive sentences, such as (10.2). It was argued that a passive was derived from an underlying or logical form that expressed the basic idea of the sentence and which was closer in structure to the active version of the sentence in (10.1). Because they were further removed from this underlying form than active sentences, it was predicted that passive sentences would be more difficult to process, and that the comprehension of (10.2) would involve greater processing demands than the comprehension of (10.1).

(10.1)   The dog chased the boy.

(10.2)   The boy was chased by the dog.

Similarly, sentence (10.4) was predicted to be more difficult than (10.3) because a negative transformation has applied.

(10.3)   That ball is blue.

(10.4)   That ball is not blue.

'Parsing' is a term associated with traditional teaching of grammar, e.g. of Latin or Greek, where texts in the language would be given to students to analyse in terms of grammatical structure. Similarly, in the psycholinguistic literature, parsing refers to the syntactic structural analysis of the input string of words.

Relative clauses in which the relative pronoun is the object of the embedded verb, as in (10.6) were predicted to be more difficult than those in which the relative pronoun is the subject (10.5). This is because the actual word order of the elements in the relative clause in (10.5) is the same as the assumed logical form of the clause (*who chased the dog* is subject – verb – object), while the surface order of the relative in (10.6) is not (*who the dog chased* is object – subject – verb). (A description of this difference in terms of constituent movements is given in Chapter 12.)

(10.5)   The boy who chased the dog ran home

(10.6)   The boy who the dog chased ran home

Early evidence for the greater complexity of passive sentences like (10.2) came from a task which measures how long participants take to match sentences with pictures showing the events described in those sentences. This task took longer for the passive versions of sentences than for the active versions. Similar findings were reported for other sentence pairings with different syntactic contrasts such as (10.3)–(10.4) (Gough, 1965; Just & Carpenter, 1971) and (10.5)–(10.6) (Fodor & Garrett, 1967). However, subsequent research found that changing the perspective shown in the pictures (so that for instance the boy is foregrounded in the picture corresponding to (10.2)) had the result that responses to passives were no longer slower than those to actives. That is, grammatical structure is not the only factor that influences comprehension, as we will see in more detail in Chapter 11.

> In **sentence–picture matching** tasks, participants are given a sentence and have to select from a set of pictures which picture best illustrates the meaning of the sentence. The accuracy in selecting the correct picture and the time taken making that selection are used as measures of how easy the sentence is to understand.

Other experimental tests of derivational complexity included a study where participants were given examples of transformationally related sentences, such as the pairs given in each of (10.7)–(10.9) (Miller & McKean, 1964). The labels at the end of the examples show the nature of the transformational relationship.

(10.7)   he caught her – he didn't catch her (AA → NA)

(10.8)   he caught her – she was caught by him (AA → AP)

(10.9)   he caught her – she wasn't caught by him (AA → NP)

In all example pairs the first sentence is an affirmative active (AA), which as we have seen was argued to be closest to the underlying logical form that was assumed to be the input to the transformations that derive the other sentence forms. In (10.7) the second sentence is a negative active (NA), and has involved a single transformation. In (10.8) the second sentence is an affirmative passive (AP), which also involves a single transformation, but a more complex one in terms of the movements of words involved. Sentence (10.9) has a negative passive (NP) sentence, which involves both the negativisation and the passivisation transformations.

For each trial, Miller and McKean presented one example pair such as (10.7)–(10.9) as a model. The participants were then given an affirmative active version of a different sentence and asked to transform it in their heads in the same way as had been shown by the example, pressing a response button to indicate when they had performed that transformation. (To check the accuracy of their transformation they were then given a list of sentences from which they had to select a sentence that matched their transformed version of the original target sentence.) The study found that the time taken to press the response button increased in line with the number and complexity of the transformations involved.

In a memory task it was demonstrated that sentences were more confusable with one another the more closely related they were in terms of transformations (Clifton & Odom, 1966). More recent research along these lines has focused on the possibility that there is a bias towards statements, since statements are closer to the 'underlying' affirmative active forms of sentences, which provide the propositional content required for comprehension. There are implications here for issues such as the use of leading questions in courts and the language used in advertising – for instance if the question 'Is brand X better than brand Y?' involves accessing the propositional content 'brand X is better than brand Y', then the question might be remembered as a claim that X is better than Y (Pandelaere & Dewitte, 2006).

In a further memory task, participants were required to memorise both a sentence and a list of unrelated words. It was found that the more complex the sentence was, in transformational terms, the fewer words the participants could reliably remember (Savin & Perchonock, 1965).

Critics of these types of experiment have argued that they only provide indirect evidence for greater complexity in language processing. This is because explicit transformation of sentences is not something we do in everyday language processing. Asking participants in an experiment to do this is therefore playing into the hands of proponents of the transformational approach to language processing. The critics agree that if we ask participants to carry out a transformation from one sentence to another then this requires some mental operations, but they question whether these are the mental operations ordinarily involved in sentence comprehension. In addition, memory tasks such as those outlined above are not measures of the immediate processing of sentences. When we understand a sentence, we do not hold it in its original form in our memory. Instead, we process it and move on. Furthermore, from an experiential point-of-view, readers and listeners have far greater exposure over their lifetimes to active than to passive sentences, a factor that must also be taken into account.

10.3 The clausal hypothesis

The clausal hypothesis is related to the derivational theory of complexity. In essence the clausal hypothesis claims that the clause is the basic unit of analysis in language comprehension. The clause is a group of words in a sentence that includes a verb. There are finite clauses, where a verb can carry markings for tense and for number agreement, as in (10.10) or (10.11) and non-finite clauses with verbs that cannot be marked in this way, such as the underlined portion in (10.12). Finite clauses can include main verb clauses as in (10.10) and (10.11), but also subordinate clauses such as the relative clause underlined in (10.13).

(10.10)　John walked.

(10.11)　They ride on donkeys.

(10.12)　John wanted <u>to leave work early</u>.

(10.13)　The man <u>who John saw</u> was very tall.

The clausal hypothesis is a special instance, for language, of a 'chunking' process. The usefulness of chunking is demonstrated in experiments in which subjects are better able to remember number sequences if they are encouraged to chunk them. So remembering a telephone number as a sequence of two chunks, as in (10.14) is easier than remembering the single longer sequence as in (10.15).

(10.14)　463 5631

(10.15)　4635631

It was hypothesised that language chunking might proceed on the basis of sentence structure, i.e. that sentences are chunked into units like clauses. As a test of this, a series of experiments used what is called a click location experiment (Fodor & Bever, 1965; Garrett, Bever & Fodor, 1966; Holmes & Forster, 1970). Participants were given a printed version of a sentence, such as one of those in (10.16) and (10.17), but without the additional markings (| and /).

(10.16)　The teacher who taught the biggest cla|ss / was given extra pay by his principal.

(10.17)　The very pretty and talented blonde gi|rl / was the runner up in the Miss America contest.

The participants then heard a recording of the sentence, onto which a click (or a beep) had been added, for instance at the position indicated in the examples by |. Their task was to mark on the printed version where the click had occurred. What the experimenters were interested in was whether the nature of a syntactic boundary close to the click would affect the likelihood that the click would 'migrate', perceptually, to that boundary (the 'click displacement effect'). They found that participants were more likely to erroneously report clicks at the boundary between the subject and predicate of the main clause, marked by / in the examples, in sentences like (10.16) than in sentences like (10.17). This is because in (10.16) the subject-predicate boundary is also the end of the relative clause *who taught the biggest class*. The experimenters claimed that this result provides evidence for the clausal hypothesis.

Processing within clauses

However, critics of the clausal hypothesis point out that we must be careful to distinguish between clausal structuring and clausal processing

(Marslen-Wilson, Tyler & Seidenberg, 1978). The former is a claim that language is segmented into clauses at some stage during comprehension, but that processing can carry on during a clause. The latter is a stronger claim about clause structure, i.e. that processing is concentrated at clause boundaries. Evidence for a claim that processing does not take place solely at these points but is carried out within clauses comes from online studies of comprehension, which track word-by-word analysis of the sentence. (Contrast offline tasks. See sidebar.) One instance of this is the word monitoring task employed by Marslen-Wilson and Tyler (1980). In this task, participants are told to listen for a word which may or may not occur in a sentence which they then hear. Their task is to press a response button as soon as they hear that word, if it is present. The materials included sentences such as (10.18), a normal prose sentence, which is both meaningful and syntactically well-formed; (10.19), an anomalous prose sentence, which is meaningless but syntactically well-formed (and in fact has the same sentence structure as (10.18)); and (10.20), a scrambled prose string which is both meaningless and syntactically ill-formed.

(10.18)   Some thieves stole most of the **lead** off the roof

(10.19)   No buns puzzle some in the **lead** off the text

(10.20)   Some the no puzzle buns in **lead** text the off

In examples (10.18)–(10.20), the same target word is used (shown in bold), and it is in the same serial position in each example. Across the experiment, the position of the target words was deliberately varied, so that the effect of accumulating information across the utterance could be measured.

The results from these experiments show an overall advantage for normal prose over anomalous prose and for anomalous prose over scrambled prose. In terms of position effects, the results show first that there is no advantage for one sentence type over any of the others at the first word position. This is not surprising because when the target word appears at this position it does not yet have any contextual support. Second, in normal prose sentences (10.18) there is a marked decrease in word monitoring times the later a word is in the sentence. Third, anomalous prose sentences (10.19) also show a decrease in monitoring times, although the change across the sentence is less dramatic than for normal prose. Finally, scrambled sentences show practically no serial position effect. The key results are that when the sentence has structure, a word within that sentence can be responded to more rapidly; that this response facilitation increases as more of the sentence is heard; and that the availability of both syntactic and semantic (meaning) structure results in a faster decrease in response times than the availability of syntactic structure alone. These results support the claim that sentence processing does not need to wait until major structural boundaries, but can take place in a cumulative way as the sentence is heard (Marslen-Wilson & Tyler, 1980).

A distinction can be made between **online** tasks, which claim to measure processing as it happens, and **offline** tasks, which measure the consequences of processing, after some or all of the processing has taken place.

Normal prose is both syntactically and semantically well-formed (10.18).
   Anomalous prose is syntactically well-formed but has little meaning (10.19).
   Scrambled prose is neither syntactically nor semantically well-formed, but consists of real words (10.20).
   Jabberwocky, named after the poem in Lewis Carroll's *Through the Looking Glass*, is syntactically well-formed, but has nonwords in the place of most or all of the content words, and so has little meaning, such as *The wuggy glim vorpily thazzes a veeg.*

10.4 Explicit syntactic markers

Sentence processing can be helped by words or affixes which explicitly mark the syntactic structure, but these are often left out in English, without making the utterance ungrammatical. So in (10.21) a complementiser (*that*) and a relative pronoun (*who*) have been left out compared to (10.22), but the sentence in (10.21) remains grammatical.

(10.21)   I told Mark the woman I met had red hair.

(10.22)   I told Mark that the woman who I met had red hair.

But leaving out syntactic markers can affect processing. For instance, response times in a phoneme monitoring task were faster when explicit markers of syntactic structure were present (Hakes, 1972). Phoneme monitoring is similar to word monitoring, but requires participants to listen for a particular speech sound rather than for a word. When participants listened to a version of sentence (10.23) with the structure made explicit by the words shown in square brackets in the example, they took less time to detect the target phoneme (/p/, shown in bold) than when those words were left out. The claim is that listeners find it easier to complete the syntactic analysis when syntactic structure is more explicitly marked and are therefore better able to pay attention to the phonemes in the input.

(10.23)   The children [that were] playing in the hayloft startled the farmer's wife.

As we will see in the next section, there have been a considerable number of studies of sentence processing that have used eye movement measurements with reading tasks. These studies also show the usefulness of the explicit marking of syntax. For example, the sentence in (10.24) has effectively the same syntactic structure as that in (10.25). The only difference is the presence of the explicit marker *that* in (10.25). This marker makes it clear that the whole clause *(that) the answer was wrong* is the object of the verb *knew*, rather than *the answer* being a noun phrase object, as it is in (10.26). The difference is perhaps more obvious if you realise that in (10.24) and (10.25) it is not claimed that John knew the answer, merely that he knew it to be wrong. Evidence for the effect on processing of the presence of the complementiser (*that*) is that reading times for the word *was* were much longer in (10.24) than in (10.25) (Rayner & Frazier, 1987). This is because it is only at that point in (10.24) that the sentence structure becomes clear and different from that in (10.26).

(10.24)   John knew the answer was wrong.

(10.25)   John knew that the answer was wrong.

(10.26)   John knew the answer by heart.

Not surprisingly, the more complex a sentence structure is, the more helpful explicit markers of syntax tend to be (Morgan, Meier & Newport, 1987). Since explicit markers are words and grammatical endings that occur very frequently in the language (inflectional endings, determiners, conjunctions, etc.), as well as generally being short, they are also easier to recognise and provide useful anchor points during processing (Valian & Coulson, 1988).

Prosody and punctuation

Evidence presented in Chapter 11 shows that spoken sentences also carry further cues to syntactic structure, through the intonation and phrasing used in speech. Such prosodic phrase-structure cues perform much the same function as syntactic markers, i.e. they make the syntactic structure of an utterance more explicit. It is clear that they do not simplify processing simply by providing (arbitrary) chunking of utterances, since prosodic phrasing is not as helpful if it is not syntactically motivated.

Punctuation provides a similar marking of syntactic structure. Consider for example the sentences in (10.27)–(10.29), which would all be identical if it were not for punctuation. Note also that as you read these out or hear them in your head you will also notice how their prosody and phrasing reflects the punctuation differences. Chapter 11 presents research that shows that our processing during silent reading can be affected by this 'implicit' prosody.

(10.27)   What is this thing called love?

(10.28)   What is this thing called, love?

(10.29)   What, is this thing called love?

Line breaks can also have an effect on sentence processing (Kennedy, Murray, Jennings & Reid, 1989). You should find that the sentence in (10.30) has been made more difficult by the position of the line break, compared with (10.31). Reading time studies confirm this finding. Formatting issues such as these have practical implications, such as in the design of signs.

(10.30)   When I've finished running
          the class can we all go home?

(10.31)   When I've finished running the class
          can we all go home?

> Line break position was one factor in a study the author carried out for a road transport authority, which was concerned about the readability and interpretation of electronic motorway gantry signs.

10.5 Strategies for syntactic processing

The preceding sections have presented summaries of a few issues in sentence complexity and in syntactic marking that have implications for the syntactic processing of sentences. How, then, do we carry out the processing of sentences? How do we build sentences using the input words? It seems that there are some basic observations that need to be taken into account.

One is that discontinuous constituents are difficult to process. Compare the sentences in (10.32)–(10.34). The more material that intervenes between *rang* and *up*, the more difficult it is to process the sentence.

(10.32)   Lou rang her friend up.

(10.33)   Lou rang her friend in the Outer Hebrides up.

(10.34)   Lou rang her friend in the Outer Hebrides that she hadn't seen since their trip together to Japan the summer before last up.

Of course, sentences like (10.34), though grammatically permissible, would normally be avoided (or expressed differently). The problem with such sentences is that when we encounter the word *up* it is disconnected from what we have read or heard just prior to that point. It seems that we package up the constituents that we read or hear, and *rang ... up* no longer belongs together as a single constituent.

Another observation is that native speakers seem to have clear preferences in the structures they assign to sentences. The same is probably true of non-native speakers, though less is known about their approaches to the processing of sentences (Frenck-Mestre, 2005; Nitschke, Kidd & Serratrice, 2010). Although (10.35) is unambiguous, it is problematic. Most readers do a double-take, and have to go back and read the sentence again to get the right analysis. By contrast, (10.36) is ambiguous, but it is often hard to detect the ambiguity (which involves the relationship of *for Chris* to the preceding material – did Pat buy the book for Chris or had I been trying to find it for Chris?)

(10.35)   Sandy said that Terry will take the cleaning out yesterday.

(10.36)   Pat bought the book that I'd been trying to find for Chris.

It is argued that these effects come about because human sentence processing automatically builds the words of a sentence into particular preferred structures, so that for instance the adverb *yesterday* at the end of (10.35) is attached to the most recent verb phrase, despite the fact that the phrase is marked for future but *yesterday* indicates past. The following section presents one account of such structural preferences.

10.6 Garden paths and the sausage machine

Observations such as the two above – that sentence constituents tend to get packaged up as we read a sentence and that we have preferred ways of packaging – have led to an account of sentence processing that is nicely illustrated with garden path sentences. A garden path sentence is one which leads the reader/listener 'up the garden path' by initially inducing an interpretation which turns out to be incorrect. Typically, garden path sentences involve a misleading syntactic analysis.

(10.37)   The horse raced past the barn fell.

The example in (10.37) is a famous one in the garden path literature and comes from Bever (1970). Many people struggle for some time to work out what it means, or even that it is a well-formed sentence in English. Adding some explicit syntactic markers, as in (10.38), can help readers reach the intended meaning.

(10.38)   The horse which was raced past the barn fell.

When confronted by the sentence in (10.37), most readers initially prefer to interpret *raced* as a past tense verb, and to understand *raced past the barn* as what the horse did. It then becomes difficult to build *fell* into that interpretation, and so a revision is necessary. A successful revision will result in *raced past the barn* being interpreted as a relative clause, with *raced* as a participle rather than a past tense verb. This relative clause reading is made clear by *which was* in (10.38). Because these words are missing from (10.37), this sentence is said to contain a reduced relative. The ambiguity in (10.37) is possible because the verb *race* has the same form (*raced*) for the past tense and the past participle. The same ambiguity would not arise for a verb like *drive*, which has the past tense form *drove* and the past participle *driven*, and so *The car driven past the barn* ... could only be interpreted as a reduced relative structure.

Other interpretations of example (10.37) have been suggested, and these either involve different understanding of the meanings of one or more words (e.g. of *fell* as meaning a type of hill, as in *fell running*, and of *barn fell* as therefore a type of fell or the name of a particular fell), or require some additional punctuation, e.g. a semicolon after *past* (*The horse raced past; the barn fell*). It is interesting that both of these suggestions follow the stated preference of interpreting *raced* as a past tense verb.

Garden-path type sentences are not hard to find in everyday life. The following are examples from newspaper headlines:

(10.39)   Man held over betting shop killings freed
Eye drops off shelf
Two sisters reunited after 18 years in checkout queue
Hospitals are sued by 7 foot doctors

The removal of grammatical information such as function words in newspaper headlines does of course add to the level of ambiguity by removing explicit markers of syntax which, as we have already seen, make an important contribution to comprehension.

One account for the garden path experience has been called the sausage machine (Frazier & Fodor, 1978). The name derives from the way the human sentence processor packages the input words into strings of phrases much as a machine manufacturing sausages packages the contents into strings of sausages. The sausage machine is a parser, i.e. it analyses sentences according to their syntactic structure. The parser is driven by some key principles, including the following. First, the goal of its operations is to build a syntactic tree, also known as a phrase marker. It does this by including each word in turn as it is encountered (i.e. read or heard). Second, the parser is deterministic. This means that it can only

A relative clause in English is a who-, which- or that-phrase that modifies or selects a noun, as in *The dog which has three legs* or *The man who was replaced by Bert*. (The relative clause is underlined in each case.) **Reduced relatives** are relative clauses without *who, which* or *that*, and with no auxiliary. So *The man replaced by Bert* contains a reduced relative. Note that the first part of this example could be a sequence of subject and past tense verb: *The man replaced* ... This is not true of all reduced relatives (compare *The woman I love* as a reduced form of *The woman who I love*).

build one tree at a time. It can therefore be contrasted with parallel processing models in which multiple interpretations can be entertained at the same time. Third, the sausage machine parser tries to keep the syntax as simple as possible. It also tries not to leave too much material unattached, i.e. not built into the syntactic tree under construction.

Late Closure and Minimal Attachment

Two parsing strategies are proposed to help the parser meet these criteria. These are Late Closure (10.40) and Minimal Attachment (10.41).

(10.40)   LATE CLOSURE: When possible, attach material into the clause or phrase currently being processed.

(10.41)   MINIMAL ATTACHMENT: Attach incoming material into the phrase marker being constructed, using the fewest possible nodes consistent with the well-formedness rules of the language under consideration.

These strategies are best explained through examples. Consider the possible analyses of the sequence *Before the police stopped the driver* in (10.42) and (10.43), as shown in the syntactic tree structures below each example.

(10.42)   Before the police stopped the driver he was getting nervous.

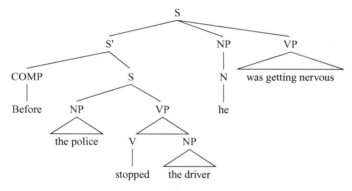

(10.43)   Before the police stopped the driver was getting nervous.

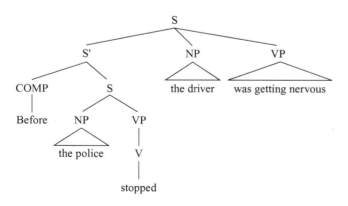

> The triangle used in the syntactic trees, e.g. between an NP node and *the police* in (10.42), is a device used to acknowledge that the constituent has internal structure (in this case the NP is made up of a determiner and a noun), but that this internal structure is not important to the analysis being discussed.

When it gets to *the driver*, the sausage machine (i.e., it is argued, the reader) prefers the interpretation represented by the tree structure in (10.42) because – obeying the principle of Late Closure in (10.40) – this NP is added to the current constituent, as the object of the V (*stopped*) inside the VP. This corresponds to a transitive reading of the verb *stopped*, with *the driver* as its object. In (10.43) *stopped* is being used intransitively, i.e. with no explicit object. In this case the first clause is closed early, after *stopped*, and *the driver* is the subject of the second clause (*... was getting nervous*).

Consider now the sequence *Karen knew the schedule* in (10.44) and (10.45). We see that it too has two interpretations, as shown in the different syntactic analyses of the same string of words. In both analyses *the schedule* is attached within the VP that was started with *knew*, i.e. Late Closure is being followed. In (10.44), the NP *the schedule* is the direct object and is attached to the verb phrase using no new nodes. That is, there are no syntactic nodes between this NP and the VP. The NP is said to be minimally attached. However, in (10.45) an intervening S (sentence/clause) node needs to be posited. This is because *the schedule* is now not the simple object of *knew*. Rather, it is the subject of a subordinate clause, *the schedule was wrong*, and it is this complete clause that is the object of *knew*. The tree diagram shows the additional S node required between the highest VP and the NP *the schedule* for (10.45), indicating the *non*-minimal attachment of that NP into the tree.

(10.44)   Karen knew the schedule by heart.

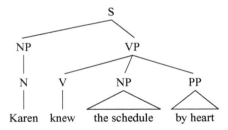

(10.45)   Karen knew the schedule was wrong.

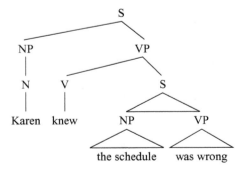

The evidence for these processing strategies comes from garden path experiences. These experiences can be measured in eye-tracking experiments that record participants' eye movements as they read (Frazier & Rayner, 1982; Rayner & Frazier, 1987). If a participant is reading a sentence like (10.43), then when they reach the word *was* their gaze lingers on that word, and they show regressions (backtracking, or backwards eye movements) to earlier parts of the sentence. This does not happen when they reach the word in the equivalent position (*he*) in (10.42). The preference according to Late Closure is for *the driver* to be the object of *stopped*, and this analysis is pursued in both sentences. Such an analysis becomes problematic in (10.43) once the word *was* is encountered, because this signals that *the driver* should be interpreted as the subject of the second clause (and *stopped* is being used intransitively, i.e. *the police* stopped themselves, not someone else). Similar findings apply to Minimal Attachment ambiguities, such as (10.44)–(10.45).

Consider now the sentence in (10.46). Does this sentence mean that Sam figured out that Max wanted to take the book, or does it mean that Max wanted to take out the book, and that is what Sam figured?

(10.46)   Sam figured that Max wanted to take the book out.

Earlier in the chapter we considered a similar example with the discontinuous constituent *rang ... up*. The more material that intervenes between the two parts, the more difficult the sentence is to process. This is reflected in a preference for interpreting (10.46) with the second of the meanings given above, i.e. that Max wanted to take the book out. That interpretation has *out* belonging to *take*, with two intervening words (or one intervening NP constituent), rather than to *figured*, with seven intervening words (and a string of intervening constituents). These attachments are illustrated in (10.47).

> Measuring participants' eye movements as they read (Chapter 9) provides information about a range of aspects of comprehension. Initially eye-trackers were rather invasive (as well as expensive), and required the participant to have their head clamped in place with their chin resting on a piece of equipment similar to those used by optometrists. More recently, eye-tracking has used micro-cameras mounted in special spectacles, or even infra-red web-cameras mounted on computer screens.

(10.47)

The preference follows a principle called Right Association (Kimball, 1973), which states that new nodes are preferentially attached to the lowest node (if the strategies of Late Closure and Minimal Attachment do not indicate otherwise). This is shown by the lower of the two dashed connecting lines in (10.47).

10.7 Syntactic category ambiguity

According to the syntactic parsing approach discussed in the preceding section, the syntactic processor cumulatively links words into a syntactic tree structure as they are encountered, as has been illustrated in earlier examples. For this to happen successfully, the processor needs to know what kind of word it is dealing with at each stage. However, a large proportion of words in all languages are ambiguous. Many involve category ambiguity, which is when the same word-form may represent more than one syntactic category. For instance *walk* can be either a noun or a verb. If it is not clear what the syntactic category of a word is, then how does the parser include it in the tree under construction? Usually, but not always, the appropriate type of word will be apparent from the structure of the tree that has been constructed up to that point. So after *Max went for a very long ...*, the noun reading of *walk* would be acceptable, but not the verb reading.

However, there are cases where the partial tree structure would allow words from more than one category. For example, if the word *trains* is encountered in the fragment in (10.48) it could be either a verb (as shown by the continuation in (10.49)) or a noun (10.50).

(10.48) I know that the desert trains ...

(10.49) I know that the desert trains young people to be especially tough.

(10.50) I know that the desert trains are especially tough on young people.

Because of parsing operations like Late Closure, Minimal Attachment or Right Association, the parser may prefer one structure – and therefore one syntactic category for the ambiguous word – over another. Sometimes, however, these parsing strategies do not lead to a structural preference for one analysis. For such cases, one solution that has been proposed is that the processor puts off attaching any additional words into the current syntactic tree until further words in the input clarify the category ambiguity. In reading experiments, such a delay should result in faster reading during ambiguous portions of the sentence, since syntactic attachments are not being made at that point, and slower reading when the disambiguating information is encountered.

Such a result was found in an eye-tracking task with sentences such as (10.49) and (10.50), which were compared with sentences (10.51) and (10.52) where the phrase *desert trains* is disambiguated by the singular or plural specification in the determiner (*this* or *these*) (Frazier & Rayner, 1987). Reading times for *desert trains* (and equivalent sequences in other sentences of this type) were longer in this region for the sentences in (10.51) and (10.52), where the syntactic category of the ambiguous words is clear and where syntactic processing can therefore proceed. By contrast, reading times in the region following *desert trains* were longer in (10.49) and (10.50). It is precisely in this region that the ambiguity is resolved.

(10.51) I know that this desert trains young people to be especially tough.

(10.52) I know that these desert trains are especially tough on young people.

Alternative accounts of category ambiguity resolution include approaches that allow multiple analyses to take place (see the discussion of constraint-based approaches in Chapter 11). That is, rather than delaying processing because of category ambiguity, the processor builds different syntactic structures immediately and in parallel, allowing for multiple syntactic analyses of the ambiguous words. Selection from amongst these structures can depend on a number of factors, including the relative frequency with which the different uses of a word are encountered (MacDonald, 1994).

10.8 Cross-linguistic evidence for processing strategies

The examples discussed above have all been from English, chiefly because English is the language of this book, and it is therefore assumed that the English examples will be most widely accessible to readers.

Much of the early research on parsing strategies did in fact focus on English, and assumed that strategies were applied equally regardless of the availability of other information. MacWhinney, Bates and Kliegl (1984), however, ran a study of English, German and Italian that showed that there is interaction between strategies and that speakers will use whatever information they can to understand a sentence. MacWhinney *et al.* asked native speakers of these three languages to carry out a simple task with short sentences in their native language. The task was to identify the agent (the entity that instigates the action shown by the verb) in simple sentences such as those in (10.53)–(10.55). These sentences were especially constructed so that the authors could examine participants' use of cues based on word order, noun–verb agreement (such as the grammatical marking of subject and object through inflections in certain languages) and animacy of the nouns.

(10.53) The eraser the pig chases.

(10.54) Licks the cow the goat.

(10.55) The dog grabs the pencil.

The authors found that native speakers of English relied primarily on word order, native speakers of German on animacy, and to a lesser extent on noun–verb agreement, and native speakers of Italian on noun–verb agreement, and to a lesser extent on animacy. Clearly a key factor in learning a strategy for processing a language is the reliability of the cues employed by that strategy. In English, word order is relatively fixed, and noun-verb agreement is absent apart from in the pronominal system (*he/ him*). Therefore it is not surprising to find native English speakers relying mainly on word order. Studies like this also show how just looking at data from English gives an incomplete view of language processing.

Further interesting work on sentence processing has compared how a particular strategy applies across different languages for very similar types of syntactic ambiguity. Particularly relevant here is the case of relative clause attachment ambiguity. Ambiguity can arise if there is more than one preceding noun that could be modified by the relative clause, as in (10.56). The ambiguity concerns who in fact had had the accident – the colonel or his daughter?

(10.56) The journalist interviewed the daughter of the colonel who had had the accident.

Following the parsing strategy of Late Closure, the relative clause should be attached to the second noun phrase in the object construction, and so will be taken to modify *colonel*. Indeed, this is the preferred interpretation for English native speakers, as shown by a simple task where participants are asked *who had the accident*? Spanish sentence grammar allows the same structure, as shown in (10.57). But for Spanish native speakers the preferred interpretation is that the relative clause modifies the first noun *la hija* (*the daughter*) (Cuetos & Mitchell, 1988).

(10.57) El periodista entravisto a la hija del coronel que tuvo el accidente.

         (lit.: *The journalist interviewed to the daughter of the colonel who had the accident*)

This difference between English and Spanish is reflected also in reading time studies with sentence materials similar to (10.56) and (10.57), but in which some aspect of the interpretation of the relative clause forces its attachment to one noun rather than to the other. That is, relative clauses were constructed with meanings that more obviously modified either the first noun (*daughter*) or the second one (*colonel*). If the relative clause modified the first noun then the English participants experienced a garden path, if it modified the second noun then the Spanish participants experienced a garden path.

Subsequent studies have extended the investigation of this ambiguity type to a range of languages that allow the same sort of structure. It turns out for example that Swedish, Norwegian and Romanian (Ehrlich, Fernandez, Fodor, Stenshoel & Vinereanu, 1999) as well as Arabic (Abdelghany & Fodor, 1999) follow the same pattern as English, with a preference for the relative clause to modify the second noun phrase, while native speakers of French (Mitchell, Cuetos & Zagar, 1990; Zagar, Pynte & Rativeau, 1997), German (Hemforth, Konieczny & Scheepers, 2000a, 2000b), Dutch (Brysbaert & Mitchell, 1996) and Greek (Papadopoulou & Clahsen, 2003) side with Spanish, and prefer to interpret the relative clause as modifying the first noun phrase. In addition, however, it has been found that structures where there are three noun phrases that are candidates for modification by the relative clause, such as (10.58) for English and the translation equivalent (10.59) for Spanish, lead to the same results for both languages, namely a preference for attachment to the most recent noun (*house/casa*).

(10.58)   The lamp near the painting of the house that was damaged in the flood.

(10.59)   La lámpara cerca de la pintura de la casa que fue dañada en la inundación.

To account for these different results for sentences with two vs three possible antecedents in the two languages, it has been suggested that there are two competing parsing strategies, and that the cost associated with one of these differs across languages (Gibson, Pearlmutter, Canseco-Gonzalez & Hickock, 1996). First, there is a Recency Principle similar to Late Closure, and which is found across all languages. This simply states that there is a preference to attach material to a recent point in the preceding structure (or alternatively that there is an increasing processing cost with more distant attachments). The second principle, Predicate Proximity, results in a preference to attach the relative clause to the noun phrase that is closest to the verb in the main clause, or that is otherwise highest in the structure (i.e. to *daughter/hija* as the object of the verb in (10.56) and (10.57), and to *painting/pintura* in (10.58) and (10.59)). The costs associated with violating this principle vary across languages, and this has to be learned through exposure during acquisition. In some languages – such as Spanish – the cost of violating Predicate Proximity is high enough to result in it being preferred over the Recency Principle in the two-antecedent cases like (10.57). However, when the highest antecedent is more distant from the relative clause, as in the three-antecedent case in (10.59), then the cost of violating Recency increases, and is greater than that of violating Predicate Proximity, and so the most recent antecedent is preferred. Additional research on second language learners suggests that – regardless of their first language and of the target language involved – these participants are more likely to make parsing decisions based on Recency. This suggests that Recency is indeed a more fundamental principle.

Summary

We have seen in this chapter a number of basic properties of sentence comprehension:

- it is widely assumed that in order to understand a sentence we need to build a syntactic structure for that sentence, and that we do this incrementally, word by word;
- explicit markers of syntactic structure help this process, reducing ambiguity and increasing the efficiency with which readers and listeners can construct syntactic trees;
- readers process sentences following a set of parsing preferences, which determine how input words are built into the syntactic tree being constructed;
- these parsing strategies include Late Closure, Minimal Attachment and Right Association, all of which are based on structural preferences;
- evidence for these preferences comes from garden path experiences, for which measurable data are provided by studies of eye movements during reading;
- parsing strategies are assumed to apply in all languages, but the details of how they apply reflect differences between the grammars of languages.

Exercises

Exercise 10.1

buffalo buffalo buffalo buffalo buffalo buffalo buffalo is, surprisingly, a well-formed sentence of English. Add explicit markers to make the meaning clear. Note that the word *buffalo* has multiple uses: 1. a type of cattle; 2. a city in New York state; 3. a verb use, meaning to bully.

Exercise 10.2

Draw syntactic tree structures (using the syntactic trees in this chapter to help you if you are unfamiliar with this type of representation) to show the two structures involved for each of the following ambiguous sentences:

1. I saw the astronomer with a telescope.
2. I saw the book that you were reading in the library.
3. Fred realised that Mary left when the party started.

Exercise 10.3

Where does each of the sentences in the pairs 1–4 below become disambiguated? In an experiment, subjects saw each sentence presented a word at a time on a screen, using the Rapid Serial Visual Presentation (RSVP) technique. After the whole sentence had been presented, they had to decide whether it was grammatical. The number after each sentence is the average time (in msec) taken to make that decision. For each pair, why do the times differ in the way that they do? Which parsing strategy – Minimal Attachment or Late Closure – is involved in each case? (You may find it helpful to draw partial tree structures for the sentences.) How would punctuation or other explicit marking of syntax help clarify the sentences?

1a.	Though George kept on reading the story still bothered him.	1545
1b.	Though George kept on reading the story Sue bothered him.	1160
2a.	The teacher told the children the ghost story that she knew would frighten them.	1359
2b.	The teacher told the children the ghost story had frightened that it wasn't true.	3150
3a.	Without her contributions the funds are inadequate.	973
3b.	Without her contributions would be very inadequate.	1985
4a.	Sally was relieved when she found out the answer to the physics problem.	1224
4b.	Sally found out the answer to the physics problem was in the book.	1647

Exercise 10.4
The word *like* has many uses, including as a discourse marker and as a quotative (*and she was like 'let's leave now'*). In its grammatical uses, *like* is far more frequently used as a preposition than as a verb. In a word-by-word self-paced reading study, participants read sentences like 1 and 2 below (they did not see the / marks). What predictions do you make for each sentence for reading times in the four regions marked by /?

1. Jack said that people / like Marty / taking such / good photographs.
2. Jack said that people / like Marty / take such / good photographs.

....

Further reading

For summaries of issues in sentence processing, see Pickering (1999) and Van Gompel and Pickering (2007). The clausal hypothesis research can be found in Fodor and Bever (1965), but see also Marslen-Wilson *et al.* (1978). For a review of studies exploring psycholinguistic support for the Derivational Theory of Complexity, see Fodor *et al.* (1974) and Johnson-Laird (1974). Early discussion of the sausage machine can be found in Frazier and Fodor (1978). Category ambiguity is discussed in Frazier and Rayner (1987), but compare MacDonald (1994).

11 Interpreting sentences

PREVIEW

In this chapter we explore how non-syntactic information is used in sentence interpretation. By the end of the chapter you should understand that:

- plausibility has an impact on the interpretation of sentences;
- there are differences between individual words of the same grammatical type with respect to the kinds of sentence structures they are found in, and this can affect the comprehension of the sentence;
- the prosodic structure of spoken sentences affects the syntactic structure assigned to the sentences;
- a range of accounts for sentence processing have been proposed which differ in how and when different information sources are used to determine the most appropriate analysis.

KEY TERMS

constraints

good-enough processing

lexical preferences

plausibility

presupposition

prosody

reversible sentences

stress shift

11.1 Introduction

Chapter 10 considered sentence comprehension from a syntactic point of view. That is, the focus was on how readers and listeners work out the grammatical structures of the sentences they read or hear, without reference to meaning. It was noted that the explicit marking of grammatical structure through function words and grammatical endings facilitates sentence comprehension. The parsing models introduced in that chapter were presented as models that build syntactic sentence trees, based on the grammatical categories of the input words and on the preferred strategies for building such trees. These strategies are based largely on common-sense notions of keeping syntactic structures simple and minimising memory load. The strategies provide an account for the garden path experience that readers (and listeners) have when processing some sentences. Such sentences have structures that are dispreferred by the operations of the parser.

The current chapter extends this survey of sentence processing by considering what use readers and listeners might make of other, non-syntactic sources of information. We first look at early research advocating the use of meaning in sentence processing before considering the opposing view, i.e. a syntax-first approach. We then consider a number of findings which demonstrate that a range of sources of non-syntactic information have an immediate impact on sentence comprehension. These sources include some of the background knowledge and presuppositions that are assumed of the reader or listener when particular syntactic constructions are used. They also include our knowledge, based on experience, of which sentence structures are typically used with specific words. More specifically for spoken sentence processing, these information sources include the prosodic structure of sentences. Finally, we will consider processing models that allow for the interaction of a number of types of information, providing a constraining influence on the interpretation of sentences.

> **Reversible sentences** are sentences in which the subject and object can be swapped over and the sentence still makes sense. Whether or not a sentence is reversible is dependent at least in part on the semantic relationships between the action denoted by the verb and the participants in that action.

11.2 Meaning and sentence processing

Some of the early psycholinguistic research confirmed the intuitive notion that meaning plays a role in the processing of sentences. One study (Slobin, 1966) compared reading times for reversible sentences (11.1) with those for non-reversible sentences (11.3). Because both chickens and horses can see, both (11.1) and (11.2) are acceptable sentences, though clearly different in meaning. However, since chickens peck and horses typically do not, the reversed version of (11.3), shown in (11.4), is less acceptable, even though it is still a syntactically well-formed sentence.

(11.1)   The chicken saw the horse.

(11.2)   The horse saw the chicken.

(11.3)   The chicken pecked the horse.

(11.4)   The horse pecked the chicken.

The results of sentence–picture matching tasks indicated that passive versions of the reversible sentences, such as (11.5), are more difficult to process than passive versions of the non-reversible sentences (11.6).

(11.5)   The horse was seen by the chicken.

(11.6)   The horse was pecked by the chicken.

It is argued that this is because for the passive versions of reversible sentences there is a plausible active sentence which has the same superficial sequence of the words *horse … see … chicken*, but a different meaning (i.e. for (11.5) there is (11.2)). The corresponding sentence for the non-reversible sentence, i.e. (11.4) for (11.6), is implausible. The result suggests that some aspects of grammar (i.e. the elements that mark the sentence as a passive sentence) are not highly constraining of the analysis.

In other experiments, overall reading times for a range of sentences were recorded, as a measure of how easy they are to process. Shorter overall reading times were found for sentences such as (11.7) in comparison with (11.8), despite the fact that the syntactic analyses would be identical.

(11.7)   They picnicked under the trees.

(11.8)   They picnicked under the teeth.

It was argued that semantic factors, i.e. plausibility, were influencing the ease of processing for sentences that were syntactically indistinguishable.

Steedman & Johnson-Laird (1978) also used sentence reading time to investigate the effect of plausibility, in their case in the processing of double-object sentences such as (11.9) and (11.10). Participants in this study read a sentence, pressed a button to indicate that they had understood it, and then answered a question that gauged what they had taken it to mean. Both sentences should be interpreted as having *the girl* as the recipient, since when there are two objects after a verb in English (and neither is introduced by a preposition, contrast *to the boy*), then the first is the indirect object or recipient. The sentences differ in that the indirect object interpretation of *the girl* in (11.10) is really the only plausible interpretation, since coats would not usually be expected to be recipients. In comparison, the objects in (11.9) are not constrained by plausibility, since either could be a recipient. The researchers found that the sentence in (11.10) took less time to understand.

(11.9)   The man took the girl the boy.

(11.10)   The man took the girl the coat.

However, both of the experimental paradigms described above (sentence–picture matching time and overall reading time) could be argued to tap into processes that occur quite late during the interpretation of a sentence. That is, they are offline measures, contrasting with the more direct online measures obtained from the eye-movement studies discussed in Chapter 10.

11.3 Syntax first

Recall that the parsing strategies approach supported by the studies presented in Chapter 10 is fundamentally syntax-driven. A strong claim made
by some proponents of this approach is that syntax (sentence constituent
structure) is logically independent of semantics (meaning, including sentence meaning). This independence has been demonstrated by linguists
using sentences such as those in (11.11) (made famous by the linguist
Noam Chomsky) and (11.12).

(11.11)   Colorless green ideas sleep furiously.

(11.12)   Accidents buy beans around the hive.

The significance of such sentences is that they are syntactically well-
formed, despite being semantically anomalous (Chomsky, 1957). That is,
native speakers generally agree that these are well-formed sentences, even
though they find it difficult to interpret their meaning. In fact, rather
than dismiss such sentences out of hand, native speakers will often try to
construct some – often poetic – interpretation.

If linguists claim that syntactic sentence structure is independent of
meaning, then it is not surprising that psycholinguists would look for
evidence that syntactic structure is independent of meaning during
sentence processing. Note that this is not a claim that other
non-syntactic sources of information are not important in processing.
Rather, it is a claim for the separation of syntactic from other information, at some stage during sentence processing. For instance, a major
proposal from the parsing strategies approach has been that syntactic
considerations determine the initial and preferred structural analysis
of a sentence, which is then compared with a semantic interpretation
generated by a separate thematic processor. If the semantic interpretation is incompatible with the initial syntactic analysis, then a revision
is necessary.

Such a position leads to claims about behavioural patterns in sentence
comprehension tasks, for example in studies of eye movements during
reading. Initial syntactic analysis should proceed without reference to the
meaning or plausibility of a sentence. Any influence on reading times in
what is known as the first-pass analysis, such as slowing down of reading
when a garden path is encountered, should instead be attributable to
syntactic factors. Non-syntactic factors should only affect later, second-
pass analysis, including regressions, i.e. the re-reading that is required for
the reader to come up with a revised syntactic analysis. Note though that
some of the regressions will be syntactically determined, as a consequence
of encountering words that have a syntactic description that does not fit
the initially preferred analysis.

This separation of syntactic and other information during processing
would clearly receive compelling support if the garden path experiences
discussed in Chapter 10 occurred irrespective of the meaningfulness of a
sentence. One set of studies (Ferreira & Clifton, 1986) took as its starting

point eye-movement patterns for participants reading sentences containing reduced relative clauses, such as (11.13).

(11.13)   The defendant examined by the lawyer turned out to be unreliable.

(11.14)   The defendant that was examined by the lawyer turned out to be unreliable.

In accordance with the Minimal Attachment strategy, the parsing preference for (11.13) is that the verb *examined* is taken to be a past tense verb, rather than the past participle form that would be part of the reduced relative. However, this preferred analysis turns out to be the wrong one in (11.13), as becomes clear when readers encounter the phrase beginning with *by*. This should result in a garden path experience, and a re-analysis of the earlier part of the sentence. Note that this preference is blocked in (11.14) by the explicit structural marking of the relative clause, i.e. the presence of *that was* rules out this past tense verb interpretation.

> The past tense or main-verb analysis of *examined* would be satisfied if the sentence in (11.13) continued along the lines of *The defendant examined the document*. An informal test of a preference along these lines would be to give participants the fragment *The defendant examined ...* and ask them to complete it.

The test, then, of a syntax-first approach is whether the garden path experience is found regardless of the plausibility of the past tense interpretation of verbs like *examined*. This plausibility was manipulated by changing the preceding noun. In sentence (11.13) it is entirely plausible that a *defendant* might examine something (e.g. a document), and so the past tense verb reading of (11.13) is initially both syntactically and semantically acceptable. However, an inanimate object such as *evidence* does not examine other things, and so the past tense interpretation of the sentence in (11.15) should be implausible.

(11.15)   The evidence examined by the lawyer turned out to be unreliable.

(11.16)   The evidence that was examined by the lawyer turned out to be unreliable.

Note that sentence (11.15) is syntactically identical to (11.13), so on syntactic grounds, garden-pathing should still be expected. What was found in the reading experiment was the same pattern of eye movements for (11.15) and (11.13), despite the implausibility of *evidence* examining something else. In addition, the same difference in reading times was found between (11.15) and the form with the unreduced relative in (11.16) as was found between (11.13) and (11.14). The interpretation of this set of results was that the syntactic preference for *examined* as a past tense verb persists, despite the semantic implausibility of that preference in (11.15).

To take another example, in both sentences (11.17) and (11.18) we again have reduced relative structures (reduced from ... *who was sent the flowers* ...). (11.17) is however less plausible than sentence (11.18), because florists tend to send flowers, but performers are likely to be sent flowers. Yet readers experience garden paths equally on both. On the other hand, (11.19) is rather implausible, but does not show garden path effects. The most coherent explanation of this set of results, it is argued, is that the purely syntactic principle of Minimal Attachment is being followed in each case, resulting in the past tense interpretation of *sent* in each sentence, regardless of plausibility (Rayner, Carlson & Frazier, 1983).

(11.17)   The florist sent the flowers was pleased.

(11.18)   The performer sent the flowers was pleased.

(11.19)   The performer sent the flowers and was pleased with herself.

These are just two examples of a range of studies that have maintained both the independence and the primacy of syntactic analysis of sentences. That is, the theoretical perspective of the researchers is that syntactic analysis can proceed without reference to other sources of information and that this syntactic analysis is the driving force behind sentence processing.

11.4 Presuppositions, plausibility and parsing

Recall sentence (11.20), which was introduced in Chapter 10 as a famous example of a garden path sentence (Bever, 1970).

(11.20)   The horse raced past the barn fell.

In the original research using sentences such as this, it was claimed that a structural preference results in the interpretion of the verb *raced* as a past tense form, rather than as a past participle in a reduced relative construction. This analysis turns out to be wrong when the final word (*fell*) is encountered; the reader is garden pathed and has to revise their analysis. No such effect would be predicted in (11.21), since the final word confirms that the past tense interpretation is the correct one.

(11.21)   The horse raced past the barn quickly.

In the preceding section we saw several examples of sentences from studies claiming syntax-driven processing which also involve this ambiguity between past tense verbs and reduced relatives. Critics of the syntax-first approach to sentence processing maintain that there are additional issues to be considered with respect to many such sentences. For instance, Crain and Steedman (1985) claim that reduced relative clause constructions such as that in (11.20) carry some assumptions or presuppositions that are not found in the past tense verb interpretation. Moreover, these presuppositions make the relative clause interpretation less plausible, in the absence of further contextualising information. These presuppositions arise primarily because the relative clause in (11.20) is a restrictive relative, as shown by the absence of commas (see sidebar). By way of contrast, (11.22) is not a restrictive relative.

(11.22)   The horse, (which was) raced past the barn, fell.

Under their Referential Hypothesis, Crain and Steedman argue that for the structure in (11.20) to be motivated we have to assume that there is a set of possible horses, and that one of these horses is being identified by

Restrictive relative clauses are relative clauses that define which of a set of possible objects, people, etc. is being referred to by the noun phrase that the relative clause modifies. Compare *Men who can multi-task are good at this* (restrictive, refers to a particular subset of men who can multi-task) and *Women, who can multi-task, are good at this* (**non-restrictive**, i.e. refers to all women). In English, non-restrictive relatives are normally indicated by commas (and by corresponding differences in the prosody of the spoken forms). In some varieties of English, the use of *that* as the relativiser is only possible with restrictive relatives (as in *Men that can multi-task ...*)

the use of the restrictive relative. In contrast, in (11.21) and (11.22) no other horses are presupposed. These sentences simply introduce one definite horse. It is claimed that it is this difference between (11.20) on the one hand and (11.21) and (11.22) on the other that explains the relative processing difficulties for (11.20), and not a garden path resulting from syntactic preferences.

If this alternative explanation is correct, then one way in which it might have its effect in terms of a processing account is as follows. When *The horse raced* has been read in (11.20) or (11.21), a syntactic ambiguity is detected which involves the interpretation of *raced* as either a past tense verb or a past participle. Because more than one syntactic analysis is available, a call is made for assistance from other information sources, including mechanisms that assess the plausibility of a sentence. The past tense verb reading is more straightforward, because the alternative, i.e. the restrictive relative reading, carries the more complex presupposition as pointed out above. The past tense verb reading is therefore the preferred interpretation. So the processing difficulty with (11.20) is argued to result from a plausibility constraint, rather than from a syntactic one.

A clear difference between this account and the parsing strategy approach outlined in Chapter 10 is the relationship between syntactic and non-syntactic information sources. In the parsing strategy account, the syntactic analysis has to have made a misanalysis (i.e. it has to be garden-pathed) before other information is used. The account sketched above makes an earlier appeal to non-syntactic information, at the point where a structural ambiguity is detected.

There are other garden path effects that might be explained in a similar way to the example above. Take for instance the sentence in (11.23). This contains a subordinate clause (*that he was having trouble with*). This particular subordinate clause is a relative clause, modifying *the wife* (i.e. it tells us which wife; this would be made more obvious if *who* were used instead of *that*).

> (11.23) The psychologist told the wife that he was having trouble with to leave her husband.

Research results show that this sentence is much harder to process than the sentence in (11.24) where the string of words after *wife* also forms a subordinate clause, but this time an object clause, i.e. a clause which is the object of *tell*. It is the X in *The psychologist told the wife X*, and it could answer the question 'What did the psychiatrist tell the wife?' Note that in this case *that* cannot be replaced by *who*.

> (11.24) The psychologist told the wife that he was having trouble with her husband.

In syntactic terms, it is argued that the Minimal Attachment strategy leads readers to prefer to interpret the string *that he was having trouble with …* as part of an object clause, and that this is why (11.23) is more difficult to process than (11.24). However, the relative clause in (11.23), like that in (11.20), is a <u>restrictive</u> relative clause, and so the sentence presupposes that there is more than one wife involved. The competing

> **Subordinate clauses** have a number of functions. Among these, they can be the subject of a verb (*That his car had broken down was obvious*), the object of a verb (*We knew that his car had broken down*), or a modifier of a noun (a relative clause as in *The car which/that had broken down was troublesome*). Subordinate clauses are frequently but not always introduced by a complementiser (*that* and *which* in the examples above).

Context sentences or paragraphs are sometimes used to test the strength of a preference for a particular interpretation of a sentence. The contexts in (11.25) and (11.26) are designed to bias the interpretation of the string *The psychiatrist told the wife that he was having trouble with ...*

explanation is therefore that it is the presence of this presupposition that makes interpretation of the sentence more complex, and not the mistaken application of a parsing strategy.

This alternative explanation is backed up by further tests by Crain and Steedman (1985) in which they altered the presuppositions associated with a sentence by preceding it with different kinds of context. These could either bias the reader towards a relative clause interpretation of *that he was having trouble with*, as would be the case with (11.25), or towards an object clause interpretation (11.26).

(11.25)   [relative clause bias]
          A psychologist was counselling two married couples. One of the couples was fighting with him, but the other one was nice to him.

(11.26)   [object clause bias]
          A psychologist was counselling a married couple. One member of the pair was fighting with him, but the other one was nice to him.

In different conditions of the experiment, each of these contexts was combined with each of the sentences in (11.23) and (11.24). Participants had to decide whether (11.23) and (11.24) were grammatical or not. Overall, there were no more 'ungrammatical' responses to relative clause structures (11.23) than there were to object clause structures (11.24). Importantly, though, the greatest number of 'ungrammatical' responses for each type resulted from a mismatch between the context and the test sentence (i.e. when (11.23) followed (11.26) or (11.24) followed (11.25)).

These findings contradict the reading studies outlined earlier, which concluded that syntactic analysis is not directly affected by semantic factors such as plausibility. Is the difference between these two groups of findings due to differences in the types of sentence used, or perhaps to differences between offline and online tasks? After all, grammaticality judgements are made some time after the sentence has been read. This means that they could be influenced by a range of other factors that may have a late effect on interpretation. These results would therefore be compatible with the notion that an initial syntactic analysis is subsequently checked by the output of a thematic, or meaning-based, processor.

The next section presents evidence of more immediate effects on syntactic processing, as the outcome of biases that result from the specific words used in structurally ambiguous sentences.

11.5 Lexical preferences

Under a syntax-first approach, when each word in a sentence is encountered it is built into the sentence tree as a member of a particular syntactic category (verb, noun, and so on), just as long as the syntactic category membership of a word is known (see Chapter 10). Any preferences for particular syntactic structures are a result of parsing operations and not of any differences in the structures associated with individual words. However, it has been claimed that not all words are equal in this respect.

For example, some verbs occur more typically in certain constructions than in others. As another example, the type of noun that is the subject of a verb can sometimes affect the interpretation of that verb. The following material gives examples of each of these.

Verb preferences

Recall that in Chapter 10 we looked at sentences like those repeated in (11.27) and (11.28). A partial syntactic tree is also given for each sentence. These sentences contain verbs (whose position is shown by the circles) that can be used in either of the two structures shown. In (11.27) the verb is followed by a noun phrase object, which is the preferred structure according to the Minimal Attachment strategy. In the more complex structure in (11.28), the verb is followed by a subordinate clause in object position. Note the extra S node between the NP *the schedule* and the VP node. This is a non-minimal attachment of the NP.

(11.27)   Karen knew the schedule by heart.

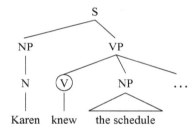

(11.28)   Karen knew the schedule was wrong.

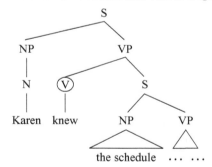

In one study, Holmes (1987) pre-tested a list of verbs to see which kind of object each verb was more likely to occur with. Two sets of verbs were then selected. In one set the verbs were more likely to be used with a noun phrase object (including verbs such as *hear, read, see, answer*). In the other, the preference was for a clause as the object (*claim, know, doubt, believe,* etc.). Pairs of sentences were made for each verb. All sentences were used in the experiment with a complement clause structure (see (11.28)), i.e. the structure that is dispreferred by Minimal Attachment. The members of each pair differed according to whether they included the complementiser *that*. Examples are given in (11.29)–(11.32).

> To provide better control over the variables used in an experiment, researchers run pre-tests. In the example here, a continuation task determined the type of syntactic structure most likely to occur with each of a set of verbs, allowing the researcher to compare verbs with NP-object and clause-object preferences.
>
> An increasingly viable alternative to pre-testing is the use of data from large language corpora, provided they have been set up to provide the right kind of information, such as the sentence structures in which a verb is used.

> In **self-paced reading** tasks, sentences are presented in chunks (e.g. word by word) on a computer screen, with the participant controlling the presentation of the next chunk by pressing a response button. The time taken to read each chunk (as registered by the button press) gives a measure of comprehension difficulty at that point in the sentence.

(11.29)   The reporter saw that her friend was not succeeding.

(11.30)   The reporter saw her friend was not succeeding.

(11.31)   The candidate doubted that his sincerity would be appreciated.

(11.32)   The candidate doubted his sincerity would be appreciated.

The task used was self-paced word-by-word reading. The crucial measure is the reading time for words in the position of *was* in (11.30) or *would* in (11.32). Before this point these sentences are perfectly compatible with the structure preferred by Minimal Attachment, but *was* and *would* make it clear that the sentence in fact involves a clause as the object of the verb (e.g. the reporter in (11.30) did not literally see her friend, but saw – i.e. realised – that her friend was not succeeding). Therefore these words are the point at which a garden path should be experienced. Note that in (11.29) and (11.31) the structure with a clause as its object becomes obvious earlier, because of the inclusion of the complementiser *that*, and so no garden path should be experienced. These sentences in (11.29) and (11.31) provide a baseline, against which (11.30) and (11.32) can be compared, to see if there is any evidence for a garden path.

The results showed that there was indeed a strongly experienced garden path. Importantly, though, this was found only for the verbs for which the pre-test had shown a bias towards a noun phrase object construction, i.e. for sentences like (11.30). When participants read sentences containing verbs with a clause object preference, such as (11.32), there was no garden path, i.e. there was no difference in reading times for *would* in this sentence compared with (11.31). This indicates that the early syntactic analysis of sentences does not simply build structures using the syntactic categories of the input words, but actually takes into account the structural preferences associated with individual lexical items.

Kennison (2002) used both self-paced phrase-by-phrase reading and an eye-movement tracking study to measure participants' processing of sentences with two sets of transitivity-ambiguous verbs that showed a preference towards either transitive usage (e.g. *read*, as in (11.33)) or intransitive usage (e.g. *perform*, as in (11.34)). The NP immediately following the verb was either an argument of the verb, as in these examples, or an adverbial adjunct, which was *every week* for the counterparts to these examples. Kennison found that after transitive-bias verbs (*read*) argument NPs (*every play*) were read faster than adjunct NPs (*every week*), but that after intransitive-bias verbs (*perform*) argument NPs were read more slowly than adjunct NPs.

> **Transitivity ambiguity**
> Many verbs of English show a structural ambiguity which relates to whether or not they have an object. So *walk* can be used intransitively, without an object, as in *She walks every day*, or transitively, with an object, as in *She walks her dog every day*. In some intransitive verb uses there is an understood object that is not made explicit, as in *She is reading*.

(11.33)   Everyone knew that Meredith read every play despite her busy schedule.

(11.34)   Everyone knew that Meredith performed every play despite her busy schedule.

Noun preferences

Nouns also enter into different structures, depending on the semantic properties of the noun. For example, some nouns denote animate entities (people, animals, etc.) that are capable of performing certain conscious and deliberate actions, while others denote inanimate entities (physical objects, etc.) that would not be expected to perform such actions. In addition, English has many verbs that exhibit transitivity ambiguity. When such verbs are used with animate entities as their subjects, then they can be used comfortably in both intransitive (11.35) and transitive (11.36) structures.

(11.35)   Even before the police stopped the driver was getting nervous.

(11.36)   Even before the police stopped the driver he was getting nervous.

When the subject of such verbs is inanimate, the intransitive reading is preferred, as in (11.37), with the transitive reading in (11.38) being less plausible.

(11.37)   Even before the truck stopped the driver was getting nervous.

(11.38)   Even before the truck stopped the driver he was getting nervous.

The parsing strategy of Late Closure predicts that verbs which can be either transitive or intransitive will always be interpreted as transitive if they are followed by a NP, because that following NP will be attached into the current syntactic tree as the verb's object. This means that garden-pathing should be found at the position of *was* in both (11.35) and (11.37), because this word indicates that *the driver* is not the direct object of *stopped*, but is instead the subject of a new clause.

In another self-paced reading task, however, Stowe (1989) found garden-pathing for sentences in which the subject of the first verb was animate, such as (11.35), but not for sentences with inanimate subjects, such as (11.37). This indicates that semantic properties of the subject noun in (11.35) affected the syntactic interpretation of the verb in the first clause, i.e. trucks are not usually expected to stop something else, but the police are. Again, this is evidence that the initial interpretation of sentences takes into account the structural preferences associated with lexical items, in this case the combination of the animacy of the subject noun and the transitivity or otherwise of the verb.

> **Punctuation**
> As suggested in Chapter 10, the sentences in (11.35) and (11.36), and many other sentences used in reading studies, would be easier to process if they were punctuated, e.g. by a comma after *stopped* in (11.35).

Thematic roles

Earlier in the chapter we encountered sentences that were used to demonstrate that the plausibility of a sentence did not have an effect on parsing preferences. The examples used the verb form *examined* in combination with different preceding nouns, as in the fragments repeated here in (11.39) and (11.40).

(11.39)   The defendant examined ...

(11.40)   The evidence examined ...

The eye movement data reported for these materials was taken to indicate that the past tense verb interpretation of *examined* was preferred (following syntactic principles) in both cases, regardless of plausibility (Ferreira & Clifton, 1986).

Thematic roles
(see also Chapter 2).
Notions such as
AGENT and THEME
relate to the part
played by an
entity in the
action of a verb,
i.e. they relate
more to meaning
than to syntactic
structure. For
example, the role
of INSTRUMENT
(thing used to
carry out some
action) is played
by *the hammer* in
each of the
following, but the
syntactic status of
the hammer clearly
differs: *John hit the
nail with the
hammer; John used
the hammer to hit
the nail; The
hammer hit the nail.*

In a further examination of such materials, Trueswell *et al.* (1994) argued that the reason no plausibility effect was found using these materials was that the plausibility difference was not strong enough. In effect, they claimed that both defendants and evidence are more likely to be examined than to do the examining. That is, they are more likely to be understood in the thematic role of THEME (or object) of the verb than in the role of AGENT (subject, in this case). To test this claim, Trueswell *et al.* carried out further experiments where the contrast between the nouns was stronger. For example, the expected role of *archaeologist* in (11.41) is much more clearly that of the AGENT of *examined* than could be argued for *defendant* in (11.39).

(11.41)   The archaeologist examined …

(11.42)   The fossil examined …

When reading patterns for sentences beginning with the fragments in (11.41) and (11.42) were compared, a clear difference was found in the likelihood of garden-pathing, reflecting this difference in the plausibility of the noun being the AGENT of the verb. The lack of such an effect in the original experiment with the materials in (11.39) and (11.40) could therefore be a result of an insufficiently distinct difference in plausibility.

The examples just discussed have shown that the same constituent, syntactically defined, can play a different role in a sentence. Another case that has been studied involves prepositional phrases (PPs). The PP (*for Chris*) in (11.43) can modify either the verb (*bought*) or the noun (*book*). Following the parsing strategy of Minimal Attachment, the preferred analysis is that the PP modifies the verb. This claim has been supported in many reading studies.

(11.43)   Pat bought the book for Chris.

However, even when PPs are in the same syntactic relationship to the rest of the sentence, they can differ in their thematic roles. This is illustrated in the examples in (11.44) and (11.45), taken from Taraban and McClelland (1988). Note that different words appear in the PP *with the …* but in both of these sentences the PP tells us something about the cleaning operation. Nevertheless, even though they are in the same structural relationship to the rest of the sentence, the roles played by the PPs in the action denoted by *cleaned* are different. *Broom* is an INSTRUMENT (a thing used to carry out the action of the verb), while *manager* is some sort of ACCOMPANIMENT.

(11.44)   The janitor cleaned the cupboard with the broom because of many complaints.

(11.45)   The janitor cleaned the cupboard with the manager because of many complaints.

(11.46)   The janitor cleaned the cupboard with the smell because of many complaints.

The sentence in (11.46) contrasts with those in (11.44) and (11.45), because the relationship of the PP to the rest of the sentence is different. The PP now tells us about the cupboard, rather than about the cleaning. (11.44) and (11.45) are preferred by Minimal Attachment, while (11.46) is dispreferred.

A self-paced reading study showed that (11.44) was easier than both (11.45) and (11.46), and that (11.45) and (11.46) did not differ. This shows that it is not just a syntactic preference that determines the interpretation of the PP, but also the thematic role. In other words, a PP modifying the verb in this sentence is expected to be in the role of INSTRUMENT rather than ACCOMPANIMENT. Other sentences in this experiment also demonstrated that the non-minimal (i.e. noun-modifying) attachment of PPs was in some cases the preferred attachment, depending on the words used in the sentence (especially the verb and the object of the verb), and that the strength of this preference also depended on the role of the PP in the meaning structure of the sentence.

As another example of how thematic role preferences can affect interpretation, consider the example in (11.47). This comes from an announcement sent out by email to staff at the author's university, warning them about impending roadworks outside the university buildings:

(11.47)   [Contractors] will be removing sections of the road and replacing the asphalt with heavy machinery.

The idea of a road surface made out of heavy machinery rather than the more conventional asphalt caused some amusement. The effect is a result of the interpretation of the PP *with ...* as showing what the replacement will be rather than showing (as intended) the INSTRUMENT of the verb action.

The examples discussed in this section show that the processing of sentences does not depend on syntactic structure alone, but that the roles that parts of a sentence play in the meaning of that sentence are important, as too are the types of structure that individual words typically occur in.

11.6 Prosody and parsing

Recall that proponents of the syntax-first approach to parsing claimed autonomous syntactic processing, but note also that they based their studies almost exclusively on reading tasks, i.e. on written sentence processing. We saw in earlier chapters that speech carries cues to syntactic structure, as well as to other types of sentence and utterance organisation, such as informational structure and focus. These are prosodic cues, which include intonation patterns as well as the stress and rhythm patterns of words, phrases and sentences. Our concern in this section is with how such cues might be used in the comprehension of sentences.

There are many well-attested effects of prosodic structure on processing, especially in word recognition, as shown also in slips-of-the-ear (see Chapter 8). But how might prosody help the parser?

Late Closure predicts that the NP following a verb like *mending* in (11.48) will be interpreted as the object of that verb. Using punctuation, in the form of a comma after the verb, signals the Early Closure interpretation, with the following NP then being in a new clause, as in (11.49). One way in

So-called comma intonation is the pattern of falling-then-rising intonation that is typically found, for instance, between a subordinate clause and a following main clause, e.g. where the comma has been placed in (11.48) or (11.49). The two parts of the intonation pattern are sometimes analysed as having two functions – the falling part indicates the end of the first clause, and the rising part indicates that there is more to come.

which prosody might influence structural analysis is therefore by providing 'comma intonation' (i.e. over *mending the* in (11.49)).

(11.48) When Mary was mending the sock, it fell off her lap.

(11.49) When Mary was mending, the sock fell off her lap.

Is there similar prosodic marking for Minimal Attachment? A comma is less likely to distinguish the pairs in (11.50) and (11.51) than those in (11.48) and (11.49), but what about prosody?

(11.50) The lawyer heard the tape and gave his opinion.

(11.51) The lawyer heard the tape was unreliable.

The 'Syntax and Speech' studies introduced in Chapter 2 considered the acoustic speech properties of a range of ambiguities, including these types, and showed that there are reliable contrasts between different versions of the ambiguity, in pausing, rhythm, amplitude and pitch contours.

The question then is whether listeners can use such information during their processing of sentences, and if so, when and how they use it. Simple continuation experiments, in which participants listen to spoken fragments of sentences and have to choose completions, have confirmed that prosodic information is used (Schafer, Speer, Warren & White, 2000; Speer *et al.*, 2011). But does prosodic information determine the initial analysis of a sentence, or is it only used in some later post-perceptual analysis? To address this, studies have used a variety of online tasks.

Marslen-Wilson *et al.* (1992) ran a cross-modal naming experiment using a set of Minimal Attachment sentences previously extensively studied in reading experiments (Frazier & Rayner, 1982; Holmes, Kennedy & Murray, 1987; Rayner & Frazier, 1987). In the cross-modal naming experiment, a spoken utterance fragment is followed by a visual probe word, and the participants' task is to read aloud the visual probe. If the probe word is related to the utterance fragment (e.g. provides a good continuation of that fragment), then participants are able to initiate their naming response more rapidly. The experiment tested whether prosodic cues can resolve ambiguity in spoken versions of minimal attachment sentences such as (11.53), just as the complementiser (*that*) resolves it in (11.52).

(11.52) The workers considered that the last offer from the management | was a real insult.

(11.53) The workers considered the last offer from the management | was a real insult.

(11.54) The workers considered the last offer from the management | of the factory.

Spoken sentence fragments were presented up to the point marked by | and followed immediately by the presentation of the visual probe word. For these examples this was the word *was*. Note that the sentence fragments up to the | in (11.53) and (11.54) contain identical word strings.

Their spoken forms in the experiment differed, however, because (11.53) was a recording from a non-minimal attachment version of the sentence, while (11.54) was from a minimal attachment version.

Marslen-Wilson *et al.* found that naming times after the minimal attachment fragment (11.54) were significantly slower than after the non-minimal attachment fragment in (11.53), even though the fragments contained identical word strings. Since the only difference between the two sentence fragments is in how they were pronounced, i.e. in their prosody, this result indicates that prosodic information is used online to resolve potential temporary ambiguities. In addition, comparison of response times for the two non-minimal attachment versions (i.e. (11.52) and (11.53)) showed that it made no difference whether or not a complementiser was present. This shows that prosodic information is just as effective in online parsing as explicit syntactic marking.

Similar results were found in an experiment using utterances involving the Late Closure strategy (Warren, Grabe & Nolan, 1995). Warren *et al.* used sentence fragments like (11.55), followed by a visually presented continuation word for naming (e.g. *arise*) that was only compatible with the early closure interpretation of the fragment (i.e. closure after *Hong Kong*, rather than after *problems*). When the spoken version of the utterance was taken from a late closure reading, naming times were significantly slower.

(11.55)   Whenever parliament discusses Hong Kong problems …

By manipulating the recordings that were used, Warren *et al.* also showed that participants were sensitive to the presence or absence of phonological processes like stress shift. Stress shift is a phenomenon in English (and in some other languages) that prevents two stressed syllables from being too close together (or clashing). For instance, the main stress that is on the second element of *Hong 'Kong* would be expected to shift to the first element when the word *problems* is in the same prosodic constituent, giving *'Hong Kong 'problems*. It is considerably more likely that *problems* will be in the same constituent as *Hong Kong* in the late closure reading.

Structuring utterances through the placement of prosodic breaks can have a profound influence on the preferred analysis. For example, Pynte and Prieur (1996) ran a word monitoring task using sentences such as (11.56) and (11.57). (The experiment was conducted in French, but the structures are equivalent.) The target word was the final word in each sentence, i.e. the noun in a PP which is in a structurally ambiguous relationship to the preceding material, since it could modify either the verb or the object noun. (Note that participants did not know that the target word was going to be the last one in the utterance, and indeed in filler trials in the experiment the target word appeared in many different positions, and possibly not at all.) Word monitoring times in Pynte and Prieur's experiment showed that a prosodic break after the verb made the attachment of the PP to the noun easier to process. This is because the break forces the linking of the PP to the noun *guards* rather than to the verb *informed* by putting it in the same prosodic phrase as *guards*, and separating it from *informed*.

> Filler trials are often used in experiments to disguise the regularities of the test trials, so that participants are not using some irrelevant cue for their responses.

(11.56)   The spies informed the guards of the conspiracy.

(11.57)   The spies informed the guards of the palace.

The effects of prosody also depended on the preferred argument structure of the verb. A verb like *inform* seems to expect a prepositional phrase as part of the sentence (i.e. we normally inform someone of or about something), but a verb like *choose* does not. So a prosodic break after *informed* made a major contribution to the interpretation of the sentence in (11.57), but a prosodic break after *chose* in (11.58) played a less significant role, as the preference was already to interpret the PP as a modifier of the object noun (which works for (11.58) but not for (11.59)).

(11.58)   The student chose the apartment with a balcony.

(11.59)   The student chose the apartment with care.

Other research shows that listeners are sensitive to the use of prosody and intonation to mark focus, and that focus can influence structural attachments (Schafer, Carter, Clifton & Frazier, 1996). Recall the relative clause (RC) attachment ambiguities discussed in Chapter 10. These are NP1-of-NP2-RC structures, where the RC can modify either NP1 or NP2 – see the underlined portion of (11.60). The preference shown in reading time studies with English materials is for the RC to modify the second noun phrase (so the mechanic was repairing the plane). Schafer *et al.* showed that this preference can be altered in spoken versions of these sentences by stress placement. That is, the relative clause is most likely to be taken to modify whichever of the NPs (*the propeller* or *the plane*) is in focus, as marked by stress on that NP.

(11.60)   The sun sparkled on the propeller of the plane that the mechanic was repairing.

These findings indicate that the input to the sentence processing system can be enriched by the prosodic features of spoken utterances, and that these features interact with structural and lexical preferences in interesting but complex ways. Interestingly, further research has indicated that prosodic structure may play a role in sentence processing even when participants are reading silently. That is, there is implicit prosody that we 'hear in our heads' when reading, and which can help structure the input (Fodor, 2002).

11.7 Constraint-based accounts

The preceding sections have introduced a range of factors that influence the interpretation of sentences. Many of the experimental results presented in those sections indicate developments beyond the syntax-first approach introduced in Chapter 10. We can think of the syntax-first approach as an example of a restricted account of sentence processing, in which only certain types of information are used in the initial analysis of sentences, even when other sources of information would potentially be useful. These restricted accounts usually assume that sentence comprehension involves serial processing, in two senses of this term. The first sense is that one source of information is processed before others, e.g. syntactic information before semantic. The second sense is that one sentence structure is considered at a time, meaning that a new revised analysis of the input is required if the first analysis fails.

Unrestricted accounts of processing, by contrast, claim that many or all types of information can be used during processing, including at the earliest stages. Such accounts often also allow multiple sentence interpretations to be considered in parallel, with the different possibilities ranked or weighted according to how well they fit the evidence from the multiple information sources. They are also usually interactive, in that the different information sources are involved in an interplay that moves the processor towards a coherent interpretation. Different versions of this type of account differ in their details, for instance in the nature and frequency of the interaction of information sources.

Weak interactive accounts include those that maintain that the interaction between syntactic and other sources occurs only when the syntactic analysis requires it. This can be seen as an extension of the syntax-first approach, in that the syntactic parser usually remains the central driving force in sentence interpretation. These accounts differ from the syntax-first approach, though, because instead of blindly pursuing an analysis based on default parsing strategies, it is assumed that the processor will cast around for information from non-syntactic sources whenever it encounters a structural ambiguity, such as whether an ambiguous verb is being used transitively or intransitively, or whether a PP is modifying a verb or a noun.

In addition there are strong interactive accounts, where the non-syntactic sources play a more determining role in sentence analysis, and are not subservient to a central syntactic processor. These include constraint-based approaches (Boland, Tanenhaus & Garnsey, 1990; MacDonald, 1994; Taraban & McClelland, 1988; Trueswell *et al.*, 1994). These accounts claim that each of the various types of information available to a reader or listener is used to determine the analysis of a sentence. Frequently, but not always, constraint-based accounts assume a parallel processing approach, with multiple alternative analyses being assessed. These alternatives may be in competition with one another, in which case the processing difficulty associated with a particular sentence will depend on the strength of the competition between this and alternative analyses. This is reflected in 'digging-in' effects. Commitment to one particular interpretation results in inhibition of competing interpretations. In the absence of correcting information, the competing interpretations become increasingly inhibited, resulting in a more severe garden path experience. In example (11.61), the initial preference to see *the town* as the object of *invaded* has to be undone (i.e. results in garden path effects) when *was* is encountered. In (11.62), the text that is read after *town* does not contradict the late closure of the first clause, and the garden path effect on encountering *was* is even stronger (Ferreira & Henderson, 1991).

(11.61)   After the Martians invaded the town was evacuated.

(11.62)   After the Martians invaded the town that the city bordered was evacuated.

Individual investigations of constraint-based sentence processing have tended to focus on specific types of constraint, adding detail to the overall picture of what drives sentence interpretation. Some of these studies have, as in some of the examples referred to earlier, taken as their starting point published materials claimed to exhibit garden-pathing, and have attempted to determine whether there are non-syntactic properties of the sentences that might cause or allow the garden path to occur.

Further factors that have been shown to influence sentence processing include fictional contexts that provide a motivation for a sentence that might otherwise be anomalous. For instance, when participants read the sentence in (11.63), their knowledge of the world will generally tell them that it contains an anomaly, as cats do not pick up chainsaws. In the fictional world of Tom and Jerry cartoons, however, this sentence is not odd.

(11.63)   The cat picked up the chainsaw.

> The **N400** (i.e. negative 400) effect is well attested in ERP studies. It is a negative-going deflection in electrical activity which is strongest at around 400 msec after the beginning of a critical stimulus

An experiment presented sentences like (11.63) following neutral or fictional contexts (Filik & Leuthold, 2008). The experiment measured event-related brain potentials (ERPs) as a measure of brain activity while participants performed a reading task. An index of semantic processing, the N400 effect (see sidebar), showed a significant reduction in processing load when sentences like (11.63) followed an appropriate fictional context.

11.8 Hybrid accounts

An alternative to both the garden path (GP) model and the constraint-based approaches introduced above is the unrestricted race model (for further discussion see Van Gompel & Pickering, 2007). This model proposes that when an ambiguous sentence is encountered, the various possible analyses are involved in a race, with the winner being the analysis that is built fastest. The speed with which an analysis is constructed depends on the strength of the information supporting it, and so from this point of view it is similar to constraint-based models and unlike the GP model, which assumes a single syntactic analysis is pursued. Like the GP model, however, it assumes that a syntactic analysis is built before it is evaluated on the basis of plausibility. The model also differs from the constraint-based models in that it assumes no competition between the different analyses.

These three model types (GP, constraint-based, unrestricted race) make different predictions about the set of sentences in (11.64)–(11.66), where the structural ambiguity concerns whether *retiring* modifies the first or second full NP (e.g. *the bodyguard* or *the governor* in (11.64)). First, the GP model predicts a preferred syntactic analysis of attaching the modifying phrase to the second NP, just as was seen earlier for relative clause attachment ambiguities (see p. 192). This would mean that both sentence (11.64) and sentence (11.66) would be straightforward, since this syntactic preference is not contradicted by the subsequent semantic interpretation. In (11.65), however, the attachment of *retiring* to *the province* will present an anomaly to the semantic interpreter. Second, constraint-based models predict that since both resolutions of the ambiguity remain possible in (11.64), these will be in competition with one another, making this sentence more difficult to process than (11.65) and (11.66), which are are semantically disambiguated (only the governor can retire, not the province).

(11.64)   I read that the bodyguard of the governor retiring after the troubles is very rich.

(11.65)   I read that the governor of the province retiring after the troubles is very rich.

(11.66)   I read that the province of the governor retiring after the troubles is very rich.

Finally, however, the unrestricted race model predicts that the globally ambiguous sentence in (11.64) will be easier than the sentences in (11.65) and (11.66). In all three cases, the model predicts that each syntactic analysis is developed, but the fastest one will be selected. In (11.64) the processor will sometimes come up with one analysis, and sometimes with the other, but in neither case is there any conflict with a subsequent plausibility analysis as both interpretations are possible. In the case of the disambiguated sentences in (11.65) and (11.66), the syntactic processor similarly sometimes reaches one analysis and sometimes the other, and some of the time this will be contradicted by the plausibility analysis, so that overall (11.65) and (11.66) should throw up more processing problems than (11.64). In a study measuring eye movements during the reading of such sentences, Van Gompel *et al.* (2005) found precisely this result – (11.64) was easier to read than the others.

11.9 Good-enough processing

An alternative view of sentence processing is presented by 'quick-and-dirty' or 'good-enough' processing accounts (Ferreira, Bailey & Ferraro, 2002; Townsend & Bever, 2001). These argue that the compositional approaches of both the Garden Path model and constraint satisfaction models are too powerful, and that readers (and listeners) will often interpret a sentence on the basis of partial or superficial information. Indeed, in many contexts in which language is naturally used (e.g. noisy rooms with multiple speakers), partial information is all that is available. Rather than following detailed parsing strategies, it is argued, readers or listeners construct good-enough analyses based on lexical meaning and surface word order.

Evidence cited for good-enough processing includes a sort of priming task. Participants had to make a response to the final word *cocktails* in sentences like (11.67)–(11.69). In both (11.67) and (11.69), but not in (11.68), this word is preceded by a related word *bartender*. A detailed structural analysis should result in a closer connection between these words in (11.67), where these nouns are subject and object of the same verb, than in (11.69). However, response times to the final word were faster in both (11.67) and (11.69) than in (11.68). It is argued that a similar link is made between *bartender* and *cocktails* in (11.69) to that in (11.67) because of an initial good-enough analysis based on the meanings of the words in the sentences.

(11.67)   The boy watched the bartender serve the cocktails.

(11.68)   The boy saw that the person liked the cocktails.

(11.69)   The boy who watched the bartender served the cocktails.

(11.70)   While Anna dressed the baby played in the crib.

The sentence in (11.70) is similar to others that we have discussed in this and the previous chapter in the context of the parsing strategy of Late Closure. According to proponents of good-enough processing, the initial misanalysis (of *the baby* as the object of *dressed*) results not from the application of a detailed sentence parsing strategy such as Late Closure but simply from a superficial good-enough analysis. It is argued that the parsing strategy approach should result in reanalysis (on encountering *played*) which replaces the initial parse. However, it was found that after they had read the sentence participants replied 'yes' not only to the question 'Did the baby play in the crib?', but also to the question 'Did Anna dress the baby?' That is, they ended up with a representation of the sentence in which *the baby* was not only the subject of *played* but also the object of *dressed*.

In the context of second language processing, this sort of good-enough processing has been seen as part of shallow processing (Clahsen & Felser, 2006) that learners rely on particularly at the early stages of acquisition.

Summary

In this chapter we have seen that a number of additional sources of information – beyond syntactic information – influence the analysis of sentences. These include:

- plausibility;
- lexical bias;
- prosodic information.

We have also seen that there is a range of different sentence processing models, which include:

- the syntax-first approach introduced in Chapter 10;
- accounts that allow weak interaction between information sources, under the control of the syntactic component;
- more strongly interactive accounts such as constraint-based models;
- hybrid models that give preference to syntactic analysis over plausibility analyses, but without claiming strong parsing preferences.

Exercises

Exercise 11.1
Give a rank ordering for the sentences below in terms of their grammaticality. What properties of the sentences do you think led you to give them that rank ordering?

1. The postman delivered the junk mail threw it in the trash.
2. The tenant delivered the junk mail threw it in the trash.
3. Postmen delivered the junk mail threw it in the trash.
4. Tenants delivered the junk mail threw it in the trash.

Exercise 11.2
Sentences 1 and 2 below contain words from four grammatical categories: nouns, verbs, determiners and prepositions. Replace the words in each sentence with their grammatical category labels. Each sentence contains a prepositional phrase that modifies some other part of the sentence. Underline the prepositional phrases, and taking plausibility into account put a box around the word that you think the prepositional phrase in each sentence modifies.

1. The spy saw the cop with the binoculars.
2. The spy saw the cop with the revolver.

Exercise 11.3
In an experiment, sentences 1 and 2 below provided context sentences for the test sentences in A and B. Each of A and B proved to be easier to understand after one or other of the context sentences. Which context sentence best suits each of A and B? Why? What does the result of the experiment tell you about the information sources that are used in the interpretation of PP attachment ambiguities?

1. Once inside he saw that there was a safe with a new lock and a strongbox with an old lock.
2. Once inside he saw that there was a safe with a new lock and a safe with an old lock.
A. The burglar blew open the safe with the dynamite and made off with the loot.
B. The burglar blew open the safe with the new lock and made off with the loot.

Exercise 11.4
Taraban & McClelland's self-paced reading experiment described on p. 188 also used the examples below. What are the syntactic attachments of the PPs (underlined) in these three sentences? Two of the PPs have the same syntactic attachment but different thematic roles. Which of these would you predict would be the preferred thematic role? Which PP(s) is/are compatible with Minimal Attachment?

1. The hospital admitted the patient <u>with cancer</u> while the other incoming patients waited.
2. The hospital admitted the patient <u>with bodyguards</u> while the other incoming patients waited.
3. The hospital admitted the patient <u>with apologies</u> while the other incoming patients waited.

Further reading

For review chapters on sentence comprehension that include reference to many of the issues discussed in this chapter, see Pickering (1999) and Van Gompel and Pickering (2007). The use of prosody in sentence processing is discussed in more detail in the review chapters by Warren (1999) and Speer and Blodgett (2006).

12 Making connections

PREVIEW

This chapter looks at how connections are made between elements within and across sentences. It focuses largely on comprehension, but includes also some discussion of how speakers mark these connections. By the end of the chapter you should understand, amongst other things, that:

* speakers use devices for showing the links between related information and that listeners follow strategies in their interpretation of such links;
* understanding discourse frequently involves the listener in making inferences based on what has been heard;
* listeners are sensitive to how speakers mark information as being new to the conversation rather than information repeated from earlier in the conversation.

12.1 Introduction

The links between sentences or between turns in a conversation are critical to our understanding of utterances (Clark, 1996). We have seen in previous chapters how the context provided by a sentence or paragraph can influence the interpretation of an ambiguous sentence. In the current chapter we consider different kinds of relationship within and between sentences. These include the relationship between pronouns or other devices and the previously mentioned items to which they refer. They also include informational structure, with speakers indicating that some elements in the discourse are already known to the speaker and listener and that some elements are new information. We also consider how it is that readers and listeners can work out with great efficiency what the links are between elements in these and other kinds of structure.

12.2 Mental model building

The term **mental model** refers to the conceptual notions that speakers or writers want to convey, or to the abstract representation of what a reader or listener understands. These mental models clearly involve more than just the words and language structures being expressed, as they are determined also by the experiences of each individual.

The interpretation of longer stretches of text or speech, e.g. of more than one sentence, requires both the integration of information from different parts of the input and the construction of a mental model (Johnson-Laird, 1983) of what is being read or listened to. What evidence is there that listeners or readers build their own mental models? First, early studies showed that listeners integrate information that they have heard, rather than remembering it as separate pieces of information. For example, Bransford and Franks (1971) presented participants with jumbled lists of sentences, including (12.1)–(12.3). Later the participants reported that they had heard the sentence in (12.4), which had not in fact been presented to them. This clearly indicates the integration of the sentences in (12.1)–(12.3) into a single mental representation.

(12.1)   The ants were in the kitchen.

(12.2)   The ants ate the sweet jelly.

(12.3)   The jelly was on the table.

(12.4)   The ants in the kitchen ate the sweet jelly that was on the table.

Second, further studies also showed that the mental representations formed during listening or reading involve more than just the integration of information in the input. They are also based on the constructive use of world knowledge and the making of inferences about the situation being portrayed in the text (Bransford, Barclay & Franks, 1972). So, for instance, participants who heard the sentence in (12.5) confused it in a later memory test with (12.6), but participants who had heard (12.7) did not confuse that sentence with (12.8). This difference arises because the mental models associated with (12.7) and (12.8) are different – in (12.7) the fish swam beneath the log, but not beneath the turtles, who were to one side.

(12.5)   Three turtles sat on a floating log and a fish swam beneath it.

(12.6)   Three turtles sat on a floating log and a fish swam beneath them.

(12.7)   Three turtles rested beside a floating log and a fish swam beneath it.

(12.8)   Three turtles rested beside a floating log and a fish swam beneath them.

So discourse comprehension involves the construction of an abstract representation, using world knowledge and inferencing skills.

Given this evidence that the words and phrases of the input become interpreted as part of a more abstract mental model, it is interesting to speculate how long information from the text remains available during subsequent processing. Dell *et al.* tested this in a self-paced reading task using groups of four connected sentences (Dell, McKoon & Ratcliff, 1983). The first three sentences, e.g. (12.9) to (12.11), appeared in their entirety one after another, and a final sentence, (12.12), was presented word-by-word. This final sentence was interrupted by a probe word, which appeared at one of the points marked by subscripts in (12.12) (at different points for different participant groups). Participants had to decide whether the probe word had appeared anywhere in what they had read over this series of four sentences.

(12.9)   The burglar surveyed the garage set back from the street.

(12.10)   Several milk bottles were piled at the curb.

(12.11)   The banker and her husband were away on vacation.

(12.12)   The$_1$ burglar$_2$ slipped$_3$ away$_4$ from the$_5$ street lamp$_6$.

Two of the probe words were *burglar*, which is referred to explicitly in the final sentence, and *garage*, which is in the same earlier sentence as *burglar*. A third probe word was taken from a different sentence in the sequence, in this case the word *bottles* from the second sentence. The processing measure from the experiment is how much more rapidly each probe word was responded to, relative to a baseline condition. The result showed that there was an immediate benefit for both the repeated word (*burglar*) and the word from its earlier sentence (*garage*), as soon as the noun phrase *The burglar* is read (i.e. at point 2), but the advantage for the word from the same earlier sentence (*garage*) drops off rapidly (points 3 through 5). There was no such advantage at any stage for the control word (*bottles*) from a different earlier sentence. This indicates that in the reader's mental model there is still an association of *burglar* with *garage*, which has been set up in the first sentence, so that *garage* is reactivated when *burglar* is repeated.

Neuroimaging studies of discourse processing have compared brain activity during the comprehension of isolated sentences with that found

> Baseline conditions are used to get a measure of how easy or difficult a stimulus is to process in the absence of an experimental manipulation, so that the effect of the manipulation can be assessed.

during the comprehension of stories and/or of texts longer than individual sentences, such as interconnected pairs of sentences (see discussion of inferences and anaphora below). The general consensus is that discourse processing involves additional brain areas and that many of these additional areas are also involved in more general cognitive processing, including those that are typically involved when people attribute mental states to others (so-called 'Theory of Mind' processes) (Bornkessel-Schlesewsky & Friederici, 2007). This pattern of neural activity fits well with the notion that in developing an understanding of connected text we need to build a mental model of the discourse, based on our own experience and often projecting beyond it.

12.3 Inferences

Successful comprehension depends on the listener or reader making inferences about the discourse situation, i.e. understanding more than the surface meaning of sentences. Consider the exchange in (12.13)–(12.14).

(12.13)   *Man at railway ticket counter*: Which platform for the next train to Palmerston North?

(12.14)   *Ticket agent*: Platform 2, but it's a stopping train. The 1:45 will get you there sooner.

The ticket agent has made an inference that the man asked about the next train to Palmerston North because he wants to go to Palmerston North, and a further inference that he wants to get to Palmerston North as soon as possible. But neither of these things was actually stated by the man. If this inference is wrong, e.g. if the man wants to see off somebody who he knows is getting the next train to Palmerston North, for instance, then the additional information in the ticket agent's response is irrelevant. If however the inference is correct, then the man may continue the discourse as in (12.15).

(12.15)   Thank you. One ticket for the faster train then please.

Notice that his use of the expression *the faster train* depends on the way in which the prior discourse has unfolded. If this has been his first request, then the ticket agent would not necessarily know which train he wanted a ticket for.

Inferences based on the preceding discourse are important for our successful and efficient processing of sentences, including the grammatical relations between elements within and across sentences. In a cross-modal naming study, Tyler and Marslen-Wilson (1982) found that listeners very rapidly use their understanding of the preceding discourse, and inferences based on this understanding, to sort out which protagonists are likely to be the subject and object of incomplete phrases like *Running towards*... The researchers presented to their participants spoken passages like (12.16), ending with one of the spoken fragments in (12.17), (12.18) or

(12.19). At the offset of this fragment the participants saw one of the visual probe words HIM or HER for reading aloud (naming).

(12.16)   As Philip was walking back from the shop, he saw an old woman trip and fall flat on her face in the street. She seemed unable to get up.

(12.17)   Philip ran towards

(12.18)   He ran towards

(12.19)   Running towards

The grammatical subject of *ran* in the fragment in (12.17) is an explicit repetition of *Philip* from the preceding discourse. In (12.18), the subject is *he*, and the preceding discourse has only one male protagonist, Philip. In both these cases it should therefore be obvious that HIM is an inappropriate continuation word after ... *towards*, while HER is appropriate. In (12.19) there is no explicit subject in the fragment, but the logical inference from the preceding discourse is that it would similarly be Philip who is running, and that the most appropriate object of the preposition *towards* is again HER. Tyler and Marslen-Wilson's results showed that the inappropriate probe word (HIM) was responded to more slowly than the appropriate word (HER) for all three continuations in (12.17), (12.18) and (12.19), and that there was no difference in the patterns of results shown by participants in the three conditions. In other words, when the fragment is (12.19), the participants are able to make the logical inference that the argument structure of *ran* will include *her* rather than *him* as the object of *towards*. What is more, they do this as efficiently in this condition as they do when the subject of *run* is made explicit.

12.4 Anaphora

It is clear that an important aspect of language comprehension is the making of connections between the different parts of a discourse. In order for a larger stretch of speech or text to make sense, it has to show both coherence and cohesion. Coherence requires that there is consistency between the events or states in series of sentences. We have seen in the previous section that this often involves making the appropriate inferences. To take another example, the sentences in (12.20) work as a connected pair as long as we make the interpretative connections that allow them to make sense together (e.g. that the man and Jane are strangers, that the man asked Jane for directions, and so on).

(12.20)   A man stopped Jane in the street the other day. She hates giving directions to strangers.

Lack of coherence can cause delays in processing. It takes longer to decide that *he* refers to *Henry* in (12.22) than it does in (12.21), even though *he* can only refer to *Henry* and not to *Jane* in both cases (Stevenson & Vitkovitch,

> **Coherence** refers to how sentences or phrases belong together in terms of their meaning, i.e. they make sense in the discourse context. **Cohesion** involves the textual linkage between elements. An example of this is using anaphors to refer back to previously mentioned entities.

1986). This is because picking up money is not clearly associated with jumping over a ravine, whereas falling into the river is.

(12.21)   Jane stood watching. Henry jumped over the ravine and he fell into the river.

(12.22)   Jane stood watching. Henry jumped over the ravine and he picked up some money.

Cohesion on the other hand involves making the appropriate links between the words and phrases in a text. One of the most extensively studied ways in which this happens is anaphora, which involves making connections between textual elements such as pronouns and elements earlier in the discourse which the pronouns are standing for, such as nouns or full noun phrases. For instance, the two sentences in (12.23) are interpretable as a pair because we link some anaphors (the pronouns *she* and *him*) to their antecedents (*Jane* and *a man* respectively).

(12.23)   A man stopped Jane in the street the other day. She gave him directions to the Town Hall.

> **Anaphora** is an example of repeated mention – the anaphor is the second or subsequent mention of the object, person or action referred to initially by the antecedent.

Successful interpretation of discourse therefore often requires that we can identify anaphors and link them back to their antecedents. But even when we can achieve this successfully, lack of coherence can still cause difficulty, as (12.22) has shown.

The forms of anaphors and of their antecedents play an important role in our ability to recognise them and to make the anaphoric connection. Occasionally an anaphor and its antecedent will be exactly the same phrase, as would be the case if (12.17) is used as the continuation of (12.16) above, or if the second sentence in (12.23) had started with *Jane* and not *she*. However, this is rather unusual, and can in fact seem marked if the anaphor and its antecedent are close together in the text, as they would be in (12.23).

Anaphors tend to be either pronouns, as in (12.23), or definite noun phrases (e.g. phrases introduced with *the* rather than *a*, such as *the man* rather than *a man*). Antecedents, on the other hand, will often involve indefinite phrases, particularly when they refer to entities that are being introduced into the discourse for the first time. So in (12.20) and (12.23) *a man* introduces a new entity. Given this difference between anaphors and their antecedents, if we encounter a pronoun or a definite noun phrase, then there is a good chance that this is in an anaphoric relationship to something earlier in the discourse, or to something presupposed by the speaker or writer, as was pointed out in Chapter 11 in relation to the famous garden path sentence that involves *The horse* .... If we have identified an anaphor, then we need to find the antecedent in order to fully interpret the text.

Bridging inferences
Relating an anaphor to its antecedent is something readers and listeners can do with great efficiency. Often, though, the antecedent may not be

made explicit, and so anaphor resolution requires some additional inferences to be made, referred to as bridging inferences. Making these inferences takes extra time and can result in delays in sentence processing. For
instance, Haviland and Clark (1974) found that readers show faster comprehension times for the second sentence in (12.24) than for the same
sentence in (12.25). The difference is that the anaphor *the beer* has an
explicit antecedent in a preceding sentence in the first example, but not
in the second. It is argued that additional interpretative work is required
before the reader can connect the two sentences in (12.25), resulting in
delays in processing.

(12.24)   Mary unpacked some beer. The beer was warm.

(12.25)   Mary unpacked some picnic supplies. The beer was warm.

Garrod and Sanford (1982) suggest that Haviland and Clark's effect
depends on how readily the coherence can be established between sentences. Garrod and Sanford found that the second sentences in pairs
like (12.26) and (12.27) were processed equally rapidly, even though in
(12.27) there is no explicit antecedent for *the car*. They argue that this
ease of processing of (12.27) compared with (12.25) is because *car* is
implicit in the role of *vehicle used to drive to London* in the first sentence
in (12.27), whereas *beer* in (12.25) may not be an obvious component of
picnic supplies.

(12.26)   Keith took his car to London. The car kept overheating.

(12.27)   Keith drove to London. The car kept overheating.

If the anaphor is a pronoun, rather than a full noun phrase, then it will
be less readily interpreted through bridging inferences, i.e. the antecedent for a pronominal anaphor needs to be mentioned explicitly. So the
sentence pair in (12.28) is anomalous, but that in (12.29) is not. The pronominal form in (12.28) does not work without an explicit antecedent. As
a result, there is a temptation – initially at least – to assume that *it* in
(12.28) refers to *London*.

(12.28)   Keith drove to London. It kept overheating.

(12.29)   Keith took his car to London. It kept overheating.

Instances and categories

Other investigations using techniques such as the measurement of eye
movements or reading times have shown that the degree of specificity of
the noun phrases involved can affect the processing of anaphoric relations. For instance, although each of examples (12.30) and (12.31) has
identical nouns in its antecedent and anaphor phrases, Garrod and
Sanford (1982) demonstrated through a self-paced reading task that the
processing of the sentences with more specific nouns, or instances, as

with *shark* in (12.30), is faster than that of the sentences with more general nouns, or categories, as with *fish* in (12.31).

(12.30)   A shark was seen swimming close to shore. By evening the shark had gone.

(12.31)   A fish was seen swimming close to shore. By evening the fish had gone.

Moreover, if the antecedent is an instance (*shark*), and the anaphor is the category name (*fish*), as in (12.32), then processing is faster than if the opposite is the case, as in (12.33).

(12.32)   A shark was seen swimming close to shore. By evening the fish had gone.

(12.33)   A fish was seen swimming close to shore. By evening the shark had gone.

In addition, Garnham (1989) showed in a clause-by-clause self-paced reading task that if a category name like *fish* is used with a type of verb that is more likely to be associated with the instance (*shark*), such as *attack*, then the interpretation of *fish* is that it must be a type of fish, such as a shark, that is likely to attack, and the difference between category-instance and instance-category orders is removed, so that (12.35) is now not slower than (12.34).

(12.34)   A shark attacked the swimmer. By evening the fish had gone.

(12.35)   A fish attacked the swimmer. By evening the shark had gone.

Garrod *et al.* (1990) found a similar result in an eye-movement study. Their materials involved antecedents that were either category labels or specific instances of that category (*his weapon* vs *his knife*) followed by anaphors in definite or indefinite NPs (*the knife* vs *a knife*). Antecedents that were category words (*weapon* as the antecedent for *knife*) resulted in slower reading times for the anaphor words, except when the antecedent was used with a verb that made the *knife* meaning of *weapon* most likely and the anaphor was definite (e.g. *he stabbed her with his weapon* as an antecedent phrase followed by the anaphor *the knife*). The definite description (*the knife*) is therefore quickly linked to the coherent preceding context.

12.5 Given and new

Discourse contains repeated mention of participants, objects or actions. The repeated mention could be by the same speaker or by another speaker in the conversation. A key distinction here is between new and given information. New information is information which has just been introduced into the discourse for the first time. Given information has already been established as background information. This might be as a result of explicit mention or might come about more implicitly as part of the shared background knowledge of speaker and listener.

Studies in this area have included speech production studies which have highlighted qualitative differences in how the same words are produced when they are introduced as new information compared to when they are given information. So it is likely that there will be qualitative differences in the pronunciations of the first and second instance of *bridge* in the sentence in (12.36). It is highly probable that the second mention would have a reduced vowel and less clear consonant articulations (Hawkins & Warren, 1994).

(12.36)　First they came to a wooden bridge. They crossed over the bridge and took the next turn to the right.

The second mention of bridge in (12.36) could easily be replaced by a pronoun – *They crossed over it ....*

There is also likely to be a difference in the prosodic status of *bridge* in its two uses in (12.36). In the first use it is likely that *bridge* will be in focus and accented, and in the second it will be unaccented, with *crossed* or *over* more likely to be in focus. It is this difference in prosodic status, with words being accented or not, that results in differences in the clarity of pronunciation of words. While new information is generally accented and given information is unaccented, this is not always the case. Sometimes given information remains important and remains accented, and therefore as clear as new information. Consider the two instances of *bridge* in (12.37).

> **Accented** words are words that are spoken strongly, i.e. with some degree of sentence stress. This usually coincides with the word being in focus, or being given some contrastive emphasis. Unaccented words typically have a more reduced or less clear articulation.

(12.37)　There is both a bridge and a tunnel at that point in the river. We decided to use the bridge.

Although *bridge* is given information in the second sentence, the implied contrast with *tunnel* means that it will be accented.

Comprehension studies have shown that listeners are sensitive to the appropriate level of accentedness for the information status of words. For example, Terken and Nooteboom (1987) asked listeners to verify whether each of a series of utterances was an accurate description of an arrangement of letters that they had been shown. Take as an example the sequence QPKC. If the participants heard the two sentences in (12.38) and (12.39), in that order, then they were faster in verifying the accuracy of (12.39) if 'K' was not accented, i.e. was appropriately treated as given information in the context of the preceding utterance of (12.38). So even though accentedness increases clarity and should make processing easier, when it does not match the information status of items in the utterance, it can actually slow processing.

(12.38)　The K is on the right of the P.

(12.39)　The K is on the left of the C.

Accentedness can also affect the interpretation of anaphora. For instance, in the classic examples in (12.40) and (12.41) (Lakoff, 1971) if *he* and *him* are unaccented, then they are likely to be taken to refer to *John* and *Bill* respectively, i.e. to the antecedents with the same grammatical role (i.e. *John* and *he* are both subjects of their respective verbs). If *he* and *him* are accented, as in (12.41), then the antecedents are reversed, as shown by the subscripts liking anaphors and antecedents.

(12.40)   JOHN$_i$ called BILL$_j$ a REPUBLICAN and then he$_i$ INSULTED him$_j$.

(12.41)   JOHN$_i$ called BILL$_j$ a REPUBLICAN and then HE$_j$ insulted HIM$_i$.

12.6 Fillers and gaps

> Subscripts are often used in sentence examples to show the links between related elements in the sentence. So two items that are linked will have a subscript identifier with the same letter (or number).

The discussion of anaphora above looked at the relationships between different parts of the discourse, and pointed out that the interpretation of text or speech often requires the comprehender to make links between anaphors and their antecedents. A further type of linkage that needs to be made, more usually in this case within sentences, is between elements moved to the front of a sentence and the locations in the sentence structure from which they have been moved (Clifton & Frazier, 1989). The fronted elements are known as fillers and the locations they have been moved from are known variously as traces or gaps. Because the traces or gaps have no phonological content, i.e. are not pronounced, they are also referred to as empty categories.

The most obvious fillers are wh-words or phrases such as *who* in the question sentence in (12.42), or relative pronouns as in examples (12.43)–(12.44). To understand sentence (12.42) appropriately, the comprehender needs to work out that this word represents the direct object of *introduce*, i.e. the question is asking for the identity of the direct object of this verb.

> **Wh-words** are the question words *who, what, where, when*, etc. The types of questions they are typically used in are known as wh-questions.

(12.42)   Who did John introduce to Mary?

(12.43)   The reporter who the senator attacked disliked the editor.

(12.44)   The reporter who attacked the senator disliked the editor.

To see why the comprehension of such sentences is an interesting issue, recall the principles of sentence processing discussed in Chapter 10 in connection with garden path sentences. The model introduced there as a starting point for our discussion argued that a single syntactic analysis is computed, on a word-by-word basis, just as long as the syntactic category of each word can be determined unambiguously. This analysis follows phrase structure rules (i.e. the rules that linguists might use in drawing well-formed syntactic trees), which establish the grammatical relations between words. Grammatical relations in English are largely determined by the position a word has in a structure (and so the sentences *Dogs chase cats* and *Cats chase dogs* are different, even though they contain the same words).

Building well-formed syntactic structures has the potential to become problematic when constituents have been moved from their typical positions, as in (12.42). To start with, the moved constituent, which in the case of (12.42) is the filler *who*, has to be held in memory while a place is found in the sentence to which it can be linked. It has been shown that keeping words in memory is more costly if there is a longer distance between the filler and its position in the sentence (Gibson, 1998; Warren & Gibson, 2002). Thus object relative clauses, as in (12.43), impose a greater load on working memory than subject relatives such as (12.44). In object relatives the filler represents a constituent in the position of object to the verb in the relative clause, and therefore after that verb, whereas in subject relatives the moved element comes from before that verb.

Processing of filler–gap dependencies is also made complicated, as we will see through further examples below, by the fact that it is not always easy to determine where the filler 'belongs'. This is because the gap is not usually marked in any way.

Once the gap has been identified, it is assumed that the processor has to retrieve the filler from memory and integrate it with the relevant parts of the sentence (in the case of the sentence in (12.42) this is with the verb *introduce*).

It has been argued that wh-question sentences such as (12.42) result from movement operations applied to an underlying sentence such as (12.45), and that although as a consequence these two sentences have different word orders, the argument structure of the verb *introduce* remains the same. That is, *introduce* has a subject (*John* in both sentences), an indirect object (*Mary*), and an object (which is *Bill* in (12.45), but is of course unknown and the purpose of the question in (12.42)).

(12.45)   John introduced Bill to Mary.

So for the reader or listener to interpret such sentences, the wh-word has to be identified as filling the appropriate argument slot in the sentence. The challenge for theories of sentence processing is to explain how this is achieved. Following on from the argument that wh-question sentences result from the movement of a sentence constituent from its underlying grammatical position in a corresponding declarative sentence (*John introduced X to Mary*), it is claimed that sentences like (12.42) have a gap in that grammatical position, as indicated by the underscore in (12.46). An alternative representation is to show that there is a residue or trace of that moved element, as shown by the letter t (for trace) with a subscript in (12.47). Of course, a wh-word at the beginning of a sentence may have been moved from other positions in the underlying structure, depending on what the question is. Other possibilities are shown in (12.48) and (12.49).

(12.46)   *Who*$_i$ did John introduce __ $_i$ to Mary?

(12.47)   *Who*$_i$ did John introduce t$_i$ to Mary?

(12.48)   *Who*$_i$ did John introduce Bill to __ $_i$?

(12.49)   *Who*$_i$ __ $_i$ introduced Bill to Mary?

The three main tasks that have to be accomplished in interpreting these filler–gap constructions, then, are first to identify the fillers, second to identify the gaps, and third to associate the fillers to their gaps. Most studies of filler–gap dependencies have involved wh-words, in which case the first task, finding the filler, is straightforward. But there are cases where it is not so obvious. The interpretation of the sentence in (12.50) clearly involves understanding that *Susan* is the subject of *marry*, and so it has been argued that there is an underlying gap before the infinitive verb *to marry* in this sentence. Despite the additional complications thrown up by examples such as this, we will focus here on those filler–gap sentences where the filler is more readily obvious, in the form of a wh-word.

(12.50) *Susan*$_i$ always seemed __ $_i$ to marry rich men.

Active filler hypothesis

Once a filler has been identified, the next task is to locate the gap from which it might have come. Under the active filler hypothesis (Clifton & Frazier, 1989), if there is a filler that is still active, i.e. has not been associated with a particular gap, then locating the gap is a priority. If there is only one possible gap, then this is straightforward, and cases like (12.46)–(12.49) above, as well as (12.51) and (12.52) below, are relatively easy to work out.

(12.51) *What*$_i$ did John buy __ $_i$?

(12.52) The little girl *who*$_i$ the teacher liked __ $_i$ sat on the grass.

(12.53) *What* did John buy (__) the paint with __?

But placing active fillers into gaps is not always easy. For one, there are often pseudogaps. For instance, (12.53) starts off looking like (12.51), and so there might be a gap after *buy*, just as there is in (12.51). However, there is a noun phrase after the verb that could also be the object of that verb. This does in fact turn out to be the case, and so the potential gap after *buy* is not a real one – the filler should instead be interpreted as the object of the preposition *with*. If the comprehension system initially tries to link the filler to the pseudogap after *buy*, then we have an example of a garden path, i.e. an attachment that turns out to be the wrong analysis.

(12.54) *What* did John buy (__) the paint __ $_1$ to decorate __ $_2$?

(12.55) *What* did John buy __ $_1$ __ $_2$ to paint the porch with __ $_3$?

Another issue is that there may be multiple gaps in a sentence. Take for instance the sentence in (12.54). In addition to the pseudogap after *buy*, there are two further gaps here. One is for the subject of *to decorate* (which is filled by *John*), and the other is for the object of *decorate* (filled by *what*). So the sentence in (12.54) means something like *John bought the paint in order that John could decorate what?* (12.55) is even more complex, with three actual gaps – the object of *buy* (*what*), the subject of *paint* (*John*), and the object of *with* (*what*). The first and third gaps ultimately need to be filled by the same element – the *what* (so the sentence means something like *John bought what so that John could paint the porch with it (=what)?*).

In addition, there are ambiguous sentences involving filler–gap dependencies, such as the sentences which we met in Chapter 2 in connection with *wanna*-contraction. These are where the verb has transitivity ambiguity, i.e. can be used either with or without an object, as is the case with *leave* in (12.56). The possible interpretations of this sentence are illustrated in (12.57) and (12.58). In the former, *leave* is used intransitively, and the question is about who has to leave. In the latter, *leave* is transitive, and the question concerns who Max is going to quit.

(12.56)   Who did Max want to leave?

(12.57)   *Who*_i did Max want ___ _i to leave?
          (cf. *Who*_i did Max want ___ _i to swim?)

(12.58)   *Who*_i did *Max*_j want ___ _j to leave ___ _i?
          (cf. *Which beer*_i did *Max*_j want ___ _j to drink ___ _i?)

Since wanna-contraction is more likely in the case of (12.58) than (12.57), it would appear that at least some aspect of filler–gap dependencies remains relevant to the final stages of speech production.

Processing strategies for matching fillers to gaps

It has been argued that the processing of filler–gap sentences follows processing strategies. However, as Clifton and Frazier (1989) explain, different and often conflicting strategies have been proposed as the best or most appropriate account. A few of these will be briefly introduced here as illustrations of the complexity involved.

The first is the strategy of gap as first resort (Clifton & Frazier, 1989: 281). This stipulates that the processing system (the comprehender) will postulate a gap at the earliest possible position. Since the wh-phrases we are considering here are noun phrases, this earliest possible gap will be at the first position where an NP could occur. A corollary of this strategy would have to be that if this first gap turns out to not in fact be a gap (but rather a pseudogap, see above) then the next gap position will be considered, and so on. It should be clear that this will lead to plenty of gap postulations in (12.59), with the potential gap after *ask* being cancelled when *Meg* is read, that after *persuade* cancelled when *Jill* is read, and so on. This does not seem to be a very effective strategy in cases like this. But then again, this is a rather unusual (though possible) sentence.

(12.59)   *Who*_i did Tom ask Meg to persuade Jill to inform Ted that Bob
          had spoken to ___ _i?

At the other extreme we find the strategy of gap as last resort (Clifton & Frazier, 1989: 282). In this case the approach is for the processor to delay postulating a gap until it is forced to. Now, though, this wrongly predicts that (12.60) (with *kill* used intransitively) will be no more difficult to process than (12.61). In both cases under gap as last resort there is no requirement to postulate a gap until the end of the sentence, which turns out to be correct for each sentence. Intuitively, though, (12.60) seems to be more difficult to process, and this appears to be because of the assumption of a gap after *kill*, i.e. that *kill* is being used transitively, which then has to be abandoned.

(12.60) *Who$_i$* did John kill (?__ $_i$) for the sake of __ $_i$?

(12.61) *Who$_i$* did John die for the sake of __ $_i$?

An approach that may be able to find the middle ground between first resort and last resort is one that expects gap postulation to follow lexical expectations. Verbs differ from one another in their expectations regarding transitivity, as we saw in Chapter 11. This can in part reflect the frequency with which they are used in different syntactic constructions. For example, *read* occurs very frequently with a following object, but although *walk* can take an object it rarely does so. Using this information, the processor may take a gamble, when encountering *read* with no apparent object, that there is a gap after *read* with which the filler should be linked. With *walk*, it makes a different bet, that *walk* has no object. Fodor (1978, 1989) shows that a lexical expectation account leads, correctly, to the prediction that (12.62) is easier to process than (12.63), and that (12.64) is more difficult to process than (12.65), even though (12.62) and (12.64) have the same structure and (12.63) and (12.65) have the same structure.

(12.62) *Which book$_i$* did the teacher read __ $_i$ to the children?

(12.63) *Which book$_i$* did the teacher read to the children from __ $_i$?

(12.64) *Which student$_i$* did the teacher walk __ $_i$ to the cafeteria?

(12.65) *Which student$_i$* did the teacher walk to the cafeteria with __ $_i$?

Along similar lines, *ask* prefers an object, but the verb *race* does not. In (12.66) and (12.67), therefore, there is a strong potential gap after *asked*. The filler in (12.66) is plausible here (reporters do ask witnesses), but that in (12.67) is not (reporters do not ask churches). Tanenhaus *et al.* (1985) found that the sentence in (12.66) is accepted as sensible more often and more rapidly than that in (12.67).

(12.66) The lawyer found out *which witness$_i$* the reporter asked anxiously about __ $_i$

(12.67) The lawyer found out *which church$_i$* the reporter asked anxiously about __ $_i$

In the pair in (12.68) and (12.69), since *race* does not prefer an object, a gap after *raced* is not so tempting. Correspondingly, Tanenhaus *et al.* found no difference between these two sentences, i.e. the processor does not try to fill a gap after *raced*, neither for the sentence in which it is plausible that the wh-phrase could be the object of *race* (12.68), nor for the one in which it is implausible (12.69).

(12.68) The sheriff wasn't sure *which horse$_i$* the cowboy raced desperately past __ $_i$

(12.69)   The sheriff wasn't sure *which rock*ᵢ the cowboy raced desperately
         past __ ᵢ

In some cases, the successful interpretation of a sentence requires the
processor to deal with more than one filler and more than one gap. A
strategy that has been proposed for dealing with this situation is the
most recent filler hypothesis (Frazier, Clifton & Randall, 1983). In its
simplest form, this says that where there are two gaps, the processor
should assign the most recent of two possible fillers to the first gap, and
the more distant to the second. This is illustrated in (12.70) and (12.71).
Note that in both cases the more distant (first) fillers are deliberately
chosen to be ones that could – on semantic grounds – be linked to the
'wrong' early gap (e.g. *who* could be the filler for the gap marked __ ᵢ in
(12.70), as in *Who did you want to make a potholder?*), but the preferred
interpretations are the ones indicated by the subscripts.

(12.70)   *Who*ⱼ did *you*ᵢ want __ ᵢ to make a potholder for __ ⱼ?

(12.71)   *What*ⱼ are the *boxes*ᵢ easy to store __ ᵢ in __ ⱼ?

(12.72)   John ᵢ promised Mary ⱼ __ᵢ to read the book on vacation

(12.73)   John ᵢ persuaded Mary ⱼ __ⱼ to read the book on vacation

However, Boland *et al.* (1990) show that this hypothesis does not apply in
cases such as (12.72), which can be contrasted with the superficially
similar sentence in (12.73). The difference arises because *promise* and *persuade* expect different underlying sentence structures – the subject of
promise is also the subject of the subordinate clause (i.e. *John promised
Mary that John would read the book*), while it is the object of *persuade* that is
the subject of the subordinate clause (*John persuaded Mary that Mary would
read the book*).

(12.74)   The little girl forced the snake ᵢ __ᵢ to hop over the fence

(12.75)   Which snake ᵢ did the little girl force __ᵢ __ᵢ to hop over the
         fence?

A final consideration in this section concerns the efficiency with which
comprehenders fill gaps. This is done very quickly, and Tanenhaus *et al.*
(1985) found that the anomaly is detected just as early in (12.75) as it is in
(12.74). In (12.74) *the snake* is object of *force*, but it is also coindexed with the
subject position of *to hop*. In an anomaly detection task, listeners are quick
to detect that there is something wrong with the meaning of this sentence as soon as they have recognised the word *hop*. The anomaly is that
snakes do not hop. Now consider (12.75). With this sentence the process is
more complicated. It is argued that the subject position of *hop* has to be
linked to the object position of *force*, which in turn has to be linked to the
filler phrase *which snake*. However, the anomaly with *hop* is detected just as
quickly here as it is in (12.74).

In a further study showing the efficiency of processing, Nicol & Swinney (1989) measured priming effects in the context of spoken versions of sentences like (12.76).

(12.76)   The cop saw the boy who the crowd at the party accused __ of the crime.

The task was to make a lexical decision about visually presented probe words, which were semantically related to one of the words in the sentence. These associate words were related to either *cop*, *boy* or *crowd* for the sentence in (12.76). The timing of the presentation of the probe words was such that they would coincide with the position of the gap in the spoken sentence. The appropriate filler for this gap is of course *who*, which is in turn related to *boy*. It was found that only the probe word associated with *boy* was primed (relative to a control condition). Even associates of the more recently heard word *crowd* were not primed. This indicates that the structure of the sentence is very rapidly worked out by the listener.

Summary

We have seen in this chapter that the processing of connected sentences, in either text or speech, involves complex processes of mental model building and of making connections between elements of the discourse. These processes include:

- making inferences, including bridging inferences that are based on our understanding of the world;
- making connections between anaphors and the antecedents that they relate to earlier in the text;
- recognising the differences between given information and new information, both in how they are marked in speech and in how they contribute to the information structure of the discourse;
- building structural relationships between elements that are not in their canonical sentence positions, e.g. between fronted items such as wh-words or wh-phrases and the places from which they have been fronted;
- this includes following strategies that deal effectively with filler–gap dependencies.

There is evidence from experimental studies that comprehenders follow efficient strategies to resolve these dependencies as part of understanding the discourse as a whole, and from neuroimaging studies that they bring into this comprehension process neural structures that are involved in more general cognitive processing.

Exercises

Exercise 12.1

Explain coherence and cohesion with reference to the passage in 1 below, and use these concepts to show why the passage in 2 does not work.

1. The blonde girl immediately fell asleep. When the bears returned to their cottage, they saw that she had been eating their porridge.
2. Cinderella watched the prince ride up to her house. The prince tied it up and he sacked his servants.

Exercise 12.2

Re-write the sentences below with subscripts to show the links between anaphors and their antecedents.

1. Bert asked Ernie to lend him some money.
2. John and Mary stayed until she had finished checking the book for him.
3. Joan complained to her parents that they never let her go out on her own.
4. Spike promised John that he would finish the job.
5. Spike persuaded John that he should finish the job.

Exercise 12.3

Underline the fillers and indicate the gaps in the following sentences, using underscores and subscripts where necessary.

1. Who did Mary ask to meet John?
2. Who did Mary ask John to meet?
3. Which book did you persuade John to read during the holiday?
4. What did you pack to take on holiday?
5. Which book did the choir sing that carol from?

Exercise 12.4

In the following sentence pairs (taken from Tanenhaus, Boland, Garnsey & Carlson, 1989), a. is acceptable, but b. is anomalous. At what point in the b. sentences would the anomaly become obvious? This should be different for 1 and 2. How does this difference relate to the preferred sentence structures for each of the verbs?

1a. Which customer did the secretary call on the office phone?
1b. Which article did the secretary call on the office phone?
2a. Which child did your brother remind to watch the show?
2b. Which movie did your brother remind to watch the show?

Exercise 12.5

Which of the following would prove problematic for a strategy of gap as first resort, and which for a strategy of gap as last resort?

1. Who did the manager need to dismiss?
2. Who did the teacher tell Mary to help?
3. Which friend did Pamela want to visit John?

4. Who would Steve like to see?
5. Who would Joan prefer Beth to call?
6. Which student did Peter ask to collect the books?
7. Who did Geoff choose to carry the tent?

Further reading

Johnson-Laird (1983) develops the notion of mental models. Singer (2007) and Garrod and Sanford (1994) provide review chapters on inferencing in discourse processing. For a review of research on anaphora see Garnham (1999). Clifton and Frazier (1989), Fodor (1989) and Featherston (2001) give surveys of filler–gap ambiguity resolution.

13 Architecture of the language processing system

PREVIEW

KEY TERMS

anomia

automaticity

chatterbox syndrome

informationally encapsulated

modularity

specific language impairment

stroop effect

word deafness

This chapter provides both a retrospective view over the material in the book as a whole and an opportunity to see some of the links between the various components of the language production and comprehension systems that have been presented. It also looks at the links between the language system and other knowledge systems. By the end of the chapter you should have a better understanding of, amongst other things:

- the relationship between the production and comprehension processes, particularly with reference to lexical processing;
- the relationship between visual and spoken language processing;
- the notion that there may be processing modules responsible for specific types of linguistic processing;
- the fact that researchers take differing views on the relationships of such modules to one another and to non-linguistic processing.

13.1 Introduction

The preceding chapters of this book have presented an overview of key aspects of language processing in connection with a number of areas of language structure. For example, there have been chapters on the construction of sentences during production, on the selection of words for output, and on the morphological and phonological construction of words. There have been chapters on spoken word recognition, on visual word recognition and on the processing of sentences during comprehension. On occasion, links have been made between these chapters and between the findings discussed within them. In the current chapter, we will look briefly at the relationships between these component parts of language processing, as well as the relationship between language processing and other cognitive activities. The purpose is to provide a preliminary sketch of the architecture of the language processing system, and to indicate some of the connections that exist between some of the component parts.

13.2 Modularity within language processing

The discussion of **modularity** in the context of language processing can be seen at two levels. One concerns the existence of separate modules for different types of language processing, i.e. concerns modules within the language production and comprehension system. The other concerns the relationship between the language processing system as a whole, i.e. as a language module, and other cognitive processes.

An on-going debate within the psychology of language concerns modularity within language processing, or the extent to which there are separate modules for different processing types, such as the various production and comprehension processes outlined in the preceding chapters of this book. For instance, do listeners or readers recognise words using a word recognition system that is separate from the structural analysis of the sentences that those words make up? Does the selection of the sound structure of a word during production occur as a separate processing stage from the selection of the lemma for that word based on the speaker's intended meaning? A related question concerns the extent to which processing operations at these different linguistic levels (e.g. involving sounds, words, sentences) act independently of one another. That is, while there may be separate components responsible for different types of language analysis, these components may in fact interact strongly with one another, so that recognition of words might be affected by the extent to which different words fit the developing interpretation of a sentence.

Interestingly, both the advocates of a modular approach to language processing and those of a non-modular or interactive approach cite efficiency in processing as a motivation for their respective positions. From the modular perspective, having specialised components for particular tasks means that these can get on with their jobs without distraction. From a non-modular viewpoint, it is argued that knowledge arising from one set of processes can improve the efficiency of another set of processes, by helping to eliminate at an early stage any analyses that might prove to be unnecessary or misleading.

There are a number of key characteristics to a strongly modular approach (Fodor, 1983). The first is that the language processing system is

divided into modules that are informationally encapsulated. The processes within each module are effectively sealed off from other processes.
So each module takes a certain type of representation as its input, and
derives from that an output that feeds the next module in the system. For
example, a phoneme-based word recognition module would take as its
input strings of phonemes that are the output of a pre-lexical analysis
module, and would pass on complete word-forms to a syntactic sentence
structure module. There is a strict linearity to the processing system, so
that for instance the module dealing with syntactic processing receives
input at the word level (i.e. the output of the word recognition system),
and does not itself receive input from the phonetic or orthographic level.
Note that this is a particularly strong view of modularity. Evidence that
the modules are not encapsulated in this way, i.e. that there is leakage
between the modules, or interaction between them, would be compatible
with a weaker notion of modularity. That is, one where there are modules
with specialised responsibilities, but which are not informationally
encapsulated in the manner envisaged above.

A second characteristic of modular systems is the automaticity of the
operations of each module. If the module receives some input, then it is
required to process that input and to at least attempt to generate an
appropriate output. This characteristic is reflected in the apparent obligatory nature of word recognition. The Stroop effect in word reading
(Stroop, 1935) is a classic example demonstrating this. This effect occurs
when participants are asked to name the colour in which a word is printed, and find it difficult to ignore what the word means. As a result, if they
see the word GREEN printed in red, then they experience interference
from the meaning of that word (i.e. 'green'), when trying to name the
colour red.

As well as being informationally encapsulated and automatic, it is
argued that each module contains processes which operate without us
ordinarily being consciously aware of them. In fact, many of the lower
level or more peripheral processes appear to be unavailable to conscious
inspection.

It is argued that these and other properties of the modules contribute
to the speed and accuracy of the processing system. Indeed, it is claimed
that the sheer speed and accuracy with which we process language are
factors that speak most strongly in favour of a modular system, since coordinating interactions between different processing components would
make the language system sluggish and open to error.

Modularity and syntax

The modularity of components at different levels of the processing system
is frequently discussed in connection with the role of syntactic and other
information sources during sentence parsing. As we saw in Chapters 10
and 11, the garden path model of sentence processing claims that the
initial analysis of a sentence is based on syntactic information associated
with the input word string. Although a semantic interpretation is also
constructed, it is argued that this provides input to the sentence-building

Two of the most widely investigated types of aphasia are **Broca's aphasia** and **Wernicke's aphasia**, named after the people who identified the conditions. Each type is associated with damage to a specific area of the brain, and each shows different patterns of language behaviour.

Speech sample from a Broca's aphasic:
Ah … Monday … ah Dad and Paul … and Dad … hospital. Two … ah … doctors … and ah … thirty minutes … and yes … ah … hospital
And from a Wernicke's aphasic:
Yes … well of course when they came there, I … em … he came there, I didn't know … there and I didn't know anything for it, any …

process only once the syntactic parser has done as much as it is able and encounters difficulties (as in garden path experiences). This separation of syntax and semantics means that it should be possible to develop a representation in one of these domains without developing one in the other. There is some support for independence of syntactic and semantic information that comes from the study of brain-damaged patients. An early and very influential study (Caramazza & Zurif, 1976) tested different groups of aphasic patients in a sentence–picture matching task that included sentences like that in (13.1). Broca's aphasics typically made errors in which they would choose a picture of a cat biting a dog for this sentence, i.e. a reversal error in which the superficial order of the noun phrases (*cat* before *dog*) is misunderstood to indicate who did what to whom. Wernicke's aphasics, on the other hand, were likely to make an error that involved selecting a picture with a representation of a different noun or verb (e.g. of a dog chasing a cat).

(13.1)   The cat that the dog is biting is black.

This pattern of processing difficulties suggests a separation of syntactic and semantic processes, since one can be affected without significant impairment of the other. This conclusion is supported by production data (see sidebar). Broca's aphasics have output that is non-fluent and consists mainly of content words with very little grammatical structure, and which is often referred to as agrammatic. Wernicke's aphasics, on the other hand, produce fluent and grammatically well-formed sentences, but the sentences are rather empty of meaning, because these aphasics have great difficulty in finding words. This difficulty is reflected also in problems that such aphasics have in matching object names with pictures of those objects.

Language production and comprehension data from Broca's and Wernicke's aphasics also show that content words and function words can be distinguished, in that the former are more likely to be affected by Wernicke's aphasia. Neurophysiological studies support this separation of word types. In fact, the processing of function words shows patterns of brain activity that indicate that they are more localised in the syntactic areas of the left brain hemisphere, than content words, which show broader patterns of activity, also involving right brain areas (for a summary of some of this fascinating research see Pulvermüller, 2007).

Subsequent studies of aphasia explored in more detail the notion of a syntactic deficit in Broca's aphasia. Consider for instance a task where sentences such as (13.2) and (13.3) have to be matched to their corresponding pictures.

(13.2)   The butcher weighed the meat.

(13.3)   The fireman weighed the policeman.

Broca's aphasics find it much easier to do this sentence–picture matching task with sentences like (13.2) than with sentences like (13.3) (Byng, 1988). In (13.2) the content words – *butcher, weigh, meat* – give only one plausible interpretation of the sentence, irrespective of grammatical constraints such as word order. This is because meat does not typically weigh butchers. In the case of (13.3), if – as a result of brain damage – syntactic information is less readily available to guide the interpretation of the sentence, then the content words could be in either of two relationships, since firemen can weigh policemen and policemen can weigh firemen (see the discussion of reversible sentences in Chapter 11). Therefore, without a syntactic understanding of (13.3), Broca's patients can have difficulty knowing that it is incorrect to match the sentence to a picture of a policeman weighing a fireman. But even though their syntactic processing may be impaired, such patients can bring semantic information and their world knowledge to bear in their interpretation of (13.2) and come up with a single interpretation without requiring syntactic (word-order) information about the relationships of the words to one another.

As further studies were conducted, it became clear that the syntactic deficit account of Broca's aphasia was too simplistic. For instance, large-scale studies of aphasia showed that both Broca's and Wernicke's aphasics showed similar rank ordering of different syntactic structures in terms of their levels of difficulty. As a consequence, there are some severely impaired Wernicke's patients who show a syntactic deficit in comprehension without showing agrammatic speech, undermining the notion that syntactic comprehension difficulties are linked to a syntactic deficit that affects all types of language processing. Similarly, patients were studied who showed agrammatic speech but without syntactic comprehension deficits. In addition, Broca's patients were discovered who, although they performed poorly on sentence–picture matching tasks, scored highly in grammaticality judgement tasks. (For a summary of these studies see Martin, Vuong & Crowther, 2007.)

Despite the doubt that is cast by findings such as these on the independence of syntactic and semantic processing, there are individual case studies that show quite clear dissociation, such as patient JG (Ostrin & Tyler, 1995). This patient had agrammatic speech, showed typical Broca's behaviour on sentences with the same characteristics as (13.2) and (13.3), performed poorly in online tasks that depended on intact syntactic processing, but performed well in a semantic priming task.

Other evidence from aphasics suggests that the observed patterns of behaviour derive perhaps not from a complete loss of syntactic processing capability, but from a weakening of syntactic processing, which leads to greater reliance on other sources of information during processing. This would mean that when these other sources of information are not as reliable, then the aphasics would rely on whatever residual syntactic processing they have. This was demonstrated in one study that used a plausibility task with normal controls and aphasics with syntactic comprehension deficits (Saffran, Schwartz & Linebarger, 1998). The materials included sentences such as those in (13.4) and (13.5), both of which the control participants easily marked as implausible.

(13.4)   The cheese ate the mouse.

(13.5)   The mouse is carrying the cat.

The interesting finding in the patient data is that while patients made many errors on sentences such as (13.4), i.e. responding that this sentence is plausible even though it is clearly not, they made few such errors with sentences like (13.5). In the case of (13.4), semantic knowledge indicates that only one of the NPs could plausibly be the agent of the verb *eat* (i.e. *the mouse*), and the patients relied on this knowledge in their interpretation of the sentence, responding incorrectly that it was plausible (i.e. interpreting it as *the mouse ate the cheese*). With (13.5), however, such semantic knowledge is not as constraining, since both cats and mice can carry. In this situation, it is argued, the patients were forced to make use of their residual syntactic understanding of the sentence, with the NP in subject position being interpreted as the agent, rendering the sentence implausible.

What such findings suggest is that during comprehension we call on a range of information sources, and that while these may be separately represented and differentially affected by different types of brain damage, they nevertheless interact during sentence processing. We saw in earlier chapters a range of evidence that seems to speak against a strictly modular view of language processing and in favour of interactive or constraint-based approaches to sentence processing. For instance, in Chapter 11 it was pointed out that sentence processing in reading experiments is affected by a number of non-syntactic factors, including lexical preferences. So it matters whether a verb is more likely to be followed by a noun phrase object or by a clause object. This is shown by the preferred interpretations and relative likelihood of garden path effects with *saw* in (13.6) and *doubted* in (13.7). The animacy of a subject noun is also important – if the subject is animate then verbs with transitivity ambiguity are more likely to be treated as transitive and therefore as requiring a following object, as shown by a comparison of (13.8) and (13.9).

(13.6)   The reporter saw her friend was not succeeding.

(13.7)   The candidate doubted his sincerity would be appreciated.

(13.8)   Even before the police stopped the driver was getting nervous.

(13.9)   Even before the truck stopped the driver was getting nervous.

These findings do not deny the possible existence of dedicated modules for specific language processing tasks. In contrast with more strictly modular approaches outlined above, however, it is argued that the modules are permeable and capable of sharing information with one another during processing.

In similar fashion, it was pointed out in Chapter 8 that words can be recognised earlier in supporting contexts than in isolation, suggesting that there is interaction between aspects of sentence processing and aspects of word recognition. In Chapter 3, we saw that the speech errors known as blends are likely to involve words that have both phonological and semantic similarity. This again indicates the interaction of different information sources during language processing.

The discussion of modularity above has focused on whether or not there is interaction between levels of the processing system, such as between syntactic and semantic processing or between word recognition and sentence interpretation. Another issue is whether there are separate modules for different types of processing within the same level of linguistic organisation. This is perhaps no more acute than in the context of lexical processing, which provides the focus of the next two sections. In particular, the possibility has been raised that there is not just one mental lexicon, but two – one for production and one for comprehension. Or perhaps four, with a production lexicon and a comprehension lexicon for each of spoken and written language processing. It is highly unlikely that these lexicons would be entirely separate from one another, and so a crucial issue is the point at which lexical operations might become distinct from one another in different processing domains.

13.3 The relationship of production and comprehension

Issues in language production and in language comprehension have largely been presented separately in the earlier and later chapters of this book respectively. At points along the way, however, we have seen that production and comprehension share some common properties, and that there is alignment of the needs of production with those of comprehension. This is not at all surprising, given that most language users are both producers and comprehenders. As an example, we saw in Chapter 2 that during fluent speech production speakers tend to line up their pauses with the boundaries between phrases and clauses. As a consequence, these pauses assist the listener in structuring the input into phrases and clauses. In Chapter 6 we saw that speakers frequently accompany their speech with iconic gestures that represent some salient aspect of what is being talked about, or with batonic gestures that emphasise parts of their message. Again, while these can be considered as features of speech production (and as such may facilitate aspects of the production process), they can clearly also serve processes of comprehension.

A more general question, though, concerns the extent to which the same representations and processes are used in these two aspects of language processing. Although the question raises issues in a number of areas, we will focus here on the study of the mental lexicon, and consider the level at which the representations of words as used in production and comprehension start to differ. Two relatively simplistic views are illustrated in Figure 13.1. Note that the figure includes a phonological lexicon or lexicons, i.e. it deals with spoken rather than written language comprehension and production. We will return to discussion of issues to do with written input and output in later sections.

On the left of Figure 13.1 we see that the semantic lexicon (the set of lemmas) is linked to a single set of forms in a phonological lexicon. This set of forms, which might take the shape of phoneme strings, is used to

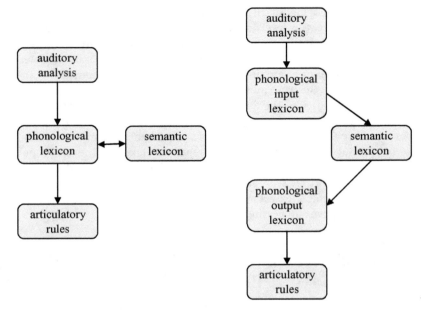

Figure 13.1
Two possible views of
the relationship between
the production and com-
prehension of spoken
words.

drive the articulatory system and is at the same time the set of representations onto which the auditory analysis of the input is mapped. On the
right of the figure we have another view, with separate form representations for output and input. This second architecture might incidentally
allow different kinds of sub-lexical representations for production and for
perception/comprehension, such as syllable structures in word production and phoneme strings in word recognition.

Researchers have looked to both experimental and clinical sources for
evidence concerning whether production and comprehension share a
common lexicon or have separate systems, at least in terms of the form-
based aspects of words. The existence of separate input and output pathways is supported by the finding that when participants have to listen for
a target word in a list of spoken words it causes little interference with
their ability to read words aloud at the same time (Shallice, McLeod &
Lewis, 1985). This is supported also by research into the neurophysiological aspects of language processing – brain imaging studies have shown
that different brain areas are activated when listening to words from
those activated during speaking, either when reading aloud or when
repeating words. On the other hand, there does appear to be some overlap
between the production and comprehension of spoken words (Indefrey &
Levelt, 2004). For instance, the production of a word in picture naming is
facilitated if a phonologically related word is heard before the naming
response is initiated (Levelt *et al.*, 1999).

Clinical evidence supporting a separation of the pathways for word
production and recognition typically includes some sort of dissociation
between aspects of production and recognition or comprehension. For
example, patients with anomia find it difficult to give the names for

objects, indicating that they have difficulty in finding words for production. Yet they can nevertheless usually recognise and understand the same words in others' speech. They are also able to speak fluently (apart from their difficulty in producing object names), and so they clearly do not have a basic problem with control of their speech articulators or with generating a plan for articulation based on word knowledge. This suggests a model along the lines of the right-hand part of Figure 13.1, with separate input and output lexicons. The anomic patients have damage to the output route from the semantic lexicon through to the phonological output lexicon.

Additionally, there are patients who show word deafness. In this condition, patients can read and write and can speak quite normally, but are unable to understand words spoken to them, although their hearing system is otherwise unimpaired. They are also unable to repeat back words spoken to them. This combination suggests that the input route through the phonological input lexicon is damaged, so that the patients cannot use auditory input to access words for comprehension or for triggering the production of words during repetition.

Further patterns of problems that patients have with repetition and other tasks require us to modify the illustration on the right-hand side of Figure 13.1, along the lines of Figure 13.2. Imagine that a participant is asked to repeat back a word that they hear. The illustration in Figure 13.2 shows three routes for doing this. The sublexical route amounts to an echoing back or shadowing of what the participant hears. This route is required for repeating nonwords, which by definition do not have a lexical representation and so would not require access to the lexical system. The lexical route is used for repeating words, but without comprehension of those words. The semantic route indicates repetition that includes understanding. Damage to one or more of these routes will lead to different symptoms. Support for the existence of the three routes would arise if the right combinations of symptoms are found across different patients. As the next paragraph shows, this appears to be the case.

First, there are patients who are particularly poor at repeating nonwords, but who can understand and repeat real words. The fact that they understand these words shows that the input route through to the semantic lexicon is intact. The poor performance at repeating nonwords suggests impairment of the sublexical route. That is, these patients have to access words from their mental lexicon in order to find a pronunciation for them, which does not help them with nonwords. By contrast, there are other patients who can repeat both real words and nonwords but have no understanding of the words they can repeat. These patients would appear to have an impaired semantic route. Note though that neither of these two types of patient, nor the combination of what they are capable of achieving, supports a separate lexical route. All we have with these patients is support for a separation of semantic and sublexical routes. Crucially though for the model shown in Figure 13.2, there are also patients who cannot repeat nonwords and can repeat words, but with little understanding of the words they repeat. Such patients have an intact lexical route, but are

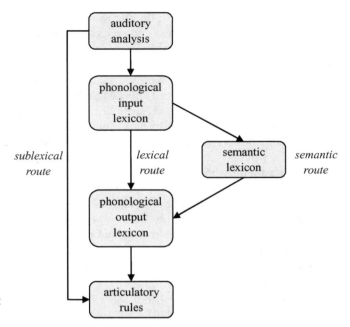

Figure 13.2
A model of three repetition routes for getting from spoken input to spoken output.

unable to make good use of the other two routes. (For further discussion of these cases, see Harley 2008, Chapter 15.)

These examples of patients with different types of impairment have not been discussed in detail here, since that would be beyond the scope of this book. They have been summarised to illustrate the complexities of the relationships between different types of processing, in this case of linguistic elements at one level, i.e. the lexical level. But they also show how considering a combination of patients with different capabilities can reveal more about the probable architecture of an intact language system than would be possible by looking at one patient – or unimpaired language user – alone.

13.4 The relationship of visual and spoken language

The similarities and differences between the processing of visual and spoken language stimuli are mentioned at various points in this book, as are the relationships between the two modalities during processing. In specific instances, such as the dual route model of reading aloud (see Chapter 9), the interaction of visual and phonological representations for words is crucial – the issue there was how we get from a visual input to a spoken output.

Some questions, however, remain. Just how much overlap is there between the representations for visual and spoken language? To what extent are the processes in the two modalities identical, similar or different? To what extent can we distinguish 'central' processes that are

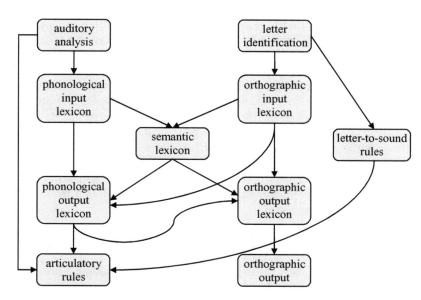

Figure 13.3
Possible architecture of the lexical system for both spoken and visual input and output processing.

common to different forms of language, and more 'peripheral' processes that are modality-specific? Examples of modality-specific differences will obviously include those that relate to the different media involved. For example, we can backtrack during reading and re-assess words that might have led us astray (as indicated in the garden path studies reviewed in Chapter 10), but this is not so easy in listening.

Figure 13.3 expands the model sketched in Figure 13.2 by adding components for visual lexical processing. The left-hand side of the figure repeats the input and output routes for spoken words, while the right-hand side adds routes for dealing with visual word recognition and production. Note the links between the orthographic input components and the phonological and articulatory output components, reflecting the different routes for reading aloud that were discussed in connection with the dual route model in Chapter 9.

Consider now evidence from studies of patients that shows how it is possible for spoken and written responses to the same stimulus to be inconsistent. Such evidence supports the notion that there are different output lexicons for spoken and written forms of words, and not just different peripheral output components for each modality. For example, when one patient was asked to identify a picture of peppers, he wrote 'tomato' but said 'artichoke'. In addition, there are patients who can provide written names for objects but who are very poor at providing the spoken word for the same objects. Some can write down words for which they can give neither a definition nor a pronunciation. Other patients show severe word finding difficulties (anomia) when speaking, yet they are able to write down the words that they are looking for. Others can write perfectly well to dictation, even of irregularly spelled words, but without understanding what they are hearing. Some patients with word deafness (see above) find that if they write down a word they have heard but not understood, then they can read what they have written and understand the word from that. These patterns of behaviour suggest a range of connections between modules, such as those suggested in Figure 13.3.

The architecture shown in Figure 13.3 is complex, but even so is something of a simplification. It seems that as more data become available from patient studies, so more and more complex interactions are required between the components in the figure in order to account for the data. It is of course possible that patients have developed strategies and alternative pathways for dealing with the difficulties they face, and that the post-trauma architecture may not accurately reflect the pathways used in so-called 'normal' language processing. Figure 13.3 is a simplification also in that it omits some detail that is almost certainly required for a full account of lexical processing.

13.5 Language and other processing systems

We have considered above the issue of modularity within language processing, i.e. whether there are separate modules for different aspects or levels of language production or comprehension. We have also looked at the number and nature of the modules that are utilised in the production and comprehension of spoken and written words, as well as the connections between them. In this section we consider another aspect of the modularity debate, namely the extent to which there is a separate module for language processing, contrasted with other cognitive skills or systems.

On a non-modular view, language, memory, reasoning, etc. can all be seen as examples of a general and powerful capacity for forming concepts and manipulating information. On a modular view, however, it is argued that there are numerous very different kinds of mental abilities, each operating in its own way, and language is one of several such modules.

Support for a modular view includes arguments along the lines of 'speech is special'. That is, there are differences e.g. between language processing and other sensory processing, so that for example speech processing and music processing involve different brain hemispherical specialisations (though with some overlap, e.g. for speech prosody and music). In addition, the processing of the visual input for sign language involves different neurological and psychological processes from those involved in processing spatial relations (though again there is some overlap). Further support for the modular view would result if there was clear evidence of separation of processes involved in language production or comprehension from central cognitive processes (i.e. those involved in memory, reasoning, etc.). The strongest sort of dissociations of this type would be double dissociations, in this case evidence not only for language deficits with preserved cognitive abilities but also for cognitive deficits with preserved language abilities.

Specific language impairment (SLI) has often been cited as a case of dissociation of linguistic and other abilities (Bishop & Snowling, 2004; Cohen, 2002; Leonard, 1998). In SLI there is early and often lasting impairment in language capabilities. This is coupled with normal performance on nonverbal tests of general intelligence. There is generally also no evidence of speech impediment or hearing loss that might explain problems at a more peripheral level. SLI speech tends to be slow and deliberate, and typically exhibits problems with grammatical forms. For instance, SLI speech does not consistently use appropriate grammatical endings, with SLI sufferers producing sentences such as *The girl is jump over the rope* or *I can see three cat*. Because there is some evidence that SLI runs in families and so may have a genetic component, it has been suggested that it may involve hereditary problems with some of the neural wiring responsible for language functions.

A contrasting set of symptoms is exhibited by so-called chatterbox syndrome (also known as Williams syndrome). Sufferers typically speak fluently and grammatically, and also score well on specifically linguistic tasks such as grammaticality judgement. In contrast to this evidence for intact linguistic skills, they show poor performance in tests of logical reasoning and in questions concerning general knowledge (Pinker, 1994).

SLI and chatterbox syndrome appear on the surface to give us a double dissociation of linguistic and other cognitive skills, which would support the existence of a separate language module from general intelligence, etc. That is, SLI has impairment of language skills with preservation of general cognitive function, while chatterbox syndrome has preservation of language skills but poor general cognitive function. However, it has been argued that SLI may be an unwitting result of difficulties in other areas which are in turn not specifically linguistic in nature. For example, SLI sufferers show an impaired ability to track where a sound is coming from. This is revealed in tasks where they listen to a sound such as a tone or click and have to point to where they think the sound is coming from. One of the early signs of children's perceptual development for language is their ability to locate the source of speech sounds. This is important for phonological development, since attention can be better directed to the input if its location can be tracked. The fact that SLI sufferers are less well able to track a moving signal may have led to impaired phonological development. In turn this may have had a detrimental effect on the course of other linguistic development. In the case of chatterbox syndrome, there are many sufferers who fail to learn to read or write, i.e. there are at least some linguistic skills (admittedly secondary skills, in terms of the development both of the species and of the individual) that are not preserved.

Visual world paradigms

More direct evidence against modular separation of linguistic and other cognitive skills includes research results that show how general knowledge is used with great immediacy and efficiency in constraining language processing. Consider for instance the bridging inferences discussed in Chapter 12 with reference to examples such as (13.10), where it is argued that the ease with which we understand the two sentences together depends on our ability to use our understanding of the world and of the fact that *car* is implicit in the role of *vehicle used to drive to London* in the first sentence.

(13.10)   Keith drove to London. The car kept on overheating.

Other evidence comes from studies of how we use non-linguistic visual information from the environment during language processing, using what is known as a visual world paradigm. Typically, this involves presenting a scene (the 'visual world') to participants on a computer screen and monitoring their eye movements as they listen to some pre-recorded instructions. The point of interest is usually where in the visual world they direct their gaze as they hear and interpret the information in the instruction. So for instance Eberhard *et al.* (1995) used different arrangements of objects and recorded participants' eye movements as they listened to spoken commands to move one of the objects. The sentences used in the command utterances investigated the parsing strategy of Minimal Attachment (see Chapter 10). This strategy predicts that the initially preferred interpretation of the instruction in (13.11) at the point that *Put the apple on the towel* has been heard will be that the apple should be moved onto the towel. This is because attachment of the prepositional phrase (PP) *on the towel* as an argument of the verb (i.e. telling the participant the goal of the *put* action) is syntactically simpler than attachment of the same PP as a modifier of the noun phrase *the apple* (where it would be telling the participant something about where the apple already is).

(13.11)   Put the apple on the towel in the box.

The sentence in (13.11) can be contrasted with the sentence in (13.12), where the phrase *that's* makes it unambiguously clear that the PP modifies *the apple*.

(13.12)   Put the apple that's on the towel in the box.

Eberhard *et al.* used the pair of sentences (13.11) and (13.12), along with others with different object names. Each sentence in a pair was listened to in combination with two different configurations of four objects. In both configurations three of the quadrants of a worktable contained an apple on a towel, a towel with nothing on it, and a box. In one configuration – the single referent configuration in Figure 13.4 – the fourth quadrant had an object not related to any of the others, e.g. a pencil. In the other configuration – the double referent configuration in Figure 13.5 – the fourth object was an apple that was not on a towel. In this case, the phrase *apple on the towel* with a <u>non</u>-Minimal Attachment interpretation (where the PP *on the towel* modifies the noun *apple* rather than the verb *put*) is made contextually relevant by the presence of the other apple, since the phrase distinguishes the two apples (one is on a towel, the other is not).

In the single referent configuration, participants' eye gaze as they listened to the ambiguous instruction in (13.11) moved first to the apple (on hearing *apple*), then to the uncovered towel (on hearing *towel*), and then at the end of the sentence back to the apple and then to the box. This pattern of eye movements, including a fixation on the uncovered towel, indicates that participants were initially garden-pathed into considering an action of moving the apple onto the uncovered towel. This contrasted with eye

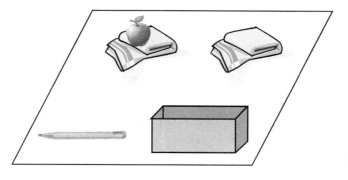

Figure 13.4
Single referent condition.

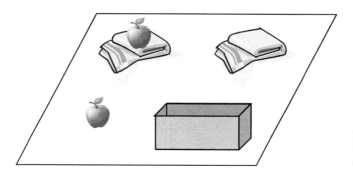

Figure 13.5
Double referent condition.

movements when hearing the unambiguous sentence in (13.12), again with the single referent condition in Figure 13.4, where participants' gaze moved only to the apple and then to the box. The phrase *that's on* in (13.12) made the interpretation clear, much as we saw for examples of explicit marking of syntax in Chapter 10.

In the double referent condition, as participants heard *the apple on the towel* in (13.11), they typically looked at both apples, but rarely at the uncovered towel. They were no longer misled by the Minimal Attachment preference into considering the towel as a goal. This indicates that the visual information in this double referent condition gives relevance to the use of the PP as a modifier of the noun phrase, and eliminates the garden path.

This example, along with other studies that have measured eye movements during spoken language processing, shows that the linkage between non-linguistic and linguistic information is an important factor in the interpretation of utterances, and can even overrule strong syntactic preferences shown in a range of other studies.

13.6 Language and the brain

Throughout this book, evidence for the representations and processes that form the subject matter of psycholinguistics has been taken from a number of areas of study. These have included the results of neurophysiological research that has investigated the areas of the brain that are involved in language processing. Since the primary purpose of this book is to introduce the reader to psycholinguistic issues of relevance to different levels or stages of language production and comprehension, this kind of evidence has been deliberately included alongside other sources of data, rather than in a separate chapter on language in the brain.

What, though, is the overall picture that has resulted from neurophysiological studies? As one review has pointed out, this picture is far clearer for comprehension than for production (Salmelin, 2007). This is above all because of artefacts in the brain activity records that are caused by movements of the vocal apparatus for speaking. This is particularly the case for fMRI recordings, where movement of the head (necessary for speaking of course) can affect the recorded images (Zeffiro & Frymiare, 2006). Unfortunately it is not possible to get the same information about brain activity from covert speech, since it has been shown that different patterns of activity are associated with inner speech and actual spoken responses. Therefore various types of comparison and normalisation are carried out to try to negate the effect of such other factors as head movement.

The general picture that emerges is that it is primarily the left hemisphere that is involved and that the processes are very fast. For example, on the basis of a review of 82 neuroimaging studies of word production, Indefrey and Levelt (2004) set out the activation patterns shown in Figure 13.6 for picture naming. There is some temporal overlap between the processes, but activation is clearly localised to particular brain areas.

MEG data from studies of word recognition show equally fast processes. For example, spoken word recognition involves acoustic-phonetic feature activation some 50–100 msec after the onset of the speech sounds, phonological analysis by 100–200 msec, and activation of lexical representations from about 200 msec onwards (Salmelin, 2007). Distinct activation patterns for speech rather than non-speech emerge about 100 msec from the onset of the stimulus. In addition, syllables heard in a meaningful context result in similarly located but markedly different levels of activation from syllables in a non-meaningful context.

In silent reading, visual feature analysis occurs around 100 msec after the presentation of a stimulus, with letter-string analysis starting at about 150 msec. Letter-string analysis is much more heavily lateralised to the left hemisphere than general visual feature analysis. Activation reflecting

Figure 13.6

Timing of activation of left hemisphere brain areas during word production (simplified from Indefrey & Levelt, 2004).

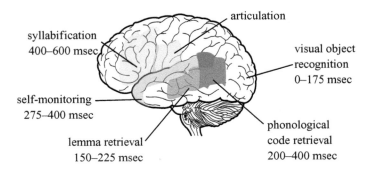

reading comprehension occurs from 200–600 msec, and it is during this period that words and nonwords become distinguished (in the relevant tasks).

Clearly, as more is learned about the neurophysiology of language production and comprehension, so we will see more rigorous defence of certain hypotheses concerning the interrelationships of the various representations and processes involved in language use.

Summary

This chapter has looked at the interrelationships between different processing components. This has included consideration both of connections between different language processing components and of the position of language processing vis-à-vis other cognitive systems. Evidence has come from studies of both normal and impaired language users, and from behavioural and neurophysiological studies. We have seen:

- that there is some evidence for separate representation for different aspects of language such as syntactic and semantic knowledge;
- that this knowledge is used in an interactive way during language processing and that there is diminishing support for a completely modular language processing system;
- that it is by no means clear at what point – from central processes through to peripheral processes – production and comprehension become distinct;
- that although there is certainly overlap in the representations used by visual and spoken language processing, it is similarly uncertain how extensive this overlap is;
- that the language system is not impervious to information from other sources, such as general knowledge, inferential processes, and non-linguistic contextual information.

Exercises

Exercise 13.1

All of the following sentences are grammatically correct. Imagine that an experimental task is to match each sentence to a picture showing the situation described in the sentence, where that picture is one of a set of pictures showing different things. For each sentence, would you predict the sentence–picture matching to be straightforward if the syntactic analysis system was restricted to (a) subject-verb-object ordering of content words, with no further grammatical information, (b) no grammatical information at all?

1. The boy stroked the cat.
2. The dog chased the cat.
3. The parcel was opened by the teacher.
4. The woman read the book.
5. The table was polished by the cleaner.
6. The tailor mended the coat.

Exercise 13.2

Consider the arrangement of shapes in panel A of Figure 13.7. The colour names on the shapes represent the colours of each one. In a test of spoken sentence processing, some participants heard sentence 1, spoken with contrastive stress on the word *large* (shown by capitals), while others heard sentence 2, without such contrastive stress. The latencies of participants' eye movements to the named object were measured, using the onset of the spoken word *blue* as the starting point from which the latencies were measured. These eye movements occurred significantly earlier for participants who heard 1 than for those who heard 2. Why?

1. Touch the LARGE blue square.
2. Touch the large blue square.

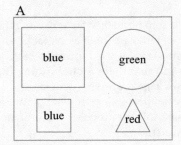
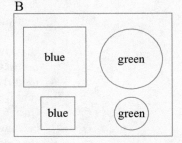

Figure 13.7
Two configurations of four objects.

Exercise 13.3

In a further set of conditions, sentences 1 and 2 above were heard in conjunction with the configuration in panel B of Figure 13.7. What result would you predict for eye movement times for this configuration?

. . . .

Further reading

The chief characteristics of a modular language processing system outlined in this chapter are based on Caplan (1992), who in turn develops the classic account of modularity by Fodor (1983). A short history of the relationship between syntax and other knowledge sources used in sentence processing, with a particular emphasis on clinical evidence, is provided by Martin *et al.* (2007). A review of MEG evidence concerning brain activity during both production and perception is found in Salmelin (2007).

Glossary

Note: The online version of this glossary (available via the web page for *Introducing Psycholinguistics*) contains additional information, examples, etc. The online version can also be used as a learning tool, e.g. by initially selecting only the terms for presentation, so that students can test their understanding of those terms. The online version can also be used to display items by topic or randomly, in addition to alphabetically as below.

accented: Of a syllable or word that is prominent by virtue of being spoken more clearly and/or more strongly, e.g. to show focus.

access: In word recognition, either making first contact with lexical entries, or retrieving information about a word from the lexicon.

accommodation: Result of errors involving word/stem exchanges, where a stranded affix takes on a form appropriate to a stem which has been moved. E.g. the plural '-s' has the sound /s/ in *pile of books* but /z/ in the error *book of piles*.

acquired dyslexia: Disruption of previously intact reading ability resulting from brain damage, e.g. after head injury or stroke.

activation: Excitation of mental representations for language, or the flow of information relating to this. E.g. in models of word recognition, a word may have a higher level of activation and therefore be more likely to be recognised if it has high frequency.

active filler hypothesis: Notion that because of memory load, the process of linking a filler to a gap must be carried out as rapidly as possible.

addition: Type of speech error where an extra word or sound is included in an utterance. E.g. *He behaved as like a fool.*

adjunct: Optional element in a sentence that may be removed without affecting structural integrity. For instance, the adverbial in parentheses in: *The student submitted his assignment (somewhat reluctantly).*

agrammatic speech/agrammatism: Non-fluent speech produced by some brain-damaged patients (typically Broca's aphasics) in which there is little grammatical structure and which consists mainly of content words.

allomorph: Variant form of a morpheme, which may depend for instance on the stem to which the morpheme is being attached. E.g. the morpheme {plural} in English has the differently sounding allomorphs /s/ in *cats*, /z/ in *dogs*, /əz/ in *horses*.

allophone: Variant form of the pronunciation of a phoneme, which may depend on the phonetic context in which the phoneme is realised. The English phoneme /p/ has an aspirated allophone at the beginning of a stressed syllable ([pʰ] as in *pot*) and an unaspirated allophone after /s/ ([p] in *spot*).

anaphor: Word or phrase that makes reference to material that has appeared earlier in the text or discourse. (This earlier material is the antecedent.) The most obvious anaphors are pronouns, but nouns, verbs and whole phrases can be anaphors.

anomalous prose: Syntactically well-formed but meaningless sentence used in experiments. E.g. *No buns puzzle some in the lead off the text.*

anomia: Speech disorder, often as a result of brain damage, resulting in difficulty with finding words and naming things.

antecedent: Word or phrase in a text or discourse that is later referred to by means of an anaphor. *Amy* (antecedent) *was pleased when she* (anaphor) *got the job.*

anticipation: Speech error where a word or sound is spoken earlier in the utterance than it should be. E.g. (self-corrected) *I suggest we kill all stone… all birds with one stone.*

antonym: Word that is opposite in meaning to some other word. Includes gradable opposites that allow some in-between value (*hot–cold*), exclusive or complementary terms (*dead–alive*), and reciprocal terms (*husband–wife*).

aphasia: Loss of language ability as a consequence of brain damage, which may result from head injury or stroke.

articulation: Final stage of the speech production process, when the sounds of words are pronounced, as the speaker implements a phonetic plan.

articulatory pause: Silence resulting from the articulatory processes, rather than a pause indicating planning processes. E.g. the silence during the closure phase of a voiceless stop like /p/ in *space*.

aspiration: Puff of air that is produced during articulation of plosive consonants (especially voiceless), at the moment when the closure is released.

association norm: List of the words produced when a target word is presented to participants and they are asked to write down the first word that occurs to them. The membership of the list provides information about the possible connections between words in the mental lexicon.

associative: Type of semantic relationship that words have with one another and which arises through their being used in the same contexts together or because the referents for these words are in the same semantic field. These relationships are argued to exist between the lemma representations of words.

automaticity: Obligatory nature of processing carried out by components in, e.g., a modular system. If the module receives some input, then that input must be processed by the module and an output generated. Cf. the apparent obligatory nature of word recognition, as reflected in the Stroop effect.

backtracking: Eye movements back to an earlier part of a text during reading.

batonic gesture: Beating gesture used for emphasis, e.g. to reinforce major stresses in the accompanying utterance.

bin model: Model of word recognition in which words are retrieved from sorted lists (bins), which have the most frequent words at the top.

blend: 1. Type of speech error where elements of two words are mixed together to produce a new word, often a nonsense word. E.g. *I must pick up my hand buggage* (blend of *baggage* and *luggage*).
     2. In general linguistic usage, word formation process where two words are combined. E.g. *smog* from *smoke* and *fog*.

body, of word: Term from the study of spelling (and its relation to pronunciation) that refers to the part of the word that makes up its rhyme.E.g. -aze in *gaze*, -oon in *spoon*.

bottom-up: Processing based on the sensory input (e.g. the speech signal) rather than on higher-level (e.g. contextual) information.

bridging inference: Connection made by the reader or listener between an anaphor and a non-explicit antecedent. E.g. between *the car* and the understood notion of car in *drove in*: *Keith drove to London. The car kept overheating.*

Broca's aphasia: Speech disorder caused by damage to Broca's area of the brain. People with this condition use mainly simple content words, omitting function words; they have trouble with parsing and in making grammaticality judgements.

Broca's area: Part of the brain which is located in the frontal lobe of the left hemisphere of the brain. It deals with grammatical processing, so people with damage to this part of the brain often have trouble with grammatical planning and parsing.

CAT scan: Computed axial tomography; imaging of the structures of the brain, based on a series of X-rays taken from different angles.

categorical perception: Hearing sounds as being clear instances of a particular phoneme, e.g. as /b/ or /p/ rather than as more or less /b/-like.

category: Semantic category: area of meaning, often referring to words from this area (e.g. types of bird);

Syntactic category: grammatical class (e.g. noun, verb);

Phonemic category: class of sounds with same property (e.g. voiced sounds).

category ambiguity: When a single word-form represents words from more than one grammatical class. E.g. *swim* as a noun or verb.

category monitoring: Experimental task where participants are given a semantic category (e.g. LIVING THINGS) and then presented with word stimuli for each of which they have to respond whether the thing it refers to is in that category.

central process: Processing which involves cognitive or conceptual aspects of language, rather than perceptual operations.

chatterbox syndrome: See Williams syndrome.

chunking: Grouping information into clusters to improve processing efficiency or to help memory processes. E.g. remembering telephone numbers as groups of three or four digits rather than as a single longer string.

clausal hypothesis: Claim that the clause is the basic unit of analysis in language comprehension. See clausal processing and clausal structuring.

clausal processing: In its strongest form, a claim that syntactic processing is carried out exclusively at the boundaries between clauses.

clausal structuring: Claim that clauses are important structural units, but that processing can take place within clauses and not just at clause boundaries.

click location: Task used to support claims of clausal processing. Participants had to mark on transcripts of speech where they heard a non-speech signal, and this 'migrated' to boundaries between clauses.

closed class: The set of function words, which cannot easily be added to. Contrast open class.

Cloze task: Experimental task where words are deleted from a sentence and participants are asked to provide the missing word(s).

coarticulation: Influence on the production of one sound from neighbouring sounds, because of how they run together in speech. E.g. /s/ at the end of *drinks* in *he drinks champagne* is more like /ʃ/ because of the sound at the beginning of *champagne*.

cocktail party effect: Ability of listeners to follow the speech of one speaker despite the fact that other speakers are talking around them. See signal continuity.

coherence: Way in which sentences or phrases belong together in terms of their meaning, i.e. they make sense in the discourse context.

cohesion: Way in which sentences or phrases belong together because of grammatical devices used to make the links between them. See anaphor.

Cohort: Model of spoken word recognition, named for the idea that a group of words is activated that share the same onset sounds. See word-initial cohort.

collocation: Words that typically occur together in a phrase or sentence. E.g. *fish and chips*, and idioms like *A stitch in time saves nine*.

competition: Notion that two or more representations (e.g. words) contest with one another during processing. See also activation and inhibition.

conceptualisation: Initial stage of language production, where a pre-verbal message is generated based on the speaker's or writer's intentions.

connected speech process: Change to the speech sounds of words that occurs late in the production process, as a consequence of coarticulation and the phonetic environment that the sounds find themselves in. E.g. wanna-contraction in *Who do you wanna see now?*

connectionism: View that representations and processes exist as patterns of interaction between processing units. Knowledge arises from statistical regularities rather than from rules.

consistency: Extent to which a spelling pattern has a predictable pronunciation across a set of words, regardless of whether that relationship follows the regular rules for the language. The <-aze> spelling in *gaze* is both regular and consistent in terms of how it will be pronounced. The <-ook> spelling in *look, book, took*, etc. is consistent but irregular (the pronunciation following rules for <-oo-> spellings would be as in *spook*).

constituent assembly: Creation of a syntactic frame for a sentence during the process of grammatical encoding.

constraint-based processing: Interactive model of language processing that claims that all kinds of information are taken into account in determining an analysis, in a probabilistic fashion.

contact: In the early stages of word recognition, the process of connecting with stored representations of words that match the phonetic input.

content word: Word from one of the categories of nouns, verbs, adjectives and adverbs. These are also known as the open class of words, since the set can easily be added to (e.g. by new product names). Contrast function word.

contingency of choice: Notion that knowing you have heard one particular word depends on your having excluded other possible words.

continuation selection: Experimental task where participants choose between possible continuations for a sentence fragment.

corpus (pl. corpora): Collection of language materials, usually analysed in some way (e.g. with part-of-speech information linked to each word). There are corpora of different kinds of text or recordings (from which frequency information can be derived), corpora of speech errors, of pause data, etc.

covert repair: When a speaker discovers that something is wrong with what she plans to say but interrupts herself before the troublesome material is actually spoken.

cross-modal: Mixed-media presentation in an experimental task, using both spoken and visual materials. E.g. in cross-modal naming an auditory stimulus is presented as a prime, with a visual probe (e.g. a word) aligned with a crucial part of the utterance.

CSP: See connected speech process.

cue integration: In perception, the ability of the listener to make use of different pieces of information, putting them together to identify a sound. Can also involve putting together cues from different sources – see McGurk effect.

cue trading: In cases where multiple cues are used to identify, e.g., a phoneme, it is sometimes the case that strong evidence from one cue will make the listener less dependent on other cues.

declarative knowledge: Knowledge we have in long-term memory, also known as 'world knowledge'.

deep dyslexia: Reading impairment where patients cannot read aloud nonsense words, but show good reading comprehension for concrete and imageable words, though not for abstract or grammatical words, and show a large number of substitutions, or paralexias.

deep orthography: Type of relationship between spelling and pronunciation where there is a high degree of irregularity. English has a deep orthography; consider the different pronunciations of the <-ough> spelling in *bough, cough, rough, though, through, thorough*.

deep structure: Underlying or logical structure of a sentence. Active and passive versions of sentences (e.g. *The dog chased the cat* and *The cat was chased by the dog*) are said to be different surface forms of the same deep structure.

definiteness: When referring to a specific item by, for example, using *the* instead of *a*. Anaphors are typically definite.

deixis: Part of message structure which deals with links to the time and place of utterance.

delimitative pause: Pause at a place where a written text might have punctuation, breaking an utterance into constituent parts and potentially aiding the listener's understanding.

derivation (morphology): Concerns the construction of new words from base forms and affixes. E.g. *brotherhood* from *brother + hood*. Compare inflection.

derivation (syntax): Process by which an underlying or logical form of a sentence is changed into the surface form that we speak or read.

Derivational Theory of Complexity: Notion that difficulty in production and/or comprehension is related to how different the surface structure of a sentence is from its deep structure, according to the rules of transformational (derivational) grammar.

developmental dyslexia: Reading difficulty that originates in childhood, where there is no obvious cause such as head trauma and where it is usually the case that the full range of normal reading skills has never been present.

deviation point: In spoken word recognition research, the point at which a nonword becomes distinct from the existing words in the language. E.g. *spoog* has its deviation point at the /g/ since this is where it differs from e.g. *spoon*.

dichotic listening: Listening using both ears, often to different stimuli in each ear, e.g. to test the right ear advantage.

dichotic switch monitoring: Task where participants listen to speech that is louder on one headphone channel than the other and while they listen this imbalance switches channels. The participant's task is to indicate when this happens, and their response can be affected by the processing load at the time of the switch.

diphone: Sequence of two sounds, importantly capturing the transitions from one sound to the next. Often used to create more natural sounding speech synthesis. Important in some models of word recognition.

distance effect: Finding that the greater the delay between an antecedent and an anaphor, the longer it takes listeners to retrieve the antecedent from memory on encountering the anaphor.

domain-specific: Characteristic of a processing module that deals only with one kind of information.

double dissociation: When two patients (or patient groups) show different patterns of ability such that one can do task A but not task B and the other can do B but not A. Often linked to physical separation of tasks in different brain areas.

double-object construction: Sentence where a verb has two objects – one is the direct object and the other the indirect object. *He sent his mother* (indirect object) *a book* (direct object).

dual-route model: Model of reading (aloud) which suggests that readers have two ways of finding the pronunciation of a word. One is through grapheme–phoneme conversion (GPC), usually used for new or nonsense words. The other is a direct route from the visual input to the lexical entry, used for practised words.

dysgraphia: Difficulty with writing processes as a result of brain damage or developmental disorder.

dyslexia: Difficulty with reading processes as a result of brain damage or developmental disorder.

edit: Stage of repair of an error or revision of an inappropriateness after the point of interruption. Often involves an editing expression.

editing expression: Sound, word or phrase (*uh, er, I mean*) which the speaker uses to inform the listener that a mistake is about to be corrected.

EEG / electroencephalography: Technique for measuring brain activity that measures electrical activity (event-related potential) on the scalp.

empty category: Another term for gap or trace. The term reflects the fact that a gap has no phonetic content, i.e. is not pronounced.

ERF / event-related magnetic field: Currents flowing over larger neuronal structures in the brain than those showing up as event-related potentials. Usually measured using magnetoencephalography.

ERP / event-related potential: Electrical activity of currents passing through the fluid surrounding the brain's neurons as they respond to an event. Measured using electroencephalography.

exchange: Type of speech error where two words or sounds are swapped. E.g. spoonerisms such as *Our queer old dean* for *Our dear old queen*.

exemplar: Rich memory representation for, e.g., words, and which includes information about the speaker (age, sex, social grouping, dialect, etc.), as well as possibly about the time and place of the utterance, etc.

eye movement: Movement of eye gaze from one position to another. Often used as a measure of the processing taking place during reading. Consists of fixations and saccades.

eye-tracking: Experimental technique which monitors eye movements during reading, to get a measure of what information readers are using to process the text.

filled pause: Type of hesitation where the speaker utters sounds while pausing. E.g. *um, eh, ah, er, mm*.

filler: 1. In a syntactic sense, the word which has moved, leaving behind a gap, or trace. So *who* is the filler, linked to the gap marked by the underscore, in *Who$_i$ did Liz introduce _____$_i$ to Matthew?*
2. See verbal filler.

filler–gap dependency: Structural relationship between a displaced element (the filler) and the position in the sentence from which it has been moved (the gap).

first pass: Initial read-through of a sentence, as measured in eye-movement studies.

fixation: When a reader's gaze rests on a particular word or part of a word, as measured by eye-tracking.

fMRI: See functional magnetic resonance imaging.

formant: Perceptually important frequency in speech (especially with regard to the identification of vowels), resulting from how the configuration of the vocal tract (throat, mouth, nasal cavity) causes some sound frequencies to resonate more than others.

formulation: Part of the language production process that imposes linguistic form on the abstract pre-verbal message.

frequency: How often something is used or encountered. This has a major influence on ease and accuracy of use.

frequency effect: Phenomenon that a linguistic unit (e.g. a word) which is used more often than another unit of the same type and which is comparable in terms of length etc. is recognised more rapidly and more accurately.

full-listing hypothesis: Idea that all forms of a word, including regular inflected forms like past tense *walked*, are listed in the mental dictionary rather than derived by rule.

function assignment: When the lemmas selected to express the message are given their roles in the sentence. Carried out during functional processing as part of message formulation.

function word: A grammatical word such as a determiner (*the, a, some, this*), preposition (*in, on, from, to*), complementiser (*because, when, that*), etc. Also known as closed class. Contrast content word.

functional magnetic resonance imaging (fMRI): Technique that measures brain activity by measuring changes in blood flow in the brain.

functional processing: Part of the formulation component in language planning, where lemmas are selected and assigned to the different jobs required by the sentence. See lexical selection and function assignment.

galvanic skin response: Measure of the skin's ability to conduct electricity. For some people, changes in this response measure are highly sensitive to emotional changes, which can in turn be affected by the language they are processing.

Ganong effect: Finding that the boundaries between phonetic categories are affected by lexical status. Thus a stimulus which is ambiguous between /d/ and /t/ is more likely to be interpreted as /d/ in the context /_esk/ because *desk* is a real word but *tesk* is not, but as /t/ in the context /_est/.

gap: Source position from which a word has been moved by a syntactic operation. Also referred to as a trace. The underscore marks the position of the gap in: *Who$_i$ did John introduce __$_i$ to Mary?*

gap as first resort: Strategy for determining where a filler has been moved from, which assumes that you allocate it to the first possible position from where it might have moved.

gap as last resort: Strategy for determining where a filler has been moved from, which assumes that the processor delays until it is absolutely forced to link the filler to a possible source position.

garden path: Sentence which misleads the reader/listener by initially inducing a structural interpretation which turns out to be incorrect. See also local ambiguity, Late Closure and Minimal Attachment.

gating task: Experimental task where participants hear edited recordings of fragments of a word and have to report what they hear after each presentation. Usually presented as incrementally larger fragments starting with the first few sounds of the word.

gender, grammatical: Basis found in many languages for grouping of words into different classes, for example into masculine, feminine or neuter. This classification need not depend on whether the referent itself is masculine or feminine etc. In German, the word for 'shoe' is masculine (*der Schuh*), 'jacket' is feminine (*die Jacke*) and 'shirt' is neuter (*das Hemd*).

gesture: Movement or posture of hands, face, body, etc. that either accompanies or takes the place of speech.

given: Information that is already part of the discourse shared between speaker and listener. Contrast new information.

global ambiguity: An ambiguity that is not resolved within the sentence. E.g. *The spy watched the man with the binoculars* (who has the binoculars?). Also known as standing ambiguity. Contrast local ambiguity.

good-enough processing: The idea that language processing does not always generate a complete analysis of a sentence, but one that is perhaps based on superficial information.

grammatical encoding: Process of generating sentences, using a string of lemmas with their functions specified. Important part of the formulation component of language production. Has the subcomponents functional processing and positional processing.

grapheme–phoneme conversion (GPC): In reading, the process of converting letters to sounds. One of the pathways in the dual-route model of reading.

graphophonic transposition: Also known as grapheme–phoneme conversion.

Guessing Game: Technique for determining the predictability of words in context, by presenting an incomplete sentence to respondents who have to make guesses as to the next word, within a specified time limit.

hemisphere: Half of the cerebrum, which is the main part of the brain.

hemispherical specialisation: Fact that each half of the brain has special responsibility for particular cognitive and motor tasks. For example, the left hemisphere has specialisation for most language faculties.

hesitation: Interruption to fluent speech, which may reveal aspects of the planning process.

homophone: Word that sounds the same as another word, and which can but need not have the same spelling. E.g. *bank* (financial institution) and *bank* (of river), *their* and *there*. Compare polysemy.

iconic gesture: Gesture that depicts what is being talked about. E.g. moving hand to show wavy line when talking about a rough sea crossing.

immediacy of interpretation: Idea that words are incorporated into the developing sentence structure one by one, as soon as they are received.

inappropriateness: Error where the speaker has not given enough information or has not been explicit enough, even though what they said is still correct. This results in a revision, rather than a repair.

indexical gesture: Gesture that involves drawing attention to something, e.g. by pointing, nodding the head towards an object, etc.

inference: Connection made to something assumed to be the case even though it might not be explicitly stated in the discourse. E.g. it might be inferred from the use of the verb *drive* that a vehicle of some sort is involved.

inflection (morphology): Affix added to word bases in order to mark grammatical function, agreement etc. (compare derivation). E.g. *-ed* added to mark past tense in English: *walked*.

informationally encapsulated: Description for a self-contained processing module.

inhibition: Reduction in activation of recognition units such as words that might result for instance from competition between such units.

inner speech: See subvocalisation.

instance: Word taken from a semantic category, as *hawk* is taken from the category *bird*.

instantiation: Type of inference that a listener draws from discourse, where they use their background knowledge to amplify something general that the speaker has said.

instrumentality: Idea that speakers choose to express information that is vital to their communicative intention, and do not explicitly express information that they can assume the listener will infer.

integration: Matching of information about possible word candidates against information about the sentence context in order to facilitate word recognition. Distinct from cue integration.

interaction: Influence on one another of different processes in different parts of the cognitive and/or language processing systems.

interactive activation: Framework for processing in which information spreads by way of activation from unit to unit within and between levels.

interruption: When a speaker stops their own utterance which is or would be errorful. Followed by editing expression (optional) and then a repair.

irregular: Language form or relationship that does not follow the rules. E.g. *feet* is an irregular plural form in English.

Jabberwocky: Sentence type made up of nonsense content words and real function words and with a grammatically correct structure. The term comes from a poem written in this style that is found in *Through the Looking Glass and What Alice Found There* by Lewis Carroll.

judgement task: Experimental task where participants evaluate some aspect of a stimulus, e.g., is it natural? a good example? acceptable? a real word?

Late Closure: One of the sentence analysis strategies proposed to account for garden path sentences. This one attaches material into the clause or phrase currently being processed, rather than to a new clause or phrase. See also Minimal Attachment. Late Closure leads to a garden path if the reader interprets *his book* as the object of *reading* in: *While Jack was reading his book fell off the table.*

left-to-right processing: Metaphor, based on the processing of writing (in languages like English), for how processing of the speech signal unfolds through time.

lemma: Abstract, conceptual, pre-phonological form of a word. Contrast lexeme.

lexeme: 1. In psycholinguistics often used for word-forms (e.g. <CAT> is the written word-form for the lemma {cat}).
2. More generally in linguistics refers to a lexical entry.

lexical access: Stage of word recognition at which stored information about a word becomes available for further processing.

lexical ambiguity: When a word has more than one unrelated meaning. See homophone. Compare polysemy.

lexical decision: Experimental task where participants are asked to decide whether a stimulus is a real word or a nonsense form.

lexical expectation: See lexical preference.

lexical frequency: How commonly a word is used. Lexical frequency has an effect on ease and accuracy of word recognition.

lexical preference: When a word tends to be used in certain sentence structures in preference to others. Our experience-based knowledge of such preferences can affect processing of sentences involving that word.

lexical selection: 1. As part of the production process, the choice of abstract forms of content words or lemmas based on the concepts that the speaker wants to express.
2. In comprehension, the process of choosing the single word that matches the phonetic or visual input.

lexical stress error: Type of speech error where the stress is placed on the wrong syllable. E.g. *tele'phone* for *'telephone*.

lexicalisation: 1. During language production, the stage of processing where we select words to express our thoughts.
2. In general linguistics, the process by which a new form becomes established as a lexical entry.

lexicality: Whether a letter/phoneme string is a real word or a nonsense form.

linearisation: Aspect of macroplanning where the order for expressing information is chosen.

local ambiguity: Ambiguity where the meaning is made clear later in the same utterance or sentence (also known as temporary ambiguity). In *While John was reading the book fell off his lap* the local ambiguity is whether *the book* is an explicit direct object of *reading*. Contrast global ambiguity.

local syntactic organisation: Level of organisation within a phrase or clause rather than across larger units. Sound exchange errors such as spoonerisms occur mainly within local syntactic units.

logical form: Underlying abstract representation of a sentence that expresses the logical relationships between entities in the sentence.

logogen: Word recognition unit which monitors various information sources and receives activation to the extent that the incoming information matches the specification of the unit. Part of the Logogen model of word recognition.

macroplanning: Process of selecting a series of speech acts to complete a communication goal. See also microplanning.

macroprocessing: In discourse comprehension, the processing involved in understanding the main ideas of a discourse.

magnetoencephalography (MEG): Technique for determining brain activity by measuring the magnetic fields created by naturally occurring electrical activity in the brain.

main clause: Clause that conveys the main idea of a sentence. Contrast subordinate clause.

main interruption rule: Rule for speech repairs which maintains that speakers correct themselves as soon as they detect an error.

malapropism: Speech error where the word produced is similar to the intended word in its sound shape, but not necessarily in its meaning. E.g. *equivocal* for *equivalent*. Named after a character in Sheridan's *The Rivals*.

masking: Experimental technique of degrading a stimulus by superimposing noise or another stimulus onto it.

McGurk effect: Perceptual phenomenon of integration, where a participant hearing the audio channel of a speaker producing one sound while seeing a video of the speaker producing a different sound will in fact report a third sound.

MEG: See magnetoencephalography.

mental lexicon: Dictionary in our head, consisting of representations for the forms and contents of words.

mental model: Internal representation that depicts a situation in the world. Part of the pre-verbal conceptualisation process in production and part of the abstract representation of meaning derived from the input during comprehension.

mentalese: Language of thought, consisting of pre-verbal message components. The output of the conceptualisation process.

metrical segmentation strategy: Process of breaking the speech input into units for processing/recognition on the basis of where the prosodically salient units are (e.g. stressed syllables in English). Accounts for some slips of the ear, such as hearing *A coke and a Danish* as *A coconut Danish*.

microplanning: Process of determining the pre-verbal message for each speech act. See also macroplanning.

microprocessing: In discourse comprehension, the processing involved in understanding a sentence and its connection with the preceding sentence.

Minimal Attachment: One of the parsing strategies which account for garden path sentences. This one uses the fewest possible syntactic nodes when attaching incoming material into the phrase marker being constructed. Minimal Attachment is claimed to result in an interpretation of *The man saw the woman with the binoculars* where the man has the binoculars. See also Late Closure.

mis-ordering error: Speech errors where linguistic units are entered in the wrong position in a structure. Includes anticipations, perseverations and exchanges.

mis-selection error: Speech error where the wrong element is inserted into the structure being produced. Includes substitutions and blends.

model: Theory of processing. Sometimes implemented as a computer-based simulation of processing.

modularity: Hypothesis that cognitive processes are divided up into separate systems.

monitoring: Attention paid by speakers to their own speech production in order to filter out infelicities or inappropriatenesses.

monitoring/detection task: Experimental task where participants respond when they see/hear a particular target item that they have been told to pay attention for. The type of target depends on what is being investigated.

morpheme: Minimal unit of meaning in a language. Can include bases/stems like *dog* and affixes like the <-s> for {plural} in English.

morpheme shift: Speech error where a morpheme (usually an affix) appears in the wrong place. E.g. *It all add ups* for *It all adds up.*

morphological decomposition: Breaking up of complex words into their component parts before looking these up in the mental dictionary during word recognition. e.g. *government* into *govern+ment*; *dogs* into *dog+s.*

most recent filler hypothesis: Claim that if you have two fillers followed by two gaps, you should assign the most recent of the two fillers to the first gap, and the more distant to the second. E.g. *What$_j$ are the boxes$_i$ easy to store __$_i$ in __$_j$?*

MSS: See metrical segmentation strategy.

multiword unit: Lexical items (i.e. individual dictionary entries) that are made up of more than one word. E.g. *point out* meaning *explain.*

naming: Experimental task where participants say a word aloud in response to a picture or a printed word, or after hearing a word.

neighbourhood: Words that can be grouped together on the basis of their similarity to one another.

neighbourhood density: Measure based on the count of words that are similar to one another. This can have an effect on both the recognition and production of a word from that neighbourhood.

neurophysiology: Study of brain structures, often to discover which parts of the brain are responsible for particular tasks, e.g. language processing.

new information: Information that has not previously been introduced to the discourse. When spoken, this information will often be accented, to ensure clarity for listeners. Contrast given information.

nonsemantic reading: When a word or text is read without the reader getting a sense of its meaning.

nonword: Form that is not a word of the language in question. Often used in lexical decision experiments. Legal nonwords have letter or phoneme strings that are permitted in the language: e.g. *wrod.* Illegal nonwords contain unexpected letter or phoneme strings: e.g. *wlod.*

normal prose: Type of sentence that is syntactically and semantically well-formed: *Some thieves stole most of the lead off the roof.* Compare anomalous prose and scrambled prose.

offline: Task carried out 'after the event' and usually without time pressure, such as an experiment where the participant makes a grammaticality judgement after the end of a sentence.

omission: Type of speech error where a word or sound is left out. E.g. *most models of acquired dyslexies – dyslexias.*

online: Task carried out while the participant is processing the input, such as pressing a response button immediately on hearing a target word in a monitoring task.

opacity: Obscurity, as when the relationship between a derived word and its stem is not obvious, particularly in a semantic sense. E.g. *casual/casualty*.

open class: See content word and contrast closed class.

orthography: To do with writing or spelling.

paralexias: Word substitutions during reading, usually as a result of language impairment. Can include semantic paralexias (reading *paddock* as *kennel*), derivational paralexias (reading *edition* as *editor*), and visual paralexias (reading *typing* as *taping*).

parallel: Of processing, when more than one option is processed or available at the same time. Contrast serial.

parallel distributed processing (PDP): Part of connectionist theory (see connectionism), proposing that the brain's processing of language is based on patterns of activation among individual processing units.

parser: Mechanism that analyses sentences according to their syntactic structure.

parsing: Process of analysing a string of words into a sentence structure.

parsing strategies: Syntactically determined preferred ways of analysing a string of words into a sentence structure. See sausage machine.

pause: Type of hesitation. Can be either silent or filled (*um, er*). Studied as a measure of planning load.

peripheral process: Process that is generally regarded to be automatic, not open to conscious control, such as the initial analysis of the speech input during listening or the final articulation of sounds during speaking.

perseveration: Type of speech error where a word or sound is mistakenly repeated in place of the intended or sound. E.g. *The hijacked plane, commandeered by six planes, or rather, six persons.*

PET scan: See positron emission tomography.

phoneme: Unit of speech sound that is capable of distinguishing one word from another. E.g. /p/ and /b/, which distinguish English *pat* and *bat*.

phoneme monitoring: Task where the participant is asked to listen for a particular speech sound and to press a response button as soon as they hear it.

phoneme restoration: Perceptual phenomenon where listeners report a word as being intact when in fact a phoneme has been replaced by a non-speech sound such as a cough.

phonetic feature: Important characteristic of a speech sound. It can help define a sound, distinguish it from other sounds, and place it into a group that shares the same feature. E.g. voicing is a phonetic feature that distinguishes /b/ (voiced) and /p/ (voiceless). /p, t, k, s, f/ and other sounds all share the feature 'voiceless'.

phonetic plan: Output of the process of phonological encoding. It is a sequence of coordinated motor commands that will drive the articulators (speech organs).

phonetic similarity: When two sounds share some properties, such as both being voiceless sounds (/t/ and /p/), or both being fricatives (/s/ and /z/), or both being labial sounds (/b/ and /m/), etc.

phonological dyslexia: Reading difficulty where patients (a) are able to read real words, both those with a regular spelling–sound correspondence and irregular words, but (b) are poor at reading pronounceable nonwords.

phonological encoding: Processes by which the sound shapes of words are specified. Component of the formulation process. The output is a phonetic plan.

phonological loop: Part of working memory which temporarily holds a small amount of phonological information.

phonological recoding: Also known as grapheme–phoneme conversion.

phrase marker: Syntactic tree, represented by nodes for sentence constituents and connecting lines showing how these constituents fit together.

physiological pause: Pauses used by speakers to regulate their breathing while speaking.

plausibility: Semantic property to do with whether an utterance is credible. Claimed to influence syntactic sentence processing.

polysemy: When a single lexeme has multiple related meanings. E.g. *point* as a geographical feature, tip of a pencil, etc. Contrast homophone.

positional processing: Part of grammatical encoding. Creates a sentence frame for the message, into which the lemmas are organised.

positron emission tomography (PET): Means of measuring brain activity by tracking emissions from radioactive substances injected into the bloodstream.

Possible Word Constraint: Ensures that the speech input is exhaustively broken into words without leaving any residual sounds. E.g. 'see' can be segmented from /siʃʌb/ because the residue 'shub' is a possible (though non-existing) word, but less easily from /siʃ/ because the residue 'sh' is not.

Predicate Proximity: Sentence processing strategy that results in the attachment of a noun-phrase modifier to the noun phrase that is closest to the verb in the main clause. E.g. *who had the accident* would be taken to modify *the daughter* in: *The journalist interviewed the daughter of the colonel who had the accident*. Contrast Recency Principle.

predictability: Likelihood of a word occurring in a given context.

prefix: Affix that is added at the beginning of a word stem to form another word. E.g. *out-* in *outstanding*.

prefix stripping: Removal of affix from the front of a word allowing its recognition via the stem.

pre-lexical analysis: Analysis of the input sound wave or the visual input that extracts relevant units for looking up entries in the mental lexicon.

pre-pausal lengthening: Increases in the durations of sounds before a pause (or the site of a possible pause), compared with their durations elsewhere. This is part of the rhythmic break that makes up a pause.

pre-selection: Early choice of a word during comprehension, e.g. on the basis of contextual information.

pre-verbal message: Abstract representation of what the speaker wants to say. Result of the process of conceptualisation. See mental model.

prime: Stimulus presented in an experiment and bearing some relationship to a subsequent stimulus (the probe).

priming: Where hearing or seeing one processing unit, e.g. a word, can affect a participant's speed and accuracy in responding to a subsequent, related processing unit.

probe: Test stimulus, especially one presented after a prime.

procedural knowledge: Type of knowledge involved in generating messages, which tells us how to perform tasks or realise goals.

procedural memory: Type of memory for how to perform tasks or realise goals.

process: Operation that is part of the production or comprehension of language. Psycholinguistics can be defined as the study of the representations and processes involved in language use.

productivity: Likelihood or predictability of a process, especially regarding whether the process is likely to apply to new forms. E.g. *-able* is a productive affix in English for making adjectives from verbs.

progressive demasking: Technique used in perception or recognition experiments where a stimulus is gradually revealed from behind a masking stimulus.

pronominal reference: Use of a pronoun (e.g. *she, us*) to refer to a person or object. Anaphors frequently involve pronominal reference.

prose: With an additional label, refers to the type of sentence used in experiments. See normal prose, anomalous prose, scrambled prose.

prosodic marking: Using increased emphasis or stress to highlight information in the replacement utterance of a repair.

prosody: Suprasegmental organisation of utterances, including intonation, stress and rhythm.

pseudogap: In filler–gap dependencies, a location where a filler could be attached, but which is in fact not an appropriate point of attachment. E.g. after *buy* in: *What$_i$ did John buy (__$_i$) the paint with __$_i$?*

pseudohomophone: Nonword that would sound like a real word if it were pronounced. E.g. *blud*.

psycholinguistics: Study of the mental representations and processes involved in language use, including the production, comprehension and storage of spoken and written language.

rapid serial visual presentation (RSVP): Experimental task where words are presented one at a time on a screen, at a pace that may be replicating the rate of presentation of words in speech.

real word bias: Tendency for processes, such as slips of the tongue, to result in an outcome that is a real word rather than a nonword.

recency: Relates to the finding that linguistic units such as words that have been used a short time ago are easier to recognise than those used longer ago.

Recency Principle: Sentence processing strategy that argues that words or phrases are attached locally to the closest appropriate structure. E.g. *who had the accident* would be taken to modify *the colonel* in: *The journalist interviewed the daughter of the colonel who had the accident.* Contrast Predicate Proximity.

recognition: Identification of a linguistic unit, e.g. as the end-point of the word recognition process.

recognition point: 1. In word recognition, the moment at which it is clear what the word is.
2. The position in the word on a left-to-right analysis of the input, and taking into account contextual constraints, at which it becomes distinct from other words. See uniqueness point.

reduced relative: Clause used to modify a noun-phrase, but from which the *wh*-word and possibly a verb is omitted. *The woman chased by Bert was anxious* contains the reduced relative *chased by Bert*, the full form of which might be *who was chased by Bert*.

referential hypothesis: Explanation for some garden path sentences that argues that they are difficult because they make unsupported assumptions about entities that have been introduced to the discourse, and not because of any syntactic difficulty.

regression: In eye movement studies, the movement of the eyes back to an earlier part of the text being read. See also backtracking.

regularity: 1. Rule-governed behaviour in inflectional processes in morphology (e.g. for past tense add <-ed>).
2. Rule-governed correspondences between spelling and pronunciation (e.g. <oo> is pronounced /u/).

repair: Speaker's own correction of an error in their speech.

repeat: Semantically non-significant repetition, which can be of a single sound or a longer sound sequence. *I f-f-finally managed to get So I ... I arrived in Rome.*

repetition priming: Task where participants respond to a stimulus that has previously been presented to them. Also refers to any change in behaviour in responding to a stimulus that is attributable to such prior exposure.

repetition task: Experimental task where participants repeat a word said to them. See naming and shadowing.

representation: Stored or constructed mental form of a linguistic unit.

restart: Point in a repair at which the speaker starts again and speaks the replacement material.

restrictive relative: Clause that modifies a noun-phrase and defines which of a set of possible objects, people, etc. is being referred to by the noun phrase. E.g. *Men who can multi-task are rather rare.*

reversibility: Semantic property to do with whether the subject and object of a sentence can be swapped to create a semantically plausible sentence. E.g. *The chicken saw the horse* is reversible but *The chicken pecked the horse* is not, since *The horse pecked the chicken* is implausible.

revision: Speaker's own correction of a mistake in speech where the original utterance was inappropriate or incomplete rather than wrong.

Right Association: Sentence analysis strategy that states that new nodes are preferentially attached to the lowest node (if the strategies of Late Closure and Minimal Attachment do not indicate otherwise).

right ear advantage (REA): Phenomenon that most people hear speech better with their right ears. Linked to hemispherical specialisation for language.

saccade: Eye movement during reading, from one fixation point to the next.

sausage machine: Model of syntactic sentence processing that packages words into phrases and other constituents, following parsing principles.

scrambled prose: Type of experimental sentence that is neither syntactically nor semantically well-formed but more like a random sequence of words. *Some the no puzzle buns in lead text the off.*

search model: Serial model of word recognition in which the input is checked against a candidate set of words one word at a time.

second pass: In eye movement studies, a re-reading of text that participants might carry out if they encounter some ambiguity.

segmentation: In speech perception, the splitting up of a string of sounds into discrete words.

selection: See lexical selection.

self-interruption: Where the speaker interrupts their own flow of speech, often to repair an error.

self-paced reading: Experimental task where participants read a passage word-by-word or phrase-by-phrase, pressing a button to get the next word or phrase displayed. The time taken to press the button gives an indication of the processing difficulty at each stage.

semantic priming: Facilitation of recognition of a word that results from prior exposure to a word related to it in meaning. Also used to refer to an experimental task exploiting this effect.

sentence–picture matching: Experimental task where participants are asked to decide whether a picture accurately describes an accompanying sentence, or vice versa.

serial: 1. Refers to how words are checked one at a time till the correct one is found (contrast parallel);
2. Information flow in one direction through the processing system (contrast interactive).

shadowing: A prolonged repetition task, where participants say aloud as quickly as possible some passage they hear over headphones.

shallow orthography: Where there is a predictable relationship between spelling and pronunciation. E.g. Italian and Māori are among the languages said to have a shallow orthography. Contrast deep orthography.

shallow processing: It is argued that second language learners often compute a superficial (or good-enough) analysis of sentences, rather than a detailed one.

signal continuity: Flow in the speech signal that indicates that it comes from a single source. Helps speakers track a voice and comprehend what it is saying. Contributes to the cocktail party effect.

silent pause: Type of hesitation where the speaker says nothing. Studied as a measure of processing load during speech production.

single modality: Method of presentation in an experimental task where the test materials are all in the same medium, typically either visual or spoken.

situational knowledge: Type of knowledge involved in discourse, which includes for example, the speaker's knowledge of the listener and of previous discourse.

situational model: Mental representation of the events being described rather than of the actual words being used.

SLIP: Spoonerisms of Laboratory-Induced Predisposition, i.e. refers to a technique used to induce the type of slip of the tongue known as spoonerisms.

slip of the ear: Misperception, resulting in the listener hearing something other than what the speaker intended.

slip of the tongue: Another term for speech error.

slots-and-fillers: Account of language production that says that first a frame is developed at some level of processing and then relevant items are slotted into the frame.

specific language impairment: Developmentally early and often lasting impairment in language capabilities, generally coupled with normal performance on nonverbal tests of general intelligence.

spectrogram: Visual representation of the acoustic analysis of speech in which time is on the horizontal axis, sound frequency on the vertical axis, and intensity shown by darkness of shading.

speech act: Performance of some action through saying something. What the speaker wants to achieve or communicate by what s/he says.

speech error: Mistake made while speaking, and which can be revealing about the processes and representations used during language production. Subtypes include anticipation, perseveration, exchange, blend, substitution, omission, addition, malapropism, spoonerism.

spoonerism: Speech error where the initial sounds of two words get swapped. E.g. *par cark* for *car park*, *start hopping* for *heart stopping*.

standing ambiguity: See global ambiguity.

stimulus onset asynchrony (SOA): Time interval from the presentation of one stimulus item to the next in experiments.

stranding: Phenomenon which occurs in speech errors when affixes stay in their correct place in the utterance when word stems are exchanged. E.g. *I went to get a cash chequed* for *I went to get a cheque cashed*.

streaming, perceptual: Separation of speech and non-speech sounds as coming from different sources – even when they are heard at the same time – by the human perceptual system.

stress pair: Pair of words that differ only in their stress placement (with, in some cases, concomitant differences in vowel quality). Many of these in English involve noun–verb pairs, e.g. *'import* (noun) vs *im'port* (verb).

stress shift: When a weak–strong stress pattern changes to strong–weak, because of a clash with a following stressed syllable. E.g. *thir'teen* becomes *'thirteen 'men*.

strong interactive: Account of interaction between language modules, e.g. in sentence processing, which argues for a high level of such interaction.

Stroop effect: When participants find it difficult to ignore the meaning of a word when they are told to name the colour in which the word is printed (e.g. RED printed in green). Reflects automaticity of processing.

subordinate clause: Clause that is dependent on or modifies an element of a main clause. E.g. the relative (who-) clause underlined in *The detective who solved the case was Poirot*.

subordination index: Ratio of subordinate clauses to total clauses; used as an indication of the syntactic complexity of an utterance or text.

substitution: Type of speech error where the intended word or sound is mistakenly replaced by another. E.g. *at low speeds it's too light – heavy*.

subvocalisation: Inward rehearsal of the spoken forms of words.

suffix: Affix added to the end of a base or stem. E.g. *-ed* to show past tense in *walked*, or *-able* in *decipherable*.

surface dyslexia: Condition where patients (a) show good reading aloud of nonsense words, indicating that they are able to make use of the spelling-to-sound conversion rules, but (b) show poor recognition and reading aloud of real words, particularly irregular words, i.e. words that do not follow the spelling–sound rules.

surface structure: Sentence structures that we produce, see or hear, as opposed to the deep structures from which they are argued to be derived.

symbolic gesture: Gesture that stands for a word or idea. E.g. a head-nod meaning 'yes'.

synonym: Word that has (approximately) the same meaning as another word. E.g. *adult* and *grown-up*, *big* and *large*.

syntactic ambiguity: When a sentence can be given more than one interpretation because the words can be arranged in more than one grammatical structure. *Put the cat in the box on the table* (i.e. put the cat that is already in the box onto the table, or put the cat into the box that is on the table).

syntactic frame: Sentence structure into which words are inserted during production.

syntactic priming: Increased likelihood of using a particular sentence structure as a result of recent exposure to the same or similar structure. Also used of a task which explores this effect, e.g. by asking participants to read aloud a sentence and then to perform some other task, such as describing a picture, for which they typically use a primed structure.

syntax and speech: Approach in the study of language production that looks for reflexes of syntactic structures in the prosodic structures of speech, e.g. in pausing and intonation patterns.

temporary ambiguity: See local ambiguity.

thematic processor: Processing component that carries out semantic analysis of a sentence. In the sausage machine approach to sentence processing this only influences parsing after the initial syntactic analysis.

thematic role: Role that an entity has in a sentence, determined by aspects of its meaning in relationship to the action of the verb. E.g. *the dog* in the following two sentences has different grammatical functions but is in the same thematic role of AGENT. *The dog chased the cat*; *The cat was chased by the dog*. Similarly, *the cat* is the PATIENT in both sentences.

thematic structure: Semantic organisation of an utterance, constructed according to the relationship each content word has to the others.

tip of the tongue (TOT): Common experience of almost but not quite remembering a word.

tongue twister: Task where the participant has to repeat a tricky sequence of words that is intended to induce speech errors. The likelihood of an error occurring is related to aspects of the production process.

top-down: Processing guided by contextual or utterance/sentence factors rather than by the lower-level input. Compare bottom-up.

trace: See gap.

TRACE model: A parallel access and strongly interactive model of word recognition. This model has been implemented in computer simulations. Similar in many respects to Cohort.

transitional probability: Likelihood of what the next word in a sentence will be, given the words in the sentence to that point.

transitivity ambiguity: Type of ambiguity involving verbs which can be used with or without an explicit object. E.g. *walk* as in *I'm walking* (intransitive) or *I'm walking the dog* (transitive).

transparency: Of morphological relationships that are obvious from the forms or meanings of the words. E.g. *mature/maturity*. Contrast opacity.

underlying form: Abstract (sometimes logical) form of a linguistic unit from which the surface form might be derived using transformations.

uniqueness point: In recognition of words in isolation from context, the point at which enough phonetic information has been heard to leave only one word-form as a possibility. Compare recognition point.

unrestricted race model: Model of sentence processing which claims that when an ambiguous sentence is encountered, the various possible analyses are involved in a race, with the winner being the analysis that is built fastest.

variability: Differences in pronunciation. Every speaker speaks slightly differently, and each speaker produces different sounding versions of the same word on different occasions. This has implications for speech perception.

verbal filler: Type of hesitation where the speaker utters words which do not form part of the message. *You know, I mean, well, like.*

visual buffer: Part of working memory which temporarily holds a small amount of visual information.

voice onset time (VOT): In plosives in consonant-vowel syllables, the time between the release of the stop closure and the start of voicing for the vowel.

vowel harmony: Agreement in the properties of vowels, as found in some languages (e.g. Turkish) between the vowels of word stems and the vowels of affixes added to those stems. E.g. an affix might have a form with a front vowel if the stem has a front vowel, but an alternative form with a back vowel if the stem has a back vowel.

wanna-contraction: Shortening of the sequence *want to* to the form *wanna*. See connected speech process.

weak interactive: Account of interaction between language modules, e.g. in sentence processing, where the interaction only takes place when one component – usually the syntactic component – requires information from other sources, e.g. to resolve an ambiguity.

Wernicke's aphasia: Speech disorder caused by damage to the brain, resulting in fluent but often nonsensical speech.

Wernicke's area: Area of the brain, towards the rear of the left hemisphere. People with physical damage to this area can speak fluently but often make no sense.

wh-word: Words like *who, what, when, where, which* and other question words such as *how*. There are also wh-phrases like *which car*. Wh-words feature in filler–gap dependencies.

Williams syndrome: Developmental disorder where a child talks fluently and grammatically but performs poorly on tests of general intelligence. Also known as chatterbox syndrome.

word deafness: When patients can read and write and can speak quite normally, but are unable to understand words spoken to them, despite unimpaired hearing.

word-form: Shape (in spelling or sounds) of a word, as opposed to its content or meaning. See also lexeme, and contrast lemma.

word-initial cohort: Group of words activated on the basis of the first few phonemes that are heard of an input word. See Cohort. The word-initial cohort for /tre/ is *treachery, tread, treadle, treadmill, treasure, treble, trek, trellis, tremble, tremolo, tremor, tremulous, trench, trenchant, trend, trepidation, trespass, tress, trestle.*

word monitoring: Experimental task in which participants are given a word and told to press a response button as quickly as they can if they hear that word in a following utterance.

word superiority effect: Finding that individual sounds or letters are recognised more rapidly and reliably when they occur in words than when they are either in nonwords or in jumbled letter strings.

working memory: Limited-capacity workbench where information is manipulated. Also known as short-term memory.

Zipf's law: Tendency for the most frequent words to be short. In the Wellington Spoken Corpus the ten most frequent words, in order, are: *the*, *and*, *I*, *to*, *a*, *you*, *that*, *it*, *of*, *yeah*. Two of these words comprise only one phoneme; six have two phonemes; and two are three phonemes long (though *and* is often reduced to two phonemes *an*, or to the single phoneme *n*).

References

Abdelghany, H. & Fodor, J. D. (1999). Low attachment of relative clauses in Arabic. Paper presented at the AMLaP (Architectures and Mechanisms of Language Processing) '99, Edinburgh, UK.

Abramson, A. S. & Lisker, L. (1973). Voice-timing perception in Spanish word-initial stops. *Journal of Phonetics*, 1, 1–8.

Aitchison, J. (2003). *Words in the Mind: An Introduction to the Mental Lexicon* (3rd edn). Oxford: Basil Blackwell.

(2008). *The Articulate Mammal: An Introduction to Psycholinguistics* (5th edn). London: Routledge.

Allbritton, D. W., McKoon, G. & Ratcliff, R. (1996). Reliability of prosodic cues for resolving syntactic ambiguity. *Journal of Experimental Psychology: Learning, Memory, and Cognition*, 22, 714–735.

Altmann, G. T. M. (ed.). (2002). *Psycholinguistics: Critical Concepts. (Vols I–VI).* London: Routledge.

Andrews, S. (1989). Frequency and neighborhood effects on lexical access: Activation or search? *Journal of Experimental Psychology: Learning, Memory, and Cognition*, 15, 802–814.

(1992). Frequency and neighborhood effects on lexical access: Lexical similarity or orthographic redundancy? *Journal of Experimental Psychology: Learning, Memory, and Cognition*, 18, 234–254.

(1997). The effect of orthographic similarity on lexical retrieval: Resolving neighborhood conflicts. *Psychonomic Bulletin and Review*, 4, 439–461.

Arons, B. (1992). A review of the cocktail party effect. *Journal of the American Voice I/O Society*, 12, 35–50.

Ashby, M. & Maidment, J. (2005). *Introducing Phonetic Science*. Cambridge University Press.

Aslin, R. N., Pisoni, D. B., Hennessy, B. L. & Perey, A. J. (1981). Discrimination of voice onset time by human infants: New findings and implications for the effects of early experience. *Child Development*, 52, 1135–1145.

Baars, B. J. & Motley, M. T. (1974). Spoonerisms: Experimental elicitation of human speech errors. *Journal Supplement Abstract Service. Catalog of Selected Documents in Psychology*.

Baars, B. J., Motley, M. T. & MacKay, D. G. (1975). Output editing for lexical status in artificially elicited slips of the tongue. *Journal of Verbal Learning and Verbal Behavior*, 14, 382–391.

Baddeley, A. D., Thomson, N. & Buchanan, M. (1975). Word length and the structure of short-term memory. *Journal of Verbal Learning and Verbal Behavior*, 14, 575–589.

Balota, D. A., Cortese, M. J., Sergent-Marshall, S. D., Spieler, D. H. & Yap, M. J. (2004). Visual word recognition of single-syllable words. *Journal of Experimental Psychology: General*, 133, 283–316.

Balota, D. A., Paul, S. T. & Spieler, D. H. (1999). Attentional control of lexical processing pathways during word recognition and reading. In S. Garrod & M. Pickering (eds.), *Language Processing* (pp. 15–57). Hove: Psychology Press.

Balota, D. A., Yap, M. J. & Cortese, M. J. (2006). Visual word recognition: The journey from features to meaning (A travel update). In M. J. Traxler & M. A. Gernsbacher (eds.), *Handbook of Psycholinguistics* (2nd edn, pp. 285–375). Amsterdam: Elsevier.

Baron, J. & Strawson, C. (1976). Use of orthographic and word-specific knowledge in reading words aloud. *Journal of Experimental Psychology: Human Perception and Performance*, 2, 386–393.

Bauer, L. (2001). *Morphological Productivity*. Cambridge University Press.

Bavelas, J. B. (1994). Gestures as part of speech: Methodological implications. *Research on Language and Social Interaction*, 27, 201–221.

Bavelas, J. B., Black, A., Lemery, C. R. & Mullett, J. (1986). 'I show how you feel.' Motor mimicry as a communicative act. *Journal of Personality and Social Psychology*, 50(2), 322–329.

Beattie, G. W. (1980). The role of language production processes in the organisation of behaviour in face-to-face interaction. In B. Butterworth (ed.),

Language Production (Vol. I, pp. 69–107). New York: Academic Press.

Beattie, G. W. & Butterworth, B. L. (1979). Contextual probability and word frequency as determinants of pauses and errors in spontaneous speech. *Language and Speech*, 22(3), 201–211.

Becic, E., Dell, G. S., Bock, K., Garnsey, S. M., Kubose, T. & Kramer, A. F. (2010). Driving impairs talking. *Psychonomic Bulletin & Review*, 17, 15–21.

Berko, J. (1958). The child's learning of English morphology. *Word*, 14, 150–177.

Bever, T. G. (1970). The cognitive basis for linguistic structures. In J. R. Hayes (ed.), *Cognition and the Development of Language* (pp. 279–362). New York: Wiley.

Bishop, D. V. M. & Snowling, M. J. (2004). Developmental dyslexia and specific language impairment: same or different? *Psychological Bulletin*, 130(6), 858–886.

Bock, J. K. (1986). Syntactic persistence in language production. *Cognitive Psychology*, 18(3), 355–387.

Bock, K. & Levelt, W. J. M. (1994). Language production: grammatical encoding. In M. A. Gernsbacher (ed.), *Handbook of Psycholinguistics* (pp. 945–984). New York: Academic Press.

Bock, K. & Miller, C. A. (1991). Broken agreement. *Cognitive Psychology*, 23, 45–93.

Boland, J. E., Tanenhaus, M. K. & Garnsey, S. M. (1990). Evidence for the immediate use of verb control information in sentence processing. *Journal of Memory and Language*, 29, 413–432.

Bond, Z. S. (1999). *Slips of the Ear: Errors in the Perception of Casual Conversation*. San Diego, CA: Academic Press.

Bornkessel-Schlesewsky, I. D. & Friederici, A. D. (2007). Neuroimaging studies of sentence and discourse comprehension. In M. G. Gaskell (ed.), *The Oxford Handbook of Psycholinguistics* (pp. 407–424). Oxford University Press.

Bransford, J. D., Barclay, J. R. & Franks, J. J. (1972). Sentence memory: a constructive versus interpretive approach. *Cognitive Psychology*, 3, 193–209.

Bransford, J. D. & Franks, J. J. (1971). The abstraction of linguistic ideas. *Cognitive Psychology*, 2, 331–350.

Brown, R. & McNeill, D. (1966). The 'tip of the tongue' phenomenon. *Journal of Verbal Learning and Verbal Behavior*, 5, 325–337.

Bryden, M. P. (1988). An overview of the dichotic listening procedure and its relation to cerebral organization. In K. Hugdahl (ed.), *Handbook of Dichotic Listening: Theory, Methods and Research* (pp. 1–43). Chichester: Wiley.

Brysbaert, M. & Mitchell, D. C. (1996). Modifier attachment in sentence parsing: evidence from Dutch. *The Quarterly Journal of Experimental Psychology*, 49A, 664–695.

Butterworth, B. (1975). Hesitation and semantic planning in speech. *Journal of Psycholinguistic Research*, 4, 75–87.

(1980). Evidence from pauses in speech. In B. Butterworth (ed.), *Language Production* (Vol. I, pp. 155–176). New York: Academic Press.

Byng, S. (1988). Sentence processing deficits: theory and therapy. *Cognitive Neuropsychology*, 5, 629–676.

Cairns, H. S. (1999). *Psycholinguistics: An Introduction*. Austin, TX: Pro-Ed.

Caplan, D. (1992). *Language: Structure, Processing, and Disorders*. Cambridge, MA: MIT Press.

Caramazza, A. (1997). How many levels of processing are there in lexical access? *Cognitive Neuropsychology*, 14(1), 177–208.

Caramazza, A. & Zurif, E. B. (1976). Dissociation of algorithmic and heuristic processes in language comprehension: evidence from aphasia. *Brain and Language*, 3, 572–582.

Carreiras, M., Perea, M. & Grainger, J. (1997). Effects of orthographic neighborhood in visual word recognition: Cross-task comparisons. *Journal of Experimental Psychology: Learning, Memory, and Cognition*, 23, 857–871.

Carroll, D. W. (2008). *Psychology of Language* (5th edn). Belmont, CA: Thomson Wadsworth.

Cattell, J. M. (1886). The time taken up by cerebral operations. *Mind*, 11(42), 220–242.

Chomsky, N. (1957). *Syntactic Structures*. The Hague: Mouton.

(1965). *Aspects of the Theory of Syntax*. Cambridge, MA: MIT Press.

(1973). Conditions on transformations. In S. R. Anderson & P. Kiparsky (eds.), *A Festschrift for Morris*

Halle (pp. 232–286). New York: Holt, Rinehart and Winston.

Clahsen, H. & Felser, C. (2006). Grammatical processing in language learners. *Applied Psycholinguistics*, 27(1), 3–42.

Clark, H. H. (1994). Discourse in production. In M. A. Gernsbacher (ed.), *Handbook of Psycholinguistics* (pp. 985–1021). New York: Academic Press.

(1996). *Using Language*. Cambridge University Press.

Clark, H. H. & Fox Tree, J. E. (2002). Using uh and um in spontaneous speaking. *Cognition*, 84, 73–111.

Clifton, C., Jr. & Frazier, L. (1989). Comprehending sentences with long-distance dependencies. In G. N. Carlson & M. K. Tanenhaus (eds.), *Linguistic Structure in Language Processing* (pp. 273–317). Dordrecht: Reidel.

Clifton, C., Jr. & Odom, P. (1966). Similarity relations among certain English sentence constructions. *Psychological Monographs: General and Applied*, 80(5), 1–35.

Cohen, N. J. (2002). Developmental language disorders. In P. Howlin & O. Udwin (eds.), *Outcomes in Neurodevelopmental and Genetic Disorders* (pp. 26–55). Cambridge University Press.

Coltheart, M. (1978). Lexical access in simple reading tasks. In G. Underwood (ed.), *Strategies of Information Processing* (pp. 151–216). London: Academic Press.

Coltheart, M., Davelaar, E., Jonasson, J. F. & Besner, D. (1977). Access to the internal lexicon. In S. Dornic (ed.), *Attention and Performance VI* (pp. 535–555). Hillsdale, NJ: Erlbaum.

Coltheart, M., Patterson, K. & Marshall, J. C. (eds.). (1980). *Deep Dyslexia*. London: Routledge & Kegan Paul.

Coltheart, M., Rastle, K., Perry, C., Langdon, R. & Ziegler, J. (2001). DRC: A dual route cascaded model of visual word recognition and reading aloud. *Psychological Review*, 108, 204–256.

Cooper, W. E. (1976). Syntactic control of timing in speech production: a study of complement clauses. *Journal of Phonetics*, 4, 151–171.

(1980). Syntactic-to-phonetic coding. In B. Butterworth (ed.), *Language Production* (Vol. I, pp. 297–333). New York: Academic Press.

Cooper, W. E. & Paccia-Cooper, J. (1980). *Syntax and Speech*. Cambridge, MA: Harvard University Press.

Cooper, W. E. & Sorensen, J. M. (1981). *Fundamental Frequency in Sentence Production*. New York: Springer.

Crain, S. & Steedman, M. (1985). On not being led up the garden path: the use of context by the psychological syntactic processor. In D. R. Dowty, L. Karttunen & A. M. Zwicky (eds.), *Natural Language Parsing: Psychological, Computational, and Theoretical Perspectives* (pp. 320–358). Cambridge University Press.

Cuetos, F. & Mitchell, D. C. (1988). Cross-linguistic differences in parsing: Restrictions on the use of the Late Closure strategy in Spanish. *Cognition*, 30(1), 73–105.

Cutler, A. (1980). Errors of stress and intonation. In V. A. Fromkin (ed.), *Errors in Linguistic Performance: Slips of the Tongue, Ear, Pen, and Hand* (pp. 67–80). New York: Academic Press.

(1983). Speakers' conceptions of the functions of prosody. In A. Cutler & D. R. Ladd (eds.), *Prosody: Models and Measurements* (pp. 79–91). Heidelberg: Springer.

(1988). The perfect speech error. In L. M. Hyman & C. N. Li (eds.), *Language, Speech, and Mind: Studies in Honour of Victoria A. Fromkin* (pp. 209–223). London: Routledge.

(ed.). (1982). *Slips of the Tongue and Language Production*. Berlin: Mouton.

Cutler, A. & Carter, D. M. (1987). The predominance of strong initial syllables in the English vocabulary. *Computer Speech and Language*, 2, 133–142.

Cutler, A. & Clifton, C., Jr. (1984). The use of prosodic information in word recognition. In H. Bouma & D. G. Bouwhuis (eds.), *Attention and Performance X* (pp. 183–196). Hillsdale, NJ: Erlbaum.

Cutler, A., Hawkins, J. A. & Gilligan, G. (1985). The suffixing preference: a processing explanation. *Linguistics*, 23(5), 723–758.

Cutler, A., Mehler, J., Norris, D. & Segui, J. (1986). The syllable's differing role in the segmentation of French and English. *Journal of Memory and Language*, 25, 385–400.

Cutler, A. & Norris, D. (1988). The role of strong syllables in segmentation for lexical access. *Journal of Experimental Psychology: Human Perception and Performance*, 14, 113–121.

De Ruiter, J. P. (1995). Why do people gesture at the telephone? In M. Biemans & M. Woutersen (eds.), *Proceedings of the Center for Language Studies Opening Academic Year 95–96* (pp. 49–56). Nijmegen, The Netherlands: University of Nijmegen.

De Ruiter, J. P. (2003). The function of hand gesture in spoken conversation. In M. Bickenback, A. Klappert & H. Pompe (eds.), *Manus Loquens* (pp. 338–347). Cologne: DuMont.

de Saussure, F. (1983 [1916]). *Course in General Linguistics* (R. Harris, trans. C. Bally & A. Sechehaye, eds.). La Salle, IL: Open Court.

Deese, J. (1984). *Thought into Speech: The Psychology of a Language*. Englewood Cliffs, NJ: Prentice-Hall.

Dell, G. S., McKoon, G. & Ratcliff, R. (1983). The activation of antecedent information during the processing of anaphoric reference in reading. *Journal of Verbal Learning and Verbal Behavior*, 22, 121–132.

Derrick, D. & Gick, B. (2010). Full body aero-tactile integration in speech perception. *Proceedings of Interspeech 2010*, 122–125.

Eberhard, K. M., Spivey-Knowlton, M. J., Sedivy, J. C. & Tanenhaus, M. K. (1995). Eye movements as a window into real-time spoken language comprehension in natural contexts. *Journal of Psycholinguistic Research*, 24, 409–436.

Ehrlich, K., Fernandez, E., Fodor, J. D., Stenshoel, E. & Vinereanu, M. (1999). Low attachment of relative clauses: New data from Swedish, Norwegian, and Romanian. Paper presented at the Twelfth Annual CUNY Conference on Human Sentence Processing, New York, NY.

Eimas, P. D., Siqueland, E. R., Jusczyk, P. & Vigorito, J. (1971). Speech perception in infants. *Science*, 171, 303–306.

Elman, J. L. & McClelland, J. L. (1988). Cognitive penetration of the mechanisms of perception: compensation for coarticulation of lexically restored phonemes. *Journal of Memory and Language*, 27, 143–165.

Emmorey, K. (2007). The psycholinguistics of signed and spoken languages: how biology affects processing. In M. G. Gaskell (ed.), *The Oxford Handbook of Psycholinguistics* (pp. 703–721). Oxford University Press.

Fay, D. & Cutler, A. (1977). Malapropisms and the structure of the mental lexicon. *Linguistic Inquiry*, 8, 505–520.

Featherston, S. (2001). *Empty Categories in Sentence Processing*. Amsterdam: John Benjamins.

Ferreira, F., Bailey, K. G. D. & Ferraro, V. (2002). Good-enough representations in language comprehension. *Current Directions in Psychological Science*, 11, 11–15.

Ferreira, F. & Clifton, C., Jr. (1986). The independence of syntactic processing. *Journal of Memory and Language*, 25, 348–368.

Ferreira, F. & Henderson, J. M. (1991). Recovery from misanalyses of garden-path sentences. *Journal of Memory & Language*, 30, 725–745.

Ferreira, V. S. & Slevc, L. R. (2007). Grammatical encoding. In M. G. Gaskell (ed.), *The Oxford Handbook of Psycholinguistics* (pp. 453–469). Oxford University Press.

Filik, R. & Leuthold, H. (2008). Processing local pragmatic anomalies in fictional contexts: Evidence from the N400. *Psychophysiology*, 45(4), 554–558.

Filipi, A. & Wales, R. (2004). Perspective-taking and perspective-shifting as socially situated and collaborative actions. *Journal of Pragmatics*, 36, 1851–1884.

Fodor, J. A. (1983). *The Modularity of Mind*. Cambridge, MA: MIT Press.

Fodor, J. A. & Bever, T. G. (1965). The psychological reality of linguistic segments. *Journal of Verbal Learning and Verbal Behavior*, 4, 414–420.

Fodor, J. A., Bever, T. G. & Garrett, M. F. (1974). *The Psychology of Language: An Introduction to Psycholinguistics and Generative Grammar*. New York: McGraw-Hill.

Fodor, J. A. & Garrett, M. (1967). Some syntactic determinants of sentential complexity. *Perception and Psychophysics*, 2, 289–296.

Fodor, J. D. (1978). Parsing strategies and constraints on transformations. *Linguistic Inquiry*, 9, 427–473.

(1989). Empty categories in sentence processing. *Language and Cognitive Processes*, 4, 155–209.

(2002). Prosodic disambiguation in silent reading. In M. Hirotani (ed.), *Proceedings of NELS 32*. Amherst, MA: GLSA, University of Massachusetts.

Forster, K. I. (1976). Accessing the mental lexicon. In R. J. Wales & E. Walker (eds.), *New Approaches to Language Mechanisms* (pp. 257–287). Amsterdam: North Holland.

Forster, K. I. & Chambers, S. M. (1973). Lexical access and naming time. *Journal of Verbal Learning and Verbal Behavior*, 12, 627–635.

Frauenfelder, U. H. & Schreuder, R. (1992). Constraining psycholinguistic models of morphological processing and representation: The role of productivity. In G. Booij & J. van Marle (eds.), *Yearbook of Morphology 1991* (pp. 165–183). Dordrecht: Kluwer.

Frazier, L., Clifton, C. & Randall, J. (1983). Filling gaps: Decision principles and structure in sentence comprehension. *Cognition*, 13(2), 187–222.

Frazier, L. & Fodor, J. D. (1978). The sausage machine: A new two-stage parsing model. *Cognition*, 6, 291–325.

Frazier, L. & Rayner, K. (1982). Making and correcting errors during sentence comprehension: Eye movements in the analysis of structurally ambiguous sentences. *Cognitive Psychology*, 14, 178–210.

(1987). Resolution of syntactic category ambiguities: Eye movements in parsing lexically ambiguous sentences. *Journal of Memory and Language*, 26, 505–526.

Frederiksen, J. R. & Kroll, J. F. (1976). Spelling and sound: Approaches to the internal lexicon. *Journal of Experimental Psychology: Human Perception and Performance*, 2, 361–379.

Frenck-Mestre, C. (2005). Ambiguities and anomalies: What can eye movements and event-related potentials reveal about second language sentence processing? In J. F. Kroll & A. M. B. de Groot (eds.), *Handbook of Bilingualism: Psycholinguistic Approaches* (pp. 268–281). Oxford University Press.

Fromkin, V. A. (1973a). Appendix. In V. A. Fromkin (ed.), *Speech Errors as Linguistic Evidence* (pp. 243–269). The Hague: Mouton.

(1973b). The non-anomalous nature of anomalous utterances. In V. A. Fromkin (ed.), *Speech Errors as Linguistic Evidence* (pp. 215–241). The Hague: Mouton.

(ed.). (1973c). *Speech Errors as Linguistic Evidence*. The Hague: Mouton.

(ed.). (1980). *Errors in Linguistic Performance: Slips of the Tongue, Ear, Pen, and Hand*. New York: Academic Press.

FSED. Fromkin's Speech Error Database, from www.mpi.nl/cgi-bin/sedb/sperco_form4.pl

Ganong, W. F. (1980). Phonetic categorization in auditory word perception. *Journal of Experimental Psychology: Human Perception and Performance*, 6, 110–125.

Garnham, A. (1989). Integrating information in text comprehension: The interpretation of anaphoric noun phrases. In G. N. Carlson & M. K. Tanenhaus (eds.), *Linguistic Structure in Language Processing* (pp. 359–399). Dordrecht: Kluwer.

(1999). Reference and anaphora. In S. Garrod & M. J. Pickering (eds.), *Language Processing* (pp. 335–362). Hove: Psychology Press.

Garrett, M., Bever, T. & Fodor, J. (1966). The active use of grammar in speech perception. *Perception & Psychophysics*, 1, 30–32.

Garrett, M. F. (1975). The analysis of sentence production. In G. H. Bower (ed.), *The Psychology of Learning and Motivation: Advances in Research and Theory* (Volume IX, pp. 133–177). New York: Academic Press.

(1980a). Levels of processing in sentence production. In B. Butterworth (ed.), *Language Production* (Vol. I, pp. 177–220). New York: Academic Press.

(1980b). The limits of accommodation: Arguments for independent processing levels in sentence production. In V. A. Fromkin (ed.), *Errors in Linguistic Performance: Slips of the Tongue, Ear, Pen, and Hand* (pp. 263–271). New York: Academic Press.

Garrod, S., O'Brien, E. J., Morris, R. K. & Rayner, K. (1990). Elaborative inferencing as an active or passive process. *Journal of Experimental Psychology: Learning, Memory, and Cognition*, 16, 250–257.

Garrod, S. & Sanford, A. J. (1982). Bridging inferences and the extended domain of reference. In J. Long & A. Baddeley (eds.), *Attention and Performance IX* (pp. 331–346). Hillsdale, NJ: Erlbaum.

(1994). Resolving sentences in a discourse context: How discourse representation affects language understanding. In M. A. Gernsbacher (ed.), *Handbook of Psycholinguistics* (pp. 675–698). New York: Academic Press.

Gaskell, M. G. (ed.). (2007). *The Oxford Handbook of Psycholinguistics*. Oxford University Press.

Gee, J. P. & Grosjean, F. (1983). Performance structures: A psycholinguistic and linguistic appraisal. *Cognitive Psychology*, 15, 411–458.

Gernsbacher, M. A. (ed.). (1994). *Handbook of Psycholinguistics*. New York: Academic Press.

Gibson, E. (1998). Linguistic complexity: Locality of syntactic dependencies. *Cognition*, 68, 1–76.

Gibson, E., Pearlmutter, N., Canseco-Gonzalez, E. & Hickock, G. (1996). Recency preference in the human sentence processing mechanism. *Cognition*, 59, 23–59.

Gick, B. & Derrick, D. (2009). Aero-tactile integration in speech perception. *Nature*, 462, 502–504.

Goldman-Eisler, F. (1961). Hesitation and information in speech. In C. Cherry (ed.), *Proceedings of the 4th London Symposium on Information Theory* (pp. 162–174). London: Butterworths.

(1968). *Psycholinguistics: Experiments in Spontaneous Speech*. London: Academic Press.

Goldman-Eisler, F., Skarbek, A. & Henderson, A. (1965). Cognitive and neurochemical determination of sentence structure. *Language and Speech*, 8(2), 86–94.

Goodman, J. C. & Huttenlocher, J. (1988). Do we know how people identify spoken words? *Journal of Memory and Language*, 27, 684–698.

Gough, P. B. (1965). Grammatical transformations and speed of understanding. *Journal of Verbal Learning and Verbal Behavior*, 4, 107–111.

Gough, P. B. & Cosky, M. J. (1977). One second of reading again. In N. J. Castellan, D. B. Pisoni & G. R. Potts (eds.), *Cognitive Theory* (Vol. II, pp. 271–286). Hillsdale, NJ: Erlbaum.

Grainger, J. & Jacobs, A. M. (1996). Orthographic processing in visual word recognition: A multiple read-out model. *Psychological Review*, 103, 518–565.

Griffin, Z. M. & Ferreira, V. S. (2006). Properties of spoken language production. In M. J. Traxler & M. A. Gernsbacher (eds.), *Handbook of Psycholinguistics* (2nd edn, pp. 21–59). Amsterdam: Elsevier.

Hadar, U. & Butterworth, B. (1997). Iconic gestures, imagery, and word retrieval in speech. *Semiotica*, 115, 147–172.

Hakes, D. T. (1972). Effects of reducing complement constructions on sentence comprehension. *Journal of Verbal Learning and Verbal Behavior*, 11, 278–286.

Harley, T. A. (2008). *The Psychology of Language. From Data to Theory* (3rd edn). Hove: Psychology Press.

(2010). *Talking the Talk: Language, Psychology and Science*. Hove: Psychology Press.

Harley, T. A. & MacAndrew, S. B. G. (2001). Constraints upon word substitution speech errors. *Journal of Psycholinguistic Research*, 30(4), 395–418.

Haviland, S. E. & Clark, H. H. (1974). What's new? Acquiring new information as a process in comprehension. *Journal of Verbal Learning and Verbal Behavior*, 13, 512–521.

Hawkins, S. & Warren, P. (1994). Phonetic influences on the intelligibility of conversational speech. *Journal of Phonetics*, 22, 493–511.

Hay, J., Warren, P. & Drager, K. (2006). Factors influencing speech perception in the context of a merger-in-progress. *Journal of Phonetics*, 34(4), 458–484.

Haywood, S. L., Pickering, M. J. & Branigan, H. P. (2005). Do speakers avoid ambiguities during dialogue? *Psychological Science*, 16, 362–366.

Heim, St., Opitz, B. & Friederici, A. D. (2002). Broca's area in the human brain is involved in the selection of grammatical gender for language production: evidence from event-related functional magnetic resonance imaging. *Neuroscience Letters*, 328, 101–104.

Hemforth, B., Konieczny, L. & Scheepers, C. (2000a). Modifier attachment: Relative clauses and coordinations. In B. Hemforth & L. Konieczny (eds.), *German Sentence Processing* (pp. 161–186). Dordrecht: Kluwer.

(2000b). Syntactic attachment and anaphor resolution: the two sides of relative clause attachment. In M. W. Crocker, M. Pickering & C. Clifton Jr. (eds.), *Architectures and Mechanisms for Language Processing* (pp. 259–281). Cambridge University Press.

Henderson, A., Goldman-Eisler, F. & Skarbek, A. (1965). Temporal patterns of cognitive activity and breath control in speech. *Language and Speech*, 8, 236–242.

(1966). Sequential temporal patterns in spontaneous speech. *Language and Speech*, 9, 207–216.

Holmes, V. M. (1987). Syntactic parsing: in search of the garden path. In M. Coltheart (ed.), *Attention and Performance XII*. Hillsdale, NJ: Erlbaum.

Holmes, V. M. & Forster, K. I. (1970). Detection of extraneous signals during sentence recognition. *Perception & Psychophysics*, 7, 297–301.

Holmes, V. M., Kennedy, A. & Murray, W. S. (1987). Syntactic structure and the garden path. *The Quarterly Journal of Experimental Psychology*, 39A, 277–293.

Hugdahl, K. & Andersson, L. (1986). The 'forced-attention paradigm' in dichotic listening to CV-syllables: A comparison between adults and children. *Cortex*, 22(3), 417–432.

Indefrey, P. (2007). Brain-imaging studies of language production. In M. G. Gaskell (ed.), *The Oxford Handbook of Psycholinguistics* (pp. 547–564). Oxford University Press.

Indefrey, P. & Levelt, W. J. M. (2004). The spatial and temporal signatures of word production components. *Cognition*, 92, 101–144.

Jacobs, N. & Garnham, A. (2007). The role of conversational hand gestures in a narrative task. *Journal of Memory and Language*, 56, 291–303.

James, D. (1973). Another look at, say, some grammatical constraints on, ok, interjections and hesitations. *Papers from the Ninth Regional Meeting, Chicago Linguistic Society*, 242–251.

James, W. (1893). *The Principles of Psychology*. New York: Holt.

Johnson, K. (1997). Speech perception without speaker normalization: An exemplar model. In K. Johnson & J. W. Mullennix (eds.), *Talker Variability in Speech Processing* (pp. 145–166). San Diego, CA: Academic Press.

Johnson-Laird, P. N. (1974). Experimental psycholinguistics. *Annual Review of Psychology*, 25, 135–160.
   (1983). *Mental Models*. Cambridge University Press.

Just, M. A. & Carpenter, P. A. (1971). Comprehension of negation with quantification. *Journal of Verbal Learning and Verbal Behavior*, 10, 244–253.

Kendon, A. (2004). *Gesture: Visible Action as Utterance*. Cambridge University Press.

Kennedy, A., Murray, W. S., Jennings, F. & Reid, C. (1989). Parsing complements: Comments on the generality of the principle of minimal attachment. *Language and Cognitive Processes*, 4, 51–76.

Kennison, S. M. (2002). Comprehending noun phrase arguments and adjuncts. *Journal of Psycholinguistic Research*, 31(1), 65–81.

Kimball, J. (1973). Seven principles of surface structure parsing in natural language. *Cognition*, 2, 15–47.

Kimura, D. (1961). Cerebral dominance and the perception of verbal stimuli. *Canadian Journal of Psychology*, 15, 166–171.

Kita, S. (2000). How representational gestures help speaking. In D. McNeill (ed.), *Language and Gesture* (pp. 162–185). Cambridge University Press.
   (2009). Cross-cultural variation of speech-accompanying gesture: A review. *Language and Cognitive Processes*, 24(2), 145–167.

Kita, S. & Özyürek, A. (2003). What does cross-linguistic variation in semantic coordination of speech and gesture reveal? Evidence for an interface representation of spatial thinking and speaking. *Journal of Memory and Language*, 48, 16–32.

Klatt, D. H. (1989). Review of selected models of speech perception. In W. Marslen-Wilson (ed.), *Lexical Representation and Process* (pp. 169–226). Cambridge, MA: MIT Press.

Klein, W. (1981). Some aspects of route directions. In R. J. Jarvella & W. Klein (eds.), *Speech, Place, and Action. Studies in Deixis and Related Topics* (pp. 161–182). Chichester: Wiley.

Krauss, R. M. (1998). Why do we gesture when we speak? *Current Directions in Psychological Science*, 7, 54–60.

Kuhl, P. K. (1987). The special-mechanisms debate in speech research: Categorization tests on animals and infants. In S. Harnad (ed.), *Categorical perception: The Groundwork of Cognition* (pp. 355–386). Cambridge University Press.

Kuperberg, G. R., McGuire, P. K., Bullmore, E. T. *et al.* (2000). Common and distinct neural substrates for pragmatic, semantic, and syntactic processing of spoken sentences: An fMRI study. *Journal of Cognitive Neuroscience*, 12(2), 321–341.

Kutas, M. & Federmeier, K. D. (2007). Event-related brain potential (ERP) studies of sentence processing. In M. G. Gaskell (ed.), *The Oxford Handbook of Psycholinguistics* (pp. 385–406). Oxford University Press.

Lahiri, A. & Marslen-Wilson, W. D. (1991). The mental representation of lexical form: A phonological approach to the recognition lexicon. *Cognition*, 38, 245–294.

Lakoff, G. (1971). Presupposition and relative well-formedness. In D. D. Steinberg & L. A. Jakobovits (eds.), *Semantics: An Interdisciplinary Reader in Philosophy, Linguistics, and Psychology* (pp. 329–340). Cambridge University Press.

Lane, H. (1965). The motor theory of speech perception: A critical review. *Psychological Review*, 72(4), 275–309.

Laver, J. (1994). *Principles of Phonetics*. Cambridge University Press.

Leonard, L. B. (1998). *Children with Specific Language Impairment*. Cambridge, MA: MIT Press.

Levelt, W. J. M. (1982). Linearization in describing spatial networks. In S. Peters & E. Saarinen (eds.), *Processes, Beliefs, and Questions. Essays on Formal Semantics of Natural Language and Natural Language Processing* (pp. 199–220). Dordrecht: Reidel.

Levelt, W. J. M. (1983). Monitoring and self-repair in speech. *Cognition*, 14, 41–104.

[1989]. *Speaking: From Intention to Articulation*. Cambridge, MA: MIT Press.

[ed.]. (1993). *Lexical Access in Speech Production*. Oxford: Blackwell.

(1999). Producing spoken language: A blueprint of the speaker. In C. M. Brown & P. Hagoort (eds.), *Neurocognition of Language* (pp. 83–122). Oxford University Press.

Levelt, W. J. M. & Cutler, A. (1983). Prosodic marking in speech repair. *Journal of Semantics*, 2, 205–217.

Levelt, W. J. M., Roelofs, A. & Meyer, A. S. (1999). A theory of lexical access in speech production. *Behavioral and Brain Sciences*, 22, 1–75.

Levinson, S. C. (2003). *Space in Language and Cognition: Explorations in Cognitive Diversity*. Cambridge University Press.

Levinson, S. C., Kita, S., Haun, D. B. M. & Rasch, B. H. (2002). Re-turning the tables: Language affects spatial reasoning. *Cognition*, 84, 158–188.

Liberman, A. M., Harris, K. S., Hoffman, H. S. & Griffith, B. C. (1957). The discrimination of speech sounds within and across phoneme boundaries. *Journal of Experimental Psychology: Human Perception and Performance*, 54(5), 358–368.

Lounsbury, F. G. (1954). Transitional probability, linguistic structure, and systems of habit-family hierarchies. In C. E. Osgood & T. A. Sebeok (eds.), *Psycholinguistics: A Survey of Theory and Research Problems* (pp. 93–101). Bloomington: Indiana University Press.

Luce, P. A. & Pisoni, D. B. (1998). Recognizing spoken words: The neighborhood activation model. *Ear & Hearing*, 19, 1–36.

MacDonald, M. C. (1994). Probabilistic constraints and syntactic ambiguity resolution. *Language and Cognitive Processes*, 9, 157–201.

MacKay, D. G. (1979). Lexical insertion, inflection, and derivation: Creative processes in word production. *Journal of Psycholinguistic Research*, 8(5), 477–498.

MacWhinney, B., Bates, E. & Kliegl, R. (1984). Cue validity and sentence interpretation in English, German and Italian. *Journal of Verbal Learning and Verbal Behavior*, 23, 127–150.

Marshall, J. C. & Newcombe, F. (1981). Lexical access: A perspective from pathology. *Cognition*, 10, 209–214.

Marslen-Wilson, W. D. (1980). Speech understanding as a psychological process. In J. C. Simon (ed.), *Spoken Language Generation and Understanding* (pp. 39–67). Dordrecht: Reidel.

(1987). Functional parallelism in spoken word-recognition. In U. H. Frauenfelder & L. K. Tyler (eds.), *Spoken Word Recognition* (pp. 71–102). Cambridge, MA: MIT Press.

(1989). Access and integration: projecting sound onto meaning. In W. D. Marslen-Wilson (ed.), *Lexical Representation and Process* (pp. 3–24). Cambridge, MA: MIT Press.

(2007). Morphological processes in language comprehension. In M. G. Gaskell (ed.), *The Oxford Handbook of Psycholinguistics* (pp. 175–193). Oxford University Press.

Marslen-Wilson, W., Brown, C. M. & Tyler, L. K. (1988). Lexical representations in spoken language comprehension. *Language and Cognitive Processes*, 3(1), 1–16.

Marslen-Wilson, W. & Tyler, L. K. (1980). The temporal structure of spoken language understanding. *Cognition*, 8, 1–71.

Marslen-Wilson, W. D., Tyler, L. K. & Seidenberg, M. S. (1978). Sentence processing and the clause boundary. In W. J. M. Levelt & G. B. F. d'Arcais (eds.), *Studies in the Perception of Language* (pp. 219–246). New York: Wiley.

Marslen-Wilson, W., Tyler, L. K., Waksler, R. & Older, L. (1994). Morphology and meaning in the English mental lexicon. *Psychological Review*, 101(1), 3–33.

Marslen-Wilson, W. D., Tyler, L. K., Warren, P., Grenier, P. & Lee, C. S. (1992). Prosodic effects in minimal attachment. *The Quarterly Journal of Experimental Psychology*, 45A, 73–87.

Marslen-Wilson, W. D. & Warren, P. (1994). Levels of perceptual representation and process in lexical access: words, phonemes, and features. *Psychological Review*, 101, 653–675.

Marslen-Wilson, W. D. & Welsh, A. (1978). Processing interactions and lexical access during word recognition in continuous speech. *Cognitive Psychology*, 10, 29–63.

Martin, R. C., Vuong, L. C. & Crowther, J. E. (2007). Sentence-level deficits in aphasia. In M. G. Gaskell (ed.), *The Oxford Handbook of Psycholinguistics* (pp. 425–439). Oxford University Press.

McClelland, J. L. & Johnston, J. C. (1977). The role of familiar units in perception of words and nonwords. *Perception & Psychophysics*, 22, 249–261.

McClelland, J. L. & Rumelhart, D. E. (1981). An interactive activation model of context effects in letter perception: Part 1. An account of basic findings. *Psychological Review*, 88, 375–407.

McGurk, H. & MacDonald, J. (1976). Hearing lips and seeing voices. *Nature*, 264, 746–748.

McNeill, D. (1992). *Hand and Mind: What Gestures Reveal about Thought*. University of Chicago Press.
    (ed.). (2000). *Language and Gesture*. Cambridge University Press.

McNeill, D. & Duncan, S. D. (2000). Growth points in thinking-for-speaking. In D. McNeill (ed.), *Language and Gesture* (pp. 141–161). Cambridge University Press.

McQueen, J. M. (2007). Eight questions about spoken word recognition. In M. G. Gaskell (ed.), *The Oxford Handbook of Psycholinguistics* (pp. 37–53). Oxford University Press.

Mehler, J., Dommergues, J. Y., Frauenfelder, U. & Segui, J. (1981). The syllable's role in speech segmentation. *Journal of Verbal Learning and Verbal Behavior*, 20, 298–305.

Merlo, S. & Barbosa, P. A. (2010). Hesitation phenomena: a dynamical perspective. *Cognitive Processing*, 11(3), 251–261.

Miller, G. A. & Chomsky, N. (1963). Finitary models of language users. In R. D. Luce, R. R. Bush & E. Galanter (eds.), *Handbook of Mathematical Psychology* (Vol. II, pp. 419–491). New York: Wiley.

Miller, G. A. & McKean, K. O. (1964). A chronometric study of some relations between sentences. *Quarterly Journal of Experimental Psychology*, 16(4), 297–308.

Mitchell, D. C., Cuetos, F. & Zagar, D. (1990). Reading in different languages: is there a universal mechanism for parsing sentences? In D. A. Balota, G. B. Flores d'Arcais & K. Rayner (eds.), *Comprehension Processes in Reading* (pp. 285–302). Hillsdale, NJ: Erlbaum.

Monsell, S. (1991). The nature and locus of word frequency effects in reading. In D. Besner & G. W. Humphreys (eds.), *Basic Processes in Reading: Visual Word Recognition* (pp. 148–197). Hillsdale, NJ: Erlbaum.

Morais, J., Cary, L., Alegria, J. & Bertelson, P. (1979). Does awareness of speech as a sequence of phones arise spontaneously? *Cognition*, 7, 323–331.

Morgan, J. L., Meier, R. P. & Newport, E. L. (1987). Structural packaging in the input to language learning: contributions of prosodic and morphological marking of phrases to the acquisition of language. *Cognitive Psychology*, 22, 498–550.

Morrel-Samuels, P. & Krauss, R. M. (1992). Word familiarity predicts temporal asynchrony of hand gestures and speech. *Journal of Experimental Psychology: Learning, Memory, and Cognition*, 18(3), 615–622.

Morris, D., Collett, P., Marsh, P. & O'Shaughnessy, M. (1979). *Gestures: Their Origins and Distribution*. New York: Stein and Day.

Morton, J. (1969). Interaction of information in word-recognition. *Psychological Review*, 76, 165–178.

Morton, J. & Patterson, K. (1980). A new attempt at an interpretation, or, an attempt at a new interpretation. In M. Coltheart, K. Patterson & J. C. Marshall (eds.), *Deep Dyslexia* (pp. 91–118). London: Routledge and Kegan Paul.

Motley, M. T. (1980). Verification of 'Freudian slips' and semantic prearticulatory editing via laboratory-induced spoonerisms. In V. A. Fromkin (ed.), *Errors in Linguistic Performance: Slips of the Tongue, Ear, Pen, and Hand* (pp. 133–148). New York: Academic Press.
    (1985). The production of verbal slips and double entendres as clues to the efficiency of normal speech production. *Journal of Language and Social Psychology*, 4, 275–293.

Motley, M. T. & Baars, B. J. (1976). Laboratory induction of verbal slips: A new method for psycholinguistic research. *Communication Quarterly*, 24, 28–34.

Motley, M. T., Camden, C. T. & Baars, B. J. (1982). Covert formulation and editing of anomalies in speech production: Evidence from experimentally elicited slips of the tongue. *Journal of Verbal Learning and Verbal Behavior*, 21, 578–594.

Murray, W. S. & Forster, K. I. (2004). Serial mechanisms in lexical access: The rank hypothesis. *Psychological Review*, 111, 721–756.

Nagel, H. N., Shapiro, L. P. & Nawy, R. (1994). Prosody and the processing of filler-gap sentences. *Journal of Psycholinguistic Research*, 23, 473–485.

Nation, I. S. P. (2006). How large a vocabulary is needed for reading and listening? *Canadian Modern Language Review*, 63(1), 59–82.

New, B., Ferrand, L., Pallier, C. & Brysbaert, M. (2006). Re-examining the word length effect in visual word recognition: New evidence from the English Lexicon Project. *Psychonomic Bulletin & Review*, 13(1), 45–52.

Newman, A. J., Ullman, M. T., Pancheva, R., Waligura, D. L. & Neville, H. J. (2007). An ERP study of regular and irregular English past tense inflection. *NeuroImage*, 34(1), 435–445.

Nicol, J. & Swinney, D. (1989). The role of structure in coreference assignment during sentence comprehension. *Journal of Psycholinguistic Research*, 18, 5–19.

Nicol, J., Swinney, D. A., Love, T. & Hald, L. (2006). The on-line study of sentence comprehension: An examination of dual task paradigms. *Journal of Psycholinguistic Research*, 35, 215–231.

Nitschke, S., Kidd, E. & Serratrice, L. (2010). First language transfer and long-term structural priming in comprehension. *Language and Cognitive Processes*, 25(1), 94–114.

Nooteboom, S. G. (1980). Speaking and unspeaking: detection and correction of phonological and lexical errors in spontaneous speech. In V. A. Fromkin (ed.), *Errors in Linguistic Performance: Slips of the Tongue, Ear, Pen, and Hand* (pp. 87–95). New York: Academic Press.

(2005a). Lexical bias revisited: Detecting, rejecting and repairing speech errors in inner speech. *Speech Communication*, 47, 43–58.

(2005b). Listening to one-self: Monitoring speech production. In R. J. Hartsuiker, R. Bastiaanse, A. Postma & F. Wijnen (eds.), *Phonological Encoding and Monitoring in Normal and Pathological Speech* (pp. 167–186). Hove: Psychology Press.

Norris, D., McQueen, J. M., Cutler, A. & Butterfield, S. (1997). The possible-word constraint in the segmentation of continuous speech. *Cognitive Psychology*, 34, 191–243.

Norris, D., McQueen, J. M., Cutler, A., Butterfield, S. & Kearns, R. (2001). Language-universal constraints on speech segmentation. *Language and Cognitive Processes*, 16, 637–660.

O'Regan, J. K. & Jacobs, A. M. (1992). Optimal viewing position effect in word recognition: A challenge to current theory. *Journal of Experimental Psychology: Human Perception and Performance*, 18, 185–197.

Ohala, J. J. & Ohala, M. (1995). Speech perception and lexical representation: The role of vowel nasalization in Hindi and English. In B. Connell & A. Arvaniti (eds.), *Phonology and Phonetic Evidence. Papers in Laboratory Phonology IV* (pp. 41–60). Cambridge University Press.

Oliphant, G. W. (1983). Repetition and recency effects in word recognition. *Australian Journal of Psychology*, 35, 393–403.

Osgood, C. E. & Sebeok, T. A. (1954a). Psycholinguistics: A Survey of Theory and Research Problems. *Journal of Abnormal and Social Psychology (Supplement)*, 49, 1–203.

(eds.). (1954b). *Psycholinguistics: A Survey of Theory and Research Problems. Indiana University Publications in Anthropology and Linguistics, Memoir 10 of International Journal of American Linguistics*. Bloomington: Indiana University Press.

Ostrin, R. K. & Tyler, L. K. (1995). Dissociations of lexical function: semantics, syntax, and morphology. *Cognitive Neuropsychology*, 12(4), 345–389.

Otake, T., Hatano, G., Cutler, A. & Mehler, J. (1993). Mora or syllable? Speech segmentation in Japanese. *Journal of Memory & Language*, 32, 258–278.

Pandelaere, M. & Dewitte, S. (2006). Is this a question? Not for long. The statement bias. *Journal of Experimental Social Psychology*, 42, 525–531.

Papadopoulou, D. & Clahsen, H. (2003). Parsing strategies in L1 and L2 sentence processing: A study of relative clause attachment in Greek. *Studies in Second Language Acquisition*, 25, 501–528.

Papçun, G., Krashen, S., Terbeek, D., Remington, R. & Harshman, R. (1974). Is the left hemisphere specialized for speech, language and-or something else? *Journal of the Acoustical Society of America*, 55, 319–327.

Parviainen, T., Helenius, P. & Salmelin, R. (2005). Cortical differentiation of speech and nonspeech sounds at 100 ms: implications for dyslexia. *Cerebral Cortex*, 15(7), 1054–1063.

Patterson, K. E. & Morton, J. (1985). From orthography to phonology: an attempt at an old interpretation. In K. E. Patterson, J. C. Marshall & M. Coltheart (eds.), *Surface Dyslexia: Neuropsychological and Cognitive Studies of Phonological Reading* (pp. 335–359). Hove: Erlbaum.

Perea, M. & Rosa, E. (2000). The effects of orthographic neighborhood in reading and laboratory word identification tasks: A review. *Psicologica*, 21, 3270–3340.

Petrie, H. (1987). The psycholinguistics of speaking. In J. Lyons, R. Coates, M. Deuchar & G. Gazdar (eds.), *New Horizons in Linguistics* (Vol. II, pp. 336–366). Harmondsworth: Penguin.

Pickering, M. J. (1999). Sentence comprehension. In S. Garrod & M. Pickering (eds.), *Language Processing* (pp. 123–153). Hove: Psychology Press.

Pierrehumbert, J. B. (2001). Exemplar dynamics: Word frequency, lenition and contrast. In J. Bybee & P. Hopper (eds.), *Frequency and the Emergence of Linguistic Structure* (pp. 137–158). Amsterdam: John Benjamins.

Pillon, A. (1998). Morpheme units in speech production: evidence from laboratory-induced verbal slips. *Language and Cognitive Processes*, 13(4), 465–498.

Pinker, S. (1994). *The Language Instinct*. Harmondsworth: Penguin.

(1999). *Words and Rules*. London: Weidenfeld & Nicolson.

Pisoni, D. B., Nusbaum, H. C., Luce, P. A. & Slowiaczek, L. M. (1985). Speech perception, word recognition and the structure of the lexicon. *Speech Communication*, 4, 75–95.

Pisoni, D. B. & Levi, S. V. (2007). Representations and representational specificity in speech perception and spoken word recognition. In M. G. Gaskell (ed.), *The Oxford Handbook of Psycholinguistics* (pp. 3–18). Oxford University Press.

Pollatsek, A., Perea, M. & Binder, K. S. (1999). The effects of 'neighborhood size' in reading and lexical decision. *Journal of Experimental Psychology: Human Perception and Performance*, 25, 1142–1158.

Postal, P. M. (1974). *On Raising: One Rule of English Grammar and its Theoretical Implications*. Cambridge, MA: MIT Press.

Power, M. J. (1983). Are there cognitive rhythms in speech? *Language and Speech*, 26, 253–261.

Prat-Sala, M. & Branigan, H. P. (2000). Discourse constraints on syntactic processing in language production: A cross-linguistic study in English and Spanish. *Journal of Memory & Language*, 42, 168–182.

Pulvermüller, F. (2007). Brain processes of word recognition as revealed by neurophysiological imaging. In M. G. Gaskell (ed.), *The Oxford Handbook of Psycholinguistics* (pp. 119–139). Oxford University Press.

Pulvermüller, F., Kujala, T., Shtyrov, Y. *et al.* (2001). Memory traces for words as revealed by the Mismatch Negativity. *NeuroImage*, 14(3), 607–616.

Pynte, J. & Prieur, B. (1996). Prosodic breaks and attachment decisions in sentence parsing. *Language and Cognitive Processes*, 11, 165–191.

Quené, H. & Koster, M. L. (1998). Metrical segmentation in Dutch: Vowel quality or stress? *Language and Speech*, 41, 185–202.

Rapp, B., Folk, J. R. & Tainturier, M. J. (2001). Word reading. In B. Rapp (ed.), *The Handbook of Cognitive Neuropsychology: What Deficits Reveal about the Human Mind* (pp. 233–262). Hove: Psychology Press.

Rastle, K. (2007). Visual word recognition. In M. G. Gaskell (ed.), *The Oxford Handbook of Psycholinguistics* (pp. 71–87). Oxford University Press.

Rayner, K. & Balota, D. A. (1989). Parafoveal preview effects and lexical access during eye fixations in reading. In W. Marslen-Wilson (ed.), *Lexical Representation and Process* (pp. 261–290). Cambridge, MA: MIT Press.

Rayner, K., Carlson, M. & Frazier, L. (1983). The interaction of syntax and semantics during sentence processing: Eye movements in the analysis of semantically biased sentences. *Journal of Verbal Learning and Verbal Behavior*, 22, 358–374.

Rayner, K. & Frazier, L. (1987). Parsing temporarily ambiguous complements. *The Quarterly Journal of Experimental Psychology*, 39A, 657–673.

Roberts, B. & Kirsner, K. (2000). Temporal cycles in speech production. *Language and Cognitive Processes*, 15(2), 129–157.

Rodd, J., Gaskell, G. & Marslen-Wilson, W. (2002). Making sense of semantic ambiguity: semantic competition in lexical access. *Journal of Memory and Language*, 46, 245–266.

Rubenstein, H., Lewis, S. S. & Rubenstein, M. A. (1971). Evidence for phonemic recoding in visual word recognition. *Journal of Verbal Learning and Verbal Behavior*, 10, 645–657.

Rumelhart, D. E. & McClelland, J. L. (1982). An interactive activation model of context effects in letter perception: Part 2. The contextual enhancement effect and some tests and extensions of the model. *Psychological Review*, 89, 60–94.

Sætrevik, B. & Hugdahl, K. (2007). Priming inhibits the right ear advantage in dichotic listening: Implications for auditory laterality. *Neuropsychologia*, 45(2), 282–287.

Saffran, E. M., Schwartz, M. F. & Linebarger, M. C. (1998). Semantic influences on thematic role assignment: evidence from normals and aphasics. *Brain and Language*, 62, 255–297.

Salmelin, R. (2007). Clinical neurophysiology of language: the MEG approach. *Clinical Neurophysiology*, 118(2), 237–254.

Samuel, A. G. (1990). Using perceptual-restoration effects to explore the architecture of perception. In G. T. M. Altmann (ed.), *Cognitive Models of Speech Processing* (pp. 295–314). Cambridge, MA: MIT Press.

Savin, H. B. & Perchonock, E. (1965). Grammatical structure and the immediate recall of English sentences. *Journal of Verbal Learning and Verbal Behavior*, 4, 348–353.

Schafer, A., Carter, J., Clifton, C., Jr & Frazier, L. (1996). Focus in relative clause construal. *Language and Cognitive Processes*, 11, 135–163.

Schafer, A. J., Speer, S. R., Warren, P. & White, S. D. (2000). Intonational disambiguation in sentence production and comprehension. *Journal of Psycholinguistic Research*, 29, 169–182.

Schegloff, E. A. (1984). On some gestures' relation to talk. In J. M. Atkinson & J. Heritage (eds.), *Structures of Social Action: Studies in Conversation Analysis* (pp. 266–296). Cambridge University Press.

Schwartz, J. & Jaffe, J. (1968). Markovian prediction of sequential temporal patterns in spontaneous speech. *Language and Speech*, 11, 27–30.

Seidenberg, M. S. & McClelland, J. L. (1989). A distributed, developmental model of word recognition and naming. *Psychological Review*, 96, 523–568.

Seidenberg, M. S., Waters, G. S., Barnes, M. A. & Tanenhaus, M. K. (1984). When does irregular spelling or pronunciation influence word recognition? *Journal of Verbal Learning and Verbal Behavior*, 23, 383–404.

Shallice, T., McLeod, P. & Lewis, K. (1985). Isolating cognitive modules with the dual-task paradigm: Are speech perception and production separate processes? *The Quarterly Journal of Experimental Psychology*, 37A, 507–532.

Shannon, C. E. (1951). Prediction and entropy of printed English. *Bell System Technical Journal*, 30, 50–64.

Shattuck-Hufnagel, S. (1979). Speech errors as evidence for a serial ordering mechanism in sentence production. In W. E. Cooper & E. C. T. Walker (eds.), *Sentence Processing: Psycholinguistic Studies Presented to Merrill Garrett* (pp. 295–342). Hillsdale, NJ: Erlbaum.

(1983). Sublexical units and suprasegmental structure in speech production planning. In P. F. MacNeilage (ed.), *The Production of Speech* (pp. 109–136). New York: Springer.

(1986). The representation of phonological information during speech production planning: evidence from vowel errors in spontaneous speech. *Phonology Yearbook*, 3, 117–149.

(1993). The role of word structure in segmental serial ordering. In W. J. M. Levelt (ed.), *Lexical Access in Speech Production* (pp. 213–259). Oxford: Blackwell.

Simos, P. G., Diehl, R. L., Breier, J. I., Molis, M. R., Zouridakis, G. & Papanicolaou, A. C. (1998). MEG correlates of categorical perception of a voice onset time continuum in humans. *Cognitive Brain Research*, 7(2), 215–219.

Singer, M. (2007). Inference processing in discourse comprehension. In M. G. Gaskell (ed.), *The Oxford Handbook of Psycholinguistics* (pp. 343–360). Oxford University Press.

Slobin, D. I. (1966). Grammatical transformations and sentence comprehension in childhood and adulthood. *Journal of Verbal Learning and Verbal Behavior*, 5, 219–227.

Snowling, M. J. & Caravolas, M. (2007). Developmental dyslexia. In M. G. Gaskell (ed.), *The Oxford Handbook of Psycholinguistics* (pp. 667–683). Oxford University Press.

Speer, S. & Blodgett, A. (2006). Prosody. In M. J. Traxler & M. A. Gernsbacher (eds.), *Handbook of Psycholinguistics* (2nd edn, pp. 505–537). Amsterdam: Elsevier.

Speer, S., Warren, P. & Schafer, A. J. (2011). Situationally independent prosodic phrasing. *Laboratory Phonology*, 2(1), 35–98.

Sperling, G. (1960). The information available in brief visual presentations. *Psychological Monographs: General and Applied*, 74(11), 1–29.

Steedman, M. J. & Johnson-Laird, P. N. (1978). A programmatic theory of linguistic performance. In R. N. Campbell & P. T. Smith (eds.), *Recent advances in the Psychology of Language: Formal and Experimental Approaches* (pp. 171–192). New York: Plenum.

Stemberger, J. P. (1982). Syntactic errors in speech. *Journal of Psycholinguistic Research*, 11(4), 313–345.

(1985). An interactive activation model of language production. In A. W. Ellis (ed.), *Progress in the*

Psychology of Language (pp. 143–183). London: Erlbaum.

Stevenson, R. J. & Vitkovitch, M. (1986). The comprehension of anaphoric relations. *Language and Speech*, 29, 335–360.

Stowe, L. A. (1989). Thematic structures and sentence comprehension. In G. N. Carlson & M. K. Tanenhaus (eds.), *Linguistic Structure in Language Processing* (pp. 319–357). Dordrecht: Kluwer.

Strand, E. A. (1999). Uncovering the role of gender stereotypes in speech perception. *Journal of Language and Social Psychology*, 18(1), 86–100.

Straub, K., Wilson, C., McCollum, C. & Badecker, W. (2001). Prosodic structure and wh-questions. *Journal of Psycholinguistic Research*, 30, 379–394.

Stroop, J. R. (1935). Studies of interference in serial verbal reactions. *Journal of Experimental Psychology*, 18, 643–662.

Studdert-Kennedy, M., Shankweiler, D. & Pisoni, D. (1972). Auditory and phonetic processes in speech perception: Evidence from a dichotic study. *Cognitive Psychology*, 3, 455–466.

Studdert-Kennedy, M. & Shankweiler, D. (1970). Hemispheric specialization for speech perception. *Journal of the Acoustical Society of America*, 48, 579–594.

Suomi, K., McQueen, J. M. & Cutler, A. (1997). Vowel harmony and speech segmentation in Finnish. *Journal of Memory and Language*, 36, 422–444.

Taft, M. & Hambly, G. (1986). Exploring the Cohort Model of spoken word recognition. *Cognition*, 22 259–282.

Tanenhaus, M. K., Boland, J., Garnsey, S. M. & Carlson, G. N. (1989). Lexical structure in parsing long-distance dependencies. *Journal of Psycholinguistic Research*, 18(1), 37–50.

Tanenhaus, M. K., Stowe, L. & Carlson, G. (1985). The interaction of lexical expectation and pragmatics in parsing filler-gap constructions. Paper presented at the Seventh Annual Cognitive Science Society Meeting, Irvine, CA.

Tannenbaum, P. H. & Williams, F. (1968). Generation of active and passive sentences as a function of subject or object focus. *Journal of Verbal Learning and Verbal Behavior*, 7, 246–250.

Taraban, R. & McClelland, J. L. (1988). Constituent attachment and thematic role assignment in sentence processing: Influences of content-based expectations. *Journal of Memory and Language*, 27, 597–632.

Taylor, W. L. (1953). Cloze procedure: A new tool for measuring readability. *Journalism Quarterly*, 30, 415–433.

Terken, J. & Nooteboom, S. G. (1987). Opposite effects of accentuation and deaccentuation on verification latencies for given and new information. *Language and Cognitive Processes*, 2, 145–163.

Townsend, D. J. & Bever, T. G. (2001). *Sentence Comprehension: The Integration of Habits and Rules*. Cambridge, MA: MIT Press.

Traxler, M. J. & Gernsbacher, M. A. (eds.). (2006). *Handbook of Psycholinguistics* (2nd edn). Amsterdam: Elsevier.

Treiman, R. & Kessler, B. (2007). Learning to read. In M. G. Gaskell (ed.), *The Oxford Handbook of Psycholinguistics* (pp. 657–666). Oxford University Press.

Treisman, A. M. (1960). Contextual cues in selective listening. *Quarterly Journal of Experimental Psychology*, 12, 242–248.

Trueswell, J. C., Tanenhaus, M. K. & Garnsey, S. M. (1994). Semantic influences on parsing: Use of thematic role information in syntactic ambiguity resolution. *Journal of Memory & Language*, 33, 285–318.

Turk, A. (2010). Does prosodic constituency signal relative predictability? A Smooth Signal Redundancy hypothesis. *Laboratory Phonology*, 1(2), 227–262.

Tyler, L. K. & Frauenfelder, U. (1987). The process of spoken word recognition: an introduction. In U. H. Frauenfelder & L. K. Tyler (eds.), *Spoken Word Recognition* (pp. 1–20). Cambridge, MA: MIT Press.

Tyler, L. K. & Marslen-Wilson, W. D. (1982). Speech comprehension processes. In J. Mehler, E. C. T. Walker & M. Garrett (eds.), *Perspectives on Mental Representation: Experimental and Theoretical Studies of Cognitive Processes and Capacities* (pp. 169–185). Hillsdale, NJ: Erlbaum.

Valian, V. & Coulson, S. (1988). Anchor points in language learning: The role of marker frequency. *Journal of Memory and Language*, 27, 71–86.

Valian, V. & Wales, R. (1976). What's what: Talkers helping listeners hear and understand by clarifying sentential relations. *Cognition*, 4, 155–176.

Van Gompel, R. P. G. & Pickering, M. J. (2007). Syntactic parsing. In M. G. Gaskell (ed.), *The Oxford Handbook of Psycholinguistics* (pp. 289–307). Oxford University Press.

Van Gompel, R. P. G., Pickering, M. J., Pearson, J. & Liversedge, S. P. (2005). Evidence against competition during syntactic ambiguity resolution. *Journal of Memory and Language*, 52, 284–307.

van Kampen, A., Parmaksiz, G., van de Vijver, R. & Höhle, B. (2008). Metrical and statistical cues for word segmentation: vowel harmony and word stress as cues to word boundaries by 6- and 9-month-old Turkish learners. In A. Gavarró & M. J. Freitas (eds.), *Language Acquisition and Development* (pp. 313–324). Newcastle: Cambridge Scholars Publishing.

Van Orden, G. C. (1987). A ROWS is a ROSE: spelling, sound, and reading. *Memory and Cognition*, 15, 181–198.

van Zon, M. & de Gelder, B. (1993). Perception of word boundaries by Dutch listeners. Paper presented at the Third European Conference on Speech Communication and Technology, Berlin.

Vanhoy, M. & Van Orden, G. C. (2001). Pseudohomophones and word recognition. *Memory & Cognition*, 29(3), 522–529.

Vigliocco, G., Antonini, T. & Garrett, M. F. (1997). Grammatical gender is on the tip of Italian tongues. *Psychological Science*, 8, 314–317.

Vitevitch, M. S. (1997). The neighborhood characteristics of Malapropisms. *Language and Speech*, 40(3), 211–228.
  (2002). The influence of phonological similarity neighborhoods on speech production. *Journal of Experimental Psychology: Learning, Memory, and Cognition*, 28(4), 735–747.

Vitevitch, M. S. & Luce, P. A. (1998). When words compete: Levels of processing in perception of spoken words. *Psychological Science*, 9, 325–329.

Vitevitch, M. S., Stamer, M. K. & Sereno, J. A. (2008). Word length and lexical competition: Longer is the same as shorter. *Language and Speech*, 51(4), 361–383.

Vroomen, J., Tuomainen, J. & de Gelder, B. (1998). The roles of word stress and vowel harmony in speech segmentation. *Journal of Memory and Language*, 38, 133–149.

Warren, P. (1999). Prosody and language processing. In S. Garrod & M. J. Pickering (eds.), *Language Processing* (pp. 155–188). Hove: Psychology Press.
  (2011). Psycholinguistics for linguists. In K. Kuiper (ed.), *Teaching Linguistics: Reflections on Practice* (pp. 98–108). London: Equinox.

Warren, P., Grabe, E. & Nolan, F. J. (1995). Prosody, phonology and parsing in closure ambiguities. *Language and Cognitive Processes*, 10, 457–486.

Warren, P. & Marslen-Wilson, W. D. (1987). Continuous uptake of acoustic cues in spoken word-recognition. *Perception and Psychophysics*, 41, 262–275.
  (1988). Cues to lexical choice: discriminating place and voice. *Perception and Psychophysics*, 43, 21–30.

Warren, R. M. & Warren, R. P. (1970). Auditory illusions and confusions. *Scientific American*, 223, 30–36.

Warren, T. & Gibson, E. (2002). The influence of referential processing on sentence complexity. *Cognition*, 85, 79–112.

Whitney, P. (1998). *The Psychology of Language*. Boston: Houghton Mifflin.

Willems, R. M., Özyürek, A. & Hagoort, P. (2007). When language meets action: The neural integration of gesture and speech. *Cerebral Cortex*, 17(10), 2322–2333.

Zagar, D., Pynte, J. & Rativeau, S. (1997). Evidence for early-closure attachment on first-pass reading times in French. *The Quarterly Journal of Experimental Psychology*, 50A, 421–438.

Zeffiro, T. A. & Frymiare, J. L. (2006). Functional neuroimaging of speech production. In M. J. Traxler & M. A. Gernsbacher (eds.), *Handbook of Psycholinguistics* (2nd edn, pp. 125–150). Amsterdam: Elsevier.

Zipf, G. K. (1936). *The Psycho-biology of Language*. London: Routledge.

Zwitserlood, P. (1989). The locus of the effects of sentential-semantic context in spoken-word processing. *Cognition*, 32, 25–64.

Index

Printed in the USA
CPSIA information can be obtained
at www.ICGtesting.com
LVHW020533110124
768609LV00036B/455

9 780521 130561